BOOK SOLD
NO LONGER R.H.P.L.
PROPERTY

D0966374

Flying the Frontiers

Volume II

More Hours of Aviation Adventure!

SHIRLEE SMITH MATHESON

Detselig Enterprises Ltd.

Calgary Alberta Canada

Canadian Cataloguing in Publication Data

Matheson, Shirlee Smith
Flying the frontiers: vol. II, more hours of aviation adventure

Includes bibliographic references.
ISBN 1-55059-131-2

1. Bush pilots—Canada—History. 2. Bush pilots—Canada—Anecdotes. 3. Aeronautics—Canada—History. I. Title.
TL523.M36 1996 629.13'0971 C96-910041-8

Detselig Enterprises Ltd.
210-1220 Kensington Rd. N.W.
Calgary, Alberta, Canada
T2N 3P5

NOTE: The people interviewed for this book used the imperial system. Rather than interrupt their narratives by adding metric conversions, we have retained imperial measurements. For similar reasons, we have not changed the word "Eskimo" to "Inuit."

Printed in Canada ISBN 1-55059-131-2 SAN 115-0324

Contents

Other Books by Shirlee Smith Matheson

Nonfiction

Youngblood of the Peace

This Was Our Valley

Flying the Frontiers, Vol. I

Juvenile/Young Adult Fiction

Prairie Pictures

City Pictures

Flying Ghosts

Dedication

This book is dedicated to the pilots and others, who, in these pages, share their discovery of personal and geographic frontiers.

A special dedication goes to Calgary pilot Roy Staniland, whose story is recounted in "A Bunch of the Boys Were Whooping It Up . . ." Roy passed away on June 4, 1995.

"Fly on, Roy-Boy."

Acknowledgements

The author's acknowledgement goes to the people whose stories are recounted in this book. Their belief in my ability to write their histories, their willingness to share some very personal anecdotes as well as photographs, newspaper clippings, charts and other statistics to support their accounts, made my work researching and writing these narratives a real pleasure.

Thanks, once again, to Calgary pilot Thomas Legg for his advice on certain scenes, and to Clark Seaborn, professional engineer, pilot, and restorer of vintage aircraft, for checking the stories for factual content.

Detselig Enterprises Ltd. appreciates the financial assistance received for its 1996 publishing program from the Department of Canadian Heritage, the Canada Council and the Alberta Foundation for the Arts, a beneficiary of the Lottery Fund of the Government of Alberta.

Preface

"Flying can be described as 95 percent boredom, and five percent panic," states an old-time bush flyer.

"Tell me about both," I say as I turn on the tape recorder.

These stories were collected by personally interviewing men and women who spend much of their lives in the air; with few exceptions, neither they nor their stories had ever been recorded. With time and fate claiming many of Canada's aviation pioneers, I felt an urgency to solicit the stories while they could still be recounted by the original leading characters.

Here, these people tell of adventures where the engineers' or pilots' decisions can mean life or death. No one is more aware of that than the person in the cockpit – often called "the busiest office in the world."

My first volume of aviation stories, *FLYING THE FRONTIERS*, published in 1994 by Fifth House Publishers, became a bestseller. In fact, I discovered so many more great stories that I was determined to put them into a second book.

With a renewed sense of adventure, I loaded up my car with a "northern" survival kit – a suitcase, a bedroll, a supply of Yukon Jack "for medicinal purposes, of course!" – and headed out.

One of my research trips took me to LaRonge, Saskatchewan, described by local pilot Mike Thomas as "a haven for bush pilots." While stopping for gas in Prince Albert, a friendly attendant asked where I was heading. I said, "LaRonge." He looked at me quizzically. "You looking for a husband?" I assured him that was not my quest. "If you are, you should be able to find one up there!" he said, smiling, as he waved me on my way.

My journeys "home" to the Peace River country – where my husband was born and raised, and where we lived for many years – resulted in several more stories for this book. While there, I not only interviewed pilots but also a famous guide and outfitter whose opinion on the effect aviation has had on the "back country" will surely cause some people's hair to stand on end.

All the stories were told to me first-hand, with the exception of "The Underwood Airship." Intrigued by the mural of the airship painted on a local building, I went to the Village of Botha office to inquire. The story, then compiled through local research and personal letters from a member of the Underwood family, tells of a little-known invention that rivals those of the Wright brothers.

Readers of *FLYING THE FRONTIERS, VOLUME II*, will meet an Oblate priest who flew throughout Canada's North; a woman who, at age 80, flight-planned solo trips from western Canada to Kansas and Vermont; a Saskatchewan pilot who owns an island in the Bahamas; one of the first helicopter pilots in the North; an engineer who earned his lifelong nickname from his early encounter with a bear; a pilot whose customer ordered him to fill his DC-4 with Ping-Pong balls; and a pilot who once guided his aircraft down the Mackenzie River with dynamite caps held between his knees, and went on to fly Mach Two – twice the speed of sound.

These adventures give a literal interpretation to "flying the frontiers," pushing the leading edge of psychological as well as physical boundaries. They take place mainly in Canadian skies, but some occur in other countries, for a pilot or engineer is not bound by a specific geography. Like the aircraft they fly, their course is defined by career choices, endurance and luck.

These short biographies feature people who flew "just for the love of it," as well as those who hovered between commerce and chaos, where their idea of a charter airline might be "a cup on the instrument panel, for a passenger to throw in money to share expenses." Also chronicled are aviation careers of more earnest types, who learned their trades through military, corporate or academic disciplines.

Added to these are thought-provoking tales of people not directly in the flying business, but whose lives were nonetheless affected by aviation. Their stories tell *our* story: how a country's development has fostered both benefit and harm; how technology has progressed beyond the realm of the ordinary person's imagination.

Flying is not a cut-and-dried occupation with prescribed expectations and rewards. Rather, it is a passion. These stories demonstrate that passion, revealed through the aspirations and adventures of those who dedicated their lives to a sometimes fatal love.

The flight plan is filed. "Foxtrot-Tango-Foxtrot – FTF, *Flying the Frontiers II* – is ready for takeoff!"

The Watcher

Pen Powell had celebrated his 40th birthday before he began flying. He was nervous and intent on obeying instructions – even when they seemed rather odd. The airstrip he practised on was no more than a farmer's field. Powell and his instructor, Bill Bale, who ran a flying school in Dawson Creek, B.C., were flying over the field, which was crisscrossed with rural roads. Powell's hands were tense on the wheel as he followed Bale's instructions to do multiple touch-and-gos: come down, land, then put on the power and take off again. Finally they came in, did a turn and Bale said, "Well, you're ready. Now land."

Powell looked down. "I can't! There's a guy coming with a team of horses, right on that road, halfway down the runway!"

"Don't worry about him," Bale said. "The main thing is to be sure you hit him."

Powell had less than a second to consider his orders. He was tense, the situation looked bad. The guy was coming closer with his team and wagon. Powell was in the air a quarter of a mile away and everything was set. He was on final approach and getting real close, had it set up just right, when Bale spoke again. "Now make sure you get him so you won't have to do it again."

Powell came in.

He was about 40 feet from the team and wagon when Bale suddenly realized that Powell meant to do it.

"For God's sake!" he yelled, and grabbed the controls.

"You *told* me to hit him. . ." Powell said shakily, when they'd finally made a successful landing,

"I didn't think you'd take me seriously!"

When Powell finally got his licence, Bale's last words to his zealous student were, "Now make sure, if a moose walks out on the runway, that you get him so he won't do that again!"

Powell can laugh about it now. "I should have realized it was his sense of humor, but he was my *teacher*, and I believed what he was telling me."

Pen Powell saw his first airplane in 1934 when he was 16 years old. He watched it fly over his family's sawmill on Charlie Lake, B.C., near Fort St. John, and he thought, "Wow!" The next year, pilot Grant McConachie flew in to Fort St. John with his Waco to "rescue a bush accident." It was the first airplane that Powell had seen land on Charlie Lake.

McConachie was as impressed with the Powells as they were with him, and he made a deal with Pen's parents, Evelyn and Walter "Red" Powell, to go into business with him by setting up a fuel depot and providing board for pilots. McConachie planned to acquire another airplane or two and start "Flight North," based on his United Air Transport contract for airmail service to Fairbanks or Whitehorse from Edmonton.

"My dad took on the gas part of it and Grant bought himself some airplanes – old Fokkers and Fairchilds, anything he could find that would fly. The pilots would take off from Charlie Lake and we wouldn't hear from them at all during their trip because there were no airports between here and there. They had to land on gravel bars in the summer, and on the frozen lakes and rivers in the winter. They'd land wherever they could fuel up again, on the Mackenzie River when they got down to Norman Wells and places like that. There was lots of fuel because of the barges working the Mackenzie system."

One winter day in 1939, Pen watched pilot Dan Driscoll climb into the open cockpit of his old Fokker Universal (G-CAFU) and take off from Charlie Lake. Five days later, the pilot came walking back. Although the aircraft was capable of handling over one-half ton of cargo, he had overloaded, picked up ice and couldn't clear the hills at the north end of the lake, so he'd gone down on the nose and wing-tip. He was injured, but he managed to get his bearings and figured the best way back, on foot, was to follow the shoreline of Charlie Lake. The lake itself is only nine miles long, but the shoreline rambles for about 27. Nobody knew there had been a problem until he came walking in.

Powell was impressed by the adventures of these northern pilots. The more he saw and heard, the more he wanted to fly.

"You'd think incidents like that would kind of scare me off, but they didn't," he says. "They intrigued me. At that time I was working for 50 cents a day. The pilots always needed help and I'd offer to go for nothing, just crawl in any place, help with unloading, anything, just to be a passenger.

"I was 16, 17, 18 years old, in that range, but I thought, 'I'll never get the chance to fly one of these.'"

In 1938, Pen married Mary "Girlie" Beattie, whose family owned the Gold Bar Ranch, 20 miles above the head of the canyon on the

Peace River near Hudson's Hope. Pen made his living through various northern ventures: operating riverboats, which he built himself; owning and operating Powell's Trucking during (and after) construction of the Alaska Highway; and operating a sawmill. In the winter of 1952, his sawmill at Cecil Lake, near Fort St. John, employed 60 men and sawed 60 000 board feet of lumber a day, in two shifts.

In 1958 when Pen Powell was 40 years of age, an Englishman named Bill Bale, who'd been an instructor overseas during World War II, advertised for students at his flying school, Silver Wings Aviation. Powell answered his ad.

"It was an experience beyond anything I'd done," Powell recalls. "I'd ridden in airplanes, but I hadn't been in one that stalled or did any of these things that you've got to go through. It was quite a thing.

"I'd never been really instructed other than in school, and I had damned little of that. I started school at Charlie Lake in 1924 – the teacher had eight grades in a little room with a gang of us in there – so I'd never been taught like this.

"I'd had nothing on triangles of velocity, wing drifts and that. Bill Bale would say, 'As you're approaching in an airplane, you don't necessarily fly from A to B to C, you fly maybe from C to B, crabbing all the time. You aim here but you're going there because you're sliding. You set your degrees with your compass.' It wasn't easy. I had to work out on paper how far the wind was angling from the west so I'd know where I was going to end up. He'd talk about things like that, and I'd wonder how I would ever learn it all."

During the first lesson, Bale had walked Powell around the airplane, starting on the left-hand side. "This is a wing here," he said patiently to his ardent pupil. "This is a door. This is what you call the fuselage, and this is an aileron. Then we've got the horizontal indicator and the elevator." In this way they circled the airplane. Finally they got to the propeller.

"This is a propeller," Bale said. "Do you know what it's here for?"

"Well, yeah, it produces the thrust that moves the airplane forward, doesn't it?"

"Yes, mostly," Bale said. "But if you're ever flying over the mountains and the bush, way up high, and that thing quits spinning around, you'll sweat like hell. It's actually a fan to keep you cool." And so the lessons continued.

Powell got his licence, but he had a small problem: no airplane. A friend from Vancouver came to the rescue. He knew of a Super Cub for sale. "You buy this airplane, and I'll finance you. I know you can pay for it." The deal was arranged and Powell got the Super Cub (CF-JXI). It didn't last long.

In an effort "to pick up the odd dollar" that first winter, Powell put skis on the airplane and took it to a seismic camp where he had a bulldozer working on contract. If a guy needed a ride to town, "he'd kind of leave a dollar or two in the airplane" and Powell would fly him in. "It was illegal, I guess. I had no charter or anything like that." But, in this way, Powell managed to pay for his airplane.

Disaster struck not long after Powell had built a fishing and hunting lodge at Carbon Lake. He planned to use the Super Cub periodically to check the lodge and to attract other flying work in connection with his business.

"On my fourth trip in there, I wrote the airplane off. Wrecked it. I had just 500 hours flying time on wheels and skis. I'd never flown in the mountains with floats on, and I got carried away in the wind. If I'd had more experience, I could have handled it."

Powell admits he had been getting away with murder with wheels and skis, but when he put on floats the wind from the mountains did him in. "I wasn't paying any attention to the wind gusts because I'd never had to, with wheels. When I put the airplane on floats I didn't realize that they were flying, too. They took me right on over."

While floats add weight, they also cause their own lift and handle quite differently from wheels. As Powell described it, "Floats are aero-dynamic, whereas wheels are just 'parasites', they don't drag."

"When you're flying with floats, you tip the airplane to bank against the air while doing a steep turn down-wind, such as in a narrow valley. The outside wing and outside float pick up speed and are really flying. The inside lower wing is almost at a stall, and the inside float is nearly still as you go around in a steep turn. I should have banked more, but with the added problem of crosswinds, the situation got out of control."

Powell knows now that he should have let the aircraft roll right over and straighten out; if he'd turned it loose it would have flown itself. He had lots of room, and that's what he would do today. But then, he froze. "Rigor mortis set in."

The airplane more or less fell into the trees, chopping the tops off 11 pine trees. Powell was hit in the face by a stick of wood. He and his passenger were marooned at the crash site for three days, with no radio or any system of communication.

Searchers, alerted by Powell's wife, Girlie, found the men sitting on the beach near the demolished Super Cub. Powell was taken to Fort St. John to be checked over by the local physician, Doctor Westover. After he had sewed up the cut, the doctor said, "What are you going to do now?"

Powell had no idea. Flying was the last thing he wanted to think about at that moment. He'd looked in a mirror and hardly recognized himself. His face was swollen and he could barely see out of one eye.

Pen Powell's first experience flying his Super Cub on floats near Carbon Lake, B.C. *Pen Powell Collection*

"I'm going to release you on one condition," the doctor said. "There is a Tri-Pacer on wheels over at the flying club. I want you to fly me in and show me your accident."

Powell started to smile.

He is ever grateful to the wise doctor, who knew that after an accident the best thing to restore confidence was to get right back into the pilot's seat.

Powell's next flying machine was a 1948 vintage four-place PA-14 Piper (CF-IXF), but it needed a lot of work. It cost him $10 000, but the airplane received a complete overhaul. The mechanic installed a new engine and new fabric, and transformed the airplane into a modern machine. Originally equipped with a Lycoming 115 horsepower engine, it now surged with the power of 160 horses.

"It was perfectly legal. That's as big as it could go and still be a Lycoming 4-cylinder engine," Powell says. "By that time I had a lot more experience or I'd have probably wrecked it, too, like I did the first one. I operated it on floats, wheels and skis. It was a fabulous airplane!"

During the time the PA-14 was being repaired, Powell read a book by John Fauntleroy Fennelly called *Steelhead Paradise* (Mitchell Press: Vancouver, 1963). Fennelly described a trip to an area 300 miles from Powell's home territory, near the head of the Skeena River. He specifically referred to two lakes that were 12 air-miles apart:

Pen's PA14 in Carbon Lake, 1961. *Pen Powell Collection*

Sustut, some 4 000 feet above sea level, and Johanson, at 5 200 feet. It was, he said, a country of "incomparable beauty."

Fennelly's description of the setting was so vivid – lakes and rivers teeming with fish that had swum 700 miles to spawn there – that Powell decided to visit the region himself.

In August, when his airplane was ready, Powell headed for Johanson and Sustut lakes. Fennelly had described looking down from the air into the Skeena River and seeing the steelhead trout resting in big holding pools. Powell flew down the river and sure enough, the fish were there. It would be a perfect spot for a fly-in camp.

But there was a problem: even though the PA-14 had four seats, Powell knew he couldn't take three passengers, along with enough fuel to get there and back. Then someone came up with an innovative suggestion: "Pull out the electrical." That meant taking off the generator, the starter and battery, removing the radios – everything electrical. Powell did it, thereby eliminating 74 pounds of weight. "When I took that weight off, I went into pretty well every lake in British Columbia, with minimum gas. I could drop into any little pothole and come out of it, easy."

These alterations had not, in Powell's opinion, jeopardized safety, but they caused some changes in his operation. Because there was no battery, he had to hand-crank the engine. Since there was only one access door, he had the choice of changing the door so he could get in, or flying from the right-hand side. He chose the latter.

Powell explains the modification: "There is only one door on a four-place PA-14 Piper aircraft, and it is located on the right-hand side. An aircraft is normally piloted from the left side, the same as a car. The pilot gets in first, then the front passenger gets in and closes the door, and the pilot starts the motor with an electric starter.

"When I removed the starter, battery, and alternator, I then had to hand-crank the engine. Normally, one doesn't ask passengers to hand-crank the engine while standing on the floats, especially late in the fall when they're covered with ice! So I decided to run the controls such as the throttle, carb-heat, and mixture with my left hand instead of my right. I'd load the passenger, and leave the aircraft tied up until I hand-cranked it and got it idling, then untie it. I'd jump into the right seat, get hold of the controls, close the door and take off.

"I modified the door by cutting it in half, welding the upper portion and having the lower half fold out like on a Super Cub so it couldn't slam shut from the prop blast.

"It was no time at all till I got used to that. It was a fabulous thing."

Then he started to fly in customers. Not having a charter licence meant he couldn't charge people for expenses, or even expect them to pay for the fuel. To make up the difference he rented out rooms at his lodge at Carbon Lake, and flew his customers where they wanted to go from there. The lodge rent was only $25 a day, "ridiculously low," and customers often booked rooms for 15 or 20 days. "But I wound up in court over it. Someone reported me."

Powell explains the circumstances that prevailed at the time:

"Around the mid-1950s into the 1960s, the government's Fish and Wildlife branch allotted all this area to outfitters. They tried to be fair: 'you've got this watershed, that's yours for bringing foreign hunters in,' and so on."

Where Powell made his big mistake was in deciding to prefabricate materials to build boats, and haul them to lakes that he flew to en route to Johanson and Sustut lakes.

Powell would strap some boat parts onto the floats; some were boxed in on the struts; other parts that could withstand water blowing back on them from the prop during takeoff were strapped underneath on the spreader bars. Long pieces (called chines), as well as other parts, such as the bottom corners that had to be kept dry so they could be glued, were carried inside along the fuselage. He removed all the seats from the airplane and laid these prefabricated sections right to the back. He found he could haul boards as long as 14 feet by shoving them right back to the tail, thereby fitting the full length of the boat inside the aircraft.

"It was definitely illegal," Powell admits, "because the boards were along the cables that went back to the rear controls, but I had them tied in so they couldn't move, and they never did.

"I'd leave home in the morning, and I'd take with me one passenger and one of these boats in the prefab stage. By that night I'd have the new boat assembled, painted and going. They were beautiful boats."

The problems came from outfitters in these areas, who saw their wilderness lakes suddenly take on the appearance of marinas as Powell brought in his brightly colored boats.

"The outfitters weren't too happy with the boats being there, and with me bringing people into their lakes to fish," Powell admits, "so they did everything in their power to destroy my boats. They fired them, they tried to sink them, everything. Of the 40 boats I built, only two survived. That's how vicious it was."

Finally an outfitter reported his actions to the law. Powell found himself the defendant in court cases that stretched over two years, involving 14 separate charges.

"They charged me with operating in different manners that I wasn't properly licensed for, operating an unlicensed charter, flying too low and scaring fish, all kinds of ridiculous things. Bootlegging was the big one. So, the MOT [Ministry of Transport] took over."

Powell won the first case – operating an unlicensed charter – and that made both him and his lawyer happy.

"The government was definitely right to a point, but I was right too," he says. "At that time there was all kinds of activity here: oil and gas exploration and drilling, and construction of every kind, as well as [big game] guides and outfitters. They all had airplanes, and none of them had charter licenses. They weren't charging, but if you went into their books you'd find items such as the gas that had been burned in their aircraft listed as part of the company's expenses.

"After my case, all the outfitters, exploration and construction companies could relax because they knew now that they had no problem. My case was precedent-setting."

Getting a licence to operate a charter is not easy. "It's like a franchise," Powell explains. "They set up an allotted area that you can operate in, and then you have to get all your permits, and follow all the regulations. There's strict aircraft maintenance rules, you have to report all movements, your rates are set. As a private pilot we don't have to list our passengers and their weights. With a charter, it's a different breakdown altogether, which is fine, but it's pretty expensive."

The rest of the charges against Powell – with the exception of the one for bootlegging – were eventually dropped.

The bootlegging charge came from an incident that seemed trivial enough. By this time, Powell had also built some cabins at Tutizzi Lake, about 30 miles east of the high Omineca mountain range, at the head of the Mesilinka River. Jack Baker, Powell's brother-in-law, also had a place there. Pen would always stop at Tutizzi Lake, and if his customers were going to use that lodge they were charged another $25 a day.

This particular time, a friend of Powell's from Fort St. John had ordered a case of Scotch whisky to be brought out to the lodge, where he'd booked a room and planned to stay a while. Pen flew out the whiskey. Then, before the two men flew over to Sustut, they took a bottle out of the case to pack with them. The American outfitter who had bought the rights to the area near Sustut Lake approached Powell as soon as he landed.

"I want to tell you something," he said in a no-nonsense tone. "We've got this area allotted for some top-notch people from L.A., and we can't allow you to bring this stuff . . ." he gestured toward Powell's passenger, then shrugged, ". . . you just can't keep coming out here."

"Well," Powell replied, "for the last 12 years I've had it allotted for some top-notch people from Hudson's Hope, Fort St. John, Dawson Creek – and even some from Vancouver! So we've got problems."

Powell's friend broke into the conversation. "Oh, quit your bargaining! Where's that whiskey?"

Powell gestured toward the plane. As the fellow brought out the bottle, he said to Pen, "What do I owe you?"

Thinking of the cost of the full case he'd delivered to Tutizzi Lake, which came to $96 and some cents, Powell said, "Just make it an even hundred bucks."

The outfitter took on a canny look. Powell suddenly realized the outfitter must have thought he had sold this fellow one bottle of Scotch for $100, thereby making a huge profit on the sale.

"He was mad at me anyway," Powell says, "so he told the law I was bootlegging. When it came up in court, as soon as the question was asked I brought my friend up for a witness. The judge believed him, so I got out of that mess."

Pen was glad to have the whole experience behind him.

Powell has helped to set a few other precedents, one which benefitted many pilots over the years. When the Town of Dawson Creek, B.C., had first considered building an artificial lake for use by float planes in 1963, Mayor Bob Trail had a hard time convincing nay-sayers that the idea would work. He phoned Pen Powell and asked for a favor. "If we wet the mud in there, can you come in, as an experiment, with your PA-14?"

With floats, Powell explains, a pilot can land on water, mud, muskeg, or grass, as long as there are no rocks. "So they cleaned up the pond, and made 'lots of stretch' for me to land on."

Bob Trail gathered the media to the site in his efforts to convince the townspeople of the need for the pond. The reporters and camera crew looked at the muddy bog. In one place, about 100 feet long, there were perhaps six or eight inches of water; the rest was mud.

"I hear there's a float plane coming in this afternoon," Mayor Trail said casually.

"There's no water! How's he going to land? What are we going to do?" The local airport crew immediately started to pump in water.

Pen knew there would be very little water – but at least it was wet. He zoomed in as planned.

"It was just soup. I set down and slid along, but you don't slide very far. There was enough water so the airplane was almost floating, put it that way. I coasted up to where it was drier, fairly near the edge, and simply stepped out."

The reporters were thrilled, and the Dawson Creek newspaper carried an enthusiastic story about the landing:

> Pen Powell . . . became the first pilot to land a plane on the $13,000 man-made seaplane base east of the city. Upon docking his Piper PA-14, Powell said Dawson Creek doesn't realize what they have, but in all his years of flying this is an ideal set-up with the base being so close to town. He landed his Piper in six feet of water at the east end of the pond, using about one-tenth of the 5,000-foot strip of water. About a million-and-a-half gallons of water are pouring into the base daily. This will be doubled shortly when two pumps are put into operation.

The citizens of Dawson Creek were now convinced that the man-made lake was not an idle whim of their mayor, who, incidentally, was also a pilot (Footnote 1).

In the early 1960s, construction began for the W.A.C. Bennett Dam (then called Portage Mountain Dam) on the Peace River near Hudson's Hope. As the flooding of the valley for the dam's reservoir would affect Powell's operation at Carbon Lake, as well as forever alter his "backyard," Powell began to fly over the area several times a day. The changes he observed from the cockpit, as the reservoir began to form behind the dam, were astounding.

In the past, as he flew his float-equipped plane through the Rocky Mountain Trench over the Peace, Finlay and Parsnip rivers, Powell had been assured of having an "airport" under him at all times. He often would land on the rivers and visit the placer miners working gravel along the beaches, or the natives paddling boats and canoes, and camping where the best fishing and hunting areas were. Often he would "hope for a storm" so he could have an excuse to land and spend the night.

"Everyone seemed to live along the rivers and I had a perfect landing strip right at their doors, with no debris, snags, or waves to worry about," Powell said. (Footnote 2).

Powell watched as the dam construction intensified. In an attempt to "do something" with 640-square-miles of forested river valley that would soon become a reservoir, contractors came in with enormous tractors tied together with heavy cables, dragging a large steel ball between them. With this equipment, they started pulling down thousands of acres of trees a day. Powell observed that most of the trees would stay down, but many rose half-way up again.

"Even before the water started to cover this mess, it was impossible for moose or caribou to make their way through it," he said. "Then as the water started to flood, the animals really got confused. As I flew back and forth each day that was flyable, the things I saw I often wish I could forget."

One day he and a friend were flying north of where the Ospika River enters the Finlay, when they spotted a large herd of moose trapped on a piece of high ground by floating debris and pulled-over trees. "We counted well over 100 moose in about a 10-acre area. The next day we flew back over the same area and it was completely covered with water, and we could see lots of dead moose floating in the debris.

"In a matter of a very short time," Powell says, "the part of the Rocky Mountain Trench that became Williston Lake reservoir behind the Bennett Dam, was transformed from one of the safest, most beautiful areas, to one of the most hazardous and ugly places in British Columbia in which to boat or operate a float-equipped aircraft."

The third airplane Pen Powell owned was a 1954 Cessna 180. It's only – and fatal – drawback was that it contained no gas gauges. He knew he could have them installed off the electrical system, but he didn't always depend on gauges. If the electrical system failed he could be lost, thinking he still had fuel. So his method was to ensure that the gas tanks were continuously topped up.

One day, after off-loading some gear for two people who were living on an island at Tuchodi Lake, he decided to fill up from one of the drums he had stored at the site. He inserted a funnel and asked Marv, one of the residents, to hand him up the gas pails one at a time.

Powell was handing back the final pail when a gust of wind blew the funnel into the water. The funnel wasn't worth much, but it was a necessary item. Marv attempted to retrieve it, but the wind blew the funnel farther out into the lake. Pen climbed down from the wing and went after the funnel himself, wading in waist-high water.

In all the commotion, he forgot a very important step – replacing the gas cap.

He taxied out to the centre of the lake, then opened wide on the throttle to get up on the floats. Marv's wife watched from the dock in

"Before." Pen taking off in his 1954 Cessna 180 on floats. Note the open gas cap on the wing. *Pen Powell Collection*

amazement as a rooster-tail of gas shot from the tank above the wing. She grabbed her camera and took a picture.

Powell, unaware of this drama, continued to fly home. En route, he flew low to check on some hunters farther down the Tuchodi River. He spied them on the mountainside and rocked his wings, interpreting their exuberant waves as an "okay" signal. He had no idea that he'd just sprayed them with gas!

From there, Powell climbed to 7 000 feet. It was a beautiful day, and he had one more stop to make – at Redfern Lake to give someone a ride in to Fort St. John. Suddenly, the engine quit. "What the hell?" There was no choke on the airplane, so he pulled the primer out and gave it a shot. Whirr! away it went. He primed it again. Nothing. He knew then what no one had been able to tell him – the gas cap was off and he was flying on an empty tank. Now he had to check out the bush for a good place to land.

It wasn't like the critical moment of takeoff, when engine failure occurs and the airplane stalls. He had lots of speed. He could even gain a bit of altitude, but he wasn't stretching his distance. He was simply, for the moment, staying airborne.

The airplane was carrying no weight, and it was a calm day – he could glide for a good distance. It seemed he'd been up there forever with nothing to do but fly around and contemplate his impending crash. He spotted a lake, but he knew it was too far away.

He turned on the ELT (Emergency Location Transmitter), gave his position to the Department of Transport, then concentrated on the matter at hand: picking a soft place to lay down the airplane.

After the silent glide, the crash was fast, loud and disastrous. Then everything became silent again. When Powell heard birds resume their chirping he knew that, whatever the damage to his airplane, he was alive.

"After." The Cessna hits the dirt after running out of gas in mid-air. *Pen Powell Collection*

"When I hit the bush, the seat came out and slammed right up into the dash. I had a four-horse Merc kicker on board that weighed maybe 60 pounds, sitting behind the seat on the floor. It flew past my head and came to rest on the ground outside. Imagine if I'd had a 100-pound bottle of propane back there! I've carried as many as ten 10-gallon drums of gas, the whole plane filled with the seat out. Imagine if I'd gone in like that!"

He emerged without a scratch.

When Powell acquired a commercial licence, he bought a new 1965 Cessna 180 (CF-SGE). Then he got a contract to haul fresh-water whitefish from Klua Lake. This venture led to his acquiring a new type of passenger. Noting that trappers always had trouble getting their dogs out to the traplines, Powell thought that maybe when he was going in for a load of fish he could haul a load of dogs. The trappers might actually give him five dollars for it.

"This worked out fantastic!" Powell said. "I hauled dogs, and I enjoyed that more, I think, than anything. We had a hell of a time getting them in there the first trip, but I just took them in one at a time and chained down to the seat ties. They were all big 100-pound dogs, and they weren't muzzled. But I got along with them."

Einar Paulson, a Swedish-Canadian trapper who hired Pen many times, was amazed at Powell's ability to handle his canine passengers. "I've never seen anybody handle dogs like you do," he said, when Pen picked him up in June at the end of the season. "Those dogs knew your airplane! Every time you went over during the winter, they were all out there yipping and barking, thinking you were coming back to pick them up."

Powell also hauled fur, sleighs, harness, anything to earn a dollar.

One time, when he was flying to the Fontas River with a load of supplies for the Indians, Powell encountered fog at the Beatton River north of Fort St. John. To avoid getting lost he decided to follow the rail line. "I had probably a 100-foot ceiling where I could see down the track, but it gradually got worse. There is a little valley where the creek comes up to the railway track, and the fog got right down in there."

He dipped to keep the track in view, when suddenly a long dark line loomed directly in front of him. A row of boxcars was sitting on the siding! "The wing just cleared those cars!"

That was the first narrow escape of the day. As long as he'd had the black strip of rail line to follow, he'd felt fairly secure. Now he had to turn back, and make a blind turn in the fog.

"The trees had snow on them, everything was white. As soon as I lost the track I was in a white world, like somebody'd put a sack over my head – and I wasn't licensed to fly IFR (Instrument Flight Rules).

"I climbed a little, not too much because I wanted to get back under the ceiling to land. I made a slow, more-or-less flat turn, banking a bit to keep from skidding. I watched my instruments as best as I could, but I wasn't absolutely certain they were accurate or that I was reading them accurately.

"Thank God I had the directional gyro compass, not just the ordinary compass. If it had happened to me with my PA-14 when I had all the electrical out of it, I'd have been in real trouble."

By that time, the boxcars were no longer a problem because Powell had veered away from the track to make his turn. Also, he knew the country was flat toward the east, so he made a slow turn in that direction, then headed back to the south from where he had come. He knew that in 25 or 30 minutes he would have a 500-to 600-foot clearance.

"I got my compass set up, and I just sat there not knowing what might happen. I soon knew my elevation with my altimeter, but I had to make sure I stayed where the railway followed the valley. I kept setting the gyro as I went along, but I set the degrees with the other compass, and just let it go. I had my directions perfect, but I was off four or five miles when I came out. That was likely the closest I came to having an accident that actually turned out okay."

Other times he was not so fortunate.

The next scrape, under eerily similar circumstances, occurred in the Peace Pass where the Peace River breaks through the Rocky Mountains.

"I was involved with another fellow on a mining venture up at Fort Ware. One day I took him and his son to view the site. The weather was fairly bad when we took off.

"On the way down we flew into the Peace Pass, which is quite bad for heavy snow. The fog was rising off the open water, and be darned if I didn't get into almost the same situation as over the Fontas."

B.C. Hydro had just built the W.A.C. Bennett Dam on the Peace River. The reservoir behind the dam was partly filled, so for the first time in history the waters of the Peace River remained unfrozen. Powell had skis on, and he could see the fog ahead. He knew he had to turn around, and he thought he could follow the bank to get back through the mountain pass.

"All at once I noticed some slashing from a logging operation on the side of the hill. I knew then I was off. There was no logging in the pass! By Jesus, I'd gone into a valley that's completely boxed in, where the mountains go straight up, opposite the Clearwater River. I knew better than to ever start up into one of those things because if you do, it's all over. When I realized where I was, I still had a 400-to-500-foot-wide area so I practically threw the airplane around.

"I put on the power and just threw that thing three-quarter way over, like a hammer stall. I went to the extreme. I had to. I lost centrifugal force – there was all this dust and stuff – but I had complete control. Then I headed back out the way I went in.

"That was a close one."

Powell has other memories of close calls in the Peace Pass area that required quick actions – some that worked, some that didn't.

One October day, he was hired to bring in two hunters and their two moose from a plateau at the head of the Stikine River at Laslui Lake. "They shouldn't have been hunting there – it's a park – but the meat had to come out, that's all there was to it. I said, 'I'll take the meat out first or the bears will get it. You guys wait here in your tents.'

"They looked a bit worried. They knew there were bears around 'til hell wouldn't have them, and wolverines."

When Powell got into the Peace Pass, the weather turned miserable. "Freezing rain was breaking down, trying to decide if it was going to be rain or snow. Every once in a while I'd see it stick, and that's dynamite. Your windscreen ices right over, clear ice, and you can't see.

You pick up weight, and your prop starts to shake from ice build-up. If it stays on it's not too bad, but sometimes a chunk will fly off and your prop is thrown off balance. The struts, your airplane's wings, everything, picks up ice. It's a horrible feeling!

"I decided to go back to Ken Kyllo's camp on Finlay Bay and land there. By that time wet snow was really coming down! When I got out of the airplane, I saw I'd picked up a bunch of ice on the fuselage just in that little while."

Powell had swung the airplane around onto some logs in the debris-strewn lake, jumped out, and tied the aircraft onto the logs. But the weight of the two moose caused the aircraft to sink quite low, and water started coming into the back of the float through the vents. Powell started to throw out the meat, to lighten the airplane before it sank completely into the lake. By the time he had it unloaded, one wing was dropping. The airplane suddenly jutted up and then settled into 15 feet of water, with one wing up and one down.

"My immediate concern was to keep the motor out of the water. My next thought was 'What the hell am I going to do?' I had two guys waiting in tents out at Laslui Lake. I should be home. And here I was with my airplane at the bottom of the lake."

Pen Powell's 1965 Cessna 180 sinking into Finlay Bay. *Pen Powell Collection*

He managed to contact pilot Jack Baker in Fort St. John, who said he'd fly down in the morning. Pen would then take Baker's airplane and fetch the two men sitting in their tents in the middle of nowhere. But what about his own airplane?

About 10 miles away, A.C. Geddes's salvage company was clearing logs off the lake, using a big barge and crane. Powell radioed their boat, and they agreed to bring the barge and crane down after hours. It was a fairly easy feat for them to tie onto the airplane and set it up on a pile of logs.

"One float had a hole from hooking onto a log when it had gone down," Powell recalls. "I took Jack's airplane into town, got a truck tube and a hand pump, and flew back. I stuck the tube inside the float, put a piece of plywood over the hole, pumped it up tight, and heck, I finished the season off – went for about six weeks – with that tube in there!

"So that wasn't a close call for me, it was just a close call at losing another airplane."

Powell's aviation jobs have varied from well-paying to non-paying. He's hauled bush men – prospectors, miners, trappers and their dogs – as well as oil and mineral exploration executives. Sometimes the jobs went smoothly; at other times they took strange turns. He relates one incident that still surprises him – because of its uniqueness and its "damned foolishness."

"Jim Burrows, a commercial pilot from Fort St. John, got a contract to haul some stuff for an oil company up at Rainbow Lake by telling the company that he had a Cessna 206," Powell relates. "He actually had one ordered, but its delivery was delayed. I'd just bought this new Cessna 180. Jim said to me, 'Will you take that job for me? They won't know the difference.' I said, 'I don't have a charter.' He assured me that everything would be looked after, so I started hauling this stuff, loading from Dawson Creek.

"Eventually, Jim was told his 206 airplane would be coming in a few days. We were behind schedule – I couldn't keep up with just the 180 – so he decided that even after his airplane arrived he would keep me on for another week. Fine."

As the job progressed, Powell figured it would be cheaper to truck the loads from Dawson Creek to Charlie Lake, and then fly them on floats from Charlie Lake to Rainbow Lake, saving about 45 miles. They followed this plan, using the two aircraft.

One day it was very hot with no wind, and Powell was concerned that he might not be able to get his airplane off the lake with a load on. Burrows loaded him anyway, "and a little too much."

He tried, but as predicted, he couldn't get up.

"If I had a little breeze, I might have made it," Powell told Burrows.

Burrows had a solution. "I'll put my 206 in the lead. You line up behind in the 180, and follow me up. All you need is a little wind."

Powell was sceptical. "I'll wait until the wind picks up."

"No, no," Burrows insisted. "There's no time. I'll taxi out, and you stay about 60 feet behind me. You'll have lots of wind."

Burrows taxied out, opened the throttle, and burst ahead.

"It worked," Powell acknowledges. "He must have created a 40-mph wind! I got the 180 on the step, but he was leaving me behind. There are steps on a float, and a vacuum is created," Powell explains. "Once you get up on the steps you're free, running on about half the float. At that point you can get your speed up and you're gone. As Burrows got more power he got more step and went a bit faster, but I was coming."

The slipstream is a vortex, a spinning funnel of air that widens out. As Powell's speed increased, he got into the narrow portion of the slipstream, and the wings lost it, although the prop still picked up some. The plane bounced, but he kept the throttle open, kept it on the step, and he was off.

"As Jim got airborne, the blast of exhaust came down. When you rear up, you put a blast onto the water. I was behind him, about 12 feet up in the slipstream of his airplane. When I came to the end of where this was, it was like somebody'd cut the rope. Down I came! Jim's dad was on the dock watching the whole show. He said if he'd had a movie camera, the footage would be worth a million dollars.

"It was my Cessna 180, only a few weeks old."

Powell takes an inventory on the aircraft he has owned: the Super Cub that he put down at Carbon Lake. The Piper PA-14 that he flew for 1 800 hours with floats – "a fabulous airplane, but it had a short fuselage and it was no good on skis, that's the only reason I got rid of it." The 1954 Cessna 180, the one he wrecked when he left the gas cap off. Then his last airplane, a 1965 Cessna 180 that he dumped into Finlay Bay, and smashed into Charlie Lake, but which lasted him until he was finished flying, in 1993.

"Two out of four were write-offs," Powell says. "Not bad. Not too bad at all."

Pilots are not always given the opportunity to evaluate their successes and failures from a comfortable pew. Pen's brother, Gary Powell, had an outfitting business on Prairie River, connected to the Tuchodi River where it drains into the Muskwa. Ninety percent of his flying was within the area. During his career, Gary owned numerous airplanes. "He had 180s and Super Cubs, all kinds of things, and he wrote off quite a few of them," Pen says. "He crashed the Super Cubs, had lots of accidents, but had never got hurt."

On October 5, 1983, Gary Powell lost his life when his Cessna 185 crashed near Dawson Creek, B.C. No one really knows what caused his airplane to go down that day.

"If you're going flying in the mountains it's going to happen," Pen says stoically. "You've got to have at least one accident to smarten you up. It's ridiculous: if you don't have one you think it never happens. Like mine at Carbon Lake when I had a lousy 500 hours; I realized very quickly that it *can* happen."

Pilot survival, according to Powell, can be credited partly to learning and remembering lessons, but sometimes to sheer luck. Powell recalls an incident that seemed minor, yet resulted in a pilot's death.

"I used to come in and land on the Fontas River quite a lot. A guy came in with a turbo Beaver right after I'd taken off. I saw him coming, so I circled around to see what would happen when he landed, because it's a tight spot. By God, he crashed into the river.

"The Beaver didn't sink. In fact, the tail stayed up out of the water. It's a narrow place, and I couldn't have got down and landed because of the tail sticking out. Also, I had a load on. I thought that someone would come out to get him in a boat – there were several Indian people around – so I took off. I couldn't do a thing anyway.

"I heard later that when he went into the river, the pilot had got out of his seat and made it into the back of the aircraft. When someone went out in a boat, the airplane was sinking to where just the pilot's head was visible. But they didn't get him out. There the guy was, screaming like hell, wanting out of that tail, but the Indians were afraid to chop a hole in the airplane. So, he drowned."

Notwithstanding his own record, Powell's 11 000 flying hours attest to a high degree of skill, a sense of adventure, knowledge of the land and an uncanny navigational sense.

"I'm not boasting or anything, but I'd think nothing of jumping into the airplane right now, taking off, and flying to Tuktoyaktuk. I'd cut right across country. I don't think about directions, I just go. I watch the flow of the rivers, and the watersheds.

"Before I went to the Arctic the first time, people said, 'You've got no idea what it's like up there! A standard compass won't work once you get north of the Arctic Circle.' 'Well,' I said, 'to hell with it, then.'"

When he wanted to install a new engine in his Cessna 180, he heard of a good deal in Winnipeg. "I just took off. I'd see a grain elevator some place and get the name off it. That would tell me where I was."

From the cockpit, Powell has carefully watched the rivers, trees, weather, animals – and construction of everything from hydro-electric dams to beaver houses. "I note what end of the slough the beaver house is on, whether a beaver has moved out or whether it's still an active house, and the size of the house which tells me the number of beaver occupying it. I can tell all this by the work that's been done around it. These things are of interest to me."

Norm Mackenzie, a trapper from the Fort St. John area, once told Powell that someone had bought a pig. "No, he has three pigs," Powell corrected. "I fly over there every day. He feeds them at six a.m."

Powell has closely observed the North's changing ecology. He has seen increasing numbers of people gain access to remote areas, and commercial enterprises – hunting, fishing, logging, hydro and mining development – take their toll. Although he's been involved in these industries himself, he is concerned about the sheer number of invasions.

Powell looks across the Peace River at Hudson's Hope, B.C., to the miles of green forest beyond. 1992. *Photo: S. Matheson*

Powell looks across his yard on the banks of the Peace River, to the miles of green forest beyond. He wonders how long it's going to last, this scene he's viewing today, the seemingly endless carpet of greenery.

"It's not going to last at all," he says moodily.

"Flying over it, I saw it all. It's terrible. For somebody who likes nature, like myself, someone who's seen it change over the years, I wish I didn't have to look out. Now, down on the ground, it's all prairie, massive dust, from clear-cut logging. I wish I could just keep looking straight ahead, which a lot of pilots do. They don't see a thing, they just sit there and look ahead and ignore the mess."

Powell doesn't excuse his own role in opening up remote areas to fishing and hunting, and two generations of his family were involved in the sawmill business. Even when the subject of hunting from airplanes is broached, he acknowledges his involvement.

"Everybody does that, including me. Let's say I need a moose real bad, and two or three miles out I 'accidentally' see a big bull moose wandering around. Well, I get home, get into my vehicle and drive back. But, I don't always get it.

"The airplane is used for spotting, that's what all the outfitters do. They spot the animals from the air all summer long; check them out, see where they're living. They say they're doing photography work and so on, but don't tell me that they don't watch where the sheep are living, where the big ones are. They wouldn't know that unless they had an airplane and did it every day. They get the animals accustomed to the airplane.

"When the season opens they know exactly where they're at because the animal's got a pattern to where he sleeps during the day, where he ranges. They get their pack horses and head up there."

Powell has always enjoyed exploring the country – taking off and going where he wants just for the sheer fun of it. With all its risks, he would still recommend flying to anybody.

"It's been fantastic," he says. "I wish I had started earlier, but I'd probably have killed myself. I saw so many of my friends out of the Fort St. John Flying Club have disasters, young guys, good guys. A lot of them got hurt and hurt bad, doing ridiculous things, trying to prove something that was practically impossible."

Pen Powell was a pilot from the age of 40 until he was 72.

"When we moved into town in 1992, there was no place to keep the float plane nearby, so I sold my Cessna 180. I'd had enough anyway. Nearly 12 000 hours."

"I saw a lot of country," Powell says reflectively. "I watched a lot of things happen."

Footnote 1:

In 1992, bush pilots flew in to Dawson Creek, Mile Zero of the Alaska Highway, to take part in Rendezvous '92, celebrating the 50th anniversary of the highway's construction. Float planes taking part in the organized flight from Edmonton, Alberta, to Fairbanks, Alaska, were able to land on this man-made lake right beside the runway at the Dawson Creek airport – the only one like it in Canada.

Footnote 2:

Excerpted from *This Was Our Valley*, Earl K. Pollon and Shirlee Smith Matheson (Detselig Enterprises Ltd., Calgary, 1989), 225-6.

Firefighter of the Northern Forest

Through others' faith in his abilities, G.T. Rowan learned to fly. He brought those skills to the forests of northern Saskatchewan, first as a pilot and then as a firefighter. He thinks often of his mentors, and the gift they gave him of an interesting and rewarding career.

"Aviation has been exciting, to say the least," G.T. states. "It changed my whole life, and I've had a good one."

Gordon Thomas (G.T.) Rowan was born March 21, 1936, at the outpost hospital in Shand Creek, Saskatchewan. His father, a World War I veteran, had emigrated from Ireland to start the homestead farm 10.5 miles north of Carragana, but the old soldier's life was interrupted by a second stint in the military in 1939. When he returned to the farm in 1945, he stayed to enjoy the freedoms for which he had twice fought.

G.T. helped out on the farm until 1955, when he opted for the higher wages of operating heavy equipment for road construction. In 1959 he married Zinnia Nazar whose parents farmed four miles from Chelen, Saskatchewan.

For the next year, G.T. continued working on construction. One of the company's owners was a pilot and took him flying in his small aircraft. Noting the young man's excitement, the boss suggested he should get a pilot's licence.

"I didn't think I had enough money, or enough time. And I didn't think I was smart enough," G.T. says. "But the boss said, 'Well, you'll never know until you try.'"

The following year, G.T. took his training for a private pilot's licence in Calgary. The course cost $380, less a federal government reimbursement of $100. By 1965, G.T. had his commercial licence (now called an Airline Transport rating).

"I knew I couldn't afford to fly as a hobby, so I figured I'd better do something drastic," G.T. says. "I bought a Calair and went into crop spraying for Frank Young's Sky Spray company out of Airdrie, Alberta. I ended up looking after that operation until 1969."

The pilots attended Olds Agricultural College for their spray licenses, where they learned about the occupational hazards. "Product labels and information pamphlets warned us about the effects this stuff could cause in later years, especially when spraying all day from a closed cockpit, in the heat. But we used precautions, and I can't recall anybody who got respiratory problems or anything."

The work involved spraying fields of flax, barley and wheat. In the fall they did brush spraying for the cattle ranchers. Like other spray pilots, G.T. learned to fly under telephone lines and over fences, and to take off from and land on roads.

The company also serviced tourist resorts. "The cottage owners at Chestermere Lake hired us to spray for bugs and mosquitos. We'd tell them when we were coming so they could cover their gardens, or make sure they didn't touch any produce following our visit until they'd sprayed it with water first.

"One morning about four o'clock, Pat Dunn and I came in to Chestermere Lake from Airdrie in two Calair spray planes. We were flying low over the gardens, less than 10 feet from the ground, when a guy came running out of his outhouse with his pants around his knees! He must have thought the world had come to an end!" G.T. laughs at the recollection. "Whoever thought there'd be someone in the outhouse at that time of the day?"

Accidents can happen, and the only airplane G.T. ever crashed was a crop duster."I was doing my turn at the end of the field in a Calair Sparrow, flying too low, and I pumped 'er into the barley field. Hit the wing tip on the ground – that started it – then I rolled it into a ball. Totally demolished it."

When the spraying season was finished in 1969, G.T. returned to Saskatchewan. There, he inquired if Norcanair needed a pilot. The company required a manager at both Uranium City and Stony Rapids, and the Norcanair crew invited him to come along in their DC-3 to check out the country.

"First we went to Uranium City. I didn't mind it, but to me it didn't look quite isolated enough," G.T. says. "Everybody said, 'You're nuts!' Then we flew over Stony Rapids and I said, 'That's where I want to go.'"

Stony Rapids barely made a smudge on the white landscape. "It didn't even look like a settlement because there weren't enough buildings. It just looked isolated, like a tourist camp would nowadays."

The hamlet had a Hudson's Bay store, an RCMP detachment, a DNR (provincial Department of Natural Resources) shop, and a federal Indian Affairs office. Calm Air had a base there, and Gulf Oil had an office and tank storage yard, run by Arnold Morburg. "They had 10 000- and 15 000-gallon fuel tanks, and that was their storage," G.T. recalls. "They used to haul fuel in on barges up Lake Athabasca. I was told that a big event in the northern communities every spring was the arrival of barges bringing in supplies."

G.T. was immediately hired to be Norcanair's base manager at Stony Rapids. Then he had to return to Calgary, to announce to his wife that they'd be moving. The response to his announcement is best left to one's imagination.

G.T. went north in the fall of 1969, and Zinnia made a trip up at Christmas in the company's DC-3, bringing a prepared dinner in boxes. As he drove his wife from the airstrip down the hill toward the river, they passed a Norcanair building.

"Is that your warehouse?" Zinnia asked.

"No," G.T. replied carefully, "that's our house."

At Christmas, the residents all got together – the Hudson's Bay and DNR employees, the RCMP, some school teachers who had stayed around, and the resident nurse, to show the newly-arrived couple that friendliness can make up for cold temperatures.

"It was cold. God, it was cold! Minus 60," G.T. recalls. "Zinnia wasn't impressed with the weather. But, after the holidays she went back to Calgary, put the house up for sale, and moved up, lock, stock and barrel, on January 17, 1970."

Not only did Zinnia move to Stony Rapids, but she also took on the job of running the base. Meanwhile, G.T. flew the company's Beaver.

"I hauled thousands of caribou," G.T. says. "The Indian chief in Black Lake, Louie Chicken, bought a 30.06 Remington rifle from the Hudson's Bay store and gave it to me to help shoot caribou. I'd take two or three native fellows with me in the Beaver, and sometimes the ladies would go too. Some of the women up there could shoot the eye out of an eagle at 200 yards. I used to take the ones who could really shoot, so we could get two trips in a day – and the days were kind of short.

"We'd land on the lake ice, with skis. The herd wouldn't run very far if we didn't do anything. We'd just sit there and they'd wander around. They're a curious animal. We'd pick out five, shoot them, cut them up, haul them home, go back, catch up to the herd again and get another five.

"We'd never gross the airplane out, but we'd fill it, have a good load, maybe four or five caribou. That way, we would stock up on meat for the winter, filling the ice-houses for the village."

G.T. also transported trappers to their cabins in the fall, taking them out on floats, picking them up at Christmas on skis, taking them back out after the holidays, and then picking them up on skis just before the ice went bad in the spring. If he got there too late, the trappers would have to wait until after break-up when the plane could come back on floats.

Fred Riddle's trapline was the farthest north, on Dament Lake in the Northwest Territories. Riddle had cabins all the way along the Thelon River, Nicholson River and Mosquito Lake area.

"The federal government had hired him to poison wolves, and he would keep the fur," G.T. says. "He'd shoot caribou, poison the meat and leave it laying out. Or he'd dig a little hole in the ice, and insert the meat so it would freeze in. That way, the wolf couldn't carry it away."

G.T. also brought school children from outlying areas such as Selwyn, Cree and Foster lakes to attend residential schools at Stony Rapids and LaRonge. "I still know a few of the kids today. They're grown men and women, and they've done well for themselves. Some of the children kept up the old skills and stayed in the bush, but the majority of them went on to higher education."

G.T. does not recall the students being unhappy at leaving home to attend school. "I never ran into any of that kind of thing. They were happy-go-lucky. Oh, a few teardrops fell, there was always that parting sadness, but they knew that if their parents could get into town, they'd see them. They were gone from September to December, then again to summer holidays. Sometimes they didn't make it home at Easter, it would just depend."

Zinnia Rowan's role in base operations became vitally important the summer that Norcanair started water-bombing for forest-fire suppression.

When the Saskatchewan Smoke Jumpers' program finished about 1966, the government began using Beavers and single Otters outfitted with water-bomb tanks, as well as the Canso.

"The Canso was the water bomber of the skies in those days. Compared to the Beaver which dropped 90 gallons of water, or the single Otter dropping 200 gallons, the Canso dropped 800 gallons. Norcanair had at that time, I believe, two Cansos, and acquired a couple more later on."

G.T. flew the single engine Beaver, which he calls "the plane of the North." Water tanks were installed on top of the floats, then two pipes called "probes" went down between the floats.

"There was a knack to pulling the nose up, bringing up the floats so water wouldn't go in. Then, when you let the floats come down a bit, the forward force drove water up through the curved spouts and into the tanks. When they were full, you'd pull up the nose, the probes would come out of the water and you'd take off, loaded, with 45 gallons in each tank.

"Once you were up and over the fire, you'd pull the 'bowden' cable which would roll the tanks over and dump the water out from the top. When you pushed the cable back in, the tanks would roll back again because they were balanced that way."

Although it was a rather old-fashioned system, G.T. says that it worked.

Flying over fires was not an easy way to make a living. G.T. recalls having to carefully watch for what they called "widow-makers."

"We'd go into a smoky area – which we shouldn't have done but most of us did anyway – to get close to the head of the fire. These widow-makers were the top parts of trees that stuck above the rest of the canopy. They were killers. They could wipe a wing off an airplane, or knock off a strut. With the Beaver, I used to fly 10 or 15 feet above the trees to get the water down into the fire."

Some of the widow-makers would be covered with foliage, some would be grey dead branches that stretched skyward. Both were difficult to see, especially if the pilot was flying into the sun, or in a smoky area.

"Nowadays we have a bird-dog aircraft that leads the bomber aircraft in and checks everything over before he gets down low," G.T. says. "And now with tankers we bomb 75 to 100 feet above the canopy, carrying straight foam so we can bomb at a higher altitude."

Demo-drop by the shoreline at Stony Rapids, July, 1970. *G.T. Rowan Collection*

Another danger for pilots fighting fires was the euphoria experienced during an exercise. "You could get 'drunk with excitement' when you were picking up in lakes, and make mistakes," G.T. says. "You might get your tanks full of water and then find that with the extra weight you couldn't clear the trees at the other end of that lake. You'd have to stop in the lake, roll the tanks over, empty the load, and take off to find another lake. But you'd get so excited, you just wanted to grab more water and get back – until you got tired."

The next danger was becoming "pooped with fatigue."

"We flew lots of hours. I guess we were money-hungry, and fires were the resources. Up north, if you had a set of bomb tanks the DNR wanted you out there. If we got the Canso in to help us, we were that much luckier."

Not only did they try to save the forests, but sometimes they had to save the people who were trying to save the forests.

"We often had to rescue people, especially firefighters, local people with axes and shovels," G.T. says. "There was no way anyone could stop some of those fires, especially if the wind switched and blew it back on them. We'd have to go in and haul them out.

"We always placed the firefighters beside a lake, bringing them in with the airplane on floats, so we could go back and get them out before they became trapped. To rescue them we'd again land on the lake, wherever the camp was. We lost quite a few tents and camping gear and stuff – we just couldn't get them out in time – but we always got the people out."

There has been no loss of human life during G.T.'s experience of fighting fires in the North, but he sometimes saw loss of animal life. "I've seen lots of small animals, like squirrels and porcupines, caught in a fire. I haven't personally seen bears, deer or moose caught, although trappers say they've found moose that were caught in a circle of fire."

One of the oddest, and most embarrassing, of G.T's northern firefighting experiences occurred while he was in Stony Rapids.

Zinnia received a call on the HF radio from Uranium City, and immediately contacted G.T. "You'd better get hold of Chick Terry [the DNR officer at Stony Rapids]. A 'tea' fire has been reported on the shoreline of Black Lake."

A "tea" fire is just a little puff of smoke, G.T. explains, as if someone had made a campfire to boil tea and left it burning.

"Who called it in?" G.T. asked.

"PWA [Pacific Western Airlines] called the station in Uranium City. They spotted the fire when they were flying over. They gave us the coordinates on Black Lake."

Chick Terry agreed that they should check it out. The bomb tanks were already on the airplane, so they quickly flew over to Black Lake. Sure enough, a little puff of smoke was wafting up, near the shoreline.

"That's weird," G.T. commented. "It's right in the middle of a birch bluff!"

The foliage was so thick they couldn't see much else, so Chick ordered G.T. to drop a little water. Then they would land on the lake, park on the shoreline, and go in to assess the problem.

The lake was very rough, so G.T. went back into the bay for the water pickup. When they spotted the fire they dropped the load and circled around to take another look. The fire seemed to have died down but they decided to give it one more load for good measure.

They picked up another load and got back to discover the fire had flared up again. This time they dived low to make sure the water really soaked well into the bush. They did that four times until they were satisfied that the fire had finally died.

Before returning to Stony Rapids, they stopped in to visit Glen Mockford at his tourist camp, called Camp Grayling, on the bay. When Glen's wife, Agath, offered them some of her fresh-baked pie, they sat down to enjoy a good visit. They had half-finished their pie when in through the door stomped a native man, one of the Sayiese boys from Black Lake.

"G.T., you're in deep trouble!" the man growled.

"Why?"

"Old lady Abraham is coming down the shoreline. Her and her old man have a rifle. They said they're going to blow that Beaver right out of the bay!"

"Why? What did I do?"

"You bombed her moosehide!"

"You've got to be joking!"

"No! She was smoking a moosehide, trying to keep that fire going while you kept bombing it! She said she's going to shoot that Beaver, and the pilot, too!"

Chick and G.T. reluctantly left their pie unfinished, jumped into the airplane, and took off.

"That story was the joke of the summer," G.T. says, "that poor lady trying to keep her fire going, with me dumping water on it. Ninety gallons to the load – and we dropped four of them!"

Luckily, no one was hurt by the impact of the water. "When she'd hear the airplane coming she'd run away. I went over a week later to visit her husband and the boys – I knew her boys real well. Everybody thought it was funny, except her. She still couldn't see any humor in it."

G.T. acknowledges that there are many unanswered questions regarding the business of forest fires. Should they be allowed to burn naturally? Should there be 'controlled-burning' to contain growth of overburden? Or should every fire be put out, pronto?

"Growth after a forest fire may come back quickly in southern regions," G.T. says, "but in the North, when those trees are burnt off that Cambrian Shield rock it takes them forever to grow again. The only real growth is along the Thelon River in the Northwest Territories, but that's exceptional. In the Stony Rapids area, or even between LaRonge and Cree Lake, it takes many years to get growth back.

"The trappers told me that in 1956 there was a fire northwest of Stony Rapids. It was still scrub when I was there 13 years later, in 1969. So, it might be okay to let fires go in areas of fast regrowth, but in the North the vegetation has nothing to root into. I've seen trees growing just out of cracks in rocks – and some lifestyles depend on that growth."

The Rowans lived in Stony Rapids from 1969 to the fall of 1972, when they moved to Prince Albert.

"I wanted a bigger airplane. That's a pilot's dream – you fly the 180 and the Beaver looks big; fly a Beaver for a while and the Otter looks big. We decided the next thing was the DC-3. That was the plane of the day – they didn't have the Fairchild F-27s yet.

"I also wanted to get on the Canso and stay in the firefighting business."

G.T. got his wish to fly a DC-3 that winter doing "skeds" (scheduled flights), while Zinnia worked in Norcanair's accounting office in Prince Albert.

In September, 1973, Norcanair bought three F-27s from Air West in Arizona. G.T. was sent to attend ground school in Phoenix. He finished the flight training back in Saskatchewan, "which was better. It was too blasted hot down there for a northern boy – 115 degrees in the shade."

He flew the F-27 on skeds, eventually clocking 1 200 hours on them. When contracts opened up to fly the Canso during the summer months of 1974 and 1975, he applied. He then flew the Canso on summertime firefighting ventures, and the F-27 on year-round sked flights. He also flew the DC-3 on fuel hauls to tourist camps, and in the winter to mining camps such as at Key Lake on skis.

"The Beaver and the DC-3 were my favorite airplanes, and still are," G.T. says.

He preferred fuel-haul flights over skeds. "Fuel barrels don't talk back to you. They don't argue. When customers ordered the fuel, we could get it there within eight hours. We didn't have to be there at 'four minutes past the hour,' that kind of stuff. Sked flying wasn't my thing. A friend of mine, Ray Cameron, calls it 'city flying'. I agree with him. It is. On sked flying you talk to the same people and follow the same route, day in and day out."

In 1976, G.T. felt it was time for a change. Again he was nudged into making that change by a friend.

"A fellow I used to fly with, Myron Barton, was chief pilot for the Saskatchewan government's outfit, Northern Air Services, in LaRonge. Myron made me an offer I couldn't refuse. I was a little reluctant to leave Norcanair, but I wanted a change. I could just see myself sitting there forever, doing the sked five days a week, with maybe a charter or two on the weekends.

"So when Myron said they wanted someone to help test-fly Grumman Trackers I was interested, and the money sounded good, so I talked it over with my wife. She said, 'I'm staying with Norcanair.' We decided that was okay, because I could live in Prince Albert anyway.

"I headed over to Calgary, and Myron got me checked out on the Grummans. He told me, 'You stay here and do the test-flying,' and then he went back to LaRonge.

The 1950-vintage Grumman Trackers had been purchased by Northern Air Services as surplus from the Royal Canadian Navy. The Ontario government had already converted some Trackers to chemical bombers, so the Saskatchewan government decided to do the same. They bought seven of them from surplus, and out of the seven they modified six for chemical bombers. Field Aviation Company Inc. of Calgary did the conversions.

"They were converting the airplane from the military version into the civvy version, totally disassembling the insides and putting in bomb tanks. These planes had flown off the light fleet aircraft carrier *HMCS Bonaventure* in the 1950s, and were used for antisubmarine patrol," G.T. explains. "They were powered by two 1 500 horsepower Wright engines (Military R1820-82). Each had a big radar unit on the bottom, and I think a crew of four: a pilot, copilot, navigator, and bombardier who did the radar work. They would track along the coast, then they'd take them out to sea on the 'Bonny', just as reconnaissance. They could carry depth-chargers and had torpedo doors in the bottom, so they could do it all if they spotted the enemy."

That summer G.T. did the water test-flying on all six Trackers in Calgary, and also did some test-flying back in Prince Albert. "Earl England was the engineer with Field Aviation, and he's now with Northern Air Services in Saskatchewan. Earl and I would repair one aircraft while we kept the other two flying, type of thing, so we kept three going for that summer. By the next summer, we had all six flying on fires."

The last Tracker to fly out of Calgary, ready to go, was christened "G.T. Rowan".

It was an innovative idea to convert the Trackers into water bombers, and G.T. is proud to have been involved. The aircraft also carried a long-term fire retardant that had 24-hour effectiveness. They were fitted with land-based equipment where water, retardant, and a "gum" that held the mix together, were put through a Berry "blender" at the base. This loading operation took just three-and-a-half minutes.

The Trackers were the only airplanes used for this purpose until the fall of 1980 when the government bought three 1943-vintage Canso PBYs from Norcanair. "We flew them to Halifax and had them totally rebuilt."

In 1986, the Saskatchewan government began purchasing Canadair CL-215 "Skimmers", and now have four. Powered by two Pratt & Whitney R-2800 CA 3, 2 100 horsepower engines, with a wingspan of 93-feet 10-inches, and a maximum lift-off weight of 43 500 pounds (after scooping their load), the huge ships can be filled with 1 200 gallons of water in a mere 10 seconds.

G.T. Rowan on the ladder of a Canadair CL-215 Skimmer, LaRonge, SK, 1993. *Photo: S. Matheson*

Then the company acquired Beech Baron B-55s, small twin engine aircraft, to be used as the "bird-dog" or lead-in airplanes.

In 1979, Myron Barton quit his job of chief pilot for Northern Air Services, and G.T. took over. G.T. is presently Operations Manager and Chief Pilot for the government's Northern Air Operations in LaRonge, responsible for the actions of the firefighting unit (now called the Fire Suppression Fleet). (Footnote 1).

G.T. explains the procedure that is followed when a fire is spotted.

"The fire could be spotted by a commercial airline crew member, by one of our local commercial operators, or by our own patrols. If there is a high fire hazard, if it's hot and dry, and if we've had any thunderstorms, then we'll have patrols out. If they spot a fire – 'a smoke' – they call up our Fire Region Coordinator in downtown LaRonge and report it.

"The Coordinator calls our dispatcher at the Tanker Base and gives the directions. We have a way of timing direction and distance so we can figure the coordinates on the map, which is given to the pilot.

"The bird-dog aircraft (the small Beech Baron) takes off first. If it's 'for sure' smoke, then the Trackers go out – the chemical bombers – in groups of three, travelling at 190 knots with a load (or 215 knots without) to the fire. Then the CL-215s go in groups of two, with one bird-dog plane assigned to each group. Cansos go as a group, also with a bird-dog. We have five groups, five Barons. We can also split the groups."

They operate from six bases: LaRonge, Flin Flon, Hudson's Bay, Prince Albert, Meadow Lake, and Buffalo Narrows. One group of three Trackers stays in Prince Albert, the other group of three stays in LaRonge. If they're needed elsewhere, they will be dispatched to that area depending on the fire hazard.

"So away they go to the fire," G.T. continues. "They have a bird-dog officer on board the Baron who is in charge of the fire. If he says, 'I want a line of chemical right here,' the Trackers go and lay the chemical in, just ahead of the fire or right beside it. When the fire burns up to it, the chemicals kill it.

"Then the 215s go out. If the fire is continuing they all work on it, dropping water and foam. If the Trackers come back they might be instructed to take another load. If the bird-dog wants to lay more line to head the fire off in another direction, or into a lake, then the Trackers come back in and we load them up. It takes three-and-a-half minutes to fill them up with 800 gallons of chemical, and back they go again. Or, the

Tanks of water, fire retardant and "gum" pumped into Grumman Trackers. The water and retardant go through a "blender" with the gum. LaRonge, SK, 1993. *Photo: S. Matheson*

bird-dog might say, 'We don't need you out there any more, the 215s can handle it.'

"That would be the procedure for a smoke being reported anywhere within a 120-mile radius of the base. If it's farther they'll go to the fire, drop their load, then go to another, closer base for a reload."

Altogether, Northern Air Services has 19 aircraft: the spotter plane (a Partenavia) sits in Prince Albert; then there are five Beech Baron 55s, six Grumman Trackers, three Canso PBY 5As and four Canadair CL-215s.

Also assisting are up to 15 helicopters, privately contracted by the Fire Management operation, a department of the Saskatchewan government.

The short season would make it nearly impossible for an individual company to get into the water-bombing business; purchase and upkeep of huge machines like Cansos, Canadair CL-215s and Grumman Trackers is difficult.

"It's a big operation," G.T. acknowledges. "Northern Air has quite a few personnel right now. In the summer we've got 75 or 80 people, including 31 or 32 pilots who work from April 15 to September 15. They have to have Airline Transport ratings and a certain number of hours. Pilots are hired on 147-day contracts, but engineers stay year-round because of the heavy maintenance program undertaken during the winter. Our turnover is minimal; some people have been here since 1977. Pilots, too, even with 147-day contracts."

G.T. attributes this low turnover to the variety and interest in the work. "The only time we've had changes is when we've gone into a different type of airplane and had to hire more crews."

Comparing the aviation field now to when G.T. started, he agrees that costs have sky-rocketed. He estimates it would now cost individuals about $30 000 by the time they got an Airline Transport rating, "whereas we got ours for around $1 000."

Pilots hired by the Saskatchewan government's Northern Air Services can expect to make, during the 147-day contract, "maybe $50 000 or $60 000 a year." It sounds good, but G.T. cautions that "they get half and income tax takes the other half."

There is one female water-bomber pilot on staff at Northern Air Services in LaRonge. "Janet Keogh is the only female captain of a water bomber in the world," G.T. says. "She's been here since 1979, and her husband flies for Northern Air Services as well. The first time I saw her, she was loading a 45-gallon drum of fuel onto a Beaver, and that's not easy!"

The pilots fly under MOT (Ministry of Transport) regulations, which specify a 14-hour duty day, which is also company policy. G.T. says he has a good relationship with MOT. "In fact three of their people train and fly with us twice a year." He does not find their regulations difficult to abide by, "as far as firefighting goes."

"In the early days the MOT's regulations bugged us young pilots, but we ignored them because they couldn't find us anyway." He laughs. "Hey! I didn't say that!"

G.T. feels that he got into aviation – and is also getting out of it – at the right time, with the economy sluggish and expenses climbing.

"Commercial aviation, as far as the bush-flying part of it goes, is history now, other than for flying into tourist camps," G.T. says. "The number of roads being built has decreased the flying by a tremendous amount. We've got a road all the way to the edge of Wollaston Lake now, and they're talking about putting one into Stony Rapids. Trapping has pretty well died away. It's going to be tough slugging for operators if they're going to stick to bush flying."

G.T. Rowan, Operations Manager & Chief Pilot, Dept. of Environment Resource Managment, Fire Suppression Fleet, LaRonge, SK, 1993. *Photo: S. Matheson*

The water-bombing business, however, still appears to be quite stable. "There's a lot of bush, expensive bush, that has to be looked after. The more tourist camps we get, the more we have to stay active. But I think the future for us will be going from piston aircraft to turbine."

With retirement coming up in a few years, G.T. has rekindled a dream he's had since youth – to own another Harley Davidson motorcycle.

"When I was a young fella, I had a Harley 45. I always wanted another one but I could never afford it. Then a couple of friends of mine in town who have Harleys, said, 'Why don't you get one?' So – what would you call it? – the boy started coming out in the old man! I decided to order the biggest Harley Davidson they had, brand-new, and that's what I did. I got an Ultra Classic Electra Glide, Road King, 1 340 cc."

The Rowans plan to tour the southern United States on the bike during the winter months.

There seems to be something about pilots that makes them yearn for the next challenge. G.T. agrees, but says that mastering the big Harley will be his last undertaking. But, another friend might just have a new idea, and G.T. could be off again on yet another adventure.

With over 15 000 hours of flying to his credit, G.T. acknowledges that aviation has given him an exciting career that has paid well, financially and personally. He thanks his old friends for giving him the push, when he was young and ready for the game.

"But believe it or not, and Zinnia says the same thing, the best years of my flying career were in Stony Rapids," G.T. says. "Just from the people we met, the socializing, the flying.

"We were young. It was all in front of us."

Footnote 1:

A sign in G.T.'s office attests to the combination of seriousness and humor he brings to the job:

> Attention: pilots with short props or low manifold pressure – please taxi closer to the ramp, as the next pilot may not be on floats.

"The Airmen's World is a Unique Place."

Keith Olson's life began in a log house in a Saskatchewan ghost town located on the Churchill River 60 miles north of Flin Flon. The town of Island Falls was abandoned in 1967 when the hydro-electric power station (where Keith's father had worked since 1929 as an electrical engineer, and later as company superintendent) became operable by remote control. The log house, however, has been retained as a historical example of northern architecture.

Keith's birth on September 1, 1937, also the date of Air Canada's inaugural flight, was prophetically announced by a card depicting an airplane.

1948, Keith Olson (11 years old) building model of a Waco Custom, Island Falls, SK. *Keith Olson Collection*

"Well before school age I was interested in airplanes, fascinated by them," he says. "I built model airplanes. Any time an airplane came to Island Falls – which was fairly frequently because there were no roads – I'd go down and talk to the pilot. I've never wanted to do anything except fly."

Keith and his younger brother lived in Island Falls until they reached 10th grade, when Keith was sent to a boarding school near Moose Jaw called Caronport. During the war, the school site had been used for an airbase.

The school's proximity to a flying club allowed Keith to

further his dream of becoming a pilot. On weekends he hitchhiked to the Regina Flying Club to take lessons from Bob Bell, an ex-air force pilot. "It took about four hours to get there and back. I had to stand out on the road, freezing, until somebody stopped and picked me up. But, I did it."

He took his first flying lesson on October 7, 1954, and made his first solo flight on the 9th, after five hours of dual instruction. He was awarded his private pilot's licence on March 2, 1955.

Following high school graduation, Olson went back to Island Falls to work at the hydro plant as a third operator. He managed to build up a "handful of hours" flying on skis with a borrowed J-3 Piper Cub owned by Jim Ripley, who ran a small outfit in Sandy Bay near Flin Flon. He had 55 hours flying time when he took Ripley's J-3 to Reindeer Lake, 80 miles north of Island Falls. On the way back, he had to fly "from lake to lake" because of heavy snow.

"I was flying very low but I was really relaxed. I kept thinking, 'This is for me!' Little did I know that I would spend many years flying the Arctic in similar stuff. I guess it was an indicator that it and I would get along well."

After a year at the hydro plant, he said, "I want to go flying." His father insisted, however, that he should have more education, so he took a three-year aeronautical engineering diploma course at the Provincial Institute of Technology and Art in Calgary.

While there, Olson got his commercial licence through the Calgary Flying Club on April 16, 1959. Again his instructors were ex-military men, Ray Scott and Jim Tattershaw. After graduating with his engineering diploma, Olson worked as a mechanic at the airport in Calgary, while looking for a flying job. (Later, while flying in the North, he wrote exams for his mechanic's licence.) The first company he applied to was Thomas Lamb Airways Ltd. (later named Lamb Airways, then Lambair), who flew across the country he'd grown up in. They said, "Come on out."

Olson and a friend owned a small Luscombe aircraft with a 65-horsepower engine, so they decided to fly to The Pas for the interview. When he arrived on Thanksgiving Sunday, no one was in the office. Olson phoned the manager at his home.

"Did you bring all your stuff?" he was asked.

"No," Olson said. "Don't you want to interview me first?"

"Naw. Go back and get it."

Olson was hired for his first flying job based on the fact that he'd even come to The Pas! He was ready to begin his commercial flying career, with barely 200 hours to his credit.

The first morning on the job, he met the crew at a local cafe. There were six Lamb sons, who all flew. The principal owner, Tom Lamb, now spent much of his time at his ranch near Moose Lake where he raised prize-winning cattle. Olson didn't meet him until he'd been with the company for several weeks.

"Everyone was really friendly," Olson recalls. "They took me over to the hangar at the base. I did 15 minutes of dual in a Cessna 180 on skis, and then a few more minutes of solo, doing circuits and practising on the lake. That was it. I passed their 'entrance exam.'"

By November, the company had him taking short trips on skis to places like Moose Lake 40 miles away, but soon he was flying to Snow Lake, Grand Rapids and Thompson. "There wasn't much work," Olson recalls. "I often wondered why they'd hired me."

In January, 1960, the company sent him to Gods Lake to stay with the Indian Agent and try to drum up some charter work. He stayed three months, picking up whatever work he could. Every so often one of the Lamb boys would come through, and Olson would hand him a roll of cash received from flying trappers and other customers around the country. Although there weren't many trips, it was good experience for the young pilot for he was left quite on his own.

He quickly learned that customers usually wanted to load twice as much cargo into an airplane as it should carry. Some trips involved taking the doors off the Cessna to get a sleigh in the back, loading supplies, a couple of dogs and two trappers, and then flying 12 miles! "A lot of work for almost nothing, but that's what you did," Olson says. "We called them 'trapper trips' and we charged a 12-mile minimum."

Olson soon met a variety of people who had come to the North seeking their fortunes – or hide-outs – as well as those who called the North their birthplace.

"There were the local types like the Indian Agent, Charlie Slade, who I'd stayed with, and the Hudson's Bay managers. In those days, people in the remote settlements really put their hearts into the communities. Some were hard workers, and some weren't.

"Sometimes I flew Indian families to their traplines. I felt a little sorry for them. The Bay would 'grubstake' them (supply their needs, on credit), and sometimes pay for the flight. They'd trap, live off the land for the winter, come back, pay off the Bay, and then have nothing left. They enjoyed themselves because they were away from the settlements, but it was sort of a dead-end thing. They could live in a tent in the summer and not feel badly done by, but as the years went by, this attitude changed. You could see problems coming. They didn't know where to fit in."

Some of his later flying jobs entailed picking up the Native children from remote settlements to take them to boarding schools. "We'd go

Eskimo family, out of food, ready to be flown in from Yathkyed Lake to Baker Lake, NWT, February, 1962. *Keith Olson Collection*

to the various Eskimo camps and take kids into Chesterfield Inlet, or to Churchill.

"I don't know how Northern Affairs worked it, but we took the kids out in the fall and brought them back in the spring. They were away not quite 10 months, whatever was sort of convenient.

"In those days, no one seemed to know just what to do with people in the North, in the Arctic," Olson says. "Should the Eskimos stay on the land, or shouldn't they? There were two schools of thought that never seemed to mesh. There still isn't any answer. But taking the kids out, I think, was the end of it, because once they'd been out they didn't mind *going* back but they didn't want to *stay* back."

Olson observed first-hand the importance of family in the Eskimo culture. "They had nothing else. They lived a harsh life, and death was imminent from starvation or illness. So, to take away the kids, it was really hard.

"They were very stoic people," he adds. "One time when we brought the kids back to Aberdeen Lake west of Baker Lake, the sea ice was so rotten I had to land on a slope on the side of a hill, on skis. These people had camped across the creek, waiting for their kids. A little girl got off the airplane with her school books and her doll. Her parents greeted her, but no one showed emotion in front of the white man. What they did was shake their daughter's hand, and you could just tell that they were so happy to see her back.

"It was heartbreaking to realize these people hadn't had their kids around for a whole winter. As soon as summer came they got to see them for a little bit, then they were off again."

Olson acknowledges, however, that the education gained did help in some ways. "The transition was inevitable, there was no way it wasn't going to happen. It was just a matter of time."

For Keith Olson, every day he spent in the North was a learning experience. When a group of prospectors came from Thompson to do some staking at the north end of Gods Lake, he got their flying contracts. One time he landed on a small lake in the spring when the snow was getting soft. As soon as he touched down he knew he was going to be stuck, so he cut the power and stopped. One of the passengers strapped on a pair of snowshoes and clambered out to discover that the airplane had settled so deeply into the snow that he could lean his elbow on the wing tip! It took them all evening to dig and tramp out an airstrip in the deep snow, and get the airplane turned.

From Gods Lake, the company sent Olson to Thompson to work on a 14-month contract for Inco (International Nickel Company of Canada Limited). At that time, the mine was set up, 2 000 single men were there, and exploration was going on all around, but smoke wasn't yet coming from the stacks in Thompson. Olson mostly made short hauls of about 50 miles, supplying the drill camps. He also made the odd trip up to Kettle Rapids, or back to Gods Lake where the company had some land staked.

"I went in to lots of places that were supposed to be secret, not only for Inco but I also took on charter flights for others if we had the time. People would stake claims and say, 'Don't tell anyone!'"

Olson quickly learned that it was a pilot's job to see all, know all and say nothing. "They beat that into our heads. They said, 'We're in the flying business, not in the business of nosing around about what our clients do.' It was a good philosophy, because if any of us had staked around, and word got out, that would have been the end of the airline business. People would have shied away from using our services."

In the summer of 1961, Olson went up to Churchill on a contract for the army who were taking aerial photographs and using tellurometers to take measurements, to correct maps of the North. Olson recalls that these instruments gave amazingly accurate readings: over eight miles – the maximum reading area – they might be out two inches at the most.

"First, we would pick a known point on the map, like a prominent rock on a lake. They'd stand the equipment up," Olson says. "We'd fly five or six miles in each direction to another point that could be recognized on a photograph, and measure the distance from one instrument to the other. We started from Churchill and worked about 600 miles, up past Baker Lake. All that time we lived in fly-infested tents, which was an experience in itself."

Olson also flew employees of the Geological Survey of Canada to northern sites. "Their idea was to walk over every piece of Canada. We'd park, they would do sort of a 'square circle' and record what they saw, even old cabins. We'd move them a few miles and they'd do it again. They also had canoes, which we had to transport on the airplane. It would get quite warm sometimes, in July, and we'd be in the water fighting off the mosquitos, wearing hip waders, and falling around on rocks trying to tie on a canoe. The bugs just about drove us nuts. We sometimes had to wear head nets. That first summer we flew all over the North, as far as the Arctic Circle.

"Then, because I hadn't got lost or otherwise come to grief, Lamb Airways decided I should go back to Churchill. I flew a Norseman (CF-INN) out of there for one year – that Norseman is at the bottom of a lake right now – and an Otter for three years, as far as the north end of Baffin Island."

Olson's favorite aircraft was the Norseman, even with its faults. "It was hard to fly in some circumstances, more of a challenge, but it's a genuine bush plane," he says. "I also loved the single Otter – it would do what the Norseman would do, but do it a lot better. You could land in a lot shorter spaces.

"The Norseman on skis in the Arctic had one major drawback: it just didn't land 'slow'. Often the snow in the North is very hard, you could walk on it and not leave a mark. To avoid damaging the aircraft, we always looked for the smoothest area to land on, such as glare ice. But on many occasions there wasn't much choice and we had to just hang on. The Norseman would land, crash! We hated that! If there was a wind it wasn't so bad, but we'd usually

Keith Olson and helper refueling Lamb Airways Norseman CF-INN, Baker Lake, NWT, January, 1962. *Keith Olson Collection*

crash to a stop, and crash taking off. Bang! Bang!

"The Otter could get off and land slower, and in shorter distances; on floats it was able to carry a bit more than the Norseman, and it had good range. The Norseman was also quite drafty – it had a little Janitrol heater under the seat, but as soon as you'd take off it would cool right down. So it was uncomfortable, whereas the Otter was better. I liked them both, though, totally different airplanes."

Olson flew on floats more often than on skis, because the airline was busier in the summer. Floats demanded a different method of flying. "You can get into a lot of trouble on floats because you can't just stop the airplane. You have to pick your water, and estimate the wind and the current to know where you should be able to stop.

"I spent my last four years with Lamb's flying out of Churchill, landing on and taking off from the ocean, so I had to really watch the swell and the weather. If I landed, was there a place to tie up? And I had to make sure I knew where I could take off from. You don't land and then say, 'I wonder where the reefs are?' because you can't see them when you're down."

In the spring he had to contend with ice clunking around in the water. Even in August, considered the best time of year to fly, sea ice would still be floating around settlements such as Igloolik on the Melville Peninsula, nearly preventing him from getting in.

Swells were Olson's worst problem when landing on the ocean. "You can see them when you fly over. If there was a storm on the east side, those waves would eventually work their way across. Or, there could be a wave coming from the north, and then another set of waves could roll in from the west. They would all meet at an apex."

One time, Olson was bringing some students down from Rankin and Chesterfield inlets to attend school in Churchill. He went into Whale Cove, picking a place that was fairly smooth to land the Otter. He came in but noted the swell, and remembers thinking, 'I don't know if I should have done this!' More kids boarded at Whale Cove, so the airplane was heavily loaded. He tried twice to get off, but because of the swell he could go only one way. As the waves came in the floats started to submerge. Olson turned off the power and aborted the takeoff. He tied up to a big fishing boat and everyone got off. They waited overnight for the waves to settle down.

"You've got to know when to quit," Olson says. "That was one of the few times – maybe the only one – that I got caught on the ocean because of the swell. You could always see it. The ocean could be perfectly calm, but in would come rollers from some previous storm."

Sometimes the tide prevented him from anchoring the airplane safely once he was down. "The first time I anchored my Beaver on the ocean bottom off Chesterfield Inlet, the water was calm as glass. I just threw the anchor out and someone came out in a boat to bring me to shore. But all night I was nervous, knowing my airplane was anchored half-a-mile out. I couldn't wait to get up in the morning to see if it was still there!"

At Eskimo Point (now called Arviat) he would tie up to an anchored raft.

The ocean at Repulse Bay, at high tide, runs into a lake that they usually landed on, resulting in a tide of its own that rises and falls 12 inches, while the ocean outside the lake rises and falls 12 feet.

The problem is the lake's rocky shoreline. If the aircraft is tied to the shore at high tide and the lake drops 12 inches, it could get hung up on the rocks. If it's tied up at low tide and the lake rises 12 inches, the aircraft might also be banged up on the rocks. So, Olson carried a little war surplus raft (which included a parachute in case a person was shot down over the ocean). "When I'd anchor on this lake, I'd have a helper with me," he says. "He would get into this raft, paddle to shore, then walk around to the upwind side of the lake and throw the raft into the water. It would drift back to me. I'd get in and paddle myself to shore."

At other places the water might be so deep that if a wind came up the anchor could drag at an angle, so he had to watch that, too. "Looking after the airplane was probably more challenging than flying," Olson says. "You were always calculating the odds. Baker Lake is 60 miles long and there is a good sweep down the lake. I used to have rows with the weather office in Churchill over their unreliable forecasts. 'It's good and calm,' they'd say, and I'd get there and it would be terrible. But in those days there weren't many recording stations and they had a tough job."

Olson got caught at Baker Lake twice in one summer when the wind came up unexpectedly during the night. "I woke up and went to the beach, and saw the waves just rolling in. We had to get a D-6 Cat to drag the airplane out of the water, up the steep beach, and onto sand until the storm passed.

"Down south you have trees around the lakes and you can get into the sheltered side. There is no shelter up there because there are no trees – and no spare parts if the aircraft gets damaged."

Being both a pilot and a mechanic proved quite useful. Although Olson wasn't a licensed mechanic when he first went north, he did what had to be done. Then Tom Lamb asked him to get his licence, because of the difficulty in finding a licensed mechanic to sign off the airplane in remote areas.

Emergency repairs had to be made, legally or illegally, to get out of a fix. "You'd do what you had to do – change a mag or patch floats. No one else was there. With the licence I could do it legally."

To patch a small hole in a float, he carried an epoxy plastic body-filler material similar to that used on automobiles. It served until he could get to the service base.

"Once, I hit a drill rod in the water south of Thompson, and it cut a long rip in the float," Olson recalls. "I got the airplane back to the dock and propped the float out of the water. I put rags in this long tear and covered the whole thing with sticky heavy drill-rod grease, almost like a glue. Then I dropped the float back into the water and flew on to The Pas."

During his years of flying in the Arctic with Lamb's, Olson never had a copilot, although he often was given a helper. "The helper was usually some chap from The Pas who wanted a job. In the winter we had to dig out our gas drums from caches here and there. We'd know they were in the snowdrift somewhere, so we'd dig and roll them out. It involved a lot of physical work, using shovels or whatever we could find."

At Baker Lake the gas was cached on the shore, but at Rankin Inlet some drums were kept out on the sea ice because the airstrip would sometimes drift in. When that happened, they had to land out on the ocean to get to the fuel. In a storm, that could be tricky.

But Olson's worst memories of arctic flying concern the ritual of starting the aircraft in the cold mornings. He would carry as many as four blowpots, but they didn't all work at one time.

"Some of those days, the only time we were warm was when we'd crawl under the tents with the blowpots. As soon as we shut them off we knew we were going to be cold for the rest of the day."

Although the flame from the blowpot was smokeless, Olson acknowledges there must have been fumes. "Maybe that's why pilots age fast," he laughs. "We tried to use ACTO, a low-grade automotive gas with less lead in it.

"We'd sit under the tarps, with no ventilation, for up to two hours with the blowpots burning away. We didn't want a draft!"

The Otters sat fairly high off the ice. When the wind was blowing, and it was 49 degrees below zero – a typical temperature at Chesterfield and other northern sites – and the tarps would be flapping, it was hard to keep in much heat.

"We must have been breathing almost pure fumes, although our eyes didn't smart or anything," Olson says. "We were out of the heavy fumes because we'd lay down with our heads near the ice, leaning on one elbow. If we sat up, the fumes would be quite dense.

"We carried brooms to brush snow off the wings, then we'd prop them up in front of the engine to hold the tarp from going right against the cowling so the heat could stay in, and put weights around the edges. If there weren't enough sleeping bags and stuff to go around and weigh down the tarp, one of us would lie on a piece of tarp to keep it from flapping, and just not move.

"We went through that operation every day. Some days it took only 20 minutes or so to get the engines warmed up, but most times longer."

Dressing for the climate threw mobility and fashion out the window in exchange for basic warmth. "I started off with a cheap parka, but eventually I got a good Woods parka with a fur-lined hood. I bought quilted nylon air force wind pants, really warm, and air force war surplus flying boots. I'd wear a couple pairs of socks along with leather slippers inside those things. Then I'd have on coveralls, and a down-filled jacket.

"I made sure my helpers were similarly dressed. We might be in the middle of nowhere and crash this airplane, so we had to be prepared to survive with what was on our backs."

Performing toilet functions when they had to overnight in the middle of nowhere in winter presented major problems. "In those days you hardly ever had to go, because you never drank anything. You didn't *want* to go to the bathroom!" Olson laughs. "It was something you tried to avoid.

"Specifically, you had to remove the one-piece coveralls, if you were going to do anything serious. So you'd plan your life even to that extent."

One time they got stuck north of Baker Lake late in the day with a storm brewing. "It was contrary to what we usually did, but Barry Gunn, the Northern Affairs representative with us – who was always weather-sensible – said he just had to get to White Lake. We went out there, landed, and he went off to the campsite. Then the weather came down. By the time he got back to the plane it was approaching dusk, and I knew we were going to have fun getting back."

Olson called Baker Lake on the HF (High Frequency) radio and was warned to not even bother coming. "Visibility is nil. You won't be able to land." Olson diluted the engine and announced, "Here we are."

And there they stayed, for three days.

If the situation had become desperate they knew they could have gone and lived with the Eskimos, but as they had sleeping robes, and the plane was large enough to allow the four men to lie on the floor, they camped inside the Otter. The primus stove kept them fairly warm during the day, but they shut it off at night. The weather blew and stormed and became ever colder. That's when the delicate problem presented itself of going to the toilet. "Nobody wanted to go out onto the ice and pull their drawers down to do the necessaries," Olson says, "but by the third day we had to do something. So, we each took turns, even though the wind was howling and we thought we'd freeze ourselves."

Flying in the North throughout the year meant dealing with darkness a good portion of the time. Keith Olson describes a typical day for a northern pilot.

"You'd get up in the dark, walk down onto the ice, and thread your way through the ice hummocks, everything black. You'd go into the airplane, get a blowpot and light it.

"Around December there's almost no daylight. At Repulse Bay, for example, there is absolutely no daylight for one day of the year. Zero. Even on a clear day the 'viz' might be eight or nine miles, max, because of ice crystals forming from fog in the air. If there was any kind of bad weather around, navigation was a real challenge. There were few radio beacons in those days so you had to navigate by map. You didn't dare get lost – how would you find your way back? How would someone find you?"

Olson flew without the aid of any electronic navigational units, except for an ADF directional finder, which was helpful when they were coming down to Churchill. "Chesterfield also had a beacon. Baker Lake had a pitiful thing they called a beacon which they replaced after I left, but it was so poor we couldn't get very far with it. Coral Harbour had a beacon.

"We usually took along a nurse and an interpreter, a DNA (Department of Northern Affairs) representative, and sometimes an RCMP constable, to record who was born, who died, what was going on, the state of their health, and check all these people out, generally. The local people knew where everyone lived, and we had a map from Northern Affairs, who had advised us which families to visit. The map described where they lived, all right, but try going out in that kind of weather to find them! Away from the settlements, there were just igloos. It was hard enough to find a house, but igloos blend in with the environment so we had to really pay attention."

Map-reading from the air was a specialized task, especially when a pilot couldn't see anything below. In the Arctic, the lakes and the land look the same. How would they know if they were over a lake, when it was frozen and snow-covered and there were no trees to mark the shoreline? The land for hundreds of miles was flat. Perhaps they might see something that looked like a shoreline, but of what lake?

Caution was the byword. "If we flew in the pitch dark, it was to some place that had lights, like Churchill. At Baker Lake they had an airstrip on the ice that was always clear of drifts. The town lights were on the side of the lake, so I could line up with the town. I did this when landing on floats as well as skis.

"We all used compasses. The magnetic compass actually worked better in the North than everybody said it did, unless you were in turbulence and were getting bounced around. We also had an astro-compass. If you could see the sun, you could get an accurate directional reading. Most of the time you couldn't see the stars up there, but if you could, that would get you within an approximate distance of where you wanted to go."

One time Olson got away late out of Churchill en route to Eskimo Point. As he flew up the coast in the dusk, heavy ice crystals further reduced visibility and he flew right past the settlement. "I was looking to my left, toward the sun, so I'd be able to see shadows from buildings in the settlement, and I flew out over the sea ice. I finally called the base and asked if they'd heard me go by. 'Didn't hear you,' they said.

"I knew I'd gone past it, but I figured once it got dark and I could see the lights of town, I could find it. I turned around and came back. By then I could see the lights, and they'd also put some flares out for me."

If Olson had to fly north in bad weather, he would choose to fly up the coast over the sea ice. "The ice is always moving. Usually there are places several miles from shore where there are cracks in the ice, called 'leads,' and I'd follow these things. The land varies in elevation – you can hit the land before you see it – but the ocean is flat and the leads are visible."

Olson has never become lost, but there was one time when he was "temporarily disoriented."

"I was in the Norseman with some schoolteachers on board, making the five-hour trip to Baker Lake from Churchill. It was a stormy day, I could hardly see anything, but I knew if I got to Baker I could land alongside the town.

"Visibility was so bad I didn't even bother trying to map-read. I could see the ground going by in bits and pieces. When I'd flown for four hours I tried to pick up the weak Baker Lake beacon, but because of the strong wind and snow static, I couldn't pick it up. Basically, I was instrument flying at 700 feet or so, and just waiting for the beacon to show up to take me in to Baker Lake.

"Then I thought, 'What will I do if the beacon isn't working and I miss Baker Lake? How can I land when I can't see the ground?' I couldn't just circle around looking for a place to land because it was blowing so hard it was impossible to see the ground. I would have to take a chance and land into the wind, hoping I didn't run into a rock pile or something. You just don't do that!

"I figured I'd better go to Plan B. I cut southeast, thinking that once I got to the coast I would recognize the landscape. I came out near where I thought I should be, on the coast between Eskimo Point and Whale Cove."

He then asked the passengers which of the two places they preferred to land. They chose Whale Cove.

"We were getting low on fuel, but I figured we could make it to Whale Cove all right. When we got there, I said, 'How about Rankin Inlet?' I actually preferred Rankin and it was only another 45 miles. It was a nicer place to stay, we had gas stored there, and the airstrip was right beside the town. If I could find the town I could find the strip. Rankin was fine.

"By the time we got there, we'd been flying for six hours and 55 minutes, and were just about out of gas. I doubt the Norseman would have flown many more minutes. I was used to the airplane, though, and I knew we'd make it on the gas I had left."

Seven straight hours in a Norseman is a tough ride. By the time they arrived at Rankin Inlet, Olson and his passengers were "just vibrating." They had taken off in the semi-darkness and were landing in the dark as well.

Snow conditions and lack of visible landmarks dictate the types of landings a northern pilot can make on skis over the rock-hard drifts.

"I liked to land parallel to the drifts," Olson says, "but if the wind was strong and I had to land into it, and if it was blowing across the drifts, I had to think: if I land crosswind, the airplane could skid sideways; if I land into the wind I'll be banging into the drifts. So that was always a decision."

Although there wasn't usually much curl to the drifts, they were hard and steep enough to damage the undercarriage just by hitting them. "The Norseman suffered every time we landed. We started off with a hydraulic wheel-ski that let us lift up the skis and land on wheels, such as for takeoffs and landings from the concrete runway at Churchill. But the metal wheel-skis couldn't take the hard drifts; the control rods would break.

"We finally had to put boards on, old-fashioned wooden skis, which stood the abuse better. But then, landing in Churchill was always a challenge because we had to land on an area of rolled smooth snow beside the long runway. It didn't matter from which direction the wind was blowing, we had to land the same way. So we'd land crosswind and skid along."

They had all kinds of adventures, trying not to run into other parked airplanes, because there are no brakes on skis.

One of Olson's more unusual experiences occurred while he was flying a Cessna 180 for Lamb Air. He had taken off from Moak Lake, the location of Inco's original find in the North, 17 miles from the new ore body at Thompson. Because the exploration camp remained in Moak Lake the aircraft was also based there, although most of the flying originated from Thompson.

Just after takeoff, Olson felt a jarring vibration. He looked down to discover that the entire left wheel and ski assembly was in the process of breaking right off at the axle. Four bolts hold the axle on, and it can get cracks through that area that can cause the whole thing to sever.

He turned and headed back to Moak Lake, listening to the loose piece whirl around, held onto the aircraft only by check cables and a brake line, and feeling the airplane shake and shudder. Finally the wheel-ski broke off and was gone. Olson breathed a sigh of relief. At least now it wouldn't wind around and do damage to the fuselage.

He could stay airborne as long as he had gas, so his best bet was to turn again and head back to Thompson. He knew that one of the Lamb Air pilots was at home, so Olson buzzed his trailer and the man came out. It took the fellow one quick look to assess the problem. He immediately jumped into his truck, drove to the base, and got on the radio.

"There's nothing hooked up on the back, on the tail," he informed Olson. "It's all clear."

Olson radioed Lamb Air at The Pas, 180 miles away, told them what had happened, and outlined his plan. "Don't worry," came the reassuring response. "Find a lake, a good place to land – and do what you have to."

Back he went to Moak Lake. He figured if he could land along the sheltered shore where the ice had frozen smooth and the snow would be deep, perhaps the leg wouldn't dig in too much and he could land

Keith Olson – a safe landing with the Cessna 180 on one ski. *Keith Olson Collection*

safely. He found a little bay indented into the bush, east of the camp, with lots of soft snow and what he suspected was good ice under the snow.

He noticed that they'd brought out the Bombardier, with the nurse, in case he did some damage to himself. Good. Might need her. Down he came.

The conditions were as he'd imagined. The deep snow caused the airplane to tilt a bit on landing. The lone ski sunk six inches into the snow, while the broken-off leg punctured through the snow and skidded along the ice for 150 feet. The airplane turned, and stopped – a smooth end to a dramatic morning.

In the spring of 1962, Keith Olson announced to the boss that he was planning to marry his childhood sweetheart, Barbara Westbury, on October 6th. He had been flying out of Churchill all that winter. To accommodate his young pilot, Tom Lamb said that he could come down and fly out of The Pas for a while, to be nearer home. Then, following the wedding, the couple could go back to live in Churchill. So, that summer Olson hauled fish with the Norseman (CF-MAM) in to The Pas, and to Wabowden, 60 miles south of Thompson. This site, originally a railroad roundhouse town, had become a centre for shipping fish because of its adjacency to the rail line.

Replacing fabric on the belly of Lamb Airways Norseman CF-MAM with cotton sheet purchased from Hudson's Bay Co., Wabowden, MB, 1962. This aircraft is now on display in Calgary in the Petro-Canada building. *Keith Olson Collection*

One day, as he approached the dock in the Norseman to pick up a load of fish, Olson noticed that the Indians were all pointing at his airplane. He got out to look. The fabric had torn off the back part of the belly, likely having rotted from years of fish drippings. But there it was, everything wide open. He flew back empty to Wabowden to see what could be done.

Connie Lamb said he would come to Wabowden as soon as he could with another airplane, but in the meantime, Olson undertook one of his many bush repairs. He went into the Hudson's Bay store and bought a cotton bed sheet, stitched it onto his airplane, slapped on some dope to hold it, and called Connie to say he'd looked after the problem. The bed-sheet patch stayed on the plane for the rest of the summer. (Norseman CF-MAM is now restored and displayed in the Petro-Canada building in Calgary).

After Keith and Barbara were married, they made their home in Churchill. They had both grown up in Island Falls, so Barbara was familiar with northern living. At Churchill she ran the base radio, which allowed her and Keith to communicate from his far-off locations. Sometimes he was away from home for more than a month at a time.

Although Barbara liked the North, she didn't have the opportunity to observe its vastness and beauty the way Keith did on flying trips. "She was mainly stuck in Churchill," Olson says. "She got a couple of trips, but with running the radio and the household – one of our children was born there – she was kind of stuck."

Olson explains that with Lamb Airways, like all such companies, when the pilots weren't flying they were expected to repair things in the hangar, or pick up freight at the CN station. Some trips might take him away for days, and when he returned he looked forward to a bit of a break. But at 7:30 a.m., a telex would come from Tom Lamb. "What are you doing today?"

Olson laughs at the recollection.

"That was Tom's style of saying, 'It's 7:30. Why aren't you in the hangar?' He was a good guy, but he didn't seem to realize I wouldn't have minded a day to just sit around.

"But," he adds, "that's the way it was. The philosophy was that you worked for the company 24 hours a day; it wasn't something stated, but expected. I was usually the only pilot at Churchill. In the summer, others would come up, but by and large, I was there alone. One airplane could handle all the work.

"It was a hard life, but we liked it."

One time Olson was flying a Single Otter (CF-MEL) from Chesterfield Inlet into Coral Harbour. It was very cold, close to 50 below. He got out of Chesterfield and went up to 8 000 feet looking for warmer air, but never found it. He knew he was over the centre of Southhampton Island but because of ice crystals in the air he could barely see the ground. Suddenly oil splattered across the windshield. The crankcase breather was freezing over and causing oil to blow out around the prop seal! He had to land.

Immediately below was an esker, a high ridge of sand. The wind had blown the top flat and smooth so it resembled a tiny airstrip. Could he land there? If not, he would have to chance landing in the drifts.

"I landed on the esker. We got out, chipped the ice out of the breather, heated up some oil in a five-gallon pail with the blowpot, refilled the engine oil tank, and took off for the remaining short hop to Coral Harbour."

Olson was flying north in the Otter (CF-MEL) one day in July, 1963, when he received a message that some boaters had become marooned on an ocean reef north of Whale Cove. When he spotted their smoke signal he landed on the ocean, but couldn't get over to the rocks because of the swell. He anchored as close as possible, and tried to think how he and his passengers could complete the rescue.

"It was a terrible place, very cold," Olson recalls. "At high tide they would have been under the waves. We had to get them off immediately."

One of his passengers, who worked for the Fish and Game branch, had an idea. "You've got a rubber raft on board, haven't you?"

"Yes, but it's just big enough for two people."

"Okay. I'll paddle over to the rock, and bring back one man at a time with me on the raft."

That is how the rescue was made. "He had the idea, and he was brave enough to carry it out," Olson said. "In this way, all were saved."

The boaters had experienced trouble with their outboard motor and had pulled onto the reef. In the middle of the night their boat floated away, leaving them marooned. Fortunately, they had carried their gasoline high onto the rock. Their signal fire, ignited from the gas, had brought their rescuers to the tiny reef in the nick of time.

In January, 1965, Olson was flying Lamb Airways' Otter (CF-MEL), hauling supplies from Baker Lake west to Schultz Lake. "Northern Affairs was setting up what was called an ECU (Emergency Camping Unit) that contained seal oil, food, and bagged dog food, to aid starving Eskimo families. Word was spread to the Eskimos in that area, around Aberdeen Lake, that if they were out of food they could go to this place and use it, rather than face starvation."

Rescuing marooned boaters from a reef in the ocean north of Whale Cove, NWT, July, 1963. *Keith Olson Collection*

Usually when he had a stopover in remote places during intensely cold weather he would leave the engine running on idle while he loaded or off-loaded. This time, when he got to Baker Lake he noticed a major oil leak. He immediately shut off the engine, and discovered the oil cooler had blown. To get another oil cooler involved radioing out, then waiting for its delivery.

Impatient to continue his deliveries, he thought he'd try flying with the belly panels off the airplane, reasoning that the weather was so cold that the slipstream would blow up onto the belly and cool the oil enough to not need an oil cooler. He removed the old one, got some copper pipe from a nearby garage, and ran a by-pass.

Then he put his experiment to work. It ran a bit hot, but he figured it would be okay. When he put a load in (causing the nose to go up a bit) it ran quite fine. He was thus able to finish his freight haul with no oil cooler. But he was stuck in Baker Lake for over a month because it stormed the whole time. When a replacement part finally came in, he installed it and headed back to his base at Churchill.

After flying for Lamb Airways for six years, from 1959 to 1965, Olson began to think about making a change. He had a family to support, and, while the money he made was adequate, it was certainly not making him rich.

"I'd had enough, basically. We'd been in Churchill four years and the Otter was Lamb's biggest airplane at the time. I asked, 'Where am I going with this outfit?' We had very few pilots in those days, and there were six Lamb brothers senior to me. I could see myself getting nowhere with the company, as far as getting into new equipment or even moving south. The novelty of living up there was wearing off, and I figured it was time to look around."

When he'd started flying to Gods Lake in the Cessna, he was making $240 a month gross, but his room and board were included. "I didn't care then if I made any money. I just wanted to fly," Olson says. "When I left Lamb's in 1965, I was lucky if I was making $1 000 a month, and I put in some long hours. I was paid by the flying hour, about $4 an hour south of Churchill, and $5 north, plus base pay. Most airlines paid so many cents a mile, which worked out to virtually the same thing."

In the summer of 1965, the family moved to Winnipeg when Olson got a job with Transair, flying a Beech 18 (CF-TAV). The job entailed bush-flying on floats off the Red River in Winnipeg on "skeds" (scheduled runs) up the lake to Berens River, Poplar River and Norway House; and about 300 miles from Winnipeg to Island Lake (one of the largest native settlements in central Manitoba), and to St. Theresa Point.

Keith Olson with Trans Air Beech 18 CF-TAV, Berens River, MB, Sept., 1965. *Keith Olson Collection*

In the winter months he flew on wheel-skis directly from the Winnipeg terminal. Olson would pull his twin-engine Beech 18 Expediter in among the big jet airplanes, and help his passengers board for trips to the northern settlements that lay along his sked run.

He liked doing skeds. What he especially liked was that he was home every night, and now he didn't have to do any maintenance. When he parked the airplane at the Transair hangar, his shift was complete. Most of his flights were in the daytime hours because his Beech 18 didn't contain any navigation equipment. "That was rather strange. With all the communication equipment available, and Transair being considered a rather large airline, although I could communicate via radio there was no ADF indicator, nothing. There was no way I could navigate in that airplane except by map."

The aircraft was kept in a hangar overnight, so it was warm when he started off in the morning, another real treat. If, however, he got caught in one of the northern settlements at night and was told it was snowing in Winnipeg, he could stay put – except then he had two engines to warm with blowpots, instead of one!

"It was an easier job than I'd had up north, much more civilized," Olson says. "Even map-reading was easier, because there were trees. I'd flown this area earlier with Lamb's so I knew the country. I could fly in worse weather in Manitoba than in the Arctic because I could see the ground. In the Arctic you push things more, handle bad weather and sort of fly to the edge because if you don't you won't get the job done. But down south it was never like that, so it was a pretty relaxed job compared to what I'd put up with."

His customers were trappers, Indian Affairs officials, numerous groups from government or mining outfits, and local residents coming to or leaving the city hospitals, but he mostly hauled mail and freight.

"With that Beech 18, I handled virtually all the service north to Norway House and the other settlements on Lake Winnipeg, and on Island Lake. There was the odd other charter, but I handled all the traffic. People didn't fly around so much in those days. Now, you have umpteen airplanes going from Winnipeg every day. Dozens of people are flying north – and the taxpayer is paying for it, I can tell you that."

Olson continued to enjoy his sked runs, and can hardly recall a morning he didn't go. "I think I turned back once. I was heading to Island Lake and got all iced up so I came back."

Olson says that he sometimes heard the Beech 18 referred to as "The Widow-Maker," and admits that "you just had to watch it."

A lot of air force people who trained on Beech 18s disliked them, saying they were hard to fly, Olson recalls. Landing was sometimes a problem because you had to wheel it on, you couldn't "stall on." That meant he had to "fly" the Beech 18 onto the runway (when there would still be sufficient airflow over the wings to be actually flying). A stall occurs when not enough air flows over the wings to keep the airplane aloft, and the whole weight of the airplane settles onto the wheels.

"If you landed at low speed, you basically lost control – it would bounce down the runway," Olson says. "Compared to other bush airplanes, the Beech landed relatively fast. Even a Norseman would land in a shorter space.

"You had to pick your water when you were on floats. Landings were fast so you could really abuse the airplane if you had rough water."

Although it never happened to Olson, he knew some pilots had problems with the Beech 18 because of an "engine-out" situation (where one engine quits). "They weren't good on one engine," Olson says. "If you were on wheels they were okay, but on floats if you got a load on they wouldn't climb. You could fly a long way but you'd lose altitude."

One time, Olson was flying Transair's Beech 18 when the retractable wheel-skis malfunctioned. He was coming down from Sandy Lake on wheels, the last stop in the spring, when he looked out and saw that one ski was down. He'd have to land on one wheel and one ski! He flew past the Control Tower in Winnipeg. They confirmed it: one ski was up and one was down.

"I figured I could put the other ski down and land at the St. Andrew's airport which was just being constructed," Olson says. "It was springtime, and there was a lot of mud and water there. I'd get the airplane dirty, but at least we wouldn't turn over."

The Control Tower called him back as he was heading north to take a look at St. Andrews. "There's a piece of snow along runway 31 where it hasn't quite melted away, where the snowblowers have blown it," the controller said. "It's a ridge about 20 feet wide and maybe 400 feet long. See if you can land there."

Back he came to check it out.

"The fire trucks and everyone were out to watch because of the possibility that I might ground-loop (flip over). Everyone, that is, except Transair whose airplane it was. They didn't bother coming out.

"I let the other ski down and landed perfectly with the two skis on this little bit of snow. The company was happy with that. Their airplane was in Winnipeg, where it was supposed to be, with no mud on it."

Olson had by now decided it was time to get off the Beech and onto larger aircraft. The company's DC-3 was the next step. They let him fly it for one month. "I liked the DC-3. It was like a big Norseman, very easy to fly. I wish I could have flown it more."

Olson also was impressed by Transair's Cansos, the flying boats, but he felt the time had come for him and the company to part. He worked for Transair not quite a year, from the summer of 1965 to the spring of 1966.

"I was promised pay raises that I never got and a few things like that, so I finally decided I'd had enough. I was complaining aloud one day in the Winnipeg Flying Club, when a friend of mine mentioned that Air Canada was hiring. I'd never even thought of them!

"I phoned, and presto! I had a job. So if I hadn't complained, or hadn't decided to have a coffee that day, I would have ended up with Canadian Airlines, presumably. That's not bad, but that's the way it would have gone."

He laughingly remembers the prophesy of his airplane design birth announcement, and his birth date coinciding with Air Canada's first flight.

Olson's training with Air Canada was a completely new learning experience, technically and socially. "There were 24 of us in the class, only four of whom were not ex-military. We came out of the bush, a totally different environment to these military guys, so we had a bit to catch up on.

"At that time the military pilots had flown fast airplanes, high. The highest I'd ever been was 8 000 feet in my Otter going into Coral Harbour, so I didn't know anything about high-altitude flying. It was difficult for some of us to get used to instrument flying."

When he passed the training course, he was supposed to start on a DC-8 but there were no DC-8s based in Winnipeg. He asked if they could change it to the Viscount, a four-engine turbo-prop aircraft that carried 48 passengers. The company agreed. He was copilot on the Viscount for a little over a year. "When the DC-9s came in and the base expanded, they started getting rid of the Viscounts, *en masse*, so we all went on DC-9s. I was on the DC-9 for eight years on right seat [copilot], then I was a captain for a few years."

The day in 1975 when Olson got his final check-ride, from which he emerged as an airline captain, was one he will never forget. "Maybe the elation came because I was so glad to be a captain – everybody wants to be one – but partly because of the ride itself. They'd told me that I would be flying to Halifax and some other places for my check ride, but that morning they decided to change it. I'd been studying that route like mad, and suddenly I was told I had to do another route!

"But, it worked out well. A rather stern instructor said some complimentary things about my flying, so nothing else mattered. That was the highlight of my whole career, becoming a captain."

With the Viscounts and DC-9s he flew back and forth across Canada. "If I had a nickel for every time I've landed in Saskatoon and Regina I'd have a lot of nickels." He also flew into the United States: to New York, San Francisco, Las Vegas and Boston. But the time came when the excitement of flying large aircraft, and being an Air Canada corporate pilot, had worn down a bit, and Olson again evaluated his career. Flying for big airlines had never been his dream. He realized he'd found flying in the North just as satisfying, but in a different way. There, he'd had to deal with the elements, and worry about the whole operation: Where was his fuel going to be? How would he look after the airplane? He'd had to find and meet his own customers, and work out all the details. He realized how much he'd liked that. "An Air Canada pilot is just somebody who sits up in the front," he mused. "The airlines wish they didn't have to pay him, but he's got to be there."

What he couldn't know was that very soon he'd be looking back to this job, and these times, as "the good old days."

In 1979 Olson became seriously ill while on vacation in Florida. "A virus started it, and my balance went," he says. "I couldn't even sit at the table. We had a group disability plan so I went on that, with reduced income plus some insurance."

Because this undiagnosed illness severely affected his equilibrium, Olson lost his medical, and therefore his job.

"After numerous tests, the doctors said, 'You'll never fly again.' And that was that. I had every test done known to man. The conclusion was that I'd always have a balance problem."

Slowly over the next 10 years he regained his balance. He then faced the process of re-qualifying. He was successful in getting his licence, and was rehired by Air Canada in 1988 to again fly DC-9s."

"My contract required that I go back to the aircraft I had left, because absence from sickness did not allow a pilot, on recovery, to jump to some other type of aircraft. I stayed on the DC-9 for a couple of years, then went on to Boeing 747s, flying to places such as Bombay and Singapore. But I missed nearly 10 years in the middle of my career."

Keith Olson's tenure with Air Canada continued until 1993, when lay-offs loomed. That fall, the company offered him a retirement package, and he took it.

Being a pensioner has its rewards, Olson says, although he misses the flying "except on those dark and stormy nights when, instead of battling the elements, I can stay home and have another cup of coffee!" But strangely, Olson's retirement has made him busier than ever.

For five of the years that he had been unable to fly, Olson became involved with Winnipeg's Western Canada Aviation Museum. "I was one of the founders, and one of the volunteers at first. Then I was their second full-time employee."

The story of his affiliation with the museum goes back even farther than that. While still working with Air Canada in 1968, he had gone to Churchill to bring back a Luscombe. On the way home he looked out the window while flying between Dauphin and St. Andrew's Airport north of Winnipeg, and spotted a twin-engine airplane down in the bush.

"That has to be a World War II aircraft!" he thought. He marked the location on the map and went back. It was a Bolingbroke (Blenheim Mark IV). He bought the wrecked aircraft and towed it to a friend's farm.

Through this acquisition, and his interest in old airplanes, Olson met pilot Gordon Emberley. When Gordon's son joined them, the conversation got around to saving airplanes. Over time, they bought some more wrecks, but no one knew what to do with them. Then someone said, "Why not start a museum as an incorporated non-profit group?"

They knew that many old Canadian planes were being bought by people from overseas or from the United States. By setting up an organization, they felt that these airplanes might stay in Canada.

"We incorporated, which meant we were a museum on paper," Olson says. "When we found a place to rent downtown, the Richardson family [whose father, James Richardson, had formed Canadian Airways in 1926], indicated they'd be willing to help. They picked up the renovation costs on the building, around $37 000, a very generous offer. With one airplane on display and another being rebuilt, we had a start. We retrieved more airplanes and stored them all over the place – I've still got several on my property."

Their efforts gained media attention, and the project was off to a good start. When the ex-TCA (Trans-Canada Airlines, now Air Canada) building came up for sale at the airport, funds were raised to buy it.

The museum's first employee was Gordon Emberley "on a half-time basis at a meagre salary," along with volunteer secretaries.

When Olson first lost his pilot's licence, he'd worked as a mechanic for a flying school, and as a volunteer with the museum. When the museum board decided they needed two employees, Olson was put on salary as the curator. When Gordon Emberley quit, Olson took on both jobs, becoming the executive director. "When the museum was well-established at the airport, with a good board of directors in place, I decided it was time to move on."

After being rehired by Air Canada in 1988, he remained on the museum board until 1990. Keith Olson's main work with the museum now is assistant editor of its *WCAM Aviation Review* magazine (edited by pilot/author Shirley Render).

"The publication makes good use of the museum's vast collection of aviation photographs. We have a fantastic collection in our archives, and a library full of photos, books and magazines."

The Olsons have three children. The eldest is daughter Shelly. Next is son Ken, a pilot with Bearskin Airlines, flying a Beech 99 out of Sioux Lookout, Ontario. At his former job with Green Airways, Ken flew an Otter (CF-MEL), the same airplane his father had flown for three years in Churchill. Olson went to see it at Red Lake. "Come on, dad," his son chided. "You should be able to fly it!"

"So," says Olson, "here was my son checking me out, as it were, in my old airplane. Talk about a sentimental journey!"

Olson's second son, Chris, has decided that he, too, would like to fly; he received his private pilot's licence in October, 1995, and is working toward his commercial licence.

Keith Olson, East Selkirk, MB, October, 1993. *Photo: S. Matheson*

Olson has seen great changes to the North in his 15 000 hours of flying, from the economic development of places such as Thompson, ("the airplane was used so much in developing that place") to social changes. "How would they ever have got up the Arctic coast and to all these northern places without airplanes?" he asks. "Transport by ship is a slow process where there's ice nine months of the year. Aviation sped up the data and the services to these places. It hastened the evolution of things."

Olson suspects that if the airplane hadn't got into the North, the native people's lifestyle would have caught up eventually. "There were years when the airplane flew up there and the native

Indians and Eskimos still lived their own way. The airplane brought benefits such as accessibility to doctors, nurses and hospitals."

Several Indian bands are now in the airline business. "The bands own them but the government puts up the money through some mechanism or other. They get grants and free flying training. I've seen both sides of the coin."

Olson has always looked at flying as a privilege. "I enjoyed doing it and I got paid at the same time. Flying is different from most other occupations, because it's something people do because they've fallen in love with it. We flew whenever and wherever we could, and our compensation was almost immaterial."

Olson believes that passion is the reason so much has been accomplished so quickly in aviation.

"The airmen's world is a unique place. That's not a grand statement, but I think it's the essence of it."

Flying Low

Omar Kirkeeng of Hudson's Hope, B.C., is a storyteller. When friends gather around the kitchen table, the fire is crackling in the stove, and the mood is right, you can count on Omar to spin a good yarn.

The 1994 edition of *Who's Who in British Columbia* relates one of Omar's adventures in 1958, when he was 17 years old. Omar was working that summer as an oiler on a dragline for McMahon Construction, doing some rebuilding work on the Mackenzie Highway, 12 miles out of High Level in northern Alberta. One day, some Forestry Department personnel pulled into camp with a big bus.

"Forest fires are burning east of Fort Vermilion," the officer announced. "We need men, right now."

They proceeded to clean out the camp, leaving behind only the waterman, cook and a mechanic. The rest of the gang was ordered to get on the bus. At High Level, the bus was loaded with more men who the Forestry people managed to drag off the street, from the bars, or wherever they could find them.

They proceeded on to Fort Vermilion, to a Forestry Department mustering point where people and equipment were being assigned to the various fires. Several men were chosen to be flown out by helicopter (a Bell 47) to a fire site. Omar was among them.

It was his first ride in a chopper, and he was excited. His enthusiasm soon dampened, however, when he saw the machine, which he describes as a "glass bubble over framework, on floats." The ride was rough, and not for anyone with a sensitive stomach.

He was even less impressed when the chopper landed and dumped them off at the site. "For firefighting equipment, I was given a water-jack, which fit on my back and held 10 gallons of water," Omar recalls. "I worked 72 hours straight, going back and forth across the river. The camp was really under-supplied. All we had to eat were prunes and cheese. I don't need to tell you what that did to our systems!"

Bell 47 helicopter on floats, similar to the one mentioned in this story. *Photo courtesy of Canadian Wings, Sept. 1965, A. LeGuilloux publishing editor.*

Finally, the fire was quelled. The Forestry Department officers thanked them for doing their bit, and started to fly the crew out again by helicopter. Omar waited his turn.

The helicopter took out two guys, and then another two, until Omar was the only one left. Back came the pilot.

"Sorry," he said. "Can't take you. We're full up with equipment and groceries."

Omar couldn't hide his disappointment. He was ragged, dirty, tired and hungry. He wanted to get back to his good-paying construction job.

"Please!" he said. "You've got to fit me in somewhere!"

The pilot thought for a moment. "The only way I can get you out is if you ride on one of those." He indicated the floats, which were equipped with straps for holding their usual cargo of fuel barrels or bulky materials that couldn't be fit inside.

Omar gulped. "Okay. Just get me back!"

He stepped into his sleeping bag, zipped it up and pulled it over his head. Then he lay down on one of the floats and the pilot strapped him up.

"I was leery of helicopters to begin with," Omar says, "so I was really no more afraid of riding on a float than inside the thing."

The pilot balanced Omar's weight with a 10-gallon drum of gas that was strapped onto the other float. Then he jumped into the cockpit and they lifted off.

Omar sensed that they had become airborne, and also that they weren't very high up. He pulled at the flap covering his head and peered out. Smoke – so dense that he could hardly see or breathe – and no more than 100 feet below him, a canopy of treetops.

The helicopter landed much sooner than Omar had expected. He felt himself being unstrapped. He sat up on the float, then stood on wobbly legs. He shucked out of the bag and looked around. No! The pilot had flown him to another fire site, just one creek over. He was stuck.

The firefighting work went on and on.

"In the evenings, the smoke was so thick it hovered three feet above the ground. It was like an endless smudge," Omar says.

Finally they beat that fire down, too, and Omar was flown back to his job site – inside the helicopter this time. But there, he received the worst news of all. The construction job was now finished and they didn't need him anymore. He was sent home, less a good portion of his anticipated summer's wages.

But, he'd had rides in – and on – a helicopter.

Pleasure Pilot

There is a pleasure in the pathless woods,
There is a rapture on the lonely shore,
There is society, where none intrudes . . .
Childe Harold's Pilgrimmage,
Canto IV (1818), Lord Byron

John William Baker, "always called Jack," was born in Cork City, Ireland, on August 22, 1909. His parents immigrated to Canada in April, 1912, on the ship *The Empress of Canada*, which followed the route and schedule of the *Titanic* by two weeks.

The Baker family settled in the East Kildonan district of Winnipeg, Manitoba, where Jack attended St. John's College, an Anglican boys' school located on Main street. Following graduation at the age of 16 from the fifth form (equivalent to grade 12), he "knocked around" Winnipeg for a while, but felt that conditions "for an up and coming young fellow like me weren't too good." He surprised his parents by announcing that he wanted to go north to seek his fortune.

"There was a big how-d'ya-do about that," Baker says, "but I got my way. I took off and went north."

Jack Baker had always wanted to see the Liard River. "I used to look at it in my geography book and think to myself, 'That river rises way up in the central Yukon! I wonder what it's like there?'"

After spending a short time at Fort Simpson, he boarded a Hudson's Bay vessel called *Liard River*, and disembarked at Fort Liard, "on the river of my dreams," about 200 miles upriver from Fort Simpson. There he stayed for the winter of 1928, trapping up the Black River (called Pettitot on the map), and helping the Hudson's Bay manager by doing everything from minding the store to cutting wood.

The following spring a scow came down the Liard River from Fort Nelson bringing Hudson's Bay Company personnel. It was a big river boat, flat-bottomed with high-flared sides made from whipsawed lumber. It travelled with the current – no engine – guided by sweeps (oars set in notches in the bow and stern for steering). When the boat docked at Fort Liard, Baker was invited to join the crew for the trip down to Fort Simpson.

One of the passengers was a man named Ike Gunnell, who was destined to direct Baker's future. He was a seasoned trapper who was bringing his winter's catch to Fort Simpson, and was much older than Baker, in his late 50s compared to Baker's age of 19.

"On the way down to Fort Simpson we were whisked along very fast by the river," Baker says. "Past the mouth of the South Nahanni River, the Liard quickens until it becomes a set of rapids. The man steering the boat wasn't being careful, and we got into these rapids. Suddenly Gunnell jumped up, grabbed the stern sweep, and yelled for somebody to get the bow sweep going. Nobody moved – they were all scared of the big rolling waves.

"I jumped across some men, grabbed the sweep and pushed it out. Gunnell was yelling instructions on what to do, and with the two of us working we managed to get the scow in closer to shore out of the big waves. Although we shipped water, it wasn't that much. We saved ourselves, anyway, from being swamped."

The result of the episode was that on their arrival at Fort Simpson Gunnell said to Baker, "I liked your action there when we needed some work on the rapids. How about throwing in with me? I hear there's good trapping down on the Mackenzie delta, on the mouth of the Mackenzie River. Would you like to join me?"

"Sure, that would be great," Baker replied, and the deal was made. Gunnell realized some $5 000 from the sale of his winter fur catch. Together they built a boat from whipsawed lumber, 30-feet long by six feet wide at the bottom, equipped it, and bought eight dogs. On Baker's 20th birthday in 1929, they headed down the Mackenzie River.

The Mackenzie delta is composed of three main areas: the west, or Peel branch, where the trading centre of Aklavik was located; the main branch called the Middle River; and the east branch which follows along the low hilly contours of the barren lands. Gunnell and Baker found a suitable spot on the east branch (about three miles below the present site of Inuvik, which did not exist then) and built their home cabin. They planned their trapline 50 miles downriver to a little island called Tununuk, and prepared for the winter.

Later that fall, Baker met an old Eskimo fellow who lived on the main channel. "He could hardly talk any English and I certainly couldn't talk any Eskimo, but he invited me, by motions, to come and live with them so I could learn how to trap, and fish under the ice, set nets, all these sorts of things. I told my partner that I was going to do that, because we didn't really have a clue how to live in that environment. I left Ike, temporarily, and went and lived most of the winter with these Eskimos, but I'd go back and forth to visit Ike, who stayed with our cabin on the east branch. The family provided me with a caribou parka, pants, boots and mitts.

"When spring rolled around I rejoined Ike. We'd had a good trapping catch, so by late May we launched our boat and worked across the delta hunting muskrats, on our way to Aklavik."

The RCMP post in Aklavik was headed by Inspector Eames, who, on February 17, 1932, led the posse that tracked and killed "The Mad Trapper," Albert Johnson.

"I was not a member of the posse," Baker says, "because I was on my trapline when Eames was forming it. I did make a special trip to Aklavik when word reached me, and offered my help, but the inspector said he had enough men."

After Baker and Gunnell had trapped together for two years, Ike's health deteriorated. "He had a bad heart, and he was getting on toward his 60s," Baker explains. Gunnell left the north and moved to Vancouver, where he died shortly thereafter. Baker stayed on his own, trapping in the delta for another five years. In 1936, the Hudson's Bay steamer brought to Aklavik two passengers from Winnipeg who represented Northern Traders, the competition to the Hudson's Bay Company. On hearing that Baker had some education, they sent for him and offered him the job of running the post at Fort Liard. The post manager had been sick and the company had to replace him.

Jack Baker, 6th from right, Easter 1932. Trappers gathering for Easter at Kost's stopping place, Aklavik. *Jack Baker Collection*

Baker accepted, and in July, 1936, he became manager of Northern Traders' post at Fort Liard.

Along with the usual furnishings in the post, Baker had inherited a still, which he refurbished and put to use. One day there was a knock on the door. Baker hadn't been expecting any visitors, and had a batch bubbling merrily upstairs. There at the door stood a policeman from Fort Simpson.

"Hello, Jack! I've come to check your fur books," the policeman said jovially.

Baker stared at him. Even from there he could hear his still working upstairs. Blurp! Blurp! Blurp! He had a little primus stove under it and the house reeked of alcohol. But there was no choice: he had to invite the policeman in.

"He persisted in wanting to check this, and wanting to check that," Baker recalls, laughing. "He knew that still was up there, but he was teasing me and there wasn't a thing I could do about it. I couldn't say, 'Get out of here, I want to shut off my still!' Oh, it was a hell of a thing. Eventually he went away."

Although Baker says he wasn't selling the liquor, it was a ticklish situation.

Up to this point in time, the fur trade was carried out over a vast, almost empty, landscape, accessible only by boat in the summer or dog team in the winter. But in the late 1930s, forces of change were in motion, insignificant at first, but becoming more important each year. One of these was the airplane.

"In the late 1920s and through the '30s there were some spectacular flights made by pilots whose names shine: Punch Dickens, Wop May, Walter Gilbert, Stan McMillan and others, but those were special missions," says Baker. "Then a hesitant monthly mail service was inaugurated between Edmonton and Aklavik in the early 1930s, which depended on open water in summer and frozen areas in winter. New types of people penetrated the North: trained prospectors, mining engineers, petroleum experts and others seeking mineral wealth that lay buried beneath the traplines."

Baker's own life changed, too.

Late one afternoon in March, 1938, a small airplane landed on skis near his lonely post at Fort Liard. Baker went down to meet the pilot, who introduced himself as Grant McConachie. He said he ran a small bush service out of Edmonton called United Air Transport.

"I'm heading for Fort Simpson but it's getting too late," the pilot said. "Could I stay the night?"

"I'd be glad of the company," Baker replied. "I've been 10 years in the North and the only people I see are the odd white fellow, a trapper or someone like that, and mostly all natives."

McConachie and Baker sat up talking half the night. McConachie explained that he was trying to get a contract to fly the mail from Edmonton to Whitehorse. The post office wouldn't issue the contract, however, until he had secured a suitable landing place and weather-reporting station between Fort Nelson and Whitehorse. "On the way up from Edmonton, we can stop in Grande Prairie, Fort St. John and Fort Nelson," McConachie explained. "Then there's this long jump between Fort Nelson and Whitehorse. There is a lake in the Yukon that would be just right, if I could get somebody to go in there and build a station for me, and run it. A trapper lives there by the name of Frank Watson, so we call the place Watson Lake for want of a better name."

"I've heard of the place," Baker said.

Then McConachie spotted a home-made radio transmitter that Baker had built from a discarded receiver and parts of the moonshine still, from plans he'd copied from a tattered *Radio Amateurs' Handbook*. Baker had been entertaining himself by "hamming it up" in Morse Code with a Hudson's Bay clerk at Fort Nelson.

McConachie was intrigued by Baker's ingenuity, and on the spot offered him the job of radio operator in the proposed site of Watson Lake.

Baker had heard that his employer, Northern Traders, was planning to sell out. He told McConachie that if the post was sold he'd stay to dispose of the company's stock. Then he wanted to go back to Winnipeg because he hadn't visited his family for 10 years.

When Northern Traders sold all their posts to the Hudson's Bay Company, Baker finalized the business at Fort Liard. Then he headed upriver to Fort Nelson in his boat, on the first leg of the trip back to Winnipeg. He stayed overnight at Nelson Forks, and caught a flight upriver to Fort Nelson.

"That was my first plane ride," Baker says. "As a matter of fact I have a rare picture taken at Nelson Forks of the famous Ford Tri-Motor (CF-BEP) that belonged to McConachie's outfit, United Air Transport. They'd landed, but during the night it sunk down into the water. Fortunately the engines were turned into the bank so they didn't get wet. We got to work digging trenches. We found some big cable at Nelson Forks, put on a Spanish windlass that had been left over from a defunct coal mining venture, and pulled up the airplane (Footnote 1).

Baker caught a ride right to Edmonton on the Tri-Motor, which was piloted by Ted Field. He took the train to Winnipeg, and enjoyed a long-overdue reunion with his parents and brother. "All the friends and relatives wanted to hear what the prodigal son had to say," he laughs. "But when the Christmas festivities had subsided, I said, 'To heck with Winnipeg. I want to go back north again.'"

On his way, he stopped in Edmonton to ask McConachie if his job offer still held.

"Oh gosh, I'm glad to see you!" was McConachie's greeting.

Baker flew on the little mail plane to Fort Nelson. There, he borrowed a dog team from a trapper, travelled the 200 miles to Fort Liard to pick up a whipsaw, broad axe, and other necessary building items, and returned to Fort Nelson within 10 days.

In early February, 1939, pilot Ralph Oakes flew him to Watson Lake, where Frank Watson and a "big fellow" named Vic Johnson met the plane. Frank and Vic had already got out a set of building logs and had nearly completed the station.

Watson died soon after Baker's arrival, but Johnson stayed long enough to help pull out more logs, cut some lumber with the whipsaw, and construct two more buildings. Then he went prospecting, and Baker was alone.

Baker's new employer, United Air Transport, sent in radio equipment, a short-wave transmitter and receiver, storage batteries and a gasoline motor generator. The Dominion Weather Service supplied weather equipment including a recording anemometer (wind speed indicator), barometers, thermometers, rain gauge and cloud atlas. Baker soon learned to take weather observations. He also increased his knowledge of Morse code (widely used at that time because of the uncertainty of microphones on the low-powered transmitters) by getting into a circuit with Royal Canadian Signals Corp at Fort Simpson and Whitehorse, who were professional operators. "I had to smarten myself up pretty fast."

Jack Baker operating a radio transmitter at Watson Lake, YT, 1940. *Jack Baker Collection*

A special long-distance radio transmitter – "it had a 248 kilo-cycle frequency homing signal, a very primitive outfit" – was sent to him from Edmonton. His job was to erect this thing, by stringing an 800-foot long aerial on 60-foot-high poles through the forested landscape of Watson Lake (Footnote 2).

"Can you believe that? You can imagine the job of me lifting those poles, watching that the aerial wire didn't catch on some tree I hadn't noticed, and making sure the guy-wires didn't tangle. Anyway, I got it up there and the thing worked."

Baker's duties included sending out three daily synoptic weather reports. He took cloud observations as to type, estimated height and direction of movement; barometer readings together with their tendencies (rising, falling, or steady); maximum and minimum temperatures; surface wind; and precipitation. He coded this information into numerical groups and sent it to the wireless stations at either Fort Simpson or Whitehorse for relay to Toronto. He also monitored daily radio "skeds" (schedules) for receiving and transmitting messages, which consisted mainly of advice regarding aircraft departures or cancellations, fuel requirements at each station, and various operational requirements. Each station had its own call: Watson Lake was CY6F; Fort St. John was CY30. Radio operators had to stand by on the hour to listen for any pertinent traffic.

He also was responsible for "dozens" of general station maintenance jobs such as keeping the radios functioning, transmitting weather advisories (apart from the synoptic, or formal, reporting), and, in the early days, checking winter ice conditions or snow depth for landings on lakes. He looked after fuel supplies such as gasoline for airplanes and for station generators, and wood for domestic heating. He ordered food, oil and other commodities for everyday needs.

The company had meanwhile changed its name to Yukon Southern Air Transport, bought some twin-engine aircraft, and increased its service from Edmonton and Vancouver to Whitehorse.

Baker asked for help, and in the late summer McConachie sent out Gordon Stock, who had little experience but was willing to learn. He took over the time-consuming outside chore of cutting wood for the station and bunkhouse, using a cross-cut saw. He refuelled the airplanes when they stopped in, and, if they stayed overnight in winter, his early-morning duties included tending the firepots that were placed under the canvas-shrouded engines. In very cold weather it took a half-hour or more to warm an airplane engine, and during this time someone – usually Stock – had to lie underneath the shroud to guard against fire.

By early November the lake froze over, which gave them a short reprieve because airplanes could land on neither floats nor skis. It was during this time that Gordon Stock fell ill.

His problems began with severe headaches, followed by monstrous swelling of his face which caused one eye to close completely. What could be done? They were totally isolated – except for radio communication. In desperation, Baker called the Fort St. John base, located at Powell's place on Charlie Lake, and asked the operator to find a doctor. Dr. Kearney responded, relaying his diagnosis through the operator. "He could die if the pressure is not relieved," the doctor said. "He has to have surgery immediately."

There was no one but Jack Baker to perform this feat.

Arrangements were made for the doctor to come to the radio station at Charlie Lake at eight o'clock that night, when communication was at its best. He would then attempt to guide the layman's hand, via a 500-mile communication link.

Baker prepared for the surgery by stocking up on clean cloths and hot water, and breaking a sterilized razor blade diagonally to get a piercing as well as a cutting edge.

That night, other radios in the circuit cleared the air to allow an open channel, so they could use microphones instead of the usual Morse key. Baker led his patient into the radio shack and sat him down. He was pretty far gone and there was no need to tie him onto the chair as the doctor suggested. Baker's hand shook as Dr. Kearney's voice was transmitted over the mike, telling him where to start cutting and how deep he should go.

"I began poking the pointed instrument into the area around Gordon's eye," Baker says. "Blood flowed. Gordon moaned and winced. I was scared, but the doctor's voice urged me on. I cut through to the infection, and it just burst out of his head! Gordon went limp in a faint."

"Lie him down on a mattress so the incision can drain," Doc Kearney said. "Cover him up, keep him warm – and hope for the best."

Baker did what he was told, cleaned up the 'operating room', and fell exhausted onto his bed. At four a.m., when he got up to take his weather observation, he checked Stock's condition. He hadn't moved. His breathing was regular, and his pulse steady.

Gordon Stock woke up in mid-afternoon the next day. "I'm hungry!" he said. It was music to Baker's ears.

"I helped him up, washed his face and gave him some soup," Baker says. "He had no memory of his ordeal, or even of several days before it."

Ten days later, a small plane came in to take Gordon Stock to the hospital in Fort St. John. Dr. Kearney looked him over and announced that nothing further needed to be done.

"But I never saw Gordon again for 30 years!" Baker says.

The war in Europe increased Baker's work at the radio station. "In the early years of the war, I'd pick up the American aircraft coming through the Northwest Staging Route from Edmonton to Fairbanks. For the first two years I was their radioman, until the Department of Transport got their radios going."

In January, 1942, word was passed to him that three B-26 American bombers were on their way north. "Fine," he thought. "They must have been notified that they can pick up my long-distance transmitter." But the planes didn't contact him. Finally, Baker sent word that they were long overdue. That was all he could report – he didn't even know who they were.

"An air force search party was sent out, but the guy who found them was a namesake of mine, Russ Baker – no relation – who I knew very well, a heck of a good pilot [Russ Baker later established Pacific Western Airlines]. Russ went in there with a German Junkers airplane on skis and located these guys near Two Bally [or Tea Boiley] Lakes, where they had force-landed. Luckily they hadn't done too much damage to the airplanes, or injured the personnel on board. I think there were eight personnel with each one of the bombers, 24 in all."

The reason for the bombers' forced landing, as explained to Baker, was that "they lost radio contact with anyone, and ran short of fuel. For some reason they couldn't pick up my signal, even though it wasn't that far.

"It took 10 days from the time they went down until they were rescued. In that country in January it's usually bitterly cold, but miraculously a warm Chinook wind had started blowing. I was talking to one of the bomber pilots and he said, 'We just lay right out on top of the airplanes! Nice and warm!' Under ordinary circumstances, it's not likely they would have survived."

(L. to R.) Art (P.A.) Taylor, officer in charge of DOT station at Watson Lake; RCMP Constable George Cameron; Jack Baker, operator and weatherman with CPA. Twin engine Beechcraft 18A sent in to rescue personnel from Million Dollar Valley, 1942. *Jack Baker Collection*

The valley where the bombers force-landed, at the head of the Smith River, has been dubbed "Uncle Sam's Million Dollar Valley," or "The Valley of Lost Planes," in recognition of the bombers – and other aircraft – that have gone down in that area.

"The bombers couldn't be taken out of the valley unless some big equipment was flown in to make a proper runway, so they were just left for many years."

While Baker was living at Watson Lake he met Clarice Beattie, whose family operated Gold Bar Ranch on the Peace River, 35 miles from

Hudson's Hope. Clarice and Jack were married at Watson Lake in 1941.

Soon after, Baker's job took him to Whitehorse, where he was promoted to Chief Dispatcher for Canadian Pacific Airlines. The Bakers stayed in Whitehorse for four years. "I got a little tired of the company red tape, and their requirements such as having to wear a uniform all the time, so I left."

For the next two years they lived at Gold Bar Ranch, where Baker ran a trapline in the mountains and along the Grahame River. "I was trying to turn back the hands of the clock, but I had to realize that trapping wasn't much of a life for a family man."

He also tried his hand at farming, but soon abandoned that idea. "The weather was uncooperative, and I wasn't cut out to be a farmer. I was too wild an individual." They moved to Fort St. John in the summer of 1948, where Baker eventually bought a small insurance agency and built it up to become a successful business.

In 1965, Baker took the notion he'd like to own an airplane. The fact that he was 55 years old was of little concern. "I've never have had any problems with studying and learning things. I took 35 hours of ground school from Norm Hill at the Fort St. John airport, and got my pilot's licence. Then I went to Calgary and bought an airplane, a darn nice little airplane, a Cessna 172 (CF-RUH)."

Jack Baker with CF-SGC Cessna 180 on floats at Charlie Lake. *Jack Baker Collection*

Baker put 600 hours on the 172 on wheels before he decided that he needed something a little bigger that could handle floats. He found a good Cessna 180 (CF-SGC), and equipped it for floats, wheels and skis. He considers the 180 the best plane he's ever owned, or flown. "For a single-engine airplane, it's great. I can take off from Charlie Lake with the biggest load you can imagine – and that's a good airplane."

Baker's brother-in-law, Hudson's Hope pilot Pen Powell, for years flew a sister ship to Baker's. "Mine is CF-SGC and Pen's was CF-SGE. They came into the country the same year. Pen was a very good pilot. He used to take some enormous loads with his airplane, too."

"I haven't built up that many hours like a lot of other pilots have done," Baker continues. "I've got about 3 000 hours, but believe me, that's a lot of flying in the bush. Transport pilots get into the airplane, go up in the air, fly across the country at a given altitude and come down again. That adds up to a lot of time, but it's a different thing.

"The bush pilot has to figure out his weather, plan how he can land somewhere, and how he can get off again after he does land. Those are little tricky things that he has to learn, and they can cause lots of trouble."

Baker has never had a flying accident, although he has been in scrapes that required some quick thinking, and a lot of hard work, to get out of them.

One such incident occurred when he was 60 years old, on a trip to his cabin on Tutizzi Lake, 200 miles from Fort St. John, in the dead of winter. Tutizzi Lake is eight miles long and one-half to one mile wide, embedded in the Omineca Mountains. "Going westward, you cross the Rocky Mountain Trench, continue west for another 60 miles, and you're right in the Omineca Mountains. It's gorgeous – on the headwaters of the Mesilinka River system."

On this cold winter day, Baker took off from Fort St. John, flew around Tutizzi Lake, picked a place that looked good to land, and came in. "As soon as I landed, I knew that I'd had it. I was right down to the belly of the airplane in snow. When I got out, I could feel the water squishing as I walked through the snow, which was up over my knees."

He knew the work that faced him, and it must be done right away before the plane froze in. He waded to shore and found a spruce tree with a lot of brush on it. He cut branches, and dragged and carried armloads of brush down to his landing spot. With a shovel, he cleared as much snow as possible from the front of the airplane.

"I couldn't lift the skis because a Cessna 180 weighs more than a ton, so I pushed the brush down in front of the skis as well as I could. It was all water down there. I stamped the area down with my big snowshoes, then I got into the airplane and gave it the gun. I rocked it back and forth, and all of a sudden it slid up onto the brush. That took all the ice and everything off the bottom of my skis. I pulled the throttle right away and just sat there on top of the brush."

It was getting late and he was very tired, so he stayed overnight in his cabin. The next day he went out and snowshoed big tracks in the "slushy, mucky, miserable" snow. Although he was healthy and strong, he hadn't snowshoed for years. To make tracks for the two skis he had to travel for a half-mile, one track down, another track back, another track down and another track back. It took all day. "I had to finally go to the cabin and buy myself a drink of whiskey and rest up.

"The next day I went out and the wind was just a-whistling. It had blown in all my snowshoe tracks! Oh yes, indeed! I could have killed the wind! So I had to do it all over again. But, to make a long story short, I managed to get out of there the next day. I just squeaked off."

Baker says the warning signs of deep snow covering overflow are usually visible: the water oozes up and gives the snow a wet icy look.

"Now I watch very carefully when I land on lakes so I don't get into deep snow conditions. I look for a place where I can see a bit of lake ice underneath the snow, where the wind has blown snow clear."

One time, Baker was flying with his business partner, Bud Hamilton. It was late on an August evening, and Baker could see there was a storm out in the mountains. He tried to get past it but a crack of lightning zapped the aircraft. "It cooked one of my radios that was on, burned it right to a crisp! It didn't hurt the airplane, but my goodness, it scared Bud and me! I had to go way into the mountains to get around the storm. I've flown through thunder storms other times, but that was the only time I've been hit."

Baker doesn't advise flying through storms, but, if there's no other choice, there are ways to pick your path. "You keep away from places where you see the lightning flashing, which you usually can if you're careful and watching."

In 1968, Baker gained his commercial pilot's licence. "I never did fly commercially, but I learned a fair amount of instrument work just for my own knowledge. I enjoy learning."

Although he later studied for IFR (Instrument Flight Rules) endorsement, he never received it. "Well, by that time I was 70 or thereabouts, and they decided they weren't going to let me fly IFR," Baker says. "I told the DOT (Department of Transport) people that if it would satisfy them I would relinquish my commercial licence altogether, which they agreed might be a good idea. So I carried on as a private pilot."

Although his radio work wasn't directly connected to flying, Baker feels that the skills he learned as an operator at Watson Lake "were part and parcel of my overall knowledge," particularly his three-year stint as a weather reporter. During his time in Whitehorse working as a dispatcher, he would go into the weather office and discuss conditions as they applied to flying.

"Weather and navigation are two of the most important things for pilots to know," Baker says. "As far as understanding the mechanics of operation, a good truck driver has to have more mechanical knowledge than a pilot. But, when you're up in the air trying to figure out where you're going and trying to outguess the weatherman, knowledge of navigation and weather are things that make a pilot, a pilot."

Baker says that since he's been flying, approximately 30 pilots have been killed in the Fort St. John area alone, mainly through imprudence. "Sometimes it's accidental, an engine might quit suddenly, but as a rule it's your own fault. You've run out of gas because you didn't carry sufficient fuel for what you were going to do. Or you've overloaded. Or your engine failed mechanically, perhaps because you didn't have a mechanic check over your airplane. Once a year I have my airplane thoroughly checked. I have to pay for it, but it's proved itself worthwhile. I've never had an accident.

"I've always been sort of a cautious fellow, I suppose," Baker concludes. "In my old trapping days I had to be damned cautious about what I was going to do. I had no one to help me if I got into trouble."

He has no fear of flying in remote areas. "At least I have a radio. In the event of a crash it will put out ELT (Emergency Location Transmitter) signals. I was the first local pilot to buy myself an ELT. Then the bureaucrats decided that particular type of ELT wasn't good enough, so I had to get a better one. But that was all right, I didn't mind that. Another couple of hundred dollars is nothing – you're always spending lots of money when you own an aircraft."

He has never needed to use his ELT, but he doesn't mind that, either.

Jack and Clarice have seven children: Vivian, Ron, Terry, Gerry, Michael, Kelly and Marty. Ron has just purchased a helicopter. Terry has a pilot's licence with float endorsement, and now flies with Jack when they make trips to the family cabin at Tutizzi Lake. Jack Baker's flying has been mainly for pleasure, but it has also given him a dramatic view of changes to the country since he was a trapper and trader in the 1930s.

"Things that were normal in our younger days have become part of the pages of history," he says. "The romance of fur, at the time when fur was king and ruled the North, has passed.

"I'm a great environmentalist, and as I fly over the country I see large areas that have been denuded by clear-cutting, and roads put in all over to oil or gas producing areas. All these things are spoiling the country, from my point of view. It was a primitive country, where

Indians were able to make a good living by trapping fur and selling it. The few white trappers who were around did very little harm, either. They were different.

"But nowadays you get camps, and big machinery coming in for logging," he continues. "Some machines used for clear-cutting are equipped with saws that cut the tree, grapple it, lay it down and then go and get another. One operator can put about 10 guys with power saws out of business. You should see the clear-cutting that goes on out west of here! It's frightful!"

His immediate sorrow is that logging is being carried out near his beloved Tutizzi Lake. "Can you believe it? That's right at the headwaters of the Mesilinka River! A company has done clear-cut logging on the Mesilinka, the Osilinka and all the other rivers around there. Now they want to go in and take this very last remnant of old growth timber. That area has been untouched since the glacial age. They've already got it staked out."

In June, 1993, Baker flew over the area and spotted a six-man camp that had been brought in by helicopter, busily surveying the land into 10-acre "cut-blocks."

Baker has spent thousands of dollars fighting logging claims around Tutizzi Lake, and he constantly monitors the activity from the air. He admits that he hasn't much hope of stopping the work, because his property is surrounded by Crown land.

"Home Sweet Home." Jack Baker's cabin at Tutizzi Lake, BC. *Jack Baker Collection*

"When I first went into Tutizzi Lake, I saw all kinds of animals – moose, bears, porcupines. Now there's nothing in there," Baker says sadly. "There are still fish in the lake, of course, and you see the odd moose track, but I haven't seen a bear in there for two years. They hear all that racket, plus the great river valleys of the Mesilinka and the Osilinka have been cut to pieces. I've got pictures. It's just awful."

Baker becomes pensive as he considers the forces that brought the change, among them the one of the things he loves most – airplanes.

"I admit that I wouldn't be over in a place like Tutizzi if I didn't have an airplane, especially at my age. I couldn't go in on foot like I used to when I was a trapper, and pack my stuff with me for many miles. But, the flying I do is not hurting anything. I don't bring anyone in to the lake for fishing other than my own family or an odd friend. It's not a commercial venture."

His thoughts become darker, as no resolution seems in sight. "You can't turn the hands of the clock back on industry, that's for sure. But there's going to be a shock that will rock them. All kinds of people will be out of work in British Columbia in the forest area, when there is no more."

Baker feels privileged to have become familiar with the wilderness, and later to have been able to afford an airplane with which to view more of it. "Nowadays, you've got to have a lot of money in your pocket to get into aviation."

Notwithstanding the financial cost, and the many sad images Baker sees from his elevated vista, he still loves to fly. "Some people enjoy golf, and want to 'live' on the golf links. I enjoy flying. I've flown into the Arctic five times, all the way to where I used to live at Aklavik – and now the new town of Inuvik."

He first flew to Inuvik in 1966, in the Cessna 172 on wheels. "When I went back in 1970 I had my 180 with long-range tanks, and on floats, which made a difference. That year they had an Arctic fly-in, sponsored by the Inuvik Chamber of Commerce," Baker says. "There were airplanes from all over, as far east as Quebec, as far west as Vancouver, and south from Texas. While I was there, I decided to fly over to Tuktoyaktuk on the coast. No one was allowed to land on the runway due to government secrecy, but they couldn't stop anyone from landing in the bay on floats. A photographer and a journalist from Victoria came with me."

When they landed in the bay, they saw that the Eskimo men had killed some white whales and dragged them onto the beach. The women were busy cutting up the meat. The photographer wanted to take a picture, so Baker asked the Eskimo women, "Do any of you talk English?" One said she did, so Baker explained that the woman with

Jack Baker talking to Mary Anik Kulayluk at Tuktoyaktuk, as she cuts up white whale meat. *Jack Baker Collection*

him wanted to photograph their activities. They agreed, and Baker continued his conversation with the one who spoke English.

"Do you know any people from Mackenzie delta?" he asked her.

"Yeah."

"Do you know any family called Kulayluk?"

"Yeah. My first husband was Kulayluk."

"Did you call him Charlie?"

"Yeah!"

"He called you Mary?"

"Yeah!"

"A long time ago," Baker said, "a white boy came, stayed all winter with old Kulayluk, and Charlie, and old Kabloyluk. And you were there. Do you remember a white boy coming?"

"Yeah!"

"That's me!" Baker said.

"Oh," she said, "They call you?"

"Jack."

"Yeah, yeah, Jack!" she said, smiling widely.

Baker couldn't believe his luck at meeting someone who remembered him, after being away from the Arctic for over 40 years. "Tuktoyaktuk is about 90 miles from Inuvik. It doesn't seem far, but Tuk is right on the coast, whereas Inuvik is on the east side of the delta, not far from where Ike Gunnell and I built our first cabin.

"She was Charlie's wife, just a young woman then," he said. "English names had been given them, like Charlie and Mary, and I think they called old Kulayluk, Rufus. Mary told me that Charlie and their two kids had been blown out to sea in a storm, and lost."

Altogether, Baker made five trips into the Arctic, the last in 1976. He has also flown to the Yukon and Northwest territories, as well as to "every major airport from Manitoba west to Vancouver Island, and to some smaller ones." But most of his flying has been done in his home territory of northern British Columbia and around Watson Lake in the Yukon.

"I've covered all sorts of desolate areas, you might say."

In August, 1994, close to his 85th birthday, Jack Baker's pilot's licence was not renewed. "The sight in my left eye didn't come up to their standard," he says. "Poor excuse! I've got lots of peripheral vision. The year before, the medical inspection went just fine. I could have fought it, I guess, but I didn't want the bother."

Jack Baker, waiting for the fog to lift at Williston Lake, BC, October, 1992. *Jack Baker Collection*

Baker still has his airplane, though. With his son in left seat and him in the right, he plans to keep on viewing his mountains and lakes from the air. "I may even take over when we're out somewhere – we'll see!" he says with a grin. "I can't hurt anything out there. After all, I'm just a pleasure pilot."

Footnote 1:

"A Spanish windlass is quite a contraption," Baker says. "It allows you to draw an object toward a firmly-anchored hold with a rope or cable; you can get a tremendous pull with it. The riverbank was too steep to be able to pull the airplane onto the ground, but once we'd lifted it up, a slim-built mechanic was able to crawl right inside those large floats through the inspection hatches, and patch them up."

Footnote 2:

To make the masts, he spliced three trees together with wire, and made a gin-pole (a tripod hoisting device, with one hinged leg) to lift them. The aerial wire had to be spread from one mast to the other while the masts were still lying on the ground, because he wouldn't be able to string them along the tops of the 60-foot masts once they were erect.

Flying on Your Own

The Bakers' large grain farm, homesteaded by Eleanor's grandfather in 1910, lay 90 miles east of Lethbridge at Nemiskam in southern Alberta.

The summer of 1953, Bill Bailey was hired to help on the farm. The young man was earning his Bachelor of Science degree in Agriculture from the University of Manitoba. When Eleanor's father was later appointed manager of the Alberta Wheat Pool in Calgary, Bill was hired full-time to manage the farm.

"I once read that the best way to ruin a good hired man is to make him a son-in-law," Eleanor laughs, "and that's exactly what happened!

Eleanor at the Edmonton airport, 1937-38.
Eleanor Bailey Collection

"Except," she quickly adds, "that the 'ruination' aspect did not really take place."

By the time they met, both Bill and Eleanor held private pilot's licenses. Bill had learned to fly at Portage La Prairie, Manitoba, earning his licence when he was in high school.

Eleanor Joan Baker was born in Calgary in the old Holy Cross Hospital on December 5, 1935, but spent her early years at Nemiskam. By the time she and her younger sister, Sandra, were in high school, the Bakers had moved their home from the farm to Lethbridge, necessitat-

Eleanor and instructor Vera Dowling (Strodl), Lethbridge, AB, 1953, with a Chipmunk aircraft. *Eleanor Bailey Collection*

ing regular weekend trips between the city and the country.

"At the time, I was dating a boy who had a pilot's licence," Eleanor says, "and I innocently kidded my dad that it would be nice if we could fly back and forth the 90 miles. So, for my 17th birthday, mom and dad gave me flying lessons."

Eleanor still has the cancelled cheque, signed by Bert and Agnes Baker, dated December 5, 1952, for $300. Her father had written on the cheque: "Good for a complete course of flying lessons at the Lethbridge Flying Club." Also saved is Eleanor's Student Pilot Permit (XD 2374) dated February 4, 1954.

Eleanor started out with male instructors, until Vera Strodl (Dowling) came to teach at the Lethbridge Flying Club. "As I recall, that was her first job in Canada. She was a kind of hero to me – a woman who was a flying instructor, backed by an illustrious career. I thought, 'Wow, this is really something!'"

Vera Strodl received her pilot's licence in England in 1937, then flew with the ATA (Air Transport Auxiliary) during World War II. She attained the rank of First Officer and built up nearly 1 000 hours on 65 aircraft types, including bombers. After the war she flew in Sweden, worked as an instructor in England, and, in 1952, with 3 600 hours of flying to her credit, she immigrated to Canada to instruct in Lethbridge.

Eleanor's initial training was in a Fleet Canuck. She liked everything about the lessons except for the mandatory spins – "my stomach still doesn't like aerobatics." After 30 hours of instruction, she got her licence in 1953, while still 17 years of age. Following Eleanor's successful completion of the course, her parents were reimbursed $100 by the government.

After high school graduation, she attended the University of Alberta, taking Home Economics, "but for most of my three years I wished I was in Agriculture."

Eleanor married Bill Bailey on May 5, 1956, right after her second year of university. At that point she announced, "I'm not going back," but pressure from parents and in-laws convinced her to finish her third year and gain her degree.

"When September came I went back to Edmonton to university and Bill stayed on the farm at Nemiskam, looking after the harvest. We did some commuting on weekends, and he'd sometimes fly up. But if I went down I had to drive because the airplane was kept at the farm. The roads weren't the best, and I can remember leaving Edmonton following Friday's classes and driving until two o'clock Saturday morning. So, they were pretty short weekends."

Bill spent the winter in Edmonton, and when Eleanor graduated with a Bachelor of Science degree that spring they moved back to Nemiskam. She never did work in the home economics profession.

Besides the home place at Nemiskam, they leased six sections – later expanded to 10 – on the Blood Indian Reserve west of Lethbridge. "We were quite busy," Eleanor says, in an understatement. Their two daughters were born while they lived on the farm, and their son was born after they moved to Lethbridge. Bill and Eleanor managed the farm until Bill got the urge to fly for a living. When they finally left, the farm consisted of nine sections of land. Eleanor's father sold the homestead place, but continued to lease the reserve land under a manager. The Baileys took over the lease again several years after they had moved to Calgary, enabling them to combine flying and farming.

"We decided we still wanted to be farmers, so we took in a partner who did the day-to-day management of the farm and we continued to live in Calgary, with Bill flying professionally. He did all our own crop spraying for years."

The Baker family's airplane was a Piper Cub, used mainly for crop spraying work. Soon, the two-place Cub was no longer large enough to include family travel, so they added a four-place Piper Pacer. Both airplanes had their limitations: the Cub was too small for the family, and the Piper Pacer was a slow airplane, not adaptable to crop spraying and not great for cross-country travel.

When the Cessna 175 came out, it appeared to be the perfect combination. "We convinced my father that this Cessna 175 would

Eleanor Bailey in the Tiger Moth, C-GABB, 1988. *Eleanor Bailey Collection*

combine the jobs of travelling the 100 miles between farms, and crop spraying. We bought it new for around $12 500.

"We thought it would be the one forever and ever, but that was only the beginning."

The Baileys have since bought and sold about 20 different aircraft, in a variety of types. Most common were Cessnas and Pipers, and then they became involved with ex-military aircraft. At one point they had six: four warbirds – a de Havilland Tiger Moth, a de Havilland Chipmunk – "It was very light on the controls and fully aerobatic! I was really in love with it" – a Harvard and a P-51 Mustang. Added to these were a Beech Queen Air, and the Super Cub used for crop spraying (after the Cessna 175 was sold).

"It was a bit much, but lots of fun," Eleanor says.

Their latest acquisitions were a 1953 North American T-28 Trojan (a 1 450 horsepower World War II trainer), a 1939 de Havilland Tiger Moth and a 1959 Piper Comanche (CF-KTU) that they originally bought in 1961, then sold, and two years later bought back.

"The Comanche is almost a classic," Eleanor says. "It's probably our favorite because we've taken most of our fun trips in it. We've flown it all around the continent, and you kind of get attached to something like that. Very reliable and economical." One time she was flying to Winnipeg in the Comanche and talking to the flight service station when a voice came on the radio, "Is that you, Eleanor?" A friend of Bill's was flying a corporate jet at 40 000 feet; she was flying at 7 500 feet, and he had recognized her voice and her aircraft. "So we went to another frequency and had a chat for a few minutes."

But the airplane that Eleanor considered the most fun was their 1939 Tiger Moth, "although it wasn't an easy airplane to fly. It was very heavy on the controls for its size and had no inherent stability."

Bill has also owned and flown a number of airplanes that Eleanor didn't fly. She never got involved with the P-51 Mustang which they owned for a number of years, nor any of the several Harvards. "I should probably have got checked out in them, but we had the Tiger and the Chipmunk, and I was busy flying them while Bill flew the bigger ones."

Eleanor presently holds a private pilot's licence with a night rating and seaplane rating.

"I used to say, 'I *only* have a private pilot's licence,' but I quit that. Now I say 'I have a private pilot's licence!' and I don't say it apologetically. I've flown for a long time, and I've had a lot of fun.

"I suppose getting a commercial licence would have been a good thing to do, for upgrading and for the training. But an instrument rating is difficult to maintain if you're not flying a lot, since you must do check rides on an annual basis. It just wasn't worth it for me."

Eleanor's flying has been strictly for pleasure, but she has nevertheless made contributions to the field of aviation, through memberships and executive positions in organizations that promote flying.

"When we were first married and actively farming, we were very involved with the Alberta Flying Farmers and International Flying Farmers," Eleanor says. "Bill was on the board of directors for the International Flying Farmers. In 1961 he was president of the Alberta Flying Farmers and I was the queen. It's a position elected by the membership, and not necessarily the president's wife; it just happened that the year Bill was elected president, I was elected queen. It's more of an honorary position, you're a kind of hostess for the chapter."

One of the Alberta Flying Farmers' earlier projects was to have a landing strip constructed on the Canada/U.S. border at Coutts, Alberta, and Sweetgrass, Montana. The Alberta group worked with the Montana Aeronautics Commission and succeeded in getting the strip built. "That enabled us to land close by the customs office, so the officer could drive up to check us out. Before that we had to go to Great Falls if we were southbound, or come to Lethbridge or Calgary when northbound."

The organization also worked on improving various rules and legislation that affected aviation and farming. "At one time there was a movement afoot to not allow farmers to air-spray any of their neighbor's crops. The Flying Farmers protested and got the rules changed so you could crop-spray within a 25-mile radius of your farm."

Through the Flying Farmers, Eleanor met a woman pilot who was a member of the 99s, and who convinced her to join that organization. This International Organization of Women Pilots was started in Long Island, New York, in 1929; Amelia Earhart was one of the original founders and the first president. When women pilots had sent out letters asking others if they'd be interested in forming an organization, 99 of them had replied, hence their name. Now, it is a world-wide organization with a membership in excess of 7 000, from virtually every country of the free world.

"There was an Alberta chapter in the 1950s, but when they got down to only five members, they folded," Eleanor says. "In 1961, I joined the Montana chapter because there wasn't a chapter here, so I had to fly down for the meetings. Then I started talking to other pilots at the fly-ins, and in 1968 we began reorganizing the 99s in Alberta. I was the first chairman. We became quite active, with about 35 members."

The Alberta 99s then got the idea to host the start of the Powder Puff Derby, an "All-Woman Trans-Continental Air Race" (Incorporated). "The criteria to win the race involves speed, but there are certain stops you have to make. Participants must use stock airplanes, not modified, and there are various other rules," Eleanor explains.

When they approached the board of directors, however, the main objection to their plan was that the race had never before been started, or finished, outside the United States. "We convinced them that there was no reason not to start the race in Calgary – and we won them over."

In 1971, the Powder Puff Derby was scheduled, for the first time, to start in Calgary and end in Baton Rouge, Louisiana. It took the Alberta group two years of preparation. To put on an event of that magnitude, the group needed money.

"One of our fundraising projects was ferrying aircraft. We contacted the Cessna Aircraft company and the local dealers. Four of us flew via commercial airlines to the Cessna factory in Wichita, Kansas, and picked up four brand-new airplanes (a 150, two 172s, and a Cardinal) for dealers in Western Canada. We were paid a few hundred dollars, which helped our treasury."

Two of the pilots ferrying the aircraft had to land at a ranch strip in Wyoming when they ran into a snowstorm. They spent the night with the farm family, then carried on the next day. "I think the ranchers were a bit surprised to see two women flyers walking out of the airplanes."

The week prior to the race was extremely active as the Alberta chapter of the 99s finalized arrangements for tours, receptions and events such as a Western Night, a convention-type rodeo and a trip to Banff. "It was a big project. I was Start Chairman, and our whole chapter put a lot of effort into it," Eleanor says.

The "impound date" was June 30, 1971, when the 150 entered airplanes were to be in Calgary for inspection to ensure they were, in fact, stock (not modified). Takeoff date was July 5. After making several mandatory stops on the way, the race finished in Baton Rouge on July 8, covering 2 442 miles.

Eleanor flew down in a rented Comanche (theirs was having a major engine overhaul) to observe the finish of the Powder Puff Derby. Three other members who had also worked on the race went with her. She then flew back the 2 442 miles from Baton Rouge to Calgary in one day. "We had an invitation that night to a pre-Stampede party, so I wanted to get home for that. I went to the party, had half a drink and that was it! I hadn't realized how tired I was."

After the big event, however, there seemed to be a decrease in interest among the Alberta 99s in keeping things rolling. They lost a number of members who had stayed on to help with the race, then dropped out for one reason or another until they were down to less than 10. "One year we didn't have any officers, we were just kind of in limbo. Burned out, I guess."

Later, the group rebuilt to its present number of 30 members. Eleanor says that the international organization is comprised of a "real cross-section" of professional and private pilots, including a couple of astronauts. "Sally Ride was a member for a number of years, and Bonnie Dunbar. We have a lot of airline and military pilots. We also have a variety of ages, from new pilots as young as 17, to grandmothers. Two or three charter members have maintained their licenses and are still active. When you think it started in 1929, these are amazing women."

Eleanor herself was winner of a flying competition, the Calgary Stampede Air Race, sponsored by COPA (Canadian Owners and Pilots Association). This annual "fuel/time efficiency dash" to the Calgary Stampede used to be held early in July. Eleanor won on July 10, 1967, for achieving an almost perfect score on her flight from Lethbridge to Calgary in an Aero Commander 100, "which I wasn't too familiar with, but things worked out well."

Another race, the Governor General's Air Rally, also sponsored by COPA, was organized out of Estevan, Saskatchewan. There, the participants had to follow a triangular course. Eleanor won a prize in this event also – flying through a Saskatchewan dust storm.

Dust storms are a particular menace to pilots, especially when flying VFR (Visual Flight Rules). The dust comes up in convection circles, rising in cones. It's carried by the prevailing winds, and severely obscures visibility of landmarks. The pilot must fly at a lower altitude than normal to be able to see the ground, but must also be aware of the highest obstacle in the area, such as any radio tower.

The lower you get, however, the less distance you can see, but if you get too high, the dust will obliterate all landmarks.

Radio contact is essential and navigation skills must be excellent, with a pilot competent in dead-reckoning as well as using ADF (Aircraft Directional Finder).

The Baileys' interest in ex-military aircraft led to their owning some unusual aircraft and participating in interesting events.

"Any ex-military airplane is called a warbird," Eleanor explains. "We had a Tiger Moth, a Harvard and a Chipmunk, which were trainers. Then we had the P-51 Mustang built by North American Aviation, with a 1 750 horsepower Rolls Royce engine. The P-51s were fighters used in Europe in World War II, replacing Spitfires and Hurricanes. They had longer range, were faster and were probably one of the finest fighter airplanes built. We had ours for eight years, and took it to many air shows from western Canada to Texas."

Members of the Western Warbirds at the Namao Air Show in 1984. Eleanor Bailey is in the front row – the lone woman. Husband Bill Bailey is in the back row, 3rd from left. *Eleanor Bailey Collection*

Along with this interest came affiliation with a group called the Western Warbirds, comprised of members who own, fly or love ex-military airplanes. At the present time, there are about 80 members across western Canada and more in the United States. Some, like the Baileys, owned several warbirds.

Eleanor's favorite was their de Havilland Tiger Moth (C-GABB), a British open-cockpit biplane painted in wartime colors, which she delighted in taking to air shows and fly-ins.

The DH82-A Tiger Moth was built by the de Havilland Aircraft Company in Hatfield, Herts, England, in 1939. There are now less than 12 of the "A" model with the open cockpit in Canada.

Unfortunately they could not locate the airplane's wartime record, but the last civilian owner in England was the Coventry Gliding Club, who used it as a glider tow plane. It was then sold to Clay Henley of Athol, Idaho. The Baileys bought it in 1976, had it fully restored, and have flown it since 1978.

When flying it to air shows, Eleanor complements the vintage look by wearing helmet, goggles and scarf.

"The first time I wore these things, photographs were being taken and they wanted to see the scarf flying out behind me. I must have tied a slip-knot because the scarf became tighter and tighter. I had to tug at it to keep from choking! I learned to tie a proper knot so it wouldn't pull in.

"I once ruined a real aviator's white silk scarf when the end frayed out after I'd been flying for an hour, with it flying out behind me. So now if I do anything like that, I keep it tucked in until necessary, then let it go."

The P-51 Mustang was another favorite aircraft, but it was sold in the early 1980s for economic reasons. "After we bought it they started to become quite valuable, and now are probably worth a half-million dollars," Eleanor says. "You get to the point where it's too valuable to fly in case you have an accident, or you can't afford the insurance. Engine overhauls are expensive; at that time, they cost around $50 000 U.S. We still miss it, and have regrets that we sold it, but at that time it was the right thing to do."

While they still owned the P-51 Mustang, they frequently flew to Harlingen, Texas, to attend and participate in the Confederate Air Force air show, sponsored by a group similar to, but larger than, the Western Warbirds.

The Bailey's P-51 lacked a back seat, so Eleanor flew with 10 others from the group in a B-25 bomber. But there was one requirement to catching a ride in the bomber: everybody had to take a turn flying, whether or not they were a pilot, although a competent pilot would remain in the cockpit. When Eleanor's turn came, the captain, Bud

Granley, (an ex-RCAF pilot and now a United Airlines captain), told her to get into the left seat.

"We were over Texas at that time, going by Houston, and it was busy," Eleanor says. "The B-25 was leading the formation of a number of other airplanes. I looked around – and Bud was gone. He was in the back, taking pictures. I was all alone, leading this great formation – and having a wonderful time!"

The following year there still wasn't a second seat in their fighter Mustang, so Eleanor flew the Comanche to Texas, taking three passengers. The warbird planes left Calgary earlier as they were to rendezvous with several other aircraft in Billings, Montana, then fly further south for the night. "The weather forecast we got wasn't too accurate, and the warbird contingent had to make some detours. We also were diverting around some weather. Then we had to try to find them."

Eleanor called in to a flight service station. "Have you got a flight plan on a B-25 and four P-51s?"

Long pause. "As in *World War II*??" the fellow asked, in an unbelieving tone.

Eleanor says that she has been generally well-received by the predominantly male flying community.

"I've never had any problems with discrimination. Quite a few years ago when we had our Chipmunk, a number of the Western Warbirds

Eleanor Bailey in Chipmunk C-FQKV. *Eleanor Bailey Collection*

also had Chipmunks. They used to fly in formation and do a lot of air shows together. When I was asked to fly with them, I realized that they'd accepted me."

Although her acceptance could be partly based on the fact that her husband is also a pilot, "I'd like to think that whether Bill was a flyer or not, I would be accepted on my own."

Eleanor Bailey has never had an accident in over 2 000 hours of flying, to all areas of the United States from Los Angeles to Albany, New York, to Mexico and to the Bahamas. She has flown as far east in Canada as Quebec City. Her northern excursions have taken her to the Peace River area of Fort St. John and Dawson Creek, to just inside the Arctic Circle at Fort Yukon, and to Fairbanks, Alaska, as well as to "most of the in-between places." She has flown to various areas of British Columbia, taking both the Chipmunk and the Tiger Moth to Oliver, B.C., for the Western Warbirds' annual meetings.

In July, 1979, the Alberta government sponsored a tourist promotion called "Stamp Around Alberta," giving out "passport" books which they encouraged people to have stamped as they visited various tourist zones in the province. Eleanor decided it might be fun to visit *all* the designated zones in one day.

"I flew about 1 200 miles that one day, stopping at airports in each zone and meeting with an official to have my passport stamped," she says. They landed at, and took off from, Banff, Spirit River, Swan Hills, Drayton Valley, Edmonton, Vegreville, Camrose, Drumheller, Brooks, High River, and then flew back to Calgary.

"Twelve hundred miles in one day is a fair amount of flying. With the Comanche averaging 165 miles per hour, it took over 12 hours," Eleanor says. "The starts and stops took a while. Some places had presentations, some put on luncheons, that kind of thing."

Bill Bailey's professional flying had begun in Calgary with Roy Moore, who was the Piper dealer at that time and later started International Jet Air. He flew with Moore for a number of years, then with Chinook Jet Charter.

In 1969, when Bill was flying charters with International Jet Air, his job took him away from his family over the Christmas holidays. There was nothing he could do about it – Dr. Charles Allard's family had booked him for a trip to Mexico.

Eleanor and the children weren't too happy about it, but they realized that was his job.

"Maybe the kids and I can come," she said hopefully.

"Sorry, you can't," he replied. "Not in the company aircraft."

"No – but why can't I fly down, too? The kids and I can all fit into the Comanche. Then we can have Christmas together!"

Eleanor had done a fair amount of cross-country flying by that time, although she'd never gone so far by herself with the children, who were 12, 11 and six years of age. From Lethbridge they flew south to Great Falls, Montana, where she cleared customs. On December 23, she walked into the weather office to get a briefing. "What? A woman flying alone – with your children? Where are you headed?"

When Eleanor replied brightly, "To Mexico for Christmas!" he just rolled his eyes and gave her the information.

They stayed overnight in Las Vegas, then in Mazatlan, and by the third day at noon they were in Puerto Vallarta. Bill met them at the airport.

"How did it go?"

"Fine!" Eleanor replied. "We had good weather all the way." The children now are grown, but they'll never forget that Christmas vacation.

Both the Bailey's daughters, Kathy and Karen, started taking flying lessons, although Kathy didn't finish because of other interests. Karen, the eldest, went on to get her commercial multi-engine instrument rating. Their son, Norman, lost his life in a traffic accident in 1981, just short of his eighteenth birthday.

Following his employment with International Jet Air, Bill became chief pilot for Dome Petroleum Ltd., followed by a nine-year stint as chief pilot for Burns Foods. He was also employed with a private jet operation flying a Hawker Siddeley 125 which involved a lot of flying to Europe. His last corporate flying job was with Bow Valley Resources, and Sulpetro flying Lear Jets. The company sold its airplanes in 1986 "when the energy crunch came," and he retired.

"At that time the Calgary airport was a pretty dead place," Eleanor says. "It used to be the corporate aviation capital of Canada. Then it became difficult to find a corporate airplane around!"

Rather than look for another flying job, the Baileys worked on their 334-acre grain farm east of Calgary at Indus. Then they rented the farm out, and in 1994 sold even the home place.

Nowadays, both the Baileys actively take part in fly-ins, fly-bys and air shows. In 1993 a reunion was held in Nanton, Alberta, to honor the Dambusters, a squadron of pilots who in World War II flew Lancaster bombers. "They had developed and dropped a round bomb that basically bounced on the water and hit against the dams, and succeeded in destroying some dams in Germany that had been elusive until that time. Several of us did a fly-by for them. I had the Tiger Moth, and there were two Chipmunks, and two Harvards."

Over the past years, members of the Western Warbirds have attended reunions of the British Commonwealth Air Training Plan at Claresholm, Alberta, and Portage La Prairie, Manitoba, and put on air shows for them. These events are pleasurable for people who put their airplanes on display, as well as for members and visitors.

Another side of the coin are air shows that are open to the public. Although most people respect the fragile nature of the aircraft on display, there are always those who don't. "Some children and their parents seem to think that anything on display is public property, and you find them climbing on your airplane without permission," Eleanor says. "There is a black walkway on the wing. We have to caution them to keep their feet on it or they could puncture the fabric or dent the aircraft.

"My Tiger Moth is made of fabric and very delicate. I almost have to put a fence around it at an air show because people often poke it, not realizing how fragile it is. One fellow found a half-eaten hamburger stuffed up the exhaust pipe of his Harvard at a fly-in breakfast. It would probably have blown out when he started the engine, but it could have made the engine backfire and caused some problems."

Eleanor Bailey feels she has experienced some of the best years of aviation. Concerned for the future of flying, particularly in Canada, she cites the problems of increased costs, problematic regulations and general changes to the industry.

"In the future, I don't think there will be the fun. People can't afford it. Everything is more regulated. You can't go to some airports now without certain equipment in your airplane. I couldn't take the Tiger Moth in to Calgary because I didn't have a Mode C Transponder in it, a special instrument that allows your location and altitude to show as a little blip on a screen in the Control Tower. I couldn't put one in because that airplane didn't have an electrical system. You hand-propped it, there was no starter."

She understands that for safety's sake the airplanes now must be better equipped than in former times, and she did install a battery-operated ELT in the Tiger. She herself prefers to land at smaller airports on the outskirts of big cities.

The difficulty in establishing a career in the aviation business is, and always will be, hinged on gaining the necessary experience. "Everybody now requires that you have experience, and whether you're a male or female pilot, building hours is one of the toughest things."

When Bill was chief pilot for various companies, he received many job applications from young men or women who had graduated from flying schools and had 100 hours, or perhaps a brand new commercial licence but no experience. "And that's where so much expense comes in."

In 1994, when Eleanor and Bill sold their farm near Calgary they also sold their two warbirds, the de Havilland Tiger Moth and the North American T-28 Trojan, leaving only the Piper Comanche.

The T-28 was sold to Victoria Air Maintenance in Victoria, B.C., and the Tiger Moth went to the Reynolds Museum in Wetaskiwin, Alberta.

Although bidding farewell to the Tiger was an emotional experience, Eleanor is happy that it found a good home, and will be part of the museum's flying display at air shows and fly-ins.

Adding to the goodwill attitude of the transaction is a story about how the museum gave the Tiger Moth a new name.

"They used to refer to the aircraft as 'Eleanor's Tiger,'" Eleanor says, "but the owner of the museum didn't like it being called *Eleanor's* Tiger. It was now *his* Tiger. So, to resolve it, my name was painted on the side. Now when the guys are deciding what aircraft they're going to take to a show, instead of saying 'Take Eleanor's Tiger,' they say, simply, 'Take Eleanor!'"

Eleanor Bailey continues to enjoy flying, and in 1994 she attempted a flight to Provideniya, Russia, in the Comanche with two women friends, Arlene Smith and Marg Ross, as passengers. After completing a pile of paperwork they started off, flying from Calgary to Whitehorse and then on to Fairbanks, Alaska.

Because of weather, however, their stay in Fairbanks dragged on for several days. "We just couldn't get out of there VFR to get to Nome. We tried it one day, got less than 100 miles, and had to turn back. We checked in and out of the same hotel in Fairbanks three times."

Finally the weather cleared so they could get to Nome, but then weather on the Russian side started to deteriorate. They couldn't take the chance of going to Nome and having an interminable wait there. They decided to fly north to Fort Yukon inside the Arctic Circle, and then to Dawson City and home.

Although they didn't succeed in making it to Russia, Eleanor is glad that she attempted the trip. "People asked why I would want to do that. Well, because it was something I'd never done. It was a challenge getting as far as we did – and getting through all that paperwork!"

Eleanor's advice to anyone planning to fly to Russia for pleasure would include a long lecture about the bureaucracy one must prepare for. "Plan to take about two months for the paperwork. Be meticulous when filling out all the forms. It takes a lot of time and patience."

The Baileys now live for part of the year in Arizona, and the rest of the time in Big Fork, Montana, on Flathead Lake. They keep their one remaining aircraft, the Piper Comanche, at a little airport nearby. "Now we're into a new field," Eleanor says. "We have a boat, for the first time in our lives." The Baileys have also pursued a third mode of travel. Each has a Honda Gold Wing motorcycle.

"I guess it was one of those situations, 'if you can't beat 'em, join 'em,'" Eleanor laughs. "When I first met Bill, he had come from Manitoba to Alberta riding an ex-army Harley-Davidson 45 (cubic inch) motorcycle. I guess back in his mind he always wanted to have another bike. In 1983 he bought a Honda Gold Wing, a nice big touring bike.

"I wasn't too interested, but he thought I should get involved so he bought a bike for me, a Honda Silver Wing. I'd never ridden a motorcycle before. It was too big, and a little top-heavy. For a beginner, it wasn't right."

Eleanor took riding lessons, and now has a 1 200 cc Gold Wing. Together, they've made a 7 000 mile motorcycle trip to Kentucky, and a trip to the Harley Davidson rally at Sturgis, South Dakota. "There were 100 000 motorcycles or more in town – traffic jams of Harleys! It was incredible!" The trip involved riding 4 000 miles in 10 days.

Eleanor is adamant that she'd rather have her own bike than be a passenger. "I don't like looking at the back of somebody's helmet. I'd rather look out myself. It's kind of like the airplane in that respect – I'd rather fly my own than be a passenger."

The Man with Three Names

*C*ampbell can't be held responsible for his history being chronicled under various names. It began with his parents calling him "Jack" (his dad's name was John but he was called Jack), although the name Jack never appeared on any of Campbell's birth certificates. Instead, one document says *Colin* Campbell was born in Sudbury, Ontario, on April 7, 1913. Another states that *Colin Norman* Campbell was born in Sudbury, Ontario, on April 7, but five years later in 1918. The matter got complicated from there.

The Campbells lived in Levack, a mining site just out of Sudbury where father Jack Campbell worked as an electrician. The family moved to Toronto when young "Jack" was three. He grew up in North Toronto, and attended Northern Vocational and North Toronto High schools where he finished grade 12.

TCA Captain Colin Campbell in cockpit of Northstar (1950) writing out in-flight passenger report for stewardess. *Colin Campbell Collection*

While in school "Jack" Campbell and his older brother Archie incorporated as Campbell Brothers, and began to weather-strip and insulate houses. The young entrepreneurs eventually took over the Canadian Johns Manville distributorship for Ontario. By 1940, the company was referring to the Campbell brothers as the "Wonder Boys" of the Toronto building industry (Footnote 1).

When their father's job at Toronto Hydro was cut back, he had just bought a house on Roselawn Avenue in Toronto. The boys paid off the mortgage.

"When I started in business, I was 14," Campbell says. "My brother did sales and I did the practical work. I'd get up early, go down to the shop, get the men out on their jobs, and then ask one of them to drive me to school – in my car, a 1931 Ford roadster. I was too young to get a licence."

After school, one of his workers would pick him up so he could inspect the jobs and line up further work.

"We had 35 men, six trucks and five cars operating out of North Toronto, so we were pretty busy."

Young "Jack's" interest in flying came about through this business. He often had to make personal visits to work sites or to insurance company offices throughout Ontario. Still without a driver's licence, Campbell had to get someone to transport him to these meetings.

When they successfully bid a job for International Nickel in Sudbury to insulate one of the big chimneys, it meant driving all night from Toronto to make a 6:30 a.m. interview at Copper Cliff. Along the way Campbell happened to see a billboard sign at Ramsay Lake: Learn to Fly!

He turned to his driver: "Let's go in and see what they're talking about."

Ken Saunders was running the flying school.

"What do I have to do?" Campbell asked.

"Just learn to fly," was the nonchalant reply.

"How long does it take?"

"That depends on you."

"When can I start?"

"Any time you can produce $22.50."

Campbell returned to the flying school following the insulation job meeting, and that afternoon he took lessons for four-and-a-half hours. "They counted each half-hour as a lesson, so I did nine lessons, and then I went solo in the evening."

He took the exam and flight test on floats in Toronto Bay (the present location of Toronto Island Airport), thereby being licensed to fly before he could drive. He then rented aircraft – usually a Waco 10 on floats – to fly to his various interviews around the province.

"In 1934, they didn't require a birth certificate for flying, but they sure did for driving. My pilot's licence was under the name of *Jack* Campbell, which at the time I thought was my name."

When he visited the government office to get his birth certificate so he could apply for a driver's licence, he discovered there was no record of a Jack Campbell with his birth statistics. There was, however, a *Colin Norman* Campbell, born in 1918. He went home, perplexed. "What *is* my real name?" he asked his parents. "Colin Norman," they replied.

Later, another birth record emerged listing plain *Colin* Campbell born in Sudbury in 1913. When he tried to explain the error to the government office, their response was, "Impossible!" So, throughout his life, Colin Campbell has carried two birth certificates. Some of his licenses are based on one record, some on another, "whichever is handiest."

Campbell laughs about it now.

"There is a mix-up," he admits, "but I'd never try to straighten out the government."

The Campbell brothers continued their business until World War II broke out, when they became instructors with the British Commonwealth Air Training Plan.

"I was in first, and after about a year Archie came in. I checked him out on Ansons in Regina." Prairie Airways had a full complement of pilots to train observers at No. 3 Air Observer School in Regina, but the No. 6 school that had just opened in Prince Albert was in dire need of civilian pilots. They had begun using American pilots because of the shortage of qualified Canadians (Footnote 2).

In 1941, the BCATP sent Campbell from Regina to Prince Albert to train pilots on twin-engine Ansons, doing "circuits and bumps," and also to train the air observers (navigators). "We would go out for three, four, or five hour trips, mostly at night, to try to get them lost and see if they could find their way home."

Campbell had meanwhile put in an application with TCA (Trans-Canada Airlines, which became Air Canada in 1965), but his work with the British Commonwealth Air Training Plan had priority. In 1942, the government, which still hadn't sorted out his birth statistics, gave him a message that he'd been hired by CPA – Canadian Pacific Airlines Limited.

"I thought they'd got things backwards again."

When he received a call from Herbert Hollick-Kenyon, a famous aviator who was then Canadian Pacific Airlines' first pilot training superintendent, he realized the message had been correct. The Prince Albert flying school was now owned by CPA, and the company had another assignment for him."We want you to come up to Fort McMurray and work for us here, because of your float time," Hollick-Kenyon said.

Colin Campbell's wife, Eleanor Mary Dewar, while working as a stewardess for TCA, 1945. *Colin Campbell Collection*

Campbell left Prince Albert in 1941 to go north. "I had flown 2 230 hours with BCATP, all in military aircraft, but received no military recognition. I was in Fort McMurray with CPA until the fall of 1942, when I left to go to TCA. Finally."

At the time, the two airline companies were not the competitors they are now considered to be, Campbell says. "In those days, CPA was a smaller outfit, in the midst of buying out various airways. They had a lot of problems with seniority and stuff.

"I went with Trans-Canada Airlines, and I spent the next 13 years with them, from 1942 to 1955."

In 1946, Campbell married a TCA flight attendant (then called a stewardess), a pretty young woman named Mary Eleanor Dewar. In those days, flight attendants had to be registered nurses, so Mary Eleanor was also a RN. The couple eventually had three children: Neil, born in Toronto; Colin, born in Montreal; and daughter Barré, born in Toronto. During the next 40 years, the family would make their home in various places around the globe, depending on Colin's business base.

On February 24, 1949, Campbell set a record for west-to-east Atlantic flight. Newspapers carried the event, via CP (Canadian Press):

> Captain Colin N. Campbell flew his four-motored North Star from Montreal to London in 10 hours and 11 minutes, chipping 19 minutes off the mark set last year.

> ... his air speed at the 21,000-foot cruising altitude was a normal 246 miles per hour. A following wind sometimes reaching 170 miles pushed him along at a ground speed of 416 miles an hour. Campbell made the 2,000-mile stretch of Atlantic between Gander, Newfoundland, and Ireland in four hours and 56 minutes without even pushing his plane.

In fact, the Irish landfall navigator, Paddy McClintock, had trouble keeping the fix lines on his chart ahead of the plane.

> "When we were heading for the Irish coast, I spotted some lights," Campbell recalled, "and asked the navigator what they were."
>
> "It must be a ship," he replied.
>
> "'It must be a big one,'" I said. "'It's got cars running around the deck!' We had hit the coast spot on course."

The North Star aircraft that Campbell flew for TCA came into being because the government, who owned Trans-Canada Airlines, decided to build an airplane (Footnote 3). The resulting DC-4M aircraft, M1 and M2, were named North Stars.

Although the new four-engine aircraft was launched in style on July 22, 1946, by Mrs. C.D. Howe (wife of the Minister of Reconstruction) breaking a bottle of champagne over its nose, not all reports on the craft were positive.

The Montreal *Gazette* (July 25, 1946) derided the hodge-podge construction features, calling the DC-4M, which was based on an American aircraft design and featured British Rolls-Royce Merlin engines, "nothing more or less than a straight assembly-job" with dubious aeronautical qualities. The *Globe and Mail* likewise knocked the North Star, while the Toronto *Star* rose to its defence (Milberry, p. 59).

Colin Campbell continued to fly the machine, keeping his opinions on its performance, and that of his employer, to himself.

Although Campbell's tenure with TCA had its ups and downs, he says that once – just once – the corporation showed him that "it almost had a heart."

In 1948, before the days of gate and boarding passes, there was often confusion in the terminal building. Several airplanes would be lined up, all looking the same, so it was inevitable that some passengers would get on the wrong one. Although the stewardesses would count heads, the number could come out right if two people had boarded the wrong planes.

This happened one time when Campbell was piloting a North Star from Toronto to Winnipeg with 25 passengers on board. They were near Sault Ste. Marie when the stewardess addressed the captain.

"We've got a problem."

"What is it?"

"There's a woman on board who's supposed to be going to Chicago to get married – this afternoon!"

"Tell her we'll buy her a drink in Winnipeg," Campbell said.

A few minutes later, the stewardess returned. "The passengers are upset. They think you should take the flight to Chicago and drop her off."

"The airline might have a little objection to that," Campbell laughed.

But the stewardess kept returning with repeat messages. The woman was crying, the passengers were sympathetic – and the captain should darned well do something about it!

"Can't you ask?" the stewardess implored.

Campbell got on the radio and related the story to Bill English, vice-president of operations at head office in Montreal. Believing that English would think he'd gone mad, Campbell was surprised to hear him say, "Hey, Colin, you're current on Chicago, aren't you?"

"Yes."

"If you get all the passengers on board to okay it, we'll put you into Chicago."

Campbell called the stewardess. She complied – and the flight was rerouted. While in Chicago, they also picked up the other mistaken person who'd ended up on the flight to Chicago instead of Winnipeg, and took him on to Winnipeg.

That situation was unusual, and probably never happened before or since. "You couldn't just take any pilot, you had to be current on the run into Chicago, which I happened to be."

From holding a favored position as senior captain with the airline, setting trans-Atlantic records and redirecting flights to escort brides to their weddings, in 1952 Campbell found himself in the opposite corner. The switch came quickly and resulted from forces that he could not anticipate.

T.C.A. PLANE FLIES PAST COLONY DUE TO GEAR FAILURE, states a Bermuda newspaper report:

> Due to a communications failure, a Trans-Canada Airlines plane from Canada missed Bermuda on Wednesday night and touched down at Kindley [Air Force base] three hours late after travelling about 200 miles south south-west of here . . .
>
> . . . with a full load of 46 passengers, the plane missed the colony due to failure of a navigational unit and inability to pick up radio beacons from Bermuda.
>
> When Captain Colin Campbell, the pilot and a senior captain of the line, realized that he had missed Bermuda and was west of the colony, he was in a heavy overcast and had to fly some distance

to get out of it in order to make an astral fix on his position. He was returning to the colony when picked up by the rescue planes.

Campbell tosses aside the clipping in disgust.

"They said that I should have picked this up! I don't know how you 'pick it up' when you've got a professional navigator on board and you can't read a thing on the radio, unless you can recognize the ocean waves or something. We couldn't even see them when we were on top of the overhead!"

Campbell itemizes what went wrong:

"The navigator was supposed to take astro shots, which he didn't take; he just kept adding a few minutes onto the ETA (Estimated Time of Arrival). We couldn't even get a clearance. I had to get on CW (Continuous Wave radio, which is on the key) to get clearance."

The situation occurred, Campbell says, as an indication of "how bad conditions were." The company had taken radio operators off the job about six months earlier, because they felt that the AIRINC (a circle of high frequency radio stations that formed a ring around the North Atlantic Ocean) radio cover and the VHF (Very High Frequency) were sufficient, and that radio operators were not needed. They did leave the keys, however, as well as the RDF (Radio Direction Finder), and the CW equipment. They also continued to carry navigators on board, whose equipment consisted of astro navigation with a periscopic sextant and LORAN "A" (Long Range Navigation, a system by which navigators received the radio signals of two pairs of radio stations of known location, and used them to establish location of a ship or aircraft).

These systems work fine, Campbell agrees, except when a number of negative conditions occur at once.

This particular flight was routine, weather was excellent, top of the overcast was 20 000 feet, and the base was about 18 000 feet over the ocean. They did a normal range airways navigation down to Nantucket, and then went on astral navigation when the navigator reported that the LORAN in the aircraft was out of service (it was normal procedure to go on astral whether or not the LORAN was working). They also had dual ADF (Automatic Direction Finders) on the airplane as navigation aids.

When they were about 20 minutes ahead of their ETA, Campbell called New York to request descent clearance in to Bermuda. No answer. He tried again. No answer. He tried the whole AIRINC screen around the ocean. No answer.

Campbell went back to the key, called CQ (a code meaning: anyone who reads – answer!), and succeeded in hearing from Ascension Island via a ground wave (a short wave skip radio condition), as they were on the CW circuit. Ascension Island got through to New York, and obtained clearance for Campbell to let down to Bermuda.

He dutifully let down, and broke out about 18 000 feet. But where was Bermuda? Visibility was approximately 100 miles so they *should* have been able to see it!

The situation that topped off this chain of events, "the thing that really made me mad" as Campbell says, was that he could pick up only a very fuzzy signal on the ADFs. He could hear "BDA," the identification of Bermuda, on the non-directional beacon, but very faintly. He pointed the ADFs to the station, one on the radio range at Bermuda and one on the Bermuda beacon, until both were pointing straight ahead.

"How close is your ETA?" Campbell asked the navigator.

"I think we should add another 20 minutes," came the reply.

Campbell continued to let down. The navigator added a further 20 minutes. They held at 10 000 feet to lengthen their visibility range. The ADFs still pointed straight ahead, and the navigator continued to stretch out the ETA until he'd added three 20-minute segments.

Campbell called up the navigator. "We're over the middle of the ocean and we don't have enough fuel to get to the mainland. How sure are you of our position?" Then, severely, "Do you actually know our position at all?"

No, the navigator replied, he wasn't really sure.

"What about the three star-fixes you took?"

The navigator had pre-plotted all the three-star fixes, as he usually did, and hadn't taken a fix. But, he reasoned, as both ADFs were pointing straight ahead, Bermuda must be there.

At this point, Campbell took matters into his own hands.

With one ADF he tuned across all four bands, from very low up to fairly high frequency, switching channels, trying desperately to get something. Suddenly, he heard a voice over a commercial radio station. In a stroke of incredible fortune, the announcer was giving a "station i.d. break."

"This is Norfolk, Virginia," the announcer's voice crackled.

Campbell swung into action.

"I did what we call a 'wing-tip null orientation,' which the airline didn't approve of. It's a method of finding your position on a non-directional beacon, like a broadcast station; if you can find that, you can get a fix. It's not what you call a Class A fix, but it's fairly accurate within 100 miles."

He discovered that they were 1 000 miles from Norfolk, which made them about 220 miles southwest of Bermuda – and they were supposed to be north. "*Bermuda was behind us!*" fumes Campbell. The two ADFs still resolutely pointed straight ahead. Campbell had to make a decision, and he had to make it fast.

"I had nothing else to go on, so I turned around and headed back up, because I knew we didn't have enough gas to get to the mainland. By this time we were a couple of hours overdue, and we still couldn't get through to anybody."

The passengers were, of course, quite concerned.

"This is your captain speaking," Campbell announced. He told them, simply, that they'd had radio trouble and were having problems with the navigation equipment. But, he assured them, he had managed to get a fix on their position, and they were now heading for Bermuda. They would be going in quite low – just above the water.

Campbell knew he didn't have enough fuel to climb up through the overcast to 20 000 feet to take a fix. By flying low, he would be able to take advantage of the "cushion" of air between the wing and the water, which would allow him to pull back on his power and still remain airborne.

Heading on a directional bearing of 045 to Bermuda, and by cruising through the night air about 50 feet "more or less" above the calm ocean, he was able to stretch three hours of fuel into three hours and 40 minutes. He pulled the prop pitch back to 1 200 rpm, with a wide-open throttle. That went against Rolls Royce's recommended operating procedure, but this was an emergency and saving fuel was of paramount importance.

"I stayed on the step, you might say, so she didn't drag," Campbell says.

They took the key and wired it up to the yoke, while Campbell continued to call CQ on CW. No answer. He gave his position blind on voice, HF. No answer.

"We still hadn't been able to talk to anybody," Campbell says. "I couldn't even get back to Ascension Island! We couldn't take a fix. If I climbed high enough to get above the cloud to get a three-star fix, it would take all the gas I had. And those planes didn't float worth a damn!"

Suddenly, a call came through on VHF. An Albatross, flying out of Bermuda for the U.S. Coast Guard, had discovered them! Campbell answered, and was asked for his position.

"I got a poor fix," he replied, "but as near as I can tell from dead-reckoning, we're 75 miles southwest of Bermuda on a course of 045."

"We're right near there, but don't see you," came the reply. "Turn your landing lights on."

"I've had them on for two hours!" Campbell responded."You might be looking too high, we're about 50 feet off the water. Do you have flares?"

"Yes."

"Fire one!"

The red flare burst into the sky at "one o'clock."

Campbell saw it, and turned his landing lights on and off to signal his position.

"I've got you in sight now," the Coast Guard operator said. "We'll swing around and come in alongside."

"What's my position?"

They told him – and Campbell realized he'd been out only six miles on the fix he had taken!

"How's your fuel?"

"I have eight tanks – all of them reading empty, and they have been for a while."

The Coast Guard was then flying B-29s (SuperFortress aircraft), which carried boats slung underneath them, for Search & Rescue operations.

"Do you think you can make it?" they inquired.

"I don't know," Campbell replied. "Just keep those boats handy!"

Finally, he was assured that he need only to "get over that little hump and land in the field."

Then the tower came on. "You're clear for a left-hand circuit. Wind is 15 knots southwest."

Yeah, sure. "We'll land straight in," Campbell replied.

"You'll be landing downwind," the tower warned.

Campbell had no choice: he came straight in. He swung around and taxied up the hill, but didn't quite make it to the usual spot on the ramp. About 60 feet short of the parking area, all engines faltered for lack of fuel.

Campbell stepped out of the cockpit and faced his passengers. "Welcome to Bermuda," he said.

Campbell's troubles were not yet over. TCA immediately suspended him pending investigation, while his flight was sent on to Barbados and Trinidad under another captain. Campbell was stunned. He requested that their local-based pilot check out the ADFs while the aircraft remained on the ramp, and also en route to Barbados. There they were, both still pointing south, but identifying Bermuda, BD and BDA.

"That's impossible!" the pilot exclaimed.

"I don't care if it's impossible or not – it's right there in front of you. And that's just *one* of the things that got us into trouble!" Campbell said.

The problem was eventually discovered: the ADFs were actually directing them to San Juan, which was on the same frequency, both for the radio range and non-directional beacon. The beacon at San Juan was the same frequency as the range at Bermuda; the range at San Juan was the same frequency as the beacon at Bermuda. They had been getting "skip conditions" and were heading for San Juan, with near-empty fuel tanks (frequencies were altered immediately).

The FAA (Federal Aviation Agency) and U.S. Search and Rescue officers were stumped over how a scheduled flight could become so lost. "Didn't you receive the message from Washington?" they asked Campbell.

"What message?"

"There was a magnetic storm over the North Atlantic. Everyone was warned to be very careful of all radio aids."

"When was this message issued? To whom?" Campbell asked. "I never got it!"

An immediate investigation resulted, with the discovery that the message had been sent to Dispatch in Montreal, who hadn't posted a NOTAM (Notice to Airmen: advice regarding changes to conditions at an airport or on the airways) or directly given pilots this information.

In retrospect, Campbell believes that the magnetic storm caused his navigation problem. He further believes there was a connection to his situation and others associated with ships and aircraft lost in the famed Bermuda Triangle.

"That's the first thing the pilots' association said to me, and I believe it, based on what I've read about what happened to those army machines and the boats. They were obviously not where they thought they were."

What made Campbell angry was the potential damage to his reputation. "They tried to make me look ridiculous. The fact is, they didn't give out information on that magnetic storm over the ocean, which probably was the main contributing factor. They decided in Dispatch Office in Montreal that it wasn't important, and it turned out to be very important.

"The navigator didn't take the fixes he was supposed to take – he'd pre-plotted all of his flight plan and didn't know where he was. They did fire the navigator, and they didn't fire me. If I was at fault I'd have been fired, that's for damn sure.

"They blamed our other problems on 'atmospheric circumstances' on the radio. That was all TCA had to say. They wrote me a letter saying I was returned to service only because there had been extenuating circumstances – but since I was considered to be a professional pilot, I'd better not miss that island again! That's when I got fed up."

The Bermuda situation in 1952 has Campbell still feeling burned about the way it was handled by the company.

"Instead of being happy about no fatalities and no damage to the airplane, they wrote me that nasty letter. I wrote back and said, 'Hey, you have professional navigators on board who are supposed to tell the captain where they are.' The company said, 'The captain is supposed to be able to handle any position in the airplane.' I said, 'Fine.'

"I took 30 days off and went to Nav School. I took astronavigation at the company's expense and got my ticket. I said, 'Now you can take the navigators and you can keep them.'"

From then on, Campbell would order the navigator to "go and sit with the passengers in the cabin," because he wasn't needed in the cockpit. (Many years later, they pulled the navigators off.) As far as Campbell was concerned, he held the same licence so the navigators weren't necessary. "I couldn't trust them. And that annoyed them."

Campbell and his family were then based in Tampa, Florida. He made a scheduled TCA flight once a week to Mexico City and back; on another flight in the same week he connected to Nassau (Bahamas), to Jamaica, back to Nassau and Tampa. That was the extent of his weekly schedule. "We had one crew down there, that was all, so we virtually had our 'own little airline.'"

A local TCA navigator named Frank Coughlin, also stationed at Tampa, wanted to fly. Campbell accommodated him, especially on the seven-hour weekly flights to Mexico City, on which they carried neither passengers nor freight ("We flew there just to hold the run"). During the flight Campbell would say, "Okay, Frank, you climb into the left seat and steer. I'll navigate over, and you navigate back."

But one day the crew received a visit from Jim Brown (not his real name), a TCA check pilot for the North Atlantic. His purpose was to give Campbell a check ride during the trip to Mexico City. Although he wasn't due for his check, Campbell obliged.

"Take a three-star fix," Brown ordered.

Campbell took a three-star fix on the periscopic sextant and plotted it out on the charts.

Because Brown wasn't a navigator, he asked Frank Coughlin to check the fix. The navigator's job didn't come under the pilot's section, however, so Coughlin didn't work for Brown, he worked for another supervisor.

Coughlin just laughed. "I know it's right," he said to Brown. "*You* check it."

"That started a sort of 'battle of wills' in the aircraft, you might say," Campbell recalls.

When they arrived at their destination, Campbell mentioned that he'd been concerned about the difficulty of getting a good load off in Mexico City, because of the city's high elevation and temperature. He had been talking to a BOAC (British Overseas Airways Corporation) crew that flew fully-loaded North Stars (or Argonauts, as they called them) into Nairobi (Kenya) in Africa, which is 2 000 feet lower than Mexico City (Nairobi alt. 5 542 ft.; Mexico City alt. 7 440 ft.). He'd asked how they managed it with full loads. The answer seemed simple: "Use the high-speed blower for takeoff."

The blowers are super-chargers, Campbell explains, with low-speed (11 000 rpm), and high-speed (33 000 rpm) capacities. Their function is to compress the air going into the engine, which allows an aircraft to gain takeoff power at greater elevation.

Campbell's next question to the BOAC crew was, "How do you get approval to use it?"

"Rolls Royce makes the engine, and they have given approval to use high blowers at altitudes over 5 000 feet," was the reply. "And you use five degrees of flap instead of 15 degrees for takeoff. The Douglas company approves of these flap settings. That's how we get a full load out of Nairobi" (Footnote 4).

Campbell had written to TCA suggesting that this system of operations might be feasible for Mexico City. This action had brought Brown in, to give Campbell a check ride and to find out just what was going on.

At midnight, they received clearance to return to Tampa. Campbell went through his run-up, and got takeoff clearance. But something was wrong – the flaps weren't where Campbell had set them. When Brown, who was sitting in the jump seat, momentarily removed his headset, Campbell said to the copilot, "Did you pull the flaps up to five degrees?"

"No, I never touched them."

Campbell sat still, at the end of the runway.

Brown replaced his headphones. "What's the delay?" he asked.

"I'm going to watch those flaps," Campbell said calmly. "When they get back up to where I set them, we'll take off."

"That was your idea," Brown said hotly. "You're the one who came up with the five-degree theory."

When they landed at Tampa, Campbell turned in his resignation. But a surprise awaited the disgruntled pilot. The airline didn't want to lose him. "The superintendent and the vice-president of operations came down to Tampa and tried to talk me out of leaving. But I said, 'No. A couple of incidents like this, that's enough. I'm disillusioned with the airline, and there's no point in your having me here.'"

In his 13 years with Trans-Canada Airlines, Campbell had flown the early Lockheeds, right through to the Douglas DC-3s and DC-4s. As the bigger airplanes came along, he'd been checked out on them also, from North Stars to Bristols.

And so, Colin Campbell's association with Canada's preeminent airline came to an end. He left TCA in 1955, and went into business for himself.

With partner Jack Sanderson, Campbell bought a Beaver and leased a de Havilland Dove, and began running Executive Air Service out of Toronto. This business lasted 18 months.

He describes the job as "flying people around who had more money than brains." Their most frequent customer was a construction millionaire "who'd been thrown out of Canada for cheating on highway construction jobs, and who wasn't allowed to bid any more." As Campbell recalls, this person had billed the Ontario government for 14 bridges, and built only 12.

And then Russ Baker of Pacific Western Airlines called. He'd acquired a contract for work on the DEW Line, and he needed help.

The DEW (Distant Early Warning) Line is an automated ring of radar stations constructed north of the Arctic Circle from Greenland to Alaska, designed to warn the U.S. and Canada of approaching enemy aircraft. At that time, its construction was partly completed. Baker told Campbell that Tommy Fox's company, Associated Airways, had held the prime contract, but now it had been awarded to him, Russ Baker.

"Russ had very little experience with heavy aircraft, but he was a good talker," Campbell recalls. "I knew Russ from before. He said, 'If you're free, come on out here.'"

After taking over from Associated Airways, Russ wanted to employ his own crews to fly the airplanes but he didn't have anybody qualified to check them out. With Campbell's experience of flying various types of aircraft, ("a couple of pages of them") he was exactly the person Baker needed.

Campbell became operations manager for Pacific Western Airlines out of Edmonton, and started checking out pilots on Yorks, DC-3s, C-46s "and all that stuff." It took a while: there were 94 airplanes which included the bush aircraft. As time went on, Campbell had Stan McMillan do the bush work with float machines, and he concentrated on operations associated with the DEW Line.

One of Campbell's assignments was to negotiate with Federal Electric for the re-supply contract of providing the camps with everything from groceries to equipment. The work called for DC-4s, which PWA didn't have. Baker made an arrangement to buy two DC-4s from a company in Los Angeles, and asked Campbell to go and check out the aircraft.

The North Star and the DC-4 were roughly the same airplane with different engines, so Campbell was fully qualified for the job. When he arrived in California, he saw two very sorry-looking airplanes. Fuel dribbled from the tanks in amounts far exceeding the maximum allowable "seven drops a minute." He got on the phone to Russ Baker.

"We can't take these airplanes! I can't walk under the wings without an umbrella!"

"They told me they'd zero-timed them!" Baker said, meaning the aircraft were to have been repaired to new condition.

"Well, they sure didn't! And the engines are in the same shape."

"They're supposed to be overhauled!" Baker exclaimed.

"Ha!" Campbell snorted. "They've been given a 'Varsol-overhaul' – they've been washed!"

"But we've got to have them!" Baker said. "July 1st, 3:00 in the morning, we have to be out of here to start work. We're nearly down to the last day."

"Russ, I'm not even going to fly these things," Campbell stated.

"They that bad?"

"Yes."

"Well, find us an airplane. We've got to have a '4'."

Campbell went to Oakland to see California Eastern (now World Airways). They had a DC-4 and were interested in leasing it. Campbell took it. Because of the DEW Line operation, Canada's Ministry of Transport would allow the aircraft to be flown under "N" (American) registration (N 75000) if the pilot had either a Canadian or American licence.

"I borrowed a copilot from the Flying Tigers in Burbank, took the airplane up to Vancouver, picked up a MOT [Ministry of Transport] guy, and flew up to Edmonton. We got out right on schedule."

Campbell again plunged into the task of checking out crews. "It's not a big deal to go from a C-46 to a DC-4, it takes about 20 hours of flying, but to get that 20 hours is tough when you're running a schedule with the same airplane."

They made three round trips each week from Edmonton to Cambridge Bay, over to Pin Main (commonly called Cape Perry) across the channel from Banks Island, into Fairbanks. In the midst of a knock-out schedule of flying, maintenance and training, Campbell received a call from the U.S. Navy's Rear Admiral in Fairbanks, who was running Federal Electric in the capacity of logistics officer. The company was taking over from Northern Electric who had built the DEW Line, and had just completed an inventory check.

"Come to Fairbanks, right now! We've discovered a major discrepancy in 'stores', and we believe you're responsible."

Campbell was dumbfounded. He flew up to Fairbanks and met with the Rear Admiral, who informed him that they were missing 100 000 gallons of aviation fuel, in 45-gallon (or 55-gallon American) drums, at Pin Main.

"You're the only outfit operating out of there. You must have used this fuel," the Rear Admiral accused.

"We didn't touch it. We had our own cache up there!" Campbell replied.

The argument went on for a half-day. Finally Campbell said, "Look, we're not getting anywhere. Account for it somehow, just don't blame us for taking it."

But they did. Their report stated that it was believed Pacific Western Airlines had used the fuel, although they diplomatically added, "by mistake." The record looked bad.

The northern ice doesn't thaw until late in the year, sometimes not until August, and it starts forming again the end of September. In early August, an amazing sight presented itself in Pin Main: along the trenches between the runway and the parking ramp rested row after row of 55-gallon drums – full of 100/130 octane fuel. The cache had been covered by deep snow and ice, and the U.S. Air Force simply hadn't been able to find it.

Campbell started to grin as he looked at the rows of fuel barrels. Taking out his camera he snapped some pictures, and the next time he was in Fairbanks he went to see the Rear Admiral.

"Have a look at these."

"What is it?"

"100 000 gallons of fuel at Pin Main."

The Rear Admiral's face turned red. "Well, I'll be damned."

"You'll do a little more than be damned, or I'm going to sue you," Campbell said grimly.

"Oh. Well, I'll write you a letter."

Which he did – a very nice letter, an extremely nice letter. He apologized for believing that Pacific Western Airlines had stolen the fuel. He had brought the matter to the attention of the U.S. Air Force (fuel was delivered to Pin Main by the U.S. Navy for the U.S. Air

Force), saying that the company was innocent. And, because the fuel had already been written off their inventory, they were going to make PWA a gift of the rediscovered cache.

It was an appreciated bonus for the struggling airline.

"Oh boy!" Campbell says. "At that time we were paying $3.25 a U.S. gallon for it up there – and he gave us 100 000 gallons! It took us into the black.

"A C-46 holds 1 200 gallons of gas. When I had to fuel up this airplane to go up to the DEW Line, I'd have to phone the bank for credit. That's the pressure we were under at that time.

"It took about two-and-a-half years to make a go of it. When we first took over from Associated Airways, right away we were $3 million in the hole, that's the debt we assumed."

Although they had assets such as the airplanes, Campbell says "airplanes are a liability unless you've got a use for them."

Campbell worked for Russ Baker until Russ died on November 15, 1958.

"I think what killed Russ was that we got a monthly statement showing we'd paid off the debt and made some money. I think so, because he celebrated. He had a heart attack on the drive home."

Campbell remembers Baker as being "a jovial type, a hell of a nice guy. A lot of people didn't like him, but I got along with him."

When Russ Baker died, Campbell's contract with PWA was near completion.

"At that time, there was a big hassle about who was going to be president. I didn't want to get involved with that. I said, 'You guys go ahead and fight it out.'

"You don't realize how much infighting goes on in an airline," Campbell says, "especially when you're taking in other airlines. You've got seniorities and all this stuff to sort out, and everybody winds up mad at you; if one side's satisfied the other side's madder than hell. They all figured I'd be elected president, and I didn't want that. It's a miserable life. So I said, 'You guys argue about it amongst yourselves. Just leave me out of it.' They said, 'Well, fine. Will you work for the airline?' I said, 'No.' They said, 'Why not?' and I said, 'I worked for Russ. I had a contract with Russ for three years, and the three years is up next week. I'll just finish the contract.' Which I did."

Campbell says he never hesitated to quit a job if things weren't going right. "If there wasn't a job flying, I'd create one. I'd talk people into doing stuff with airplanes. You can do that."

Colin Campbell's next career step was to hire a man named Jim Keir as a pilot, and buy two refurbished DC-4s. The two men started a company called Territorial Bulk Distributors, to work with the oil patch. Keir had been with Imperial Oil for a long time and he knew the people. In discussing the needs of the oil business, they decided it might be possible to get a lot of business with a major airplane, because when the oil patch had trouble they had big trouble. An example was when the oil crew had to ream out a hole.

This procedure occurs when the well bore deviates off centre. The drill string can't go in or out because of the bend, so the next step is to put down a reamer to straighten out the hole.

"A rig was having trouble getting the bit out of a hole where they'd drilled down about 4 000 feet. The drill pipe had twisted off. Using a 'fishing tool,' they tried to grab it and pull it back out, but that was impossible because of the bend in the pipe. They needed a reamer, so they phoned me up."

"Is your airplane available for charter immediately?"

Campbell assured them it was.

"Okay. Go down to Ogden, Utah, pick up three reamers and bring them up to Fort Nelson."

"Okay, when do you want me to leave?"

"Five minutes ago. Get those things up here just as fast as you can."

Campbell took an extra crew along and flew to Ogden, where they loaded the reamers onto the airplane – about seven tons worth. There was some other equipment also, but this weight presented no problem for the DC-4 which could carry 11 tons. They tied everything down, refuelled the airplane, and flew back to Fort Nelson. The company was waiting for them, with trucks to haul the equipment out to the hole.

The rig crew was impressed with the cargo capacity of the big airplanes. They'd started drilling the year before and still had to drill two more holes, so they had a lot of work in that immediate area. Their only problem was how to get materials and supplies directly to the drill sites.

"We talked to Texaco people, who were there with Parker Drilling. To get to their rig site at Sandy Lake, 212 miles north of Fort Nelson in the top northeast corner of B.C., they had to wait for winter roads. Then they had to worry about crossing major rivers to get into the area.

"So Jim Keir and I talked to the company officials in Calgary, and convinced them that we could get our DC-4 in by building an airstrip. They said it couldn't be done. It was all clay ridges, swamp and muskeg, and it would be impossible to get a decent airport in there."

But Campbell and Keir thought otherwise.

"Let's be practical," Campbell said. "You stick pipe down 6 000 or 8 000 feet. How much does it weigh when you pull it out of the hole?"

"Tons!"

"What's the rig resting on?" Campbell asked.

"It's got to be on a clay ridge."

"So, let's build an airport on that clay ridge."

The company officials looked at each other. "How much would that cost?"

"You already have a D-4 Cat with a blade on it at the rig. Using an Otter on floats, we'll bring up fuel and oil for the Cat. We'll also bring a farm wagon, in parts that can be reassembled on site."

The deal was struck.

As soon as the ground froze, they took in six men, a "yellow dog" pump, a "whale" or "bladder" tank for water, and the farm wagon. They bladed off a level spot, scraped down hillocks, and filled all holes until the area was table-flat. Then they built up the sides of the ice strip like those surrounding a skating rink.

They pumped water into the whale tank from a small nearby lake, using the yellow dog pump. Then they drove around the site sprinkling water from a spray bar affixed to the back of the farm wagon, on which rested the water-bladder tank, pulled by the Cat. The ice over ground

A DC-4 hauling drilling mud in to the strip built under Campbell's supervision at Sandy Lake, BC. *Colin Campbell Collection*

was solid and reliable. The last step was to back-grade in some sand and run the wagon and spray-bar over, giving it another coat of ice. That provided braking action.

"It took us seven days to build that runway," Campbell says proudly. "We built a nice 7 000 foot-long strip, 300 feet wide, and sent them a bill for $8 500. They couldn't believe it."

Then they began to haul in supplies. The first item needed was fuel, to run the rig, and the camp for cooking and heating. They installed a huge whale tank in the airplane, filled it with 3 000 U.S. gallons of diesel (which made them only a couple of hundred pounds under-weight on the airplane), took off from Fort Nelson, went in and landed on their new strip. No problem.

Pilot Mike Thomas, who was flying a Beaver in the area at that time, says he had noticed this strip out in the middle of nowhere and wondered if he should chance landing on it. He was quite amazed to see Colin Campbell swoop down and land a DC-4!

Campbell laughs. "We were delivering 22 000-pound loads into that strip, keeping them supplied. We were able to get that rig going 90 days early, which meant a lot of money to them. Then they got 'welled down' with the hole and they lost circulation. This meant that the drilling mud wasn't coming back to surface, but was seeping out a fissure in the formation, perhaps through a prehistoric river bed. The job then was to keep pumping in material to keep the gas down, while trying to plug the hole in the bottom.

"They asked us to fly in strip plastic, so they could put that down the hole and try to seal it off. We did, but that didn't work. Next, we brought in a couple of planeloads of golf balls, sawdust and Ping-Pong balls."

Campbell describes the fun of loading a DC-4 to the roof with Ping-Pong balls. "We closed the cockpit door and put in these boxes of Ping-Pong balls. Then we opened the boxes and dumped them in from the front, all the way to the back of the airplane. That way, we filled the airplane absolutely full. The last thing we did was take away flexible pieces of plywood and close the doors.

"When we reached the site, I parked the airplane, got out the front cockpit exit and said to the guys, 'Don't open the door until I get my camera!' When I was ready, they opened the door, and boom! They nearly drowned in Ping-Pong balls."

The oil companies were happy with Territorial Bulk Distributors, and so were Campbell and Keir. They decided to apply to the Ministry of Transport in Ottawa for a charter to fly throughout the Arctic and sub-Arctic regions, delivering petroleum products and draft beer in barrels.

The company's mandate was "to distribute the products it sells to dealers into and from the Northwest Territories and Yukon, to and from the rest of Canada, by the use of all modern methods of transportation, including modern freight aircraft and helicopters." Their application was for a licence to haul freight – and freight only – in Canada. "With freight charters you can go anywhere; we weren't going to carry passengers or run a schedule airline. Each flight would be paid for as it went."

On August 23, 1958, Campbell inquired by letter to the Lockheed Aircraft Corporation about the feasibility of using a Hercules for transporting POL (Petroleum Oil Liquifying, a general term meaning petroleum products) in northern regions. Most of the proposed sites had 4 500 foot-long runways. It would be necessary to land at 121 600 pounds, but takeoff would be in the vicinity of 82 000 pounds. They were considering a tanker type of operation, which would entail pumping fuel oil, aviation gas, or regular gas, out of the aircraft into ground tanks at these northern points.

(What wasn't mentioned in the letter was their ultimate plan of hauling an entire oil rig inside the aircraft!)

Their inquiry came to naught.

"Ottawa said if we included the price of air transportation we needed a charter, so our licence application was turned down," Campbell says.

"They don't like me in Ottawa," he adds. "And they were protecting Northern Transportation, a Crown corporation."

The defeated proposal ended his partnership with Jim Keir. They did not operate long enough to make much money.

Undaunted, Campbell soon found new work for his DC-4s: using the same airplanes, he bought into a company with Bill Bale, a man who was familiar with the construction business. The new company was called Yukon Construction.

"As I said, an airplane is a liability if you don't have any work for it," Campbell says. "For example, just to park it at the airport costs $100 a day, and we had two DC-4s [plus one that was leased]. We and the bank, of course. So we had to use the airplanes or let them go."

At one point, the bank seized two of their airplanes and parked them out at the airport. The bank wanted its money, and wasn't concerned – or knowledgeable about – possible deterioration of these assets. Campbell approached the manager.

"You know, it might end up costing you an awful pile of money to seize those airplanes," he said.

"How so?" inquired the bank manager.

"Well, you'll have to pay the parking fees, for starters. And if you don't run the engines up at least once a week, they'll be ruined." He paused for effect. "And there are lots of other things on airplanes that could deteriorate because of non-use. . . "

"So what do you suggest?"

"We want to bid a job at Cambridge Bay, to build the airport there," Campbell said. "All we need is some backing money and the airplanes so we can bid on flying stuff up."

"We'll have to think it over."

Campbell shrugged. "You've got yourself some airplanes. If you keep them in shape, I'm sure you'll eventually get your money out of them. If you don't – they're going to be good only for scrap."

While they were mulling this over, Campbell walked over to the Bank of Montreal. The manager there showed immediate interest in his proposal. In the end, Campbell talked them into putting up bidding as well as operating money, taking the airplanes over from the first bank, and getting them back into the air so Yukon Construction could try to pay them off.

"We had to bid against a big company, Pitts Construction, but we won the contract at Cambridge Bay. We did the job, and we made money, which paid off the airplanes. We eventually sold one to Calm Air in Manitoba."

Everyone should have been happy: the bank had its money and Yukon Construction was successful. They owned outright two DC-4s.

"But typical government – they'll make it expensive if they can," Campbell adds. "The MOT wrote me a letter, saying because Yukon Construction didn't have any experience running airplanes – the *company*, never mind the individuals – that we were back to the basic engine times, which meant 1 000 hours between overhauls."

He felt that 1 000 hours was an unnecessarily short time for a safety check, especially when their flight plan would take them over largely uninhabited territory. If they crashed, the only ones they'd hurt would be themselves. "The closest we came to any living soul on our flight path was 30 miles. We were running mainly out of Fort McMurray and Edmonton, flying direct to Cambridge Bay. There wasn't a thing along the route!"

Oddly enough, they could fly the airplanes in the United States for 2 200 hours between overhauls. So, an idea formed. The Cambridge Bay job progressed to the point where they were able to do the work using only one airplane. Campbell took the second DC-4 down to Oakland and had it converted from a freight to a passenger aircraft. He formed a company called Majestic Charters, and applied for a U.S. charter to fly passengers out of Teterboro, New Jersey (an airport on the edge of New York City), to Gatwick, England.

He got his American charter with no problem. "They gave me a book, said 'These are the rules you follow,' and that was it." A difference between aviation rules in Canada and the United States can be illustrated by what followed:

"Just to show you how the MOT ruling affected the operation," Campbell says, "we would run freight to Cambridge Bay, up to 1 000 hours on the four engines. Then we'd fly that airplane down to Cut Bank, Montana, and the other DC-4 would come from New York to meet it. We'd line them up, take the engines off one and put them on the other. The new engines would go on the freight machine, and the engines with 1 000 hours on them would go on the passenger plane. Then we'd fly the extra 1 200 hours off those engines, taking passengers across the North Atlantic, until we'd reached the maximum 2 200 hours allowed on them.

"But we couldn't fly freight to Cambridge Bay with engines over 1 000 hours because it was considered 'too dangerous'! We had only two pilots on board the airplane going north, while the charter airplane carried 52 passengers. And we never had to shut down an engine."

For a period of 18 months in 1958 and 1959, Yukon Construction flew supplies north during construction of the Cambridge Bay airport. With their second DC-4, Majestic Charters flew out of Teterboro, New Jersey, to Gatwick, England.

When the Cambridge Bay airport job was completed, Campbell found another job for one of his DC-4s. He took a two-month flying contract with the United Nations, flying white refugees out of the Belgian Congo, during the time that country was being released from Belgium and gaining its independence.

For Campbell, this job was simply another way of putting one of the DC-4s to work.

"We didn't do any actual *work*," he laughs, "but we got paid. One time we flew five gallons of ice cream, that was the only load we ever had. We went into an airport just outside the Congo, picked up the ice cream for some United Nations general, and went back. That was my only trip."

They were based at Stanleyville airport for the two-month duration (now called Kisangani, Stanleyville is a port and commercial centre in northeastern Zaire, on the River Zaire). Although their purpose was to act as stand-by crew, Campbell's DC-4 came back riddled with bullet holes. Luckily, no one was inside the aircraft at the time, so damage was minor.

"Oh hell, that was nothing," Campbell shrugs. "My DC-3 being shot up in Iran a few years later was more exciting than that."

Campbell regards this first shoot-up as an accident – "some idiot practising with his gun."

While stationed at Stanleyville, Campbell met some unusual characters. One such person was "Crazy" Gonzales.

"He wanted to come to work for me," Campbell explains. "I first met him in the Belgian Congo when he bummed a ride up to Gatwick, and that's where we parted company. He was from Columbia or somewhere around there, and was on his way back. But this industry is funny: by just giving him a ride, people associated me with him, but that's the only dealing I ever had with him. Really. He kept bugging me to hire him, but I wouldn't."

Although Gonzales said he was a pilot, Campbell never saw his licence. He heard that Gonzales was later caught running guns, munitions and ammunition out of the United States.

Another character was a gunrunner who had a series of registrations taped onto his airplane. He'd fly it under British registration and get clearance to land in France. As soon as he got in to France, he'd pull off the tape to reveal French registration. He had as many as six registrations on the same airplane, one taped underneath another. "He travelled around for a long time, until he finally got caught," Campbell says, "but he made a lot of money."

In 1960 and 1961 Campbell worked for the toy company Fisher-Price, based in Holland, New York. He ran their moulding shop, and also did some executive flying. He took on a second job flying DC-4s from Los Angeles to Liverpool, where he met Cubana crews. They invited him to Havana to discuss a contract to fly agricultural products from Canada to Cuba.

Campbell had flown North Stars during his tenure with TCA so, in 1961, when the company was selling the aircraft, he bought three of them for his newly-formed company, International Air Freighters. The company operated on a Cuban licence, which stipulated that a Canadian operator be allowed to fly trips to Cuba on a one-for-one basis.

Campbell hired three ex-TCA pilots, Stan Hegstrom, Al Burns and Willy Milne. Another pilot, Clif Wenzel, was hired later. Cargo hauled to Cuba ranged from chicks to piglets, powdered milk and pharmaceuticals; return flights might carry anything from seafood to watermelons. The company even carried passengers on occasion, including Cuba's UN ambassador and his family. Despite a U.S.-Cuban trade embargo, an agent in Toronto was on hand to receive the shipments and reroute them to the United States. As author Milberry says, "So much for the Cuban trade embargo!" (Milberry, p. 213).

Colin Campbell's happy passenger. One trip involved hauling a load of pigs in a Northstar from Toronto to Havana, non-stop, in 1961. On other trips, he transported 7.5 million day-old baby chicks, (90 000 per trip). *Colin Campbell Collection*

As business increased, International Air Freighters was making several flights each week, which encouraged them to add an ex-Cuban DC-4 (CF-NWM) to their fleet.

But still, revenues didn't exceed expenses, and after a little more than a year (May, 1961 to July, 1962) International Air Freighters shut down, "and the North Stars were left to languish at Malton for several years until they were scrapped" (ibid., p. 213).

"I got out right at the end of the Cuban haul. A Toronto stockbroker decided he had always wanted to be president of an airline, so he bought the company from us," Campbell says. "In the end, we had two DC-4s from Cuba that went with the sale in lieu of payment for flights, plus the North Stars."

From 1962 to 1966, Campbell made aircraft deliveries "all over the world. And in 1966, he began flying for a company called Mount Royal Air. One of their customers was Weather Engineering, based out of Montreal, whose business was cloud seeding. The enterprise didn't work as well in Canada as in other places, says Campbell, mainly because of complaints that we were stealing rain from one province to give to another." Campbell considers this to be pure nonsense and even more, a cover-up.

"A lot of Canadian aircraft operators got much of their business from fighting fires, and still do – and that's not the way to put out a forest fire. I proved it up in Labrador. They had tremendous fires going there around 1966. They'd been fighting them for three weeks and they still had 40 fires going, big ones, some they didn't even know were burning out in isolated areas. I took an airplane up there, seeded the cloud, and put the fires out in 30 hours."

When Campbell went to the main office in St. John's to send in his time for the Labrador assignment, the manager asked, "Do you think you can do anything about the Avalon Peninsula? It's tinder dry. Fire hazard is extreme, over 90 percent. Can you wet it down any?" They got out a weather map, which showed that an upper trough was coming across. Good.

Approximately three hours after this conversation took place, Campbell and his crew went out and seeded clouds. The fire hazard in Newfoundland's Avalon Peninsula was brought to under 40 percent overnight.

Based on his experience with Weather Engineering, and later, nine years cloud seeding in Iran for The Tehran Regional Water Board, Campbell feels that the business of fire suppression is "patronage to people who work with the government." In the fire-suppression business, money is paid for putting out fires. Interlopers are not welcomed.

"When we were in Labrador, there wasn't one operator there who would sell me a gallon of gas. I had to go to the air force to get gas. Why? They didn't want us fighting fires. *They* were getting paid to fly the firefighters and their equipment in and out. It was a lucrative business. Still is. All we needed was some cloud and we could put the fire out. That's it."

Then Mohammed Riza Shah Pahlevi inquired of Weather Engineering if cloud seeding would work in Iran. The company meteorologist and others, including Campbell, went over to assess conditions, and told him it would.

"Good," said the Shah. "Come over."

Later, Campbell took on the contract personally. His sojourn in Iran lasted from 1968 to 1978, fulfilling three, three-year contracts. Campbell's direct communication with the Shah of Iran extended, in the years to follow, from business to mutual respect, and friendship. "I used to play poker with him almost every Friday night that he could make it."

One of Campbell's flights in Iran involved a trip that he considered fairly normal, but one which the Shah classed as "service above and beyond the call of duty."

It began with a phone call from the Shah. One of his ministers had suffered a heart attack at Bandar Abbas, located south on the Persian Gulf. This man was not only a valuable member of the government, but was also a close personal friend to the Shah. Because of the difficulty in getting into the area, compounded by a fierce sandstorm, and the airport being just partially built, the air force had refused to go. So had the airline.

"Would you try?" the Shah asked.

"Well, I'll try but I can't guarantee anything."

"Do you know the area?"

"Never been there," Campbell replied. "How close can I get fuel?"

"You can get fuel at Shiraz, and go from there."

Campbell got out his map. "Okay, I'll go to Shiraz, gas up, and take a crack at it. Have you got a chart of the airport you're building? Send it over."

Campbell plotted to go around the end of Queshm Island in the gulf, and then head straight in, which he figured should bring him dead-on the end of the runway.

"Tell them to get some flarepots out," he instructed.

"You're not going in at night!" the Shah exclaimed.

"I'm surely not going in during daylight! You can see way better in a sandstorm at night than in the day."

So off he flew in a DC-3. "I hadn't told my wife any details, just that I had a trip down to Bandar Abbas, because she used to worry."

He picked up the patient and flew him to the hospital in Shiraz, where he recovered. "It was pretty routine," says Campbell, "but the Shah made a big deal out of it. He sent a major from the Savack [a division of the army], who was the Shah's personal bodyguard, to the house. It was really comical because his English wasn't that good, you know."

"You must be available for Monday evening!" the major announced to a surprised Mrs. Campbell.

"What for?" she asked.

"I just deliver message," said the major. He turned on his heel, and left.

When Colin returned, she confronted him. "What's going on?"

"Well, you'd better wear your fancy clothes," Campbell said mysteriously.

"Why? Where are we going?"

"To the Shah's palace. He wants to see you!"

And so they went, all dressed up, to the Gulistan Palace in Tehran.

"Talk about royalty, Holy smokes!" Campbell says. "They made a big presentation and gave me a watch, which weighs half a pound. I can't even wear it. It's of gold and silver, made by a Swiss manufacturer, and was worth, at that time, $1 500. It's engraved in both Farsi

Colin Campbell with some of his gifts from Iran. *Photo: S. Matheson*

and English: 'C. Campbell, thank you for a job well done, Minister of Water and Power, Rohnni.' I've still got it.

"Then he said to my wife, 'Hold out your hand.' She held it out, and he poured into it a handful of loose diamonds!

"My wife still didn't know what this was all about. Many of the people didn't speak English. The Shah spoke 26 languages, and could read and write them all. He went to Oxford University, so his English was good."

"Mrs. Campbell," said the Shah, "I gather your husband did not tell you!"

"No, he didn't say a thing. What did he do?"

"He went down and brought my friend out of Bandar Abbas when nobody else would do it."

Besides the watch and diamonds, other gifts presented by the Shah to the Campbells included a hammered ornamental tray four feet in diameter, designed by one of the country's top artists. A gift from the Sheik of Sharjah was a belt and dagger inscribed in Arabic, representing a "key to the country" of the United Arab Emirate of Sharjah, (one of seven Arab sheikdoms located on the Persian Gulf coast of Arabia, between Qatar and the Musandam peninsula, formerly known as the Pirate Coast).

When the government minister had recovered sufficiently to be returned to Tehran, he refused to get on the airline's 727s or 737s. Again the Shah phoned Campbell.

"You must have given him a good trip. He wants you to go down and get him, or he says he won't come!"

So Campbell again flew to Shiraz in his humble DC-3.

The cloud seeding enterprise also went well. Basically, when Campbell arrived the country had run out of water.

"They had built a major system of catch basins and power stations [the Karaj and Sefid Rudd dams] to supply the city of Tehran with water and power. The dams had been built and completed for 11 years, but they'd never got enough water in them to even start the turbines, let alone supply any water or power.

"Within four years, they asked me to stop cloud seeding because the reservoirs were full and they were afraid the dams might break."

Campbell says, however, that there was an ongoing dispute over whether their work brought on the rain, or whether it had come naturally.

"A natural phenomenon!" he scoffs. "In the Gazvin Plain, east of Tehran, south of the Elburz Mountains, the plains were a desert! I have pictures of them. I flew from one end to the other, 150 miles by 95 miles, and there wasn't a tree or anything. Nine years later I took a picture on the same run, and everything was green. There hadn't been anything growing on the Gazvin Plains for about 1 200 years. Would you say it was coincidence – or what?" (Footnote 5)

Not all of Campbell's experiences in Iran were positive. There was an element of danger, and Campbell met it full-force one day when he was starting up his airplane on the military tarmac. "When I first went over to Iran on my own, following the contract with Weather Engineering, I'd park my DC-3 at the Hajj Terminal. It was a special terminal built to accommodate the huge increase in traffic when Muslims were making the walk to Mecca. That's called the Hajj [or hadj], which means pilgrimage.

"Hundreds of thousands of them fly as far as Jeddi, then on to Medina in Saudi Arabia, and walk to Mecca," says Campbell. "It's quite a deal. But there are so many that most major airports have another terminal building strictly for the Hajj. They gave us a lot at the Hajj to park our aircraft, because the walk only takes place at certain times of the year. When the Hajj was on we couldn't park there, and so they asked us to park over on the military side of the airport, which we did."

One day, Campbell prepared to make a flight. He hopped onto an airport vehicle, and, with its lights flashing away, scooted over to his airplane. He entered the cockpit, did his check, fired up the engines, released the brakes and BAM! No windshield, no front end, no instrument panel!

"A soldier with a machine gun blew the front end off my airplane!" Campbell says. "Right in front of my face! My feet were underneath, on the pedals."

The shots had come from the side, from the wing tip, and missed the pilot by mere inches.

"What could I do? Nothing. I just stopped the airplane and waited. Sure enough, an officer came out. He rounded up a guy who could speak English to tell me that they apologized very much, but the kid who'd fired on me couldn't read English – likely couldn't read at all – and he had been told to stop any airplane from moving. He was on guard duty, so, he stopped me.

"It took them three months to rebuild the airplane. I got a holiday, came home."

While Campbell didn't exactly get "danger pay" for the job, he acknowledges that "I got paid pretty well for being over there."

His work in Iran finished around 1978, "when the Shah got thrown out of his country. The Moulas, the Ayatollah [Shi'ite Muslim spiritual leader in Iran] came in and said it was against Allah to seed the clouds, so I quit."

While the Campbells were living in Iran, they purchased a farm in Manitoba located north of Brandon near Gladstone. The reason for buying the farm came from a comment made by James George, a Canadian Ambassador stationed in Iran.

"Guess what the government's doing over in Canada now?" Jim George said. "They're paying farmers not to grow wheat."

Campbell laughed. "That's a gift! I've got more experience not growing wheat than anyone!"

"Well, why don't you go back there and buy a farm?"

"That's not a bad idea," Campbell said.

That summer, the family went shopping for a farm. The one they chose was owned by a retired couple, whose people had owned the property for several generations.

"As soon as we bought the farm, we got a permit book from the Canadian Wheat Board," Campbell says. "I grew buckwheat, corn, sunflowers, all kinds of cash crops. We lived on the farm for about six years after returning from Iran."

Soon after their return, Colin journeyed to Edmonton for a reunion with his old friends in Edmonton's Quarter Century Aviation Club. There, he was pleased to run into Jim Keir, with whom he'd operated DC-4s for Territorial Bulk Distributors. Jim (since deceased) had formed Keir Airways. Ten years had passed since Campbell had last met with his club members, and he was shocked to discover that quite a few of them weren't around any more.

In 1979, Campbell started flying C-46s for Jack Anderson's company, North Coast Air Services. The company was based in Prince Rupert, B.C., but Campbell's work included cargo flights from Winnipeg up to the Kewatin district in northern Manitoba, servicing freight contracts for the Hudson's Bay Company.

"I went out to the coast, picked up the C-46s, flew them back, did a contract in Manitoba, took them back to the north coast and then worked with the float machines. When we got another contract, I went back with the '46s again.

"We finally sold the '46s to Lamb Air. I stayed with Lamb Air to check their people out – it takes quite a while to do that. Then the company folded and I had to reclaim the '46s. North Coast sold them to Air Manitoba [then Ilford-Riverton]."

Living on the farm became difficult with more and more work being based from the west coast, so the Campbells left the farm in 1981 and moved to Prince Rupert.

Beaver CF-OMI, North Coast Air Services, Prince Rupert, flown by Colin Campbell over the Pacific Ocean in the 1980s. Note the weight and balance line on the floats to ensure the aircraft is not overloaded or unbalanced. (This aircraft was bought new by the Catholic church and flown by Father Leising.) *Colin Campbell Collection*

Campbell was operations manager for Anderson's North Coast Air Services, and also flew a variety of airplanes in addition to the C-46s, including Beavers, Huskies, Mallards, and Cessna 180s and a 310, on floats. His route included Queen Charlotte Islands, and the north coast of B.C., from the Alaska border (Wrangell and Ketchikan) south through the Douglas Channel to Bella Bella, and down to Vancouver, "a good-sized route."

Personal tragedy struck the family while they were living in Prince Rupert. Mary Eleanor Campbell died from cancer in 1985, three weeks short of their 40th wedding anniversary.

"I left North Coast Air Services right after she died in 1985," Campbell says. "Jack and I parted on excellent terms, but I didn't want to stay."

Campbell's next contract was with Trans-Provincial Airlines, flying freight to Johnny Mountain Gold Mine. This gold-producing mine was built on the mountain, downstream on the Iskut River (which runs through Canada and into Alaska), not far from Wrangell, Alaska. The company used Twin Otters and other aircraft for flying personnel and freight to the site.

"I got Trans-Provincial Airlines the contract to fly freight up to Johnny Mountain," Campbells says, "but big airplanes were needed to do the work. So I phoned New Zealand and got a price on some Bristols" (Footnote 6).

Campbell personally bought two Bristols from Hercules Airline. He borrowed a crew from the airline and flew these two aircraft from New Zealand to Canada. Then he made a trade with the New Zealand Air Force Museum in Christchurch for one of their Bristols in exchange for a "rebuildable" Bolingbroke.

"A museum in Mount Hope, Ontario, had a Bolingbroke in bits and pieces, and they wanted $2 000 for it. I said, 'Let's be practical, I'll give you $1 000.' They said okay, but you'll have to take it away. So I traded the Bolingbroke at Mount Hope for a Bristol at the Christchurch museum, and flew that Bristol Freighter back to Canada. I got my third Bristol, which I also sold to Trans-Provincial Airlines so they could do the work on Johnny Mountain."

The next step of getting the Bolingbroke over to New Zealand was also handled smoothly. "The New Zealanders owned some C-130s, but the servicing had to be done in England. So, on their way home from a trip to England, they stopped in Hamilton, loaded the Bolingbroke into the C-130, and flew it back to New Zealand."

Campbell believes that two of the Bristols are still in Terrace, B.C., scheduled to be sold, while one was sold in England.

But once again, Campbell encountered problems with MOT's rules regarding the number of hours allowable on an engine.

"In Canada, 'basic engine times' for commercial airplanes cannot exceed 1 000 hours between overhauls," Campbell says. "It puts Canada at a distinct disadvantage when you're competing with any other country. ICAO (International Civil Aviation Organization), with headquarters in Montreal, set safety rules for the world. The Bristol company sets their number of engine hours at 3 300 between overhauls; Canada says 1 000. That makes it impossible. The Bristol has two engines; it costs $60 000 to overhaul one engine, $120 000 for both."

Campbell contacted Bristol executives at their office in England, who in turn contacted the Ministry of Transport in Ottawa to reiterate that the manufacturer's recommendation were safe. The MOT was not moved.

"It's ridiculous," Campbell says. "That's why I have so many licenses. If I have a job to do that requires a Canadian licence, I renew it – *if* I can't do it with any other licence. Otherwise, I wouldn't touch it. They're very impractical.

"The most dangerous time for a new engine is when you first hang it," Campbell explains. "If there's anything wrong, it's going to show up then. After you've got 1 000 hours on it, you've got it in good shape" (Footnote 7).

Campbell's next career phase was something quite different, again. In 1988, he went down to the Antarctica to fly a DC-4 for a northern carrier.

"We flew from Punta Arenas in Chile to a place called Patriot Hills near the South Pole. We landed on the ice without any preparation, where the wind had blown the ice clear." These rather difficult conditions held no element of concern, Campbell says, because "I know a DC-4 pretty well."

His job was to transport tourists. "They'd sell a package of tours to go down and climb the highest mountain or whatever; then they'd give out certificates saying the people had done it. We would land them out on the ice, they'd ski to the South Pole, then we'd pick them up and take them home."

Campbell's opinion of this sort of business, and the customers who go for it, is that "the people had to have more money than they knew what to do with."

The adventure was not a positive one for Colin Campbell.

"I went down to find there was no gas at the south end, and we had to make the round trip without stopping for long because of the temperatures. We could shut the engines down for about 40 minutes, that would be the maximum. We had to fill the aircraft tanks with fuel, carry fuel in barrels in the airplane, and carry the passengers in with the fuel. To do the round trip, we had to overload the airplane 25 percent."

Campbell was about ready to retire but not completely, and he had agreed to the contract, but when he saw what was involved he had second thoughts. "I said I'm not going to fly 23 hours out of a day – go down to Patriot Hills in the South Pole area and back to Punta Arenas in Chile – with a single crew."

Campbell produces one of the flight plans for the DC-4, which substantiates his concerns:

"From Punta Arenas, which is designated as SCCI (international airport code for Punta Arenas), direct to Patriot Hills, time: 21 hours 10 minutes – that's round trip flying time – 10 hours and 35 minutes each way. That was a typical flight.

"What I was worried about more than anything was losing an engine on takeoff which could result in 'piling in.' And sure enough, that's what happened."

The situation had all the makings of a disaster. They'd got up to 40 feet when an engine blew, then caught on fire.

"These airplanes have what's known as 'dump chutes' to allow us to dump off a big load of fuel in a hurry. We call it 'pulling the corks.' Four-inch diameter holes are located in the bottoms of the tanks, and you can activate them from the cockpit."

That might dump the fuel from the tanks in a hurry, but there were still barrels of fuel in the back of the airplane, along with the passengers.

"There was a guy with me who they'd sent down to be in charge of the operation. He'd been with this carrier for quite a while. He had his MOT type endorsement for a DC-4 on his Canadian licence, but I felt I needed a pilot with more experience on the equipment."

So there they were, with a blown engine and a plane loaded with 14 passengers along with fuel. Gas poured out underneath the wing, and the left outboard (Number One) engine was in flames.

"I also had a light aircraft pilot from New Zealand, Max Wenden, in the jumpseat. We had a [Cessna] 185 down there and he used to fly it. I never saw a guy get out of the jumpseat so fast, and move back in the airplane! He figured we were going to hit for sure!"

Campbell didn't need to radio the airport – everyone saw, as it happened right on takeoff at Punta Arenas. By the time they were into the turn, fire trucks were out and ready.

"It was rising ground to the left, but lower to the right. If your ground is more level, you usually turn left. But the left outboard engine had let go, and you don't turn against a dead engine, so fortunately we were turning into the flatter – lower – ground, to the right."

The airport was situated on the edge of the Straits of Magellan. Campbell headed out over the straits, which gave him 100 to 150 feet altitude, turned, and came in on the approach.

"I'm hanging onto the airplane with one hand, punching out Number One engine, selecting the fire extinguisher – you had to reach down on the floor to pull up on the fire extinguisher – and all this time I'm just on very critical stalling speed of 115 knots. We never got over 120. If it stalls, it's gone.

"I put the wheels down, the landing gear, and then adjusted the flaps. I wanted five degrees of flap. We managed to get the plane around.

"Later the copilot said, 'How'd you ever make it around?' I said, 'Just by knowing a DC-4!'"

Campbell informed the carrier how he felt about the situation. Their response was "You're fired." He said, "Fine. Good-bye."

Campbell next bought his own airplane, a DC-6, and continued to fly in the Antarctica under his newly-formed company, Antarctic Air. He did this for one year (1989-90), with a major investor. "But our customer wasn't too happy with me because I wouldn't take the thing out under adverse conditions. I said, 'If *you're* going to run the airplane, *I'm* not going to fly it.' I had them in on the purchase of the

Colin Campbell's local welcoming committee at Punta Arenas, southern Chile, on the Strait of Magellan, 1992. *Colin Campbell Collection*

airplane, so things got real nasty. Nothing came of it but a bunch of lawyers' fees."

In 1992, Campbell flew with Regal Air, a little company that did freight hauling in the Caribbean. "We ran out of New York, Fort Lauderdale, Miami, San Juan and the leeward islands down as far as Argentina. Regal Air became a subsidiary of my other company, Carricargo, for hauling cargo for the leeward islands."

But Colin Campbell wasn't as young as he once was. Depending on which birth certificate he produced, in 1992 he would have been 74 or 79 years of age. "So I sold out of the company, and I haven't done very much since. Oh, I went up north and flew a DC-3 for a while, for ATA Construction out of Norman Wells. They owned the airplane, I just flew it to give them a hand. The last time I flew it was 1994."

Although he's still flying, he is not actively involved in a commercial venture. Perhaps it's time for him to rest on his laurels: 41 000 accident-free flying hours, holding Airline Transport pilot's licenses from five different countries: Canadian licence #94 issued from headquarters, as well as licenses from United States, New Zealand, Australia and Iran. The latter licence includes credentials for Douglas DC-3s, as well as Boeing 707s, 737s and 747s, and a pass that permits him to enter all Iranian airports.

Campbell has created numerous inventions to which he holds some patents pending. Included in these are a "renewable resource clean-burning fuel," an "engine pre-start and turbo shut-down oiling system," and a "method of keeping float-equipped aircraft from sinking when floats are holed," which involves filling some internal sections of the floats with Styrofoam "peanuts."

One of his innovative ideas, also in for patent, is a "weight and balance indicator line, or mark, for use on aircraft that operate off water." It was originally adapted from the Plimsoll Mark, a load-line painted on the side of a ship's hull which shows how much cargo the ship can safely carry under different conditions.

"With the airplane fully loaded and the Centre of Gravity right on centre where it should be, the 'Weight and Balance Line' that I painted on the aircraft will be level with the surface of the water."

Simply put, if the "C of G" is too far forward, the airplane will tip nose down, and the back end of the Weight and Balance line will be out of the water while the front end will be submerged. The line would show precisely how far it is off-balance.

This instant reading gives the pilot a tremendous advantage in circumstances where somebody else is loading the airplane, or when the actual weight of cargo being loaded is difficult to estimate. The line will indicate if the aircraft is being loaded unevenly or overloaded.

Campbell says he had never seen this idea used before he began implementing it, and it's foolproof. Although it was based on the Plimsoll Mark used on ships, the difference lies in the fact that it also shows the balance.

The *Rules of the Air and Air Traffic Services*, established by Transport Canada, calculate weights and balance differently:

> Actual passenger weights should be used, but, where they are not available, the following average passenger weights, arrived at by an Airline-Transport Canada survey, may be used.
>
> In the summer (March 15-Dec. 14, incl.) males weigh 182 lbs., females weigh 135 lbs., children 2-12 yrs. old weigh 75 lbs, and infants weigh 30 lbs. But in the winter, males weigh 188 lbs., females weigh 141 lbs., and the other two stay the same. Large males, such as a football team are to be accounted for separately, at not less than 215 lbs (Section 3.1, RAC).

"That makes it nice and easy for a guy out in the bush, right?" Campbell says.

"They say that 'ignorance of the law is no excuse,'" he adds, "but if you told anybody to read this book and then keep up-to-date by reading all the amendments, his flying time would be very little.

"The Weight and Balance Line does everything that the regulations talk about, plus taking in the gas, the oil, and the pilot's weight. And one big thing that nobody can do with a bunch of arithmetic, *it tells the weight of the water that's in the floats*. All floats leak. You can have many gallons of water in the floats, and water weighs 10 pounds to the gallon. There is no way in the arithmetic here, or in this book, to account for water in the floats – which is just as big an overload as any other. And worse, because it's not visible."

The Weight and Balance line, adapted (and patent pending) by Campbell, eliminates making mathematical and balancing calculations where the weight of materials is often unknown. And it will work on any airplane on floats.

Colin Campbell's varied career has been typical, he says, of the life of an airline pilot – flying everything, everywhere.

Among his strangest cargo, he counts the golf and Ping-Pong balls flown for the oil rigs, and over seven million day-old chicks on the hauls from Canada to Cuba. Then there were the 19 penguins he flew for TCA. "I picked them up in Nassau and flew them to Vancouver for the zoo, the first penguins they ever had." The big birds were transported in the baggage compartment, which caused no problems for either birds or pilots. "But, boy, did they have a fishy smell!" One got loose at Idlewild (now John F. Kennedy International) Airport in New York. Campbell took some video footage of the chase.

When considering the number of airplanes he's flown, he can't pinpoint the best and worst.

"Airplanes are funny. Most are built for a specific job, and the trouble I find – and my criticism would be different than most people's I guess – is that some freight airplanes are built too light. You have to be extremely careful with them. They're not too bad in fresh water but when you get in salt water, the light material erodes quite fast. You have to do continuous checks to make sure they're not being eaten away. So it's hard to say what's best and what's worst."

Campbell liked the old Barkley-Grow, and the DC-3 and DC-4. "The material that the airplanes are built out of is most important. With a modern aircraft they sheet the airplane, and parts, with 'ST-75' or higher tensile strength aluminum alloys. When they first started building aluminum airplanes, they used 'ST-24' [2024.T3]."

"That's the reason there are thousands of DC-3s still around, which were built in 1934 and 1935. Airplanes built long after that, you can't find; they've been scrapped. The corrosion level is very high in ST-75 compared to ST-24, so the skin and the spars will wear. DC-3s and DC-4s don't get that corrosion, as they are made of the ST-24. In a DC-6, you're after corrosion all the time."

In 1995, at age 77 or 82, take your pick, Colin Campbell has no intention of putting a cap on his aviation career.

"I'm opening a new phase, if I can. I'm after a deal with the Ukrainian airplane, an An-225."

The Antonov An-225 Mriya heavy transport is considered to be the world's largest airplane. The one that Campbell refers to is called NATO Cossack. The features on it are thus: maximum takeoff weight: 1 322 750 pounds. Tail-span: 107 feet. Wing span: 290 feet. Overall length: 275 feet 7 inches. Height: 59 feet 8 1/2 inches. Wheel track: 29 feet. Cargo hold, length of floor: 141 feet; max. width 21 feet; maximum height, 14 feet 5 1/4 inches (just the cargo hold!). It can carry a payload of 551 150 pounds, and is powered by six big jet engines. It takes a crew of six.

Although Campbell hasn't yet flown an An-225, he anticipates no problem taking over the controls. "It's only an airplane."

His plan involves selling the Australians on the idea of shipping sheep by air, because "anywhere from 20 to 40 percent" of these animals die when they are shipped live via surface transportation. "It's hard on the sheep, and the ones who do get there are not in too good a shape."

The customers for these sheep are the Muslims in Saudi Arabia and Kuwait. Campbell explains that they have to kill their own meat, so it must be shipped live. They can't grow their own "because their land is too poor."

The deal involves an agreement with four countries. "We'd be doing it from Australia, using a Ukrainian airplane, and flying to Saudi Arabia, and Kuwait. It's being pulled together now, in 1995." When asked if he will be the captain on this venture, his answer is deadpan. "I don't plan to look after the sheep."

What about retirement? Campbell just laughs. "I've retired so often I make a career out of it!" He plans to keep on making good use of his five Airline Transport licenses and two birth certificates. He is busy right now, in fact, checking out that big Ukrainian airplane. Oh yeah, and there's those patents to look after, pilots' reunions to attend, speaking engagements, and his Canadian Aviation Hall of Fame shareholder position to maintain.

Just an average workload – for a man with three names.

Footnote 1:

A J-M (Johns Manville) Memo dated July, 1940 reads:

Youthful J-M Dealers Build Up Business 1 500 percent in Five Years

> Several days ago, Archie Campbell, half of the brother act of Campbell Brothers, Toronto, joined the First 100 Club by selling 100 jobs valued at $150 or more in one year. In a short space of five years, the Campbell brothers have become the "Wonder Boys" of the building industry in Toronto.
>
> Who are these Wonder Boys? They are Archie and Jack Campbell, 24 and 22 years of age, respectively, quiet and unassuming and with winning smiles and the will to get ahead in life. Five years ago they started in business without capital. Today they expect to do 15 times the volume they did in their first year.

Footnote 2:

Ted Barris reports on this phenomenon in his history of the British Commonwealth Air Training Plan, (*Behind the Glory*: MacMillan, Toronto, 1992):

> On December 8, 1941 – the day after the attack on Pearl Harbour – there were 6,129 Americans serving in the RCAF (more than six percent of its strength), nearly 900 Americans had graduated from the BCATP, another 650 were working as staff pilots and EFTS (Elementary Flying Training School) instructors, and 668 RCAF ground personnel. Of course, because of U.S. neutrality [in the war, up to that point], these were not highly publicized statistics (p. 116).

Footnote 3:

Milberry, Larry: *The Canadair North Star*, CANAV Books, 51 Balsam Ave., Toronto, ON M4E 3B6, 1982:

> The plant and all its equipment was owned by the Canadian government. The licence agreement giving Canada the right to build the DC-4 was completed between the Canadian government and the Douglas Company, of the U.S. The contract for DC-4 construction was awarded by the government to Canadian Vickers.
>
> An agreement was then completed whereby a new company (Canadair Limited) took over the contract and ran the plant on a management-fee basis for the Canadian government.
>
> (excerpted from letter dated November 13, 1946, from James T. Bain, Superintendent of Engineering and Maintenance, TCA, to H. Oliver West (formerly of TCA, then of Seattle).

Bain's letter goes on to extol the virtues of development plans for the aircraft that would become known as the North Star:

> The probability that a new type of aircraft for trans-ocean travel will be developed in Canada is very strong. The combination of U.S. knowledge of transport aircraft and British turbine engine developments offers possibilities for the manufacture in Canada of advanced types not available anywhere else in the world (p. 233).

Footnote 4:

Flaps are movable surfaces forming part of the wing. They extend and retract together, and increase and decrease the effective lift of the wing by altering its curve. They are controlled by the pilot.

Footnote 5:

A letter to Campbell dated January 24, 1972, from A.R. Omouni, Supervisor, Cloud Seeding Project, Ministry of Water and Power, Tehran Regional Water Co., states:

> In answer to your query of the practical results of rainmaking in Iran over the past five years that you have been conducting the operation, evaluation for the first three years of the operation was accomplished basically by two methods. First: Comparison of precipitation in seeded areas to unseeded areas. Second: Comparison of precipitation in seeded storms, to that of unseeded storms in the same area.
>
> The mean result was: 80.3 percent increase in precipitation for the three-year average.

Footnote 6:

The 44 000-pound (gross weight) Bristol Freighter, powered by two Hercules 1 980 horsepower engines, first appeared in Canada in 1946. They were found to be well-suited to the North because of their ability to carry a huge payload – up to 12 000 pounds of freight – which could be quickly loaded and off-loaded through clam-shell nose doors.

Footnote 7:

Most rules, established after long negotiations by ICAO, Campbell finds to be reasonable and valuable. They involve standardization of language and measurements for aviation.

ICAO, a special agency of the United Nations founded in 1944, promotes safe and orderly growth of civil aviation throughout the world, and standardization of safety rules. Its headquarters are in the International Aviation Building in Montreal.

"First, ICAO fought for *standard language*. It took 25 years to decide that it had to be English," Campbell says. "There were many objections, including one from the Americans who wanted the international language to be called 'American.' Never heard of that language before! But, they finally decided on English.

"The same thing with *speed*. The standard for speeds is in knots, and the reason for that is, in long-term navigation your maps are all in latitude and longitude. Latitude is 60 nautical (sea or air) miles to one degree. Why convert it back and forth? Use knots and there's no conversion.

"*Miles* are used for light airplanes, but that's optional. They can use knots or miles, it depends on the way it's calibrated. The maps are in miles. I wouldn't put kilometres into it at all.

"In *fuel*, we've got pounds instead of gallons or litres, pints or quarts, or whatever, because the crew is interested in the all-over weight of the airplane for load. If you put it in pounds, you've got what you want, so the gauges on major-sized airplanes are in pounds, the fuel flows are in pounds, and the amount of fuel consumed is in pounds. Smaller airplanes still use gallons.

"*Altitude* is another measurement that ICAO has agreed to standardize. Up to 18 000 feet, it's measured in feet. Above 18 000 feet, it's measured by *flight levels*. For instance, 20 000 feet will be flight level 200.

"*Temperatures* are all in Celsius in the *airline* business in aviation. We always use Celsius because zero is freezing. Thirty-two degrees in the Fahrenheit scale was always awkward to read, but zero is zero, it's freezing, and it made sense because you were worried about ice. When the temperature came down to zero, you started looking for ice.

"But, it's a little bit of a mix."

The Story is Not Told Until the Book is Closed

Father Leising, OMI, is a big, friendly man. At the age of 82 (in 1995), he appears some 20 years younger. He is a strong-voiced individual with strong opinions, and a personality reminiscent of the stereotyped American – hearty, hale and self-assured. The sort of man you'd trust to fly you over the unforgiving terrain of Canada's Far North. If the going got tough, he'd surely know what to do.

Father William A. Leising, OMI, 1959, at the launch of his book, *Arctic Wings* (Doubleday). Herbert Hoover (retired U.S. president) and Taylor Caldwell (U.S. author) spoke. *Father Leising, OMI, Collection*

But how and why did this man, who was educated in top colleges with the intention of becoming a doctor, choose instead to become a priest and a member of the Oblates of Mary Immaculate – a Catholic order whose mandate is to preach the Gospel to the poor? What were his rewards for following this calling, and what were his regrets?

"The story is not told until the book is closed," says Father Leising, laughing, yet serious. "You have to see the whole picture in order to form an evaluation."

William A. Leising was born on March 31, 1913, on his family's farm at East Amherst, just outside of Buffalo, New York. He is the eldest of four brothers and four sisters. The family quit farming three years before Bill left home, and turned their 700 acres of land into "a kind of village." Bill was taught the art of construction by his dad and uncles.

He excelled in school, in both academic and athletic achievements, and won a high school scholarship to attend St. Jerome's College in Kitchener, Ontario. He swam, and played football, tennis and hockey, in order to earn his letters.

He next attended the University of St. Bonaventure, a New York co-educational school founded in 1856 and operated by the Franciscan Order of the Roman Catholic Church. "When I returned to the United States, I found out how high the standard of education is in Canada," he says. "The curriculum covered at St. Jerome's was so advanced that I had spare time at St. Bonaventure to study science along with arts, leaving time, also, for athletics."

During a football game against Manhattan College in New York, Bill had the misfortune to break his ankle. After it had been attended to, he was bemoaning his accident when a man walked into the dressing room and introduced himself as William Stanton from Buffalo, New York. "I've been following all the games played by St. Bonaventure against Niagara University, Boston College and Villanova College this year," he said. "Bill, I admire your skill as a punter and half-back."

Bill smiled through his pain.

"But, I see that you're now incapacitated," Stanton observed.

Bill's friend entered the conversation. "*We're* incapacitated all right! We have dates and now we've got to cancel them."

"No, don't cancel them," replied Stanton. "I'll take you on your dates!"

The boys discovered that their benefactor was none other than the Reverend William Stanton, coach of the Ottawa University's (St. Patrick's) football team, many of whom later joined the Ottawa Roughriders.

He took the boys and their dates out in his new Chrysler and paid for dinner. On the way home, he questioned the boys about their future plans. "I'm studying engineering," said the friend.

"I hope to be admitted to John Hopkins University to study medicine," Bill said.

"Both of you have very good ambitions," Stanton said slowly, "but I have a better one.

"Bill, you want to work on bodies, and bodies die. I work on souls. They live forever. Think about that."

Stanton's words haunted Bill Leising's thoughts during the next year. That summer he consulted Paul Rust, an Oblate Father whom he had met in Buffalo. Following Reverend Stanton's and Father Rust's initiative, he decided to consider the Oblate order.

"When you go to a religious order you have much time to think during your novitiate years, and also during six years of study before you're ordained," Father Leising explains. "That's what I did."

Instead of going directly from the novitiate in 1934 to Washington, D.C., Bill Leising spent the next two years in Newburgh, New York, where he gained a Bachelor of Arts degree, majoring in Latin and Philosophy.

While at Newburgh he was asked to build a regulation-size handball court. He noticed two French priests watching as he worked, and was later introduced to the Most Reverend Bishop Pierre Fallaize, and another bearded Oblate from France, the Reverend Alphonse Mansoz.

"William," said Bishop Fallaize, "we need you in our missions."

The old Oblates began to talk about the Mackenzie River district of northern Canada, painting a vivid picture of its people, its climate . . . and its great need for missionaries.

Bill Leising was ordained on May 27, 1940, by His Eminence Francis Cardinal Spellman in Washington, D.C. This was followed by a two-and-a-half month internship at Mercy Hospital in Buffalo, to allow him to retain and build on his medical knowledge.

"I did a few minor operations like tonsillectomies and appendectomies, and spent a month in the out-patient ward. The doctors presented me with a beautiful medical kit when I left."

Father Bill, as he was called by the Oblate Brothers, arrived in Edmonton, Alberta on September 7, 1940, as a delegate at the consecration of Bishop Joseph Marie Trocellier at St. Albert. The next day he took a movie of the proceedings with a 16mm camera he had been given as an ordination present by friends. Following the consecration he went down the huge steps leading from the cathedral. "I was below the steps, getting a shot of the Bishop coming down giving his blessing, when all at once a figure loomed larger and larger. The newly consecrated Bishop walked right up to me, and I had to shut the camera down."

"You look like an American!" said the Bishop. "Are you the young man who's coming up north with us?"

"Yes, I am," said Father Leising, wondering if he'd somehow committed a *faux pas*.

"Welcome aboard!" The new Bishop clasped his hand, then added, "Why don't you let someone here take care of that camera? I want to talk with you."

And so Father Leising met Bishop Trocellier, with whom he worked for the next 17 years (until the Bishop's death November 27, 1958) as secretary, boat-builder, and later, aircraft pilot and engineer.

Following the consecration came a celebration at Edmonton's MacDonald Hotel, and the next morning they caught the Northern Alberta Railway, commonly called "The Muskeg Special", to travel north to Fort McMurray. From there they boarded the Hudson's Bay tug, *Dease Lake* on the Athabasca River, navigated up the Slave River from Fort Chipewyan to Fort Fitzgerald, then took a 14-mile portage to their mission base of Fort Smith. Here, Father Leising was reunited with Father Mansoz, who became his teacher of the Chipewyan Indian language.

That year, Father Leising and two Oblate Brothers built a 30-foot power barge. The young priest accompanied the Bishop on the boat to visit the missions around Great Slave Lake; then they sailed down the Mackenzie River to Aklavik where they sold the boat. "Every year it was the same deal – at the end of the trip we sold the boat."

From Aklavik they travelled on the mission schooner, *The Lady of Lourdes*, along the Arctic coast to the various island missions. The boat usually made three trips across the Arctic during the season from August to September, but Father Leising would often stay over at a particular mission to help out where he was needed.

In 1942 the Bishop decided the young priest should make further use of his medical knowledge, and sent him to study dentistry under Dr. Alfred Clermont, who was affiliated with the University of Alberta in Edmonton. He worked in the dentist's office for two winters as Clermont's assistant, until he qualified for a "private licence." He then went back north, and, with a dental kit donated to him by friends in the United States, he began practicing dentistry on the school students, doing extractions, restorative work such as fillings and inlays, and fittings for dentures.

His work filled a definite need in the North. "We had no dentists during the war for any of our schools, and we had over 400 students. I had to go through all of them, doing dental work while the Bishop did his visiting. I had RCMP men coming to me, Hudson's Bay men, nurses, school teachers, everyone."

Very few of the Eskimo people wanted an anaesthetic. "They would often come with a broken tooth or a root that they'd tried to take out with a hunting knife. Then I had to extract the roots, a delicate and difficult procedure."

In 1945 Father Leising was building a church in Yellowknife when he severely injured his hand. He went back to the U.S. for restorative surgery, which included the insertion of an ivory knuckle so he could again bend his finger. While in New York, he showed some film footage he had taken in the North. Cardinal Spellman immediately saw potential for attracting benefactors to fund their northern missions. He called a friend who did work for Columbia Pictures, and asked him to edit and add audio to this footage. While Father Leising waited for his hand to heal, he helped produce *Arctic Missions of the Mackenzie*, a 60-minute color motion picture. They made 40 copies in French and 80 copies in English, and thus audiences around the world were introduced to the people and customs of Canada's Far North.

Father Leising then served as "a free agent" filling in wherever a missionary's services were required. In 1950, after a two-year hitch as a replacement pastor at Aklavik, he accompanied the Bishop to Ottawa as his secretary. En route they stopped at the Polish Oblate Residence, and Father Leising took the opportunity to call home.

"A man from Toledo, Ohio, has been trying to get you on the phone," his mother told him. "His name is Monsignor Scheckelhoff. You'd better call him. He's very insistent."

Father Leising called and received phenomenal news.

Monsignor Raymond J. Scheckelhoff, director for the Propagation of the Faith in Toledo, had viewed the film in 1948 during a private showing at Radio City Music Hall in New York City. He had become quite interested in the Oblates' work in the Mackenzie district, and had since shown the film to other interested audiences. One night, a lady and her husband approached him after the show. "We want to give that Father Leising an airplane. Flying would be much easier than following a dog team."

When this message was relayed to Father Leising over the phone, Bishop Trocellier was sitting beside him. "Bishop, someone wants to give us an airplane!" he said, holding his hand over the receiver. "Shall we take it?"

"We'll take it if you'll learn how to fly it!"

Father Leising nodded happily.

Soon, Father Leising and Bishop Trocellier were introduced to Mr. and Mrs. Robert Lehmann of Freemont, Ohio.

"I have a little four-place Aeronca Sedan," Mr. Lehmann said. "My wife doesn't want me to fly anymore – she says if I keep the plane, I lose her – so I'm going to give it to you. To make it a legal contract, it will cost you one dollar."

"You just sold it," the Bishop replied with a big smile. "A sincere thank you." He turned to Father Leising. "Now you must learn how to fly."

They were told that one of the best flying schools was Parks Air Tech College of St. Louis University, in Cahokia, Illinois, just across the Mississippi River from South St. Louis, Missouri.

The airplane was in Florida, so the first week of November Father Leising flew down with a Parks pilot, Roger Heald, who would be his instructor. When they returned with the plane, his training began. Following ground school classes and 25 hours flying with an instructor, he soloed on April 1, 1951.

"I wanted education in navigation and engineering, because I was going to a place where I'd need that knowledge," Father Leising says. "They said I'd have to return two winters to get my aeronautical engineering degree, which I did."

He had just a private pilot's licence and his VFR (Visual Flight Rules) endorsement when, on May 30, he flew the red Aeronca Sedan (CF-GMC) north from St. Louis with one passenger aboard, Father John Colas. From Parks Air Tech college airport they flew via Winnipeg to Edmonton's marine air base at Cooking Lake. There, he changed to and was checked out on floats for the trip to their mission home at Fort Smith.

Although he had never before flown with floats, they didn't present too much difficulty and he was happy to have them. "I'd rather fly with floats in the north country than anything because they are the safest. You have so much water to land on, and you can even land on muskeg with them. Many times I had to land without power."

He had "a very good first year" with the Aeronca. He knew the country a little from flying with other pilots, and after a summer on floats he felt he had a handle on the operation, even though his first forced landing occurred that year.

After filling up from his 10-keg cache of aviation fuel, left on the beach at Fort Norman by a Brother, Father Leising had taken Father Victor Philip to Fort Franklin. There, he picked up Father Bernard Brown for the return trip to Fort Norman.

He was on cruise at 2 500 feet when suddenly the windshield became coated with oil. He shut the engine off immediately and let down onto the first lake he saw. While gliding down, he managed to radio out a May-day call (an international distress signal) which was heard by Moe Lynn, a Department of Transport operator at Fort Wrigley, 190 miles south. Lynn called Air Traffic Control in Edmonton: "Charlie Foxtrot – Golf Mike Charlie, four-place Aeronca Sedan is down," and he gave the location.

Meanwhile, using the two paddles strapped to the floats, the priests were able to move the plane to the eastern shore of the lake. A steady rain was falling so they spent the night in the airplane. The weather cleared by morning and Father Leising was able to check the engine to find the problem. He pulled the spark plugs and discovered that number five cylinder had no compression. Father Brown helped him remove the "jug" to have a look; there was a hole the size of a 25-cent piece on top of the piston.

"When I found the burned piston, I figured either bad fuel or a faulty engine part. If it was caused by bad fuel, what about the other pistons? We pulled number four and it was okay. This indicated a faulty piston."

At 10 o'clock that morning they were surprised to see an Eldorado Mines' Norseman, piloted by Alf Caywood, circle and land on a longer lake next to theirs. He had picked up their May-day signal and come in to see if he could help. "We need a number five piston for a 145-horsepower Continental engine!"

Caywood said he would pick up the part in Edmonton. He took Father Brown with him, so he could continue on his way to a new assignment at Nahanni, west of Fort Simpson.

"We could actually have walked back to Fort Franklin, but decided to follow the rules and stay with the plane," Father Leising says. "Two RCAF rescue planes came over that afternoon. One dropped a 10-gallon keg of gasoline that splashed on the rocks of the tundra, but a second drum landed safely in the lake. The kegs had tags on them, 'From the Red Baron,' and 'From the Red Dean of Canterbury.' They were pulling my leg, these RCAF boys, having a little fun. They also dropped a small wrench kit, which I needed, and a box of emergency rations."

The next day pilot Stan McMillan, flying for Canadian Pacific Airways, brought the new piston from Edmonton to Norman Wells. Alf Caywood delivered the gaskets and a new set of spark plugs, along with the piston, directly to Father Leising. He installed the piston, checked it out, and that afternoon took off for Fort Norman. The "unscheduled stop-over" was an occurrence that every bush pilot must deal with sooner or later.

The Aeronca Sedan was a good "starter aircraft" to the era of using airplanes in mission work, but both Bishop Trocellier and Father Leising, being in the heavy-weight class, came to the conclusion that they needed a larger plane. Besides themselves and personal baggage, their usual Arctic survival items included a tent, sleeping bags, tools, rations, two pairs of snowshoes, a .22 calibre rifle and a fish-net. They had to cross many miles of mountainous terrain, such as when flying west out of Paulatuk over the Smoking Mountains, 1 125 feet above sea level.

"The wind at that elevation was perhaps 90 miles per hour and I had only 145 horses to pull us along – not much power. The higher I'd go the stronger were the winds, so I had to just nurse the ground," Father Leising says. "I entered the Horton River Canyon to get through, rather than over, the rim of mountains. We had to fly between 400 and 500 feet elevation in order to make forward progress. Even then, our ground speed was only about 60 miles per hour."

When they visited the mission of Father Max Ruyant, north of the Anderson River delta, they would buzz the mission and then land three miles west in the rough waters of the bay in the southern part of Nicholson Island. Father Max would come out in his sea-going 'jolly' boat, bringing a 10-gallon keg of aviation fuel that had been cached there. "I needed that fuel after battling those head-winds," Father Leising says.

After a three-hour visit, they'd leave in the evening when the wind had abated. The takeoff would still be rough. Following a trip to that mission the Bishop declared, "We need something with more power up here!"

Father Leising consulted a magazine that listed used planes, and spotted a Norseman for sale "as is" at Kalamazoo, Michigan. The Bishop liked the size of the machine, having seen many of this type in the North. They went down to see it.

The Norseman, painted bright orange with blue trim, was equipped with a refrigeration unit from its former work as a shrimp boat on flights from New Orleans to Chicago. On its last run it had ground-looped, damaging a wing, the reason why it was being

Father Leising and Bishop M. Trocellier at Fort Smith, NWT, with Norseman CF-GTM on floats. Under the wing on the fuselage is the inscription "Saint Joseph, The Good Provider."
Father Leising, OMI, Collection

sold "as-is." They decided it would do.

Father Leising sold the refrigeration unit in Kalamazoo to pay for temporary wing repairs and to buy a new battery. Once again, instructor Roger Heald was called on to fly the large aircraft to Parks Air Tech College, for repairs.

After selling the Aeronca, Father Leising participated in a fund raising drive to finance the Norseman. Through his friend and former teacher, Bishop Fulton J. Sheen, he was sent on a lecture tour. Agencies in New York City and Chicago booked the venues and paid his transportation costs as well as generous speakers' fees.

In addition to his lectures, Father Leising attended aviation classes at Parks to learn how to operate an airplane on instruments. Over the course of two winters, he gained his American IFR (Instrument Flight Rules) certificate.

"It was very useful in areas with radio aids, such as out of Edmonton or Yellowknife," Father Leising says. "The DEW [Distant Early Warning] Line put in a very powerful station at Cambridge Bay. Between Yellowknife and Cambridge Bay I could usually place my flight plans, set up my destinations, and give the position of the airplane with the aid of a sextant I had on board – if I could see any of the planets, sun, moon or stars."

He flew the Norseman (CF-GTM) for six years.

"I flew Christmas mail one year, but it was difficult; I spent so much time at the airport in the morning. Fort Smith was my base. It wasn't daylight until 10 o'clock in the morning, but if I took off at five o'clock, that meant I could land at Fort Simpson in daylight. I did that several times, but it was taking big chances to fly in the dark, without lighted runways to come down on, over forests and mountainous areas on skis. A pilot could easily kill people, and himself.

"I discussed this with the Bishop. 'Is it worth it? Let's fly when we can see things, when it's safe.' He agreed I shouldn't fly during December, January or February. During those months, I could raise funds working down south on the lecture tours."

Father Leising's lucrative speaking engagements were curtailed when he developed emphysema, which he believes was caused from inhaling second-hand smoke in the lecture halls.

"I couldn't pass my pilot's physical for two months, so I stopped lecturing. That's what turned me to writing."

Using techniques learned from college creative writing courses, Father Leising began to write an autobiography describing his first 10 years in the North. The book, titled *Arctic Wings*, had a dual purpose: to raise money and to encourage vocations for the church (Footnote 1).

On July 8, 1956, Father Leising transported the Bishop and the Provincial Superior from Fort Smith to Hay River, through skies grey and smoky from forest fires. He was assisting with the Mass in Hay River when he was brought to his knees by a sudden sharp pain in the area of his liver. He began to perspire profusely and thought he might pass out. He somehow made it through the ceremony, then took some aspirins and lay down on the bed at the mission. The pain slowly receded. In the morning he set a flight plan for Fort Providence.

During the night the wind had changed to the southeast. The smoke that they had hoped to leave behind now blew their way and visibility was less than two miles as they flew at 300 feet above the western shoreline of Great Slave Lake. As they were nearing Fort Providence the pain came again, sharp and urgent, nearly causing Father Leising to pass out. His clothes were again soaked with perspiration.

Gasping with pain, he managed to land the plane on the Mackenzie River, then asked Brother Beauchemin to help him taxi it into the mouth of the little river north of the settlement. His passengers, including the Bishop and Provincial Superior, had to assist him into the mission house.

For three days Father Leising moved between consciousness and unconsciousness, with high fever and relentless pain. Because of the smoke, it was impossible for a rescue plane to come in. Fearing that he was near death, the Bishop administered the Sacrament of the Sick.

By the time the smoke cleared and an airplane could come in from Hay River, Father Leising was unconscious. He was flown to Fort Smith, and then moved onto another plane for the flight to Edmonton.

The doctors at Edmonton General Hospital discovered that his gallbladder had ruptured – while he was bringing the Norseman in over the Mackenzie River! His chances of survival were 50-50. Father Leising pulled through, however, and several weeks later he was flown back to Fort Providence to reclaim the abandoned Norseman.

"Norseman CF-GTM was my favorite airplane," Father Leising says. "It transported me and my passengers safely for many thousand hours, from 1952 to 1957." But, it was well-used when he'd bought it in Kalamazoo and it was showing its age. With the consent of the Bishop, he decided in 1957 to buy a new aircraft.

"We went to the de Havilland Aircraft Company office in Toronto, and sitting at the sales desk was the Bishop's old friend, Clennell Haggerston 'Punch' Dickins. He had given the Bishop his first airplane ride in the North," Father Leising says. "Mr. Dickins convinced us that a Beaver was exactly what we needed to replace the Norseman, because it could carry almost the same load for half the cost."

Father Bill Leising, Fort Smith, NWT, 1955, with the Norseman CF-GTM.
Father Leising, OMI, Collection

On June 15, 1958, Father Leising flew out of Toronto in the new Beaver. Its registration letters, CF-OMI, were an apt designation for an OMI (Oblates of Mary Immaculate) mission airplane.

Not only did air travel assist the Mackenzie River missions to move people and supplies quickly from one point to another throughout the vast territory, but it also added mercy flights to their services.

Father Leising once flew out a small Indian boy, the son of the park ranger who lived near Fort Chipewyan in Wood Buffalo Park. The boy had fallen on a pointed stick and had critically pierced his intestines. When the emergency call was received at Fort Smith, Father Leising was told that the boy had been haemorrhaging for 24 hours.

"A Nursing Sister and a Brother came with me from Fort Smith on this flight. I was on skis and had to land a mile-and-a-half away. The Sister and a Brother went cross-country to the tent where he was, and pulled him back on a little toboggan over that rough terrain. It was very cold, about 35 [Fahrenheit] degrees below zero. I had to stay with the airplane so I could start the engine every 10 minutes, instead of diluting the oil with gasoline which I usually did for overnight visits. The poor little boy! By the time we got him aboard the plane he'd started to haemorrhage again. But, we saved his life. Thank God for the airplane."

Father Leising's medical knowledge served him well in the North, but he was well aware that "a little knowledge can be a dangerous thing."

"I thought of that many times!" Father Leising says. "So all I carried was a kit containing a few aspirins, iodine, castor oil and bandages, things like that. The aspirins came in gallon pails, and iodine in big quart bottles."

Father Leising's experiences in both air and water transportation brought about several "inventions." One was to build extended hulls in the backs of the boats to give them more speed. "The propeller would throw the water against this false hull. Instead of the stern being pulled into the water, which happens if you have a powerful engine on smaller 16-to 20-foot boats, the propeller underneath acted as a jet. This could increase our speed from seven or eight knots to 20 knots. When you're travelling a thousand miles, it makes a difference."

On his aircraft, he always "safe-tied" various hose connections to prevent them from loosening. "You have a lot of vibration on aircraft piston engines. This is the 'gremlin' that often causes power-loss and fire. After each flight, the Brother and I would check for oil, fuel, hydraulic fluid leaks, or loose electrical connections. When we found a connection without safety wire, I'd drill holes and pull a wire through to hold it in that position so it couldn't turn open."

His idea developed from noting that some connections were safety-tied and others were not, but all were at the risk of shaking loose. "It saved a lot of time and worry – and a lot of oil splashing around – especially on all those oil valve connections where oil pressure can cause a leak."

Father Leising also became aware of the power of water on a spinning aircraft propeller. "The propeller tips on a float-equipped Norseman or on a Fairchild are not far off the water. At Fort Simpson, the Mackenzie River is three-quarters of a mile wide where the Liard River comes in. If there is a north wind blowing against the current, sometimes there will be a chop of three-foot waves when you're taking off into the wind. When you hit the tops of the waves with that fast-turning prop, the hard steel tips of the prop blades can split! When you get to the next place, you have to hone them smooth with a file.

"If it's badly pitted, with split tips, you don't get the action you should from your propeller. You reduce its potential a lot if you leave those split ends."

Father Leising adds that when new, the propeller tips were almost square like a duck's bill. They became round from being filed after many landings and long taxi take-offs made in rough water.

"One night I was landing at Fort Simpson in the Beaver and I wanted to get the wind direction and velocity from the radio station. It was getting dark and the only lights I had were from the radio tower. I couldn't contact them for love nor money. I had to make a guess on the wind velocity and direction for a float-landing on the Mackenzie River."

He came down two-and-a-half miles north of the landing dock, where he knew there would be fairly calm water. Then he had a long taxi to a sand beach. It took some time to re-shape his propeller blades before he could fly the next day.

Father Leising saw a lot of wrecked airplanes in the North. "It's unnerving to see shards of metal and bits of wing littering the landscape. You say a prayer when you fly over," he says philosophically.

He blames many aircraft accidents on something no pilot can control: downdrafts. "People not familiar with meteorology call them air-pockets, but they're downdrafts of air," Father Leising maintains. "You constantly get updrafts and downdrafts. For example, if you're in a glider over a wheat field where you get a lot of heat, an updraft will be created and you can climb up 4 000 or 5 000 feet in two minutes. In the same machine, if you get in a downdraft you can come down 2 000 to 3 000 feet in a few minutes, and you can't do anything about it. You can control it only if you have speed to get out of the draft, which could be a mile or more wide."

Father Leising's work often took him to residential schools in the North. In fact, a major portion of his job as a "missionary airman" was to bring the students.

Usually the pilot would be accompanied by a Brother, and often by the Bishop on his visitation rounds.

"In Coppermine, Father LaPointe was the missionary on the scene. He would alert the people and ask them, sometimes plead with them, to send their children to school, to give them a chance at an education. He knew their language. The Bishop too. They'd tell the parents, 'We have our school open – it's for you.'

"The parents would look at the guy who was going to take the children to school. They had seen me offer the Mass, they had heard me preach to them. They knew me, and they knew I was coming back and seeing them. Finally I gained their confidence, as did the Father. So, I was flying them to school."

Father Leising stops a moment to reflect on the impact of these visits to the native communities.

"When you have children they mean a lot to you, don't they? Supposing you were 1 500 miles from a school and some guy came along and said, 'I'd like to take your children away and educate them.' You'd say, 'Oh you would, eh? Hmmph! Will they ever come back? *How* are they coming back?'

"That was the main problem when I would land in places like Coppermine, Holman Island or Paulatuk to bring children to school. Fortunately, very fortunately, I could bring a child back home for vacation from the school with the benefit of two or three years of education. They could write their names, they could cypher, and they could teach their fathers and mothers how to write. That benefit would break the barrier. The parents would see what was being done in the school. Getting just one or two children from a settlement, bringing them back home and the parents seeing the results, solved the love-problem."

Not all parents wanted all their children to attend school. Sometimes they'd say, "You can take Maisie, but leave Pete here. He's 11 and he can work. Maisie is only seven yet. You take her to school and see what you can do with her."

"But Pete was the one I wanted," Father Leising says. "He needed the education. I'd keep Maisie for two or three years and bring her back, and then maybe Pete would go."

If Pete was 16 or so and just beginning school, he would be enroled in a class called "older grades," where students of similar age might all be starting grade one. "We couldn't put them with the little ones, so we put the older kids, 15 and 16 years old, together, boys and girls. Of course, a lot of marriages resulted from that," Father Leising smiles. "The people used to call the Bishop 'the matchmaker.'"

The children were returned "as often as I could bring them home. Sometimes every year, sometimes every five." The reason for the long delay, says Father Leising, is simply that the parents were always moving. "I might have the children aboard the airplane for a week. I couldn't find the parents! They'd be off in the barren lands, or somewhere on one of the Arctic islands. I didn't know where they were, nobody knew where they were. I couldn't find them.

"Sometime the parents would move from, say, Sachs Harbour on Banks Island over to Minto Inlet, 300 miles away, to find good fishing and sealing. 'Fred, where did they go?' I'd ask Fred Carpenter at Sachs Harbour. 'Huh! Your guess is as good as mine. When you see a tent, take a look, they might be there.' Fred Carpenter was one of these very energetic and influential Eskimos among his people, who'd had several very good years trapping white fox. He had a big schooner,

The North Star, and was sort of the 'mayor' of the settlement, not elected but chosen by the people."

Father Leising maintains that when children were reunited with their families after a long absence, there was no real sense of alienation between the child and the parents or the community. "Not so much, really. Maybe they were alienated in the sense that they had education. They often became teachers for their own parents, or other children, other people – very effective teachers. The advantages were plenty."

Children who had been in school a year or two would be taken home by airplane or by the boat, a situation that clearly showed the advantage of the former over the latter. "When we had just our boat working in the Arctic coast, sometimes it was three or four years before school children got back home. But with the airplane it was almost every year – if I could find the parents!

"I made stops at different tents, or igloo homes in winter, along the way where we thought their parents might live. If we couldn't find them, we'd bring the child back to school. Some were sad not to have found their parents. They'd go and sit in the airplane. 'Maybe my father die?' 'Oh no, I don't think so. We'll find him. Don't give up.' 'Well, I'll go back then. I want to go back to my friends in school.'

"You see, they made great friends in school, great companions for life, sometimes. And some children, when they saw their parents and the poor place in which they lived, did not want to stay with them. They asked to return to school."

In the eastern Arctic where the people had to constantly travel to look for food, life was much harsher than in the western side which is nearer the tree line, Father Leising explains. "The tree line runs on an angle from Point Barrow, Alaska, to Churchill, Manitoba. North of that is almost barren. Those Arctic islands have scattered areas of grass, rock and sand, winter and summer, very little snow, a tough place for those poor people to live. As I say in my book, I think they are some of the most intelligent people on earth, to be alive. We'd die."

If the parents refused to allow the church to take the children away to be educated, Father Leising says that decision was not disputed.

"Oh, no, that was fine. I was just as friendly with the parents who did not send their children to school as I was with those who sent their children with me. That's their privilege – it's their child, and I told them that. If the wife would ask, 'Have you any needles?' I'd say, 'Yeah, I've got a pack for you, too.' Needles, especially the three-sided leather-cutting type, were treasured by the people. Pocket knives, too, were appreciated; I always carried a spare."

At times, the parents would come into town to be with the children, especially at Christmas and Easter. "Sometimes we'd have eight or nine families come in, with their dog teams. We'd even supply feed for their dogs. The girls had a big recreation room. I remember one time I had 12 Eskimo families in that room, in sleeping bags. During the summer the Church would supply tents for the people to live in."

But the schools began shutting down as the government took over. "We had to move Aklavik because the river was cutting into the town, so in 1957 we moved the whole school, everything, to the new Inuvik townsite. That year, the government supplied new hostels in Fort Smith, Yellowknife and Fort Simpson. We flew all our children to these hostels. They stayed for the year, then we took them home."

Some of the things that Father Leising considers as positive for northern residents no longer exist: the church-run residential schools are gone, and the Oblates no longer operate aircraft in the Mackenzie district. His airplane was sold in 1965, and that is when Father Leising quit flying altogether.

"To me it was very sad, because I saw it as more than just flying an airplane. The airplane and the boats that we had on the rivers made the connection between the families, not only the missionary families – the Sisters, Brothers, Fathers – but the local people. The arrivals and departures of the boats were events. They would either be bringing their children home from school or taking them to school; bringing patients home from the hospital or sending them out for medical help; or taking people to a new location like Fort Providence or Fort Simpson to work there. Our barge carried 150 tons on the river, mostly provisions.

"The boats and the airplane made this family connection for the people, and that is what was missing afterwards. It sort of broke the connection. The people felt alone again."

Father Leising ran into an old friend recently, Father Leonce Dehurtevent, who, in his 80s, still lives at Paulatuk on the central Arctic coast. He has been there since 1948. Father Dehurtevent said to him, "Bill, you remember the last time you landed over there and you took off from Paulatuk, in 1965? That was an historical event."

"Why?" Father Leising asked.

"It was the last time I saw a Bishop come and visit me. And you brought my mail."

"I didn't know it," Father Leising says, "but that was the end of an era. After that time they would take commercial planes, and often the visitation would be 'touch and go.' But when an individual is alone in a place, a visit means an awful lot, to realize that you are part of an organization, that you belong to someone and some unit. You're not just a lone cog in a wheel."

Father Leising admits that when he bought his airplanes, he considered them the beginning of a fleet for the Oblates' work, with new priests coming in with pilot's licenses and taking over what he had started. He mentioned to Bishop Trocellier that Father Bernard Brown had a pilot's licence, but the Bishop decided one airplane was all they could afford at the time.

"I had them lined up to take over. That's why I later got the Beechcraft – a gift from Parks Air Tech College for the sum of one dollar – and why I brought it up to Edmonton and worked on it. That little plane could fly seven passengers conveniently. It would not only save a few dollars from having to rent or charter aircraft, but it would mean that we could spend two or three days and really visit, not have to follow a schedule.

"I wasn't going to fly it myself, I was looking for another pilot who could handle it and make all these connections between our schools at places like Chesterfield Inlet, Churchill and The Pas, Manitoba. You see, I had been in those places and I saw the deal," Father Leising says. "I could see why the people were reluctant. They wouldn't see their children too often. I don't blame them. Not at all.

"Father Thomas Lobsinger (now Bishop of the Yukon) at Whitehorse was also an air pilot. We had priests all over the southern part of this country where they had many airports. Another 'flying Father' is George LaGrange, who flies a little Cessna out of Fort Simpson and takes care of Fort Providence, Fort Liard, Nahanni and Wrigley. The difference is, while it is the mission's plane, it does not make the rounds of all the missions and is not at the disposal of the missions' personnel.

"There is an Oblate who flies a Helio Courier in St. Paul's Province in British Columbia, Father Brian Ballard, but he also has just a local operation."

As Father Leising looks back over his career, and his flying adventures, he admits there are things that could have been improved upon.

"I would have liked to purchase, instead of the Beechcraft, a DC-3. I could have had it from another source for the same price as I paid for the Beechcraft, one dollar, and I was ready to spend a few thousand dollars to upgrade it. The 'powers at hand' decided, however, that it would be a little too large for our operation because at the time we were beginning to close some schools. But I was looking much farther ahead.

"The only way to keep many of these places in operation was to have students. We had Cambridge Bay at that time. We could have had little airplanes bring in our students there, and then fly from Cambridge to Inuvik with 40 children, with baggage, in a DC-3, a good-sized plane. The DC-3 could have been their 'air bus.'

"But, of course, this was only my idea. Every one of us – and I guess we can say 'thank God' – has different ideas. You have yours and I have mine."

Another of Father Leising's interests, since abandoned, was the radio-telegraph network he helped to install and maintain in the Mackenzie district. The project, completed in 1960, consisted of a network of 16 stations located at the Mackenzie River missions and along the Arctic coast. This network made it possible for the Oblate Bishop, Father Provincial and the Grey Nuns' Mother Provincial to maintain contact with their personnel, as well as to serve emergency needs of local residents.

"When I left the Arctic in 1965, all stations were in working order," Father Leising says. "Since then, many missions have closed due to lack of missionaries."

It is no secret that some aspects of the missionaries' work, such as native residential schools, have met with controversy in recent years. One Catholic priest, Father Crosby, OMI, apologized during a recent annual pilgrimage at Lac Ste. Anne, Alberta, for the Church's role in taking children from their homes for the purpose of educating them. The hair on Father Leising's head stands on end when this is mentioned.

"He virtually apologized for the residential schools and their *modis operandi*, the way they worked. He thinks they sort of robbed the people of their culture. I think they advanced the culture of the people instead of robbing them, weeded out the bad practices of their culture, and enhanced it. I was there to see the results.

"I wish I had been there at Lac Ste. Anne," Father Leising continues. "I would have added a few constructive thoughts to the other side. There are two sides to every story. I would have got up in front of the people, and I would have tried to present the other side of the ledger.

"And I can say this: if I had presented the positive story, three-quarters of those Indians there would have stood up and cheered. Why? The reason they were there at Lac Ste. Anne was because of those boarding schools! They could understand when English was spoken! They learned it at the mission boarding schools. That is the thought I would have presented, a true happening that many of the young generation of Indians may have overlooked."

He takes a moment to contemplate the situation, then and now.

"We cannot stop time and progress. We had to try to think ahead to what these children were going to need in the future, and how they were going to provide for themselves. They had to know English, for example, to get work. We wanted them to keep their own language and their own culture and such, but in order to survive, to find work,

Father Leising, OMI, at the 50th anniversary of his ordination, May, 1990. He is now retired and living in Oregon. *Father Leising, OMI, Collection*

they had to know the language of the people with whom they'd be working. The language of this country is English. And this Father knew that."

The era of the Mackenzie River missionary boats and planes has come to a close. The boats are gone, the airplanes are gone, the schools are gone. During 14 years and five months of flying, from 1951 to 1965, Father Leising clocked 8 380 flying hours, and many miles on the rivers. He aims to record his northern memories. His present projects, a biography of Bishop Trocellier titled *Arctic Shepherd*, a novel, and a history of the North, are now on his computer, along with information augmented by "about 700 volumes on the North" gathered over the years.

He saw the country as it was and never will be again.

"When you come to the end of the whole story, you close the book," Father Leising concludes.

Footnote 1:

Arctic Wings was published by Doubleday of New York in 1959, with an Imprimatur (an official sanction to print) by Francis Cardinal Spellman, ArchBishop of New York. The best-seller enjoyed many more sales in the paperback edition that followed in 1965.

Queen of the Flying Farmers

Mildred Holtby Beamish was destined to be a queen. Born on February 11, 1910, at Nurse Rowe's small clinic in Lloydminster, a town that straddles the Saskatchewan and Alberta borders, her keen intellect early indicated her life would follow an unusual path.

For one thing, she was a born musician. "I never remember the time when I couldn't play the piano," Beamish says. "I was playing when I started lessons, and that was before I was six."

She started school in Kempton, Saskatchewan, followed by brief high school attendance in Lloydminster. "I was quite popular in high school because I could play music!"

The Holtbys, who had come to the area in 1903 from England with the Barr Colonists, farmed four miles north of Marshall, Saskatchewan. Mildred grew up on the farm along with her sister and two brothers, and music was part of their daily lives. Mildred's parents first taught her notes, and then a neighbor took over her tutoring.

Soon, Mildred began to play piano accompaniment for her parents' singing duet. "My dad and I used to play for dances from the time I was 10 or 11. He played the piccolo and the flute. We'd go out as a pair."

At age 14 she met the man she would marry three years later, Somerville (Somers) Beamish. Naturally, he was a musician.

"When I met Somers we formed a five-piece band. He played the violin, I played piano, Dad the flute and piccolo, Ovy [Oswald, Somer's brother] got a set of drums, and Arthur Welch was on sax. We were called BBK – Banana Belt Kempton."

Somers had a farm six miles northeast of the Holtby place, and so, when they married in 1928, Mildred just moved "across the gully".

"He was a bit older than me: I was nearly 18 and he was 30 when we were married."

When the children arrived – Eric, Gwen, Grete and Norma – Mildred continued to play for local dances and other musical events, while dutifully passing on her love of music to her students and to her own children.

"I taught my kids, or three of them, and then the oldest taught the youngest. As soon as I could do it I'd get them to other teachers, that's better. My oldest daughter Gwen ended up going to the Royal Conservatory of Music in Toronto, getting her degrees and so on. She married Ross MacMillan, Sir Ernest MacMillan's son – so she was right into the music circle" (Footnote 1).

Meanwhile, back at Marshall, "there was a beautiful field called Earlie's where any stray airplanes flying in the area would land," Mildred says. "That's where Somers met Bill Whiteley. He was a local boy who had gone into the air force, you see, and he was fairly famous around there because he was a pilot.

"So Bill took him for a ride and that was when Somers, and his brother Ovy and his wife May, got the idea they would like to fly, too."

Ovy had married May Kenderdine in 1938, whose English-born artist father, Gus, was famous for establishing the Murray Point Art School at Emma Lake (Footnote 2). Ovy and May farmed north of Lashburn, Saskatchewan.

"Somers, Ovy and May used to go down to California every winter, taking their mother with them. At that time we had a house on the farm, and a house in Lloydminster so the kids could go to high school. I stayed here in the winters with the kids while my husband was down in California," Mildred says.

In 1947, Somers, Ovy and May started taking flying lessons in California. When they returned to Canada in the spring they completed their flight training at a school in Vermilion and got their pilot's licenses.

The next step was to buy a two-place Luscombe that was initially shared between the families. They began to venture everywhere, freed by flight. After buying wheel-skis to enable them to land on snow, they would head north to explore the fishing lakes and just look at the vast country. Sometimes they were called on to offer their flying services when emergencies occurred in the small remote communities. "They used to come back and land on fields, but finally they made a strip on our own fields."

May and Ovy had no children, so were fairly free to take off in the airplane at any time of year. They flew everywhere, from the bush of Canada's Northwest Territories to the beaches of Jamaica.

Somers soon bought his own airplane. Mildred, meanwhile, was viewing all the fun from the passenger's seat, or second-hand through the others' stories. The flying bug didn't bite her for 10 more years.

"Let's see," she says, "when did I fall in love with flying? Perhaps while navigating for my husband on a trip to Texas to pick up the new Luscombe. But, I was so busy raising the kids that I wasn't worrying too much about it. When I got the kids educated and away I thought, 'Well, it's my turn now!' I went for a ride with the instructor and I fell for it right away. I was soloing very shortly, after about eight hours, and just went ahead from there."

Mildred began taking lessons on September 2, 1957, when she was 47 years of age and already a grandmother. She says that learning the basic principles of flight didn't present much of a problem because she worked hard.

"You don't get your licenses without quite a lot of studying, especially commercial and instrument. I did a *lot* of studying. I wish I was as smart now as I was then."

Her age did not present a drawback, either. "I don't remember that anybody pooh-poohed me. They were very helpful, actually, and I really appreciated it."

Mildred took her check flight on November 8, 1957, wrote and passed all five ground school tests on November 28, and got her private pilot's licence.

"We had this strip on the farm. The instructor had come out, landed the Fleet Canuck 80 (CF-ENP), and then had gone back to Lloyd. In the morning I decided I'd take the plane off, seeing as how I'd already soloed. I remember my son saying to my husband, Somers, 'You're not going to let her go alone in that bag of bolts, are you?' He didn't think much of that plane! 'Oh,' Somers said, 'she'll be all right!'

"So I went, and that was my start. It was such a wonderful feeling to get off on my own!"

By letting her be, Somers encouraged Mildred to try winging it on her own – and she's never stopped.

At first, Mildred thought she should learn to fly for safety's sake; if anything happened to her husband when he was at the controls, she'd be able to take over. "That was how I started out, but that didn't last, because I was flying for myself after that!"

Mildred obtained her radio licence on April 25, 1958, in Regina. In July of that year she broke an "old-age money bond" to pay $3 400 for her own aircraft, a Cessna 140.

The unusual thing about this flying family was that husband and wife seldom flew together. "We did very little of that. We might be going to the same destination, but in our own planes. We'd take off and then we'd chat back and forth on our radios."

They wouldn't necessarily land at the same place, either. "He'd be doing one thing and I'd be doing another. I might be going on a trip, and he might be going back to work, farming or so forth."

Mildred says that although Somers was confident flying with her, they were quite independent.

"We were both the oldest children in the family and were used to doing our own thing. We continued to do so!"

That independent spirit kept Mildred Beamish aloft until after her 83rd birthday, accumulating 3 000 accident-free flying hours. She got her night flying endorsement on June 23, 1968, her commercial licence on September 12, 1969, and passed the instrument rating exam in June, 1975. After that, there was no keeping her on the ground.

Starting with the Fleet 80, in which she took her first instruction, Mildred and her husband subsequently owned a number of aircraft (Footnote 3). Looking over the list in her log book of 10 different aircraft flown, and five that she's owned herself, brings back stories of each.

"Instructor Phil Slager 'soloed me out' in the Cessna 140 (CF-HDJ), and that is also the aircraft in which I experienced one of my few forced landings, in June, 1961," Mildred recalls.

"It had had its annual inspection the day before. When I flew it that night it didn't sound quite right. Then, in the morning when I tried it again, my husband listened to it and said, 'There's nothing wrong with it, it's just your imagination.' I started off en route to a ladies' fly-in at Medicine Hat, flying cross-country. I had my sister-in-law with me. We got as far as Provost and the engine was just clattering. I managed to get down in a pasture and land. I stopped the plane and we dashed off in case anything was going to happen, because it was making such horrible noises, but it was all right. We went to a phone and called home; they came and got us.

Mildred Beamish, 1958, with Cessna 150 CF-MJU. *Mildred Beamish Collection*

"When they went back to get the plane, they discovered that they couldn't fly it home. If I'd gone any farther, the whole thing would have fallen apart. So I was lucky that time."

Mildred describes the problem as one of those "mechanical things. I never did understand their language – what did they call it? Oh, they said that 'a pot would have fallen off.'"

Then she adds, more seriously, "I would have crashed. It would have gone out of kilter – and the weight of the plane is all-important. So that was one of them, anyway."

She traded the 140 off for a one-year-old Cessna 150 (CF-MJU), but that aircraft came to an ignoble end one March day when the hangar roof caved in on it. There had been a build-up of two feet of ice on the roof, and the airplane was wrecked.

She then bought a new Cessna 150 from Ed Dyck at Meadow Lake, Saskatchewan, in which she qualified for her commercial licence.

Although Mildred and Somers, and Ovy and May, would often fly north to fishing camps, Mildred never did fly on floats. "It would cost about $5 000 to get into them and there was no need. We could clear the runways off in the winter, so I flew wheels & skis only."

The northern flights were great fun. "When we were first flying it was something to realize that there was a strip somewhere, because there weren't so many. We'd land on them just to see what they were like. Now, there are strips everywhere."

On occasion she even landed on roadways, but caution was always foremost in her mind. She never had a serious accident, and had virtually no minor accidents.

"You have to be careful, flying. Before you go on a flight, first of all you get the weather report; then you know if you'll be going. The weather can change when you're flying but you make adjustments."

Whether or not some people are born flyers is a moot point, but some seem drawn to the excitement of flying. Mildred wouldn't approve of that view.

"If you're going to think of it as an exciting thing, you're going to have an accident. You have to be more careful than that."

So, what is the 'passion' that she expresses for flying, if not excitement?

"You're driving along the road, right? Half the roads are treed, and you don't see anything. You get up in the air and you can see everything! You don't have to be high – it's all there. The excitement is not so much the mechanics – it's floating in the air."

By 1975, shortly after Mildred had received her instrument rating, she and Somers traded their two aircraft in on a new Cessna Skyhawk 172 (C-GEBD), which Mildred flew for the remainder of her career. During the official opening and annual fly-in for Lloydminster's improved airport facilities in 1976, the newspaper noted that Mildred was the first lady pilot in, and Somers was the oldest pilot, at "a spritely 78."

In 1984, Mildred experienced a forced landing near Northway, Alaska, in the fog. She was flying the Cessna 172, on her way to Anchorage to attend the international convention of the 99s. She left Lloydminster on August 3, with pilot Karen Rutherford in the right seat and 121 pounds of cargo in the hold. As their flight would take them over mountains, and also over miles of isolated forest, muskeg and lakes, their supplies included survival gear of axes, a gun, sleeping bags and food.

On the first day, they flew directly from Lloydminster to Whitehorse. The next leg took them to the rendezvous strip just outside Anchorage where women pilots, fellow members of the 99s from all over the world, had gathered. After three days of meetings and socializing they left to return home. The weather, up to that point perfect for flying, suddenly changed when a cold front moved in. They made it from Anchorage to Gulkanen, Alaska, but travel was slow and rather hazardous with freezing snow encountered at 10 000 feet.

Soon, fog closed in and she had to put down. "I turned back and landed in a field, got down nicely. Later when everything cleared off I was able to fly out of this field, but first they had to move a horse that was there."

Other 99s returning from the convention were experiencing the same problems. They, too, had to turn back and land where they could. They'd head for the nearest town and the party would start all over again. "I ended up playing the piano in Northway, in a bar," smiles Mildred. "Being weathered in were some of the happiest times of the holiday!"

They encountered "instant fog" while flying back home over the mountains. Beamish's instrument training came into use and she turned the aircraft around and headed back into clear skies. The encounter scared her passenger, though. Because Karen Rutherford had to be back by a particular date, Mildred flew her to Whitehorse where she caught a commercial flight home.

"I came the rest of the way on my own when things had cleared up."

Four days later Mildred landed on the family farm airstrip, excited about the trip and the challenges it had presented.

The Beamishes all belonged to the Flying Farmers of Saskatchewan and were also members of the International Flying Farmers, which Mildred says is the second largest aviation group in the world. They had fun attending a number of special functions connected with these clubs. In July, 1967, Mildred Beamish was honored to receive the Saskatchewan Flying Farmer of the Year award. The Saskatchewan chapter contained, at that time, the largest number of women in all phases of the flying program.

At a fly-in of the Alberta and Saskatchewan Flying Farmers, held in Lloydminster during her year as Queen, Mildred noted the evolution in transportation that had occurred during her lifetime; from her father's arrival in the area with the Barr Colonists, travelling from Saskatoon in a covered wagon pulled by oxen, to her present mode of hopping into her own airplane and flying like a bird to her destination, it was an incredible jump.

"It's a long way in a short time, from those oxcart days to our present airplane travel," Mildred said to the assembled crowd. "I will never get over the wonder of modern transportation, and how marvellous it is to be able to meet and discuss flying and farming with people from all over the continent – thanks to the Flying Farmers."

The Saskatchewan Flying Farmers' Queen had a busy year. That summer, she cut the ribbon to open a new airport at Watrous, Saskatchewan, flying in for the event, of course (Footnote 4).

In November, Mildred gave an address encouraging safety in flying and independence in spirit to the first graduating class of pilots – 21 of them – at the Neilburg, Saskatchewan, Flying Club.

As a 99, Mildred is proud to have been a charter member when the Saskatchewan chapter was formed in 1971. She has continually served on its executive, and was governor in 1973.

"These organizations give you something to fly to, and for," Mildred says. "But a lot of women who belonged to them didn't do any flying at all; they only flew with their husbands and one thing and another. I didn't want that – I wanted to pilot my own aircraft, go places on my own."

Mildred Beamish, 1967 Queen, Saskatchewan Flying Farmers (SFF). *Mildred Beamish Collection*

Mildred often took her sister-in-law, May Beamish, on trips with her, flying to ceremonies in honor of May's father, Gus Kenderdine, at Regina, Saskatoon and Emma Lake (one when May was 90), or to aviation conventions and fly-ins around the country.

The two women would fly together to attend SFF meetings all over Saskatchewan, and also to the United States. On one such flight, Mildred and May were part of a contingent of 13 women pilots from Canada who flew in to the Havre, Montana, airport. At the time of their arrival, a 45 miles-per-hour wind was whipping up so much dust that the airplanes couldn't be seen until they were right over the end of the runway. The newspaper reported, however, that "all landed skilfully," and with local help their aircraft were tied down safely for the night. The purpose of this flight was to allow the pilots to become better acquainted with filing flight plans, checking through customs, and landing at other than their home airfields.

In 1970, at an International Flying Farmers' convention, Mildred was presented with the ladies' Most Hours Award by Kenneth Payne of Piper Aircraft Corporation, and also was given an award from the "Know Your Radio" chairman, for making the most radio transmissions during the past year.

In September of that same year, Mildred joined three other Canadian pilots to ferry new Cessnas to Canada from their factory in Wichita, Kansas. A newspaper article captures the uniqueness of the venture:

> Not too unusual? But then take into consideration this was the pilots' first time at ferrying planes, and that all were women. Three have commercial ratings and one a private licence. The four, Carole Morris of Revelstoke, B.C., Mildred Beamish of Marshall, Saskatchewan, and Eleanor Bailey and Jeannine Sprague, both of Calgary, Alberta, represent the Alberta Chapter of the 99s.

The purpose of the visit was to publicize and raise funds for the All-Woman Transcontinental Air Race, or the Powder Puff Derby.

Although Mildred has many friends who share her love of flying, such as fellow members of the 99s and International Forest of Friendship, she realizes she was always considered kind of "different" by her neighbors and family friends. "No, they didn't understand me," she says shyly. Did they think she was an oddball? "I think I was!" is her quick response. But she has never found this difference to be a problem. "I always got along with people."

The traditional difficulties women have experienced getting jobs in the aviation field have not directly affected Mildred.

"I don't think it's as bad now as it used to be. You have to have qualifications; you have to get *more* qualifications, probably, than the men get. But, women are doing well. There are problems, and then there aren't, you know," Mildred laughs. "They would actually treat me nicer.

"When you fly you're talking to various radio control people who tell you when and where to land. You have to be conversant on the radio, which I've always enjoyed doing. It gave me a back-up, I knew I wasn't alone in the air. When they heard a woman's voice, they were pretty good."

Mildred would just laugh at the surprise expressed by the radio control people when she landed and stepped out of her airplane. "I was always older than my passengers so they'd talk to them, assuming that one of them must be the pilot!"

While Mildred herself found radio communication to be helpful and pleasant, she says that "some people, especially men, would fly from here to there and never use the radio at all. They were scared to, I don't know why. I guess they just were not used to talking into things. The younger ones would be all right, but the older ones would be shy.

"I was never behind when it came to asking for help, and asking for information," Mildred says.

If she were to give advice to women who are considering entering the flying field, she'd be hesitant to suggest anything beyond the basic advice of "be cautious".

"I know some marvellous pilots who are women. I think you've got to know what you're doing, and be sure of yourself before you start talking to anyone, about anything. Don't you think so?"

She would also add that one should never take flying lightly. "Pay attention and make sure you have good instructors, because there are poor ones as well as good ones. I was lucky to have some great instructors."

Whereas it might be hard for novice flyers to know if they've got a poor or a good instructor, Mildred says that in her case she had the family background to rely on, "men who had been through the ropes. They would know. So I had a better background than a lot of people."

The flying family made many trips together. Ovy flew until the day before he died in 1980. Somers Beamish died in 1988, in his 91st year. "He more or less stopped flying when he was about 80. But, flying to that age sure beats the rocking chair," Mildred says philosophically.

On July 22, 1983, Mildred made a six-hour flight to Atchison, Kansas, to take part in the 99s Flyaway ceremony – the first time a pilot from Canada had participated in the event. Amelia Earhart's sister, then in her 80s, took part in the ceremonies.

That year, as part of the Flyaway, blue spruce seedlings were given to the pilots to bring back to their state or provincial capitals. Mildred was given four seedling trees to take to North and South Dakota, Manitoba, and Saskatchewan.

Mildred Beamish in the cockpit of her Cessna 172, 1984.
Mildred Beamish Collection

In 1991 she made a return visit to Atchison, bearing a gift from Canada: a white birch tree to be planted as a memorial to the original 99s' president, Amelia Earhart. Flying her Cessna 172 Skyhawk II, with her birch cargo, Mildred was grounded in Huron for two days because of weather. "You can have maps and instruments, but you still can't do much about the weather," she says. She continued the trip by car, an ignoble entry for a veteran flyer attending a 99s convention!

Bearing her birch tree, she and friend Nadine Cooper added it to the "Forest of Trees" on the memorial grounds in Atchison, which contains a variety of trees from all over the world. One is a "moon tree", grown from seeds that travelled to the moon and back via Apollo 14.

When interviewed during that trip, Mildred informed the newspaper reporter that, at age 81, she now required help to get her airplane out of the farm hangar, but she still did her own pre-flight checks. She added proudly that she had attended every Kansas meeting of the 99s since 1983.

Mildred averaged 300 flying hours per year for the duration of her career in aviation, with her husband, with other passengers or by herself. "When I'm alone, I can spread out my maps beside me," she says.

Mildred acknowledges that she herself has just about fulfilled all of life's wishes, even though she didn't start to fly until age 47.

"I flew, solo, pretty well all over Canada, as far north as Inuvik in the Northwest Territories, and down into the States, too. I flew to Alaska, out to the coast, and down east to Toronto quite a few times. I'd take the American route because it was easier, better country. The Canadian route from here to Toronto took you, at that time, through a lot of the north country, through Ontario bush. Although I have flown that way too, you're more isolated and there's more distances between stops. Now, it's different entirely.

"I didn't fly the mountain states very much, but I flew to Banff a lot."

One of the images that remains in Mildred's mind is spotting the incomparable turquoise beauty of Lake Louise nestled deep in the mountains, when flying "around the corner" from Kicking Horse Pass.

Although the airstrip in Banff is avoided by some because of wind tricks that can play along the high slopes of the Rocky Mountains, Mildred has never had a problem there.

"It's supposed to be a very risky one, but I'd go in the early morning or in the evening. If you go in the daytime you bounce all over, especially in Banff where you land right beside a mountain. You get all these airlifts in the daytime."

Weather at any time can be a concern to a pilot, but Mildred says, "You just put down." The word "panic" is not in any pilot's vocabulary, even when the situation looks scary.

"It's just like a door opening. You say, 'Fly the aircraft!' You just have to say that to yourself."

Speaking of a door opening, Mildred has had that happen. To both doors simultaneously, in fact, on her Cessna 172 (Footnote 5).

"They didn't fly wide open, just came ajar and were wobbling away. I slowed down the aircraft and kept up my airspeed. You put the flaps on or something like that to slow you down, but still keep good engine speed, and go along until you get somewhere where you can land."

The doors are fairly fragile things and sometimes just a bump will turn the latch off, Mildred says. "Sometimes you're flying along and both latches let loose, but the door hinges are on the front so they won't flap wide open."

The years were going by. At age 80, Mildred made one of her last long-distance solo trips when she flight-planned through from Lloydminster to Vermont, in her Cessna 172, to attend yet another 99s "Forest of Friendship" event.

"No big deal," shrugs Mildred. "I had been on other trips to the States. The main thing is getting information and planning your flight-plan across the border, but I was quite used to that. Actually, the American radio people help you a great deal. I won't say they're better than Canadians, but they're probably more used to talking on the air."

"Off to Vermont!" the 80-year-old-pilot wrote in her log book on July 18, 1990. Her landings were then dutifully recorded: Grand Forks, North Dakota; Marquette, Wisconsin; through Customs at Sault Ste. Marie, Ontario, to Ottawa, and to Vermont. Return trip: back to Toronto Island Airport, to West Branch and Pellston, Michigan; Marquette, Wisconsin; Bemidji, Minnesota; Minot, North Dakota; Regina, Saskatchewan; and to the Beamish farm on July 30, 1990. No problems.

During the last few years, when Mildred went in for her medical the doctor would ask, "Are you *still* flying?" "Of course!" she'd reply. She knows many women her age who are still flying. "I think we all fly until our medical says we're not safe in the air. By this time, a person has so much experience that they *are* fairly safe."

Mildred Beamish flew at least once a week while in her 80s, usually in the early morning or in the evening. She took to writing a "log-book," of her year's events, contained in a Christmas letter.

"January, 1990, and the beginning of my 80th birthday year!" she wrote. "A flight in 'EBD' got me off to a good start. Thanks to Eric, who cleared the runway off." The year records picking up a new car, taking a helicopter ride over the Blackcomb and Whistler area of B.C. to view their rugged peaks from her favorite vantage point, playing in musical festivals and listening to her students perform in recitals. And, always, there were new things to learn in the flying field.

Newspaper reporters continued to court the Flying Grannie. The Lloydminster *Meridian* wrote, on July 22, 1990:

> When you think of Mildred Beamish, you have to throw out any stereotypes about great-grandmothers you've been holding on to. For Beamish is as likely to be found buzzing a landing strip in her 1957 Skyhawk as she is to be found playing a soothing sonata on her grand piano.

Mildred Beamish, May, 1995. *Photo: S. Matheson*

Mildred's years of flying have left a legacy among her family and acquaintances. Her son Eric flies, although not often, and her daughter-in-law Leona is also licensed. "The thing was, my husband and I loved to fly. Our son Eric is a much, much better pilot, but it's not his main love. Our daughters never did fly. They were so busy they didn't have time for flying."

Then their grandson, Don Beamish, got his pilot's licence. He now lives on the family farm, and has inherited Mildred's beloved Cessna 172. Don's love of flying likely started, Mildred says, with his first flight with her at age three months, in October of 1965.

So Mildred concentrated on her grandchildren, and took them for plane rides "to Calgary, or here, there and everywhere." Many years later, Mildred learned that "when my kids, with their children, came to the farm, they knew they'd have to have a flight with granny. I thought they'd enjoy it, but evidently that was part of the ordeal!"

On October, 1992, the Saskatchewan Flying Farmer's hosted a "Toast and Roast," with Mildred Beamish as their subject. A poem written by Mildred's children was read at the event. Titled "The Flying Mom," it got a good laugh from the crowd, none more enthusiastic than Mildred's.

Where is our mother?
Making meals in the kitchen as she used to be?
No! Now she's a celebrity being interviewed on T.V.,
Playing piano in a bar in the North,
Flying home from Kansas with a tree,
or . . . weathered in . . . where??

The poem continues the theme, now sponsored by the next generation:

Where is Granny?
Some grannies rock and knit, and are afraid of a height.
When you visit our granny, you may go for a flight!
When you ask her advice, it's "the sky is the limit."
Our role-model Granny is right up to the minute.

And so, Mildred passes on her twin passions, music and flying, to those she loves.

In 1993, Mildred's flights included going to Edmonton "to get a chip in my LORAN (Long-Range Navigation aid)", another trip to the 99s All-Canada Meeting, a Forest of Friendship conference which honored her friend, Harvey Peacock, a Saskatchewan pilot who'd been flying for 60 years; a fly-in breakfast at Camrose, a flight with her grandson to Fort McMurray, and several flights around the province with a trainee from Australia. But at the end of the letter she lamented that she "didn't get in any long flights" over the summer.

Her log book records her last flight made on October 11, 1993, just a short spin over Lloydminster.

Mildred's flying career did not end because her licence was lifted. She simply decided, following a hip operation, it might be a good time to end it. The following year, she didn't apply for her licence. "I sort of wished afterwards that I hadn't quit. Nobody stopped me from flying, I just stopped myself. There wasn't any reason. It was silly."

Mildred Beamish and author Shirlee Smith Matheson at the Lloydminster Flying Club Awards Night and banquet, April, 1995.
S. Matheson Collection

Mildred looks around her comfortable room where she resides at the Pioneer Lodge in Lloydminster. "From oxen to aircraft –

I've had a wonderful life," she says with a soft smile.

The walls are filled with her awards and numerous photos of airplanes and family members clustered around airplanes. For many years, Mildred was Secretary for the Lloydminster and District Flying Club, and was honored by the club at a banquet and awards night held April 8, 1995. Another plaque for her wall.

"I just wanted to get up from the road and see everything," she explains. "It's a wonderful feeling, taking off by yourself in an aircraft. There's nothing else like it. You sort of feel like you're a part of the aircraft."

She looks at the awards and photos, with pride and with a certain amount of awe.

"I'm a rather timid person," Mildred says. "Sometimes I surprise myself."

Footnote 1:

Gwen Beamish's father-in-law, Sir Ernest Alexander Campbell MacMillan (who died May 6, 1973), was considered to be the statesman of Canadian music and was the first person to be knighted (1935) outside the UK for contributions to music. Enjoying an international reputation as a conductor of symphonic and choral music, he was also an organist and pianist, an educator and a spokesman for music. He led the Toronto Symphony Orchestra until 1956 and left behind 20 compositions and many arrangements.

Footnote 2:

Gus Kenderdine's friendship with Dr. Walter Murray, first president of the University of Saskatchewan, had led to his finding support for the school to become a credited part of the university's art program. In 1935, Kenderdine became the director of fine arts at the university.

In the 1950s, May donated a number of her father's paintings to the Glenbow Foundation of Calgary and to the Mackenzie Art Gallery of Regina; in the 1980s, the University of Saskatchewan was the recipient of paintings, plus over $1 million for the university's college of agriculture building.

Footnote 3:

Among the aircraft that the Beamish's have owned are Cessna 140 CF-HDJ, Cessna 150 MJU, Cessna 150 MJE, Cessna 150 XLB, and WYA, XIJ and XKQ. Mildred has also flown 1970 Cessna 172 YGE; Cessna 177 ZGS, Cessna 172 CKS; Cessna 180 RLJ (husband's plane); Cessna 172 CKK, Cessna 172 FLH; Cessna 172 CKS; Cherokee 140 YTY; Cherokee 180 FQP. Then, the last airplane she owned, a smart blue and white Cessna 172 C-GEBD*.

(*Canadian aircraft registrations were prefixed with CF- _ _ _ in the years 1929-1972. Then they ran out of letters, so started the CG series. However, the Department of Transport changed the sequence to C-F ___ and C-G ___ to ensure the full identity was given. All these identification letters must be prefixed with CF-(if old) or C-G (if new).

Footnote 4:

"The cost of building this airport, not including a $300 provincial government grant, was $659," said Chamber of Commerce president, Dr. A.W. Thomson. Then he added, "But the volunteer labor that went into picking stones, filling gopher holes and clearing scrub brush could not be measured in dollars."

Footnote 5:

The subject is addressed in *Aviation Safety Letter,* Transport Canada (Issue 1/1994):

> Since 1986, 180 incidents of doors coming open during takeoff or in flight have been reported in Canada. All aircraft types are involved, from the Concord and Boeing 747s all the way to Cessna 172s. The results have included explosive decompressions, lost doors, lost baggage, and lost people.
>
> Pilot reactions have varied among aborted takeoffs, returns for landing and emergency descents. Over the years, doors opening in flight have caused a disproportional number of accidents, considering that with a few exceptions it is not a critical emergency. The fact is that pilots get distracted and simply forget to "fly the aircraft."

Finding the Mother Lode

"When we were kids, airplanes would come and land in farmers' fields near our place at Marshall, Saskatchewan," Bill Whiteley recalls. "Sometimes they were barnstormers, and a couple of times they'd run out of gas. They just used car gas. Naphtha was expensive and hard to get.

"I'd run around and help them find fuel. Then I'd watch the pilot strain the gas through a felt hat – or a chamois if he had one – to take out the impurities and any water. The pilot would work on his airplane, get it going and fly away.

"See, our village had no running water, no power, nothing happening, this was rural living, so an airplane landing was quite fantastic! So you say, 'When did you get interested in airplanes?' I got interested the first day I saw one."

John William "Bill" Whiteley was born in Edmonton, Alberta, on October 2, 1923. His family owned one of two general stores in Marshall, the first village east of Lloydminster. He was a happy kid, even though those years are generally referred to as the "hungry '30s" and there wasn't anything extra.

Harry Wilford was a World War I veteran who ran a bake shop in Marshall. One day he got talking to the young boy about kites. Bill had never had one, so Wilford went to work. "He made me a box kite, a big one," Bill recalls. "It was so large that when there was a strong wind I couldn't hold it, which I think was an excuse for Harry because he and I flew it. Then the Wilfords left Marshall and went to North Battleford. My dad didn't have any time to play with me, so this kite went into the warehouse. It hung in there for years."

While growing up, Bill was often taken on visits to Edmonton. That was where Wiley Post (an American high-altitude pilot, and the first man to fly alone around the world) had landed on Queensway! At that time the Edmonton Municipal Airport was a grass strip out in the country, and it involved quite an expedition to get there. Bill and his old uncle would stand and watch the airplanes land.

One year, when Bill was 10, his family vacationed at Cooking Lake and Bill was treated to another exciting experience. "I was sitting on the beach with my buddy, and there was Wop May fixing a float with a pot of tar! He spilled some on himself and it burned. I heard words that I'd never heard before!"

From these dynamic events grew the desire to fly. Then along came the war. Bill's first thought was, "Hey! Now I can be a pilot."

He took all his schooling in Marshall, "with teachers that really took an interest in me," and wrote his provincial senior matriculation exams in the two-room school. After graduating at age 17, Bill found a job in a bank. He worked there until his 18th birthday, and the very day he was eligible to join, October 2, 1941, he went to Saskatoon to sign up for air force service as a pilot.

"There was no question in my mind about doing anything else, like joining the navy or the army," he says. "I wanted to be a pilot!"

He received his training in Prince Albert on open cockpit Tiger Moths – "no radios, funny old airplanes." Listed in his log book among his instructors' names are Floyd Glass and Ernie Boffa (Footnote 1).

"Boffa had 12 000 hours as an old bush pilot before he started instructing, so I had instruction from the best."

The instructors came from military as well as bush-flying (referred to as civilian) backgrounds. One major difference was that military flyers were familiar with many types of airplanes and so used a standardized approach; bush pilots often had flown just one or two different types, and they sometimes taught methods that worked best for those particular airplanes.

"They tried to ensure that air force standardization was maintained because all students were supposed to get the same training. But, if you went with Floyd Glass one time, and Ernie Boffa another, you learned different things," Whiteley says.

An example was the lesson on how to handle forced landings.

"You can handle an airplane even when the engine quits running," Whiteley explains. "The aircraft becomes a glider – it doesn't just fall out of the sky. This gives you time to look around and find a nice flat place to land. You have very little control over your rate of descent, but you can control your airspeed and land it like a glider. It's a case of judgement.

"The proper way to handle a forced landing, according to the air force instructors, was to keep working toward a field. Because you're losing height, you want just one key position before you turn in to land. Ernie Boffa thought this was kind of a waste of time. His idea of how to deal with a forced landing was what we later called a 'falling leaf'. Ernie Boffa could take an airplane, pull the nose up, stall it and kind of flip it from side to side like a falling leaf, all the way down.

"Can you imagine a man with thousands of hours trying to teach that to some kid who's got 10 hours?" Whiteley laughs. "Those guys had all kinds of tricks, but they now had to standardize young fellows who would be flying Spitfires or Lancasters, and you don't play 'falling leaves' with Spitfires or Lancasters! Ernie didn't have to fly those kind of airplanes – he would just be going back to the bush."

Whiteley would say to himself, "One day I'll be able to do that falling leaf, but in the meantime I'll do it the standard way."

All instructors taught the students to plan ahead for emergencies: to consider, if their engine quit, could they make that lake? Could they use that road? "That was just one of the airmanship rules.

"But when you learn to fly Tiger Moths in about 80 hours you don't know much about flying," Whiteley concludes.

One thing Whiteley noticed among the students then, and later when he became an instructor himself, was that kids who had grown up in rural areas seemed to be more mechanically inclined than city kids. "Farm boys know how to mend things. They can do a lot with a piece of baling wire, because all their lives they've been around machinery."

The air force students went from Tiger Moths to twin-engine Cessna Cranes – "quite a jump." At that point, Whiteley got his wings and was posted overseas, prepared for "fight or flight," with 250 hours flying time.

It first appeared that the RAF (Royal Air Force) wasn't too impressed by his 'colonial' credentials. "I had my log book transcribed before I left Canada, which showed that I'd taken pressure chamber tests. Maybe because of my size, and also because I was in good shape then and I didn't get any bends, my log book said I was recommended for special high altitudes. I immediately thought, 'Oh boy, Spitfires! Mosquitos!'

"My first assignment with the RAF was flying wimpy Wellington torpedo bombers at 50 feet! I'm serious! That's the way we had to fly them over the ocean. If you're going to run in on targets, you have to do it straight and low-level. I wasn't too impressed with that."

When he finally did get on Spitfires, it often involved low-level flying. Even the name of their missions sounded feeble. Their Fighter Command was sent on "sorties", while the Bomber Command had "designated *raids*".

Bill Whiteley spent four years overseas. He married an English girl, Eileen Garnham, who was also in the RAF, in 1945 while in England.

Before returning to Canada, the military gave him a choice: he could serve the remainder of his time with the Army of Occupation – "I didn't know what that was but it didn't sound right to me, somehow" – or serve in the Far East with the "Tiger Bomber Force." He chose the latter and was transferred back to Canada in 1945, bringing his British bride.

"I was on my embarkation leave, visiting my sister in Calgary prior to departing to the United States for training, when the war ended in Japan. I got a telegram saying 'Report to Regina for your discharge.' And suddenly I was out of the service and back to Marshall, Saskatchewan."

He didn't want to get into the grocery business, and he didn't want to go back to the bank. He wanted to fly, but he didn't know where to start looking for a job. He was one of many ex-air force pilots who'd come back, and meanwhile the aviation industry at home had been established, and filled, in his absence.

Then he had a bit of luck: a Piper Cub landed in his father's field near the village late one afternoon because of impending bad weather. Whiteley drove out in his car to greet them.

"Hello! What's your problem?"

"We sure need some gas, and the weather doesn't look very good."

The couple introduced themselves as Mr. and Mrs. Leo McKenna. Whiteley took them home for supper, and they stayed the night.

"Of course we got talking. He was a Piper agent, and this was the first aircraft he was flying to Edmonton to show and sell, to set up his agency there," Whiteley recalls. "He'd already set up agencies in Saskatoon and Regina, and he was planning to set them up in Edmonton, Calgary and Vancouver."

It didn't take long for the McKennas to learn of Whiteley's flying experience, and of his yearning to continue in the business.

"You wouldn't be interested in coming flying for me, would you?" McKenna asked.

"Oh! I sure would!"

The next morning, McKenna and his wife left in their two-place aircraft to get organized in Edmonton; Whiteley was to come later after he got a commercial licence. "It was no big deal because I was current, and they couldn't ask me any questions that I shouldn't know. I had the required flying time, just had to write the exam. I talked to an old gentleman named Ken Saunders, a chief inspector who'd got his licence with the Wright brothers! He was very pro-military, so that helped."

McKenna's Piper agency was called Canadian Aircraft. It occupied a portion of the hangar at the Edmonton Municipal Airport, where Tommy Fox had the Taylorcraft agency and operated Associated Airways; on the other side of the field was Maurie Fallow of Keith and Fallow who had the Aeronca agency. They were all in competition.

The company's first job was to find a way of getting their airplanes out from Hamilton, so they put an ad in the paper: "Is anybody interested in flying an airplane?"

The response was overwhelming, including some from men who didn't even have pilot's licenses. But one of their respondents was an air force friend of Whiteley's, Bill Meaden, who came in with his log book.

Meaden went to Ontario and brought back the first Piper Cub, and shortly thereafter, Whiteley and another ex-air force pilot picked up the next two.

"I figured I should know how to do this if I was going to be hiring guys for the job – and it was quite a ride," Whiteley says. "We came from Hamilton through the States, around Chicago to Great Falls, Montana; into Alberta through Lethbridge, and up to Edmonton – in those 60-mph airplanes bucking a 30-mph wind! It took a week! They had 65-hp Continental engines, no radios, fixed props, two dials, and that was it. We brought back two, and sold them for $2 600 each. When you think about it, you could buy a Hudson car in 1946, a tremendous car, for $2 300. You could buy a Ford for $1 200 or $1 400. Those sales got us started."

Whiteley was an employee, not a partner, but he did everything he could to move airplanes. "We'd get a call from someone in Lloydminster, Vilna or Vegreville, saying, 'I'd be interested in a demonstration,' so away we'd go. We sold quite a few."

One day he went to Vilna, Alberta, where the population was largely comprised of people of European descent, to show the airplane to a man who'd been in the air force. "When we went to a village like that we first had to find a place to land, as close in as possible, being careful of the fields. With a little airplane, the best places to land were stubble or summer-fallow fields, especially in the autumn because you could see if they were dry. Usually, if the farmer had recently worked a field it was safe to go in with an airplane – usually – but you still looked around to make sure. If a field had hay on it, there might be rocks or gopher holes.

"I found a field outside of Vilna, and right away I was surrounded by kids. They'd let them out of school to come and see the airplane! I had to be careful because they were all around."

The first thing Whiteley said was, "Whose field is this?"

"Old Joe Kapushky's."

"I'd like to talk to him, to make sure it's okay that I'm sitting here."

At that point Mrs. Kapushky arrived, a shyly smiling little old lady. The people talked to her in Ukrainian, and Whiteley said, through an interpreter, "You'd better come for a ride, and see your place from the air."

She shook her head, "No!"

But the people urged her, "Go on!"

In the meantime Whiteley had sent a message to the fellow who was interested in buying, to tell him where he was.

Mrs. Kapushky got into the airplane, in the seat directly behind the pilot. He strapped her in. She seemed a little leery, but they'd all coaxed her so she was in for the ride.

Whiteley took off. He got just high enough to clear the fence when Mrs. Kapushky threw her arms around him from behind and yelled, "No!" plus some strong Ukrainian words that Whiteley knew meant "Stop! I want out!"

She had him throttled! "Okay, lady, I'll stop," he said through his closing larynx. "Just let go!"

He made the fastest circuit of his life – and he wasn't very high. He got down, stopped, turned in his seat – and there she sat, all smiles, looking out and waving to her anxious relatives who were standing around in the field.

When the sale was made, the salesperson/pilot would usually offer to go with the purchaser to try out the airplane on different fields. One of Whiteley's sales was to an oil man who was doing seismograph work in the districts from Lloydminster to Provost. He thought the little airplane would just be perfect, but he didn't want to learn to fly himself so he hired an ex-air force pilot. When Whiteley met the hired pilot, he said, "Let's fly this around for the afternoon, go to St. Albert. I'll show you what it will do in all sorts of fields, in summer-fallow, in pastures."

The air force pilot looked at him disdainfully. "I've flown everything, Mosquitos . . ."

"This isn't a Mosquito!" Whiteley interjected.

"Ah, don't worry."

The second time the pilot took it out he put it on its back near Provost, and the oil man had to write it off.

"So," Whiteley concludes, "there are pilots – and there are pilots."

Whiteley found it fascinating to meet legendary pilots who had flown out of Edmonton for the past decade, such as T.P. (Tommy) Fox, who was then a partner in Associated Airways Limited.

"I was there when he brought back the Anson after he'd cut nine feet off the wings. They were flying fish, on skis. One of the guys caught a wing-tip on a snowdrift and crimped the end.

"I talked to Tommy afterwards. He said, 'I looked at this thing, and there was four feet, from the aileron out, all twisted up. It wouldn't fly like that, so I went to a rib and cut the wing-tip off. I taped it up, stood back and looked at it. No, it wouldn't fly like that, either. So I went over and cut the same amount off the other one, and taped it up.'

"I was at the airport when he came back," Whiteley says. "The Anson came in and I thought, 'Gee, I've never seen one like that!' Well, right away, the DOT (Department of Transport) lifted his licence for 30 days for flying an airplane that wasn't airworthy. But I asked Tom, 'You didn't play with it on the way down, did you?' He said, 'Oh God, no. I was careful on the way down.'

"I asked him at what speed he thought it was going to stall, because that would tell him what to land at. He said, 'We had lots of length on the lake, and we were on skis. I just poured the coal to it. I didn't try to lift it off, it lifted itself off when it came un-stalled, and I noted the speed. Then I knew what to land it at.'

"He was also the guy who said to me, 'Don't ever forget to put something under your skis in the winter, or you won't be able to move that airplane in the morning. Spruce boughs, anything.' I learned all kinds of things from these people, lots of tricks."

Whiteley stayed with McKenna's Piper agency for a year, until a new adventure presented itself.

Bill Whiteley had sold an aircraft jointly to Bill Meaden and Doug Tod, an ex-air force navigator from Taylor Flats, B.C. It was a three-passenger Cub Cruiser, with "wet" wings (tanks in the wings), and had a range of 600 miles. Tod wanted to go to the Peace River country to see what was going on, so up they went with Meaden flying.

(L. to R.): Instructor Bill Whiteley, student Jack Patterson, owner of Patterson's Menswear, with partner and ex-Air Force pilot Doug Tod fueling J3 at Dawson Creek's old airstrip in 1947. *Sam Side Collection*

They did some barnstorming, but the two men didn't hit it off too well together.

Tod came back to Edmonton to see Whiteley. "That country is ready to go with an airplane, but Bill Meaden's not interested. You should come!"

They talked it over, with Tod insisting on one thing: "Before we go, we've got to get a charter. There's no point going in there and just hop-scotching around."

They were advised to see Cy Becker, an Edmonton lawyer who specialized in aviation and was known to all the old aviation guys. "He took kind of a shine to us and went to work on it," Whiteley said. "It took quite a while but nobody else was there and he got us a charter."

Their charter licence covered northern Alberta, northern B.C. and the Northwest Territories, based at Dawson Creek and Fort St. John. It allowed them to do recreational flying, barnstorming, charter work, contract work and instruction.

Bill Whiteley and Doug Tod were the principals of the company, which they registered as Inter-Provincial Airways. Its assets were the Cub Cruiser and a J-3 Cub, "where the side goes down and the top goes up, no doors, one seat front, one seat back," which they planned to used for instruction. Whiteley got his instructor's licence before they left.

Now they were into a new business with barely a nickel between them, and Whiteley had a wife and little daughter to support. Whiteley's first job was to find a place for his family to live in the town, which was then at the end of the rail line. The only house he could find to rent was very small, with no running water and an outdoor toilet. "Eileen was an English girl, she'd never lived in a place like that. She was not impressed! If I hadn't been able to get away in the airplane sometimes, it would have been terrible!" Whiteley laughs.

The town welcomed the new enterprise. The Dawson Creek "airport" had one airstrip, constructed by the Americans during the war, and not much else.

"When we were there in 1946 they still had a tethered balloon that went up a couple of thousand feet for telecommunications. The tether was a LORAN (Long Range Aerial Navigation) aerial, one of three satellites. The one airstrip, which ran alongside the hospital, had been hardtopped but had been let go, so it was a bit broken up. That's what we used. We had to make little hangars for our airplanes."

Their business got off to a good start with instruction and charter work. As soon as they advertised flying lessons, they received 15 responses from students of all ages – "young fellows, old fellows, businessmen, women – it was fairly busy."

In the meantime, Doug Tod also got his pilot's licence.

"Instructing wasn't difficult, it was very easy as a matter of fact," Whiteley says. "One strip, and we had the only aircraft. There was nobody controlling, no radios, we did our own thing. I could give instruction in a real hurry, whereas in a normal airport it takes hours. I spent as much time on the ground briefing as in the air, so there was no question about what the student was to do. When we were in the air, I'd sit in the rear cockpit with the student in the front where the instruments were so he could see where he was going. I had a removable stick in the back, which would be taken out when we had a paying passenger."

Their first charter work was with the government's Department of Forestry, going on forestry patrols and looking for fires. The not-so-great thing about getting contracts from the B.C. government was that their pay came months later; in the meantime, the fledgling company had bills for oil, insurance and payments for airplanes. "Sometimes it was pretty thin going."

From the departments of Health and Welfare, and Indian Affairs, they got contracts to fly the nurses on their visits to Moberly Lake on call-out or to administer vaccinations and to visit the schools. "When the Indians came in for treaty money was the perfect time for the nurse to visit, because she could get them all at once. You'd never find them once they went back out into the bush."

One time he took the nurse, Marjorie Leach, out to Moberly Lake, and was to come back to pick her up the next day. He was on skis, and it was right around spring break-up time. "We put the big wide Tiger Moth skis on the three-passenger Cruiser, which gave the aircraft better buoyancy on the soft snow, but they were heavier and the airplane had to work a little harder getting off."

Overnight, a warm Chinook wind came through. There was enough snow to get off the strip at Dawson Creek with skis, and he assumed it would be cooler out in the hills. It was, but it was still very soft, and the nurse was bringing a patient back, adding extra weight. To aid takeoff from Moberly Lake, Whiteley got kids to push the airplane around on the sticky snow.

When they arrived back at Dawson Creek there was no snow. The strip, which was lined with wide ditches, had now filled with water. Whiteley sized up the situation, and saw an answer.

"Look, Marjorie," he said, "I'm afraid you're going to get wet because there's only one place to land."

They landed in the ditch, skimming along like a water-skier. As long as he kept up his speed he knew they could keep going to the end; then he ran the airplane up onto the dirt bank. They got out and stepped into two feet of water. Later on, he rolled the aircraft up and changed the skis to wheels.

One time he had to go north of the Peace River to a new community east of Fort St. John, to bring in a patient who'd suffered an appendicitis attack. He went in with the Cub on wheels – "not Weldy Phipps' big tundra tires, but they were pretty big."

When Whiteley looked for a place to land he judged the ground by its color. "Wet is dark. If you see a light color you know there's a rise and it's dry." He had to land near the schoolhouse and little store, and he could see people standing outside. Everyone was looking up, all the school kids, people on horseback – likely not having seen an airplane before. None would know what he needed for a field. The nearest he could come was a small field next to the road, but it was black. Right in the middle, however, he saw some light-colored ground, which looked dryer. He went as low as possible to take a good look, then circled and came in for a landing. The aircraft rolled a bit and bogged down.

He explained the situation to the people, telling them he needed their help. They immediately got horses and some rope, and towed the airplane onto the road. "I had to make sure they put the ropes in the right places, and pulled very gently so they didn't pull the wings off." But when he looked at the road his spirits sank. Solid mud! Apart from being sticky, it would pick up on the prop, too. "The prop will pick anything up, if it's down on the ground, and loose. It was something else to worry about."

"I can take off if we can get this road dried and packed a bit," he said. A dozen kids had the time of their lives! For a half-hour they galloped the horses up and down, "pounding the hell out of this road, packing down the mud." They finally got it to a point where it was more solid, and he managed to get out with his seriously-ill patient.

"You always think afterwards, 'Gee, if I'd busted the prop the patient would be in trouble – and so would I!'"

There is a lake in the Rocky Mountains south of Chetwynd, B.C., that used to be called Rocky Mountain Lake, and is now known as Gwillim Lake. At that time, the only way to get there was with pack train. One day, a group of big-game guides and outfitters who were operating out of Dawson Creek came into the office of Inter-Provincial Airways. They introduced themselves as Ross Tipton, the Young brothers, and an old bush-man named Milo Dirney. They had been taking in hunters with pack trains past Gwillim Lake to a big hill called Bullmoose Mountain, close to where the coal mine is now, to hunt for sheep, grizzly and goat. They explained that after leaving the highway it was a two- or three-day pack trip before they got in to big-game country.

The purpose of their visit was to inquire if Inter-Provincial Airways could fly passengers from Dawson Creek in to their camp at Gwillim Lake.

"But we're not on floats," Whiteley said.

"We'll cut a strip – how big do you need?"

Looking back on it now, Whiteley says that he made a mistake. "I showed them how good the Piper Cub was, how it could get off and land in a short distance, but I cautioned them that the big trees had to come down to accommodate the wingspan."

"Don't worry, we'll get horses in there, cut the trees, pull stumps. We'll make you a good strip."

When Whiteley was told the strip was ready, later in the summer, he went to have a look. They had done their work, all right. The aircraft wingspan was 25-feet, and they had cut trees to allow three feet extra on each side. The strip was cleared for 200-feet in length, but abruptly at the end loomed 50-foot-high trees. There was no way he could get in there. He dropped them a note asking them to widen the strip and cut off the big trees at the end – even if they left the stumps.

"The first time I went in I was a little bit leery. The bank rose about 20 feet high off the lake, and that's where the strip started. On that first approach and landing I was twitchy, knowing that at a certain point I was committed and I couldn't go around again.

"But I went in, and it worked. I asked them to make more changes, get rid of a few humps here and there, and I never had an accident there.

"I've never had an accident at all, ever, not even dented one up," he adds. "Just lucky."

That contract started a larger operation for Inter-Provincial Airways. The outfitters advertised in *Field and Stream* magazine, and attracted game hunters from New York State to California, who paid good money to come up to Canada and hunt. They flew into Dawson Creek or Fort St. John, and Whiteley would take them to the strip out at Gwillim Lake.

The outfitters lived in the bush year-round, and ran trap-lines in the winter. They killed for meat only when needed. When Whiteley stopped at their camp, he would see quarters of moose or deer hanging on ropes from tree branches 20 feet high, "above the fly-line". The meat would drain, so when they let it down there was a crust at the end, which they sliced off and gave to the dogs. "And then," says Whiteley, "you've got real fine meat."

They once gave him a moose roast that weighed 20 pounds. He took it home to his wife and she was dumbfounded. Even its appearance did nothing for her appetite, and she didn't have a clue how to cook it in the cantankerous wood-stove. She bravely stuffed it into the oven, which it filled entirely. "We didn't cut it into smaller pieces, nor did we put things with it, which we should have," Whiteley says. "Have you ever smelt moose roasting? It can get pretty high."

In the winter, the guide-outfitters also caught lake trout in Gwillim lake, which they called "land-locked salmon" – a beautiful pink fish. They netted them by cutting a hole in the ice, pushing down a plank with a net on it and jigging it across under the ice. When it got far enough, they cut another hole and pulled it up. When they caught the fish they threw them up onto the ice, stiff and straight as sticks of wood. Whiteley would make twice-weekly trips, flying their fish out to Dawson Creek.

He was getting used to hauling almost every kind of cargo, but he still had some surprises coming. One was his assignment to haul live beaver.

"An old gentleman who lived up the Alaska Highway toward Muncho Lake used to 'farm' beaver," Whiteley recalls. "He felt it was wrong to deplete the stock. He took only a certain number of beaver every year, and he had a good stock of them."

There was a little valley not far away that he wanted to stock with beaver, and he asked Whiteley if he could take two beaver, enclosed in wire cages, in there for him. There was a small meadow to land on.

"I hope you've got them caged good, because if those guys get out and start biting or using their tails, I'll be in trouble," Whiteley said.

He hauled the two beaver without incident, and as far as he knows the beaver lived happily ever after in the valley.

Possibly the strangest – and most dangerous – order he ever received was to fly dynamite. Whiteley was sitting in his office in Dawson Creek when he received a call from a man in Edmonton, who worked for a company who put barges in the river at Waterways, north of Edmonton, to haul goods down the Mackenzie River to Aklavik. They'd had a short season of open water. He told Whiteley that four big barges and a tugboat had to be ready to go in the spring and then get back before freeze-up.

"How can we help you?" Whiteley asked.

"One of the barges left Aklavik too late in the fall – got caught in ice on the way out," the man said. "We had to pull it up on shore at Fort Good Hope." There it was. "In the spring when the ice went out, icebergs the size of a back-lot pushed up against it. It's costing us hundreds of dollars a day to have the thing sitting there.

"We've been trying to pick-axe the ice out, but it's impossible," he added. "We're going to have to blast. What would you charge to take up 500 pounds of dynamite?"

Whiteley hadn't the foggiest idea, so he just blurted out a price. "$500."

"You're on," said his caller.

Whiteley figured that he could have said $5 000 and got the job.

"We'll have the dynamite flown up to Fort St. John with an Anson tonight."

Something sounded odd. "If you can do that, why don't you take it all the way up with the Anson? What do you need me for?"

"The little strip up there is grass. I'm pretty sure it's underwater, and the Anson would probably sink in. You wouldn't." Whiteley's aircraft (the Cruiser) was on wheels, but equipped with big tires and was a lighter airplane. It seemed to make sense.

Then Whiteley said, "Did you check this out with the air force?"

The RCAF was still operating the airport at Fort St. John, and Whiteley knew all the guys who worked in the tower from his years in the military.

"You've got to get permission from the air force to bring this stuff into the airport," Whiteley insisted.

"I haven't got time for that."

"Well, it's your dynamite," Whiteley said. "How will I know it when I see it? I don't even know what I'm looking for."

"It looks like apple boxes. There'll be four of them, and two other boxes. We'll leave it in the infield. You'll be able to see it."

There was a triangular runway at Fort St. John. No matter what runway an aircraft landed on, it would be easy to leave the boxes on the grass in the centre area.

Whiteley went to Fort St. John early in the morning and flew around. He couldn't see anything in the infield. He landed anyway and went in to the tower to talk to his friend, Percy Pigeon, who had flown in the Dambusters squadron. Whiteley always checked in there, especially if he was going back into the hills. Their aircraft had no radios, so he'd simply say, "Hey, I'm going for two days. If I'm not back, you know where I'm heading and what I'm flying."

Now he greeted his old friend casually, but felt he was playing a cat-and-mouse game."Hi, Perc, how are you?"

"Fine, Bill."

"Uh, did you have an Anson come in here in the last day or two?"

"Yeah, one came in last night. You know what the @*!# did? He left enough dynamite on that infield to blow up this camp!"

"Oh, did he, Perc? Where is it now?"

"It's down in the 'ammo' hut."

Whiteley could feel the heat creep up his collar. "God, Perc, I've got to have that," he said, and told the story.

"I'm just writing my report. This guy should go to jail!" Pigeon said.

He didn't write the report, and he did send an airman down with Whiteley to get the dynamite. It was heavy stuff, and they were quite careful when hauling it out to the airplane. There was also a bigger box and written on it was the advice to "Handle With Care." They looked inside and found it contained a coil, "the fuse, the stuff you light and it goes along, zzzzz."

Then there was a small box.

"I don't know what's in this," the airman said, and tossed it to Whiteley. He caught it and opened it, to discover it contained the caps. He'd heard they could go off if they were dropped.

"Well," he thought, "I've got dynamite, fuses and caps. And I've got a landing field up at the other end – I think. Real fun."

He first had to go to Fort Nelson for gas, then cut across to the Mackenzie River. He could follow the Canol (Canadian Oil) pipeline pretty well all the way, but it was over rugged country. If a guy went down in that area, he'd be a long time walking out. He always carried survival gear, snares for rabbits, a bit of rations, but no gun – "I never carried a gun."

He was flying with the dynamite in the back seat when the thought came to him, "If I have to go down, I don't want to be searching for those caps." He tucked the box between his knees. If he had to force-land he could just throw it out.

He made it to the site and found the strip to be a bit wet but it looked all right. He came in for a landing.

Everything went fine. The dynamite got unloaded, and Whiteley had enough gas to get back to Fort Nelson.

"I got back, and I got $500."

He admits that he had many such experiences flying in the North, when he wondered how the story might end. "You always did. I used the Alaska Highway as a landing strip a lot. It was gravel, but once you did it a few times you got to know it. It wasn't very wide and there were big trees on each side. If you went off, you'd had it. But, you got used to it."

One unforgettable customer was Snuffy Johansen, an old guide-trapper who came in to Dawson Creek one winter looking for Whiteley.

"I don't have any money, but I've got a little story to tell you," Johansen said. "This last fall I had a pack train in through the Peace Pass, with three hunters. There's no road in there, just a narrow gorge.

I was working on the west side of the Parsnip River, the original gold country, in the Manson Creek and Germanson Landing area.

"When we were coming out, one night a bad thunderstorm hit and the horses got away. We took whatever food we could carry and started to walk out. We followed a dry riverbed and came to a drop-off from what had been a waterfall, something like Niagara. We couldn't go down it, but there was no way anyone could come up that way, either. And there, on a bar, I saw the gold."

Bill Whiteley was spellbound. He leaned closer to catch every word.

"I scooped some up and put it into a can, and I didn't say anything to those guys. If they'd panicked, we'd never have got out of there."

His voice fell to a whisper. "I found the mother lode."

Of course, over a beer this sounded pretty good, Whiteley says. But the man stated for a fact that all the gold he'd been seeking for a lifetime was there. It was safe – nobody could come up that dry waterfall cliff from the other way.

Then the man said, "Would you take me out in the spring? If I can see that bar, then I've found it."

"I can't land in there," Whiteley said.

"No, I know that. I just want to see it. I can tell from the air."

Whiteley thought about it.

"We'll shake on it," the old man said. "You grubstake me, take me in, and it's 50-50."

What did he have to lose? A few dollars for gas, a grubstake for the old man, and maybe . . . just maybe, he *had* found the mother lode.

He flew the old guy in. It was a rough ride through the pass and quite a long distance. He had to use the "wet-wing" Cruiser with its long range because there was no place to land.

He followed Johansen's directions, and suddenly the old prospector nearly jumped out of the airplane! There it was, exactly where he'd remembered! Whiteley couldn't see anything unusual about the area, but the prospector definitely recognized it.They came back, Snuffy got his grubstake, and away he went.

"I never heard from him again, and never heard of anybody finding him," Whiteley says. "I don't know what happened. I guess the bears got him. That's a true story. I could show you that spot on the map. Someday, I'm going back to find it."

Bill Whiteley becomes quiet for a moment, thinking about his plan, reconsidering a dream that has been sidetracked for 50 years. He'd have to get together a grubstake, maybe hire a helicopter. He sighs.

"Aw, I'm getting a little long in the tooth myself. But from flying over, I still remember exactly where it was, exactly the river."

(L. to R.): American pilot Stan Fletcher, AME Hal Billings, Bill Whiteley recording fuel, future pilot sitting on the pump looking on, at Dawson Creek's original airstrip, July 31, 1948. *Sam Side Collection*

In July, 1948, Inter-Provincial Airways struck another first in Dawson Creek. Bill Whiteley and local flying enthusiast George Schmidt experimented with making rain by dropping dry ice on a formation of clouds. The first trial was made on June 29, when the two flyers took a 12-pound block of dry ice, and after pulverization, dropped it on the clouds over the village from an airplane. It didn't work, and the men figured they weren't up high enough.

The second time, on July 3, they used a fire extinguisher that sprayed a larger amount of dry ice under pressure. They climbed to 7 500 feet to get above a bank of cumulus clouds, then sprayed the clouds for a distance of about four miles.

It took six minutes to spray and come down below the clouds. By then, it was raining hard. The local newspaper reporter declared that this might be the first experiment with dry ice carried out in Western Canada, and added that if any farmer or others in the district would supply the dry ice and fuel for the airplane, Bill and George would gladly donate their time.

The company now had four airplanes. They'd added another Cub, and a Fleet Canuck leased from K.O. Aspol, the local Ford dealer who Whiteley had taught to fly.

For licensed commercial flying operators, the regulations were stiff. The airplanes had to be checked every week, every so many hours, by a licensed engineer. The company didn't have a licensed engineer.

Howard Russell was an engineer working for CPA (Canadian Pacific Airlines). He had previously worked for Yukon Southern Air Transport, and had lost an arm when a pilot inadvertently left switches on when the prop was being swung. Yukon Southern had given him a lifetime work contract, and when they were bought out by CPA the contract was carried on. Russell could pick his spot. He chose Fort St. John because he liked it and his family was there. Whiteley got to know Russell, who offered to travel the 45 miles to Dawson Creek every Sunday and check their airplanes.

"We did all the work on them, and Howard signed them out," Whiteley says. "I think we paid him $10 an airplane a week. We were absolutely legal.

"CPA knew what Howard was doing, I'm sure, but we weren't interfering with CPA's business."

At that point a man named Sam Side, whom Whiteley had trained with in the air force, came into the picture. Side had bought a twin engine Cessna Crane from War Assets and found he couldn't use it. He called Whiteley and asked if he would like to buy it. The price was $1 200. Whiteley told him they would like to have it but they didn't have any money.

(L. to R.): Sam Side, flying Dr. Kearney into the Rhowade Reservation near Pink Mountain, with Native trapper and dog team. Many Natives were dying of diptheria. *Sam Side Collection*

George Schmidt, another man who Whiteley had taught to fly, owned North American Trucking, one of the biggest companies operating on the Alaska Highway. Whiteley mentioned this airplane to Schmidt. "It's a good buy, but I don't have $1 200."

"We'll get it, don't worry," Schmidt said.

After its purchase, they made several trips in the Crane, taking George Schmidt to Great Falls, Montana, or wherever he wanted to go, but the airplane was available to the company at all times. In one case they used it on an emergency flight to Edmonton. The trip was made as quickly as CPA could have done, and they were able to fly directly to a waiting ambulance.

But that flight prompted a letter from CPA: "We understand that you're using the services of our engineer, Howard Russell. We have informed Mr. Russell that this has to stop."

Howard Russell didn't want to lose his good job, of course, and now that CPA perceived that Inter-Provincial was cutting into their business, he had to make a choice. He stayed with CPA, and the little airline had to find an engineer. "When you don't have any money, how are you going to hire someone?" Whiteley asks.

It so happened that a young man working in Dawson Creek for CN Telegraph named Stan Fletcher had an A&C engineer's licence. "He said he'd come and work on the airplanes in his spare time, which really kept us afloat, but for any of the major overhauls we had to take the airplanes to Edmonton."

By 1948, although there seemed to be lots of business, it was still a constant struggle to survive. "Things financially were getting real tough, payments on the aircraft, insurance was high. There were two separate types of insurance, flight risk when an airplane's flying, and ground risk. We always had to carry liability to satisfy charter requirements for the government, and the flight risk – they went together – but ground risk was optional. We'd never had any problems, so we took off ground risk."

Within a month they lost two airplanes.

"Easy to explain," Whiteley says. "Wintertime, skis, a lot of rough snowbanks on the lake, Piper aircraft goes over onto its nose, busts off a wing-tip. It wasn't a write-off, but the plane wasn't usable.

"The other one broke a ski, cartwheeled. It wasn't damaged bad, but enough to put it out of commission. Had to go to Edmonton."

Just then, he received a letter from the RCAF. Whiteley explains that when you got out of the air force you belonged to a certain class of the reserve, and could get called back into service again if you were needed.

"We understand you've continued flying, and have an instructor's licence," the letter read. "Are you interested in coming back to the air force?"

"Oh, boy, was I! So was Eileen. Living was tough, money was tough, nothing was working."

The Whiteleys left Dawson Creek in 1948, after being there for two years. Although he says he has no regrets about pulling out, Bill Whiteley recognizes that the business held great promise and he could have been part of it.

"I sold my share. Sam Side came in, and Doug Tod was still there. I took whatever I had and paid what we owed, Imperial Oil and all of them, so the company didn't owe any money. I didn't owe a cent, but I didn't have any either.

"If a guy had had some business sense, and a little backing, and could have hung in there until business came along, and the helicopter business developed, all that stuff . . . but it didn't happen. So I went back into the air force, and had a wonderful career."

Whiteley was looking forward to something different. He got his wish. The air force sent him to Trenton, Ontario, and suddenly he was into a new game. The first thing they did was put him through a series of courses – to be an instructor.

"You see," Whiteley explains, "there's the difference between flying 'an airplane' like our old friends would have done – they were used to their Norseman or Waco or whatever – and flying a number of airplanes. The air force took a different approach: they said, 'An airplane's an airplane. If you can fly one, you can fly them all.' I had to take an air instructor's course, which wasn't bad because I had some background in it. They lined up all the airplanes – Harvards, or Expediters, twin engine, that's what the kids were being taught on – and, because they had all these airplanes at Central Flying School in Trenton, they said, 'It's good experience to learn to fly them all. There's a Lancaster – go and fly that Lanc.'

"When I got out of the Lancaster, I flew a Mitchell. Got out of that, and into a Vampire. No dual controls on these airplanes. You get in by yourself and they say, 'This does this and that does that, and lots of luck.'"

Bill Whiteley listed the various aircraft in his log book, which now reads like an inventory of the National Aviation Museum: "Single engine: DH 82, de Havilland Tiger Moth. An Auster. Pipers, all kinds; Cessnas, 152s, 172s; a Walrus, an old RAF flying boat, a one-engine plane, but they were still using them during the Second war; Harvards; Spitfire; Mustang, P-51s; Bellanca; Norseman; and Fleet. They're all similar – all single engine.

"Then we got into twins and multi-engine – some have four: an Oxford, Wellington, Warwick, Mitchell, Dakota, Lancaster, Expediter, Cessna Crane and Anson.

"Now we're into jets: a Vampire – that was the first one we ever had in the air force, a cute little rascal. No dual. They gave you a book and said, 'Read this, this is what happens. The first time you go up, do a circuit. But don't lock the canopy seal until you get airborne, because if you wreck it on the runway we won't be able to get in and you'll burn to death.' Okay.

"I remember the guy telling me this. The surprising thing about it, it's a small airplane with a tiny cockpit and the windscreen is very close. The Vampire 'knelt'. The power against the brakes compressed the front oleo [nose gear]. I was sitting right against the windscreen as the nose went down, compressing. I took the brakes off and the nose jumped up again, and away I went. God!

"I'd left the canopy seal open like they told me. I got the wheels up and everything, and I was supposed to be doing a circuit. When I got airborne, I put on that canopy seal and I thought I'd gone deaf! I thought everything had quit! I'd never flown in such a quiet airplane. And suddenly I was 50 miles away and flying at 10 000 feet! That's exaggerating a little bit, but not much."

The Vampire was his first type of jet. "Next came the T-33s, you see them all the time; the Tutor, that's what the aerobatic teams used; F-86 Sabres, used in wartime, in Korea; and a Gnat, a British type; the CF-100, the twin-engine all-weather fighter that we used in NORAD [North American Defense Command, coordinator of continental defense network], when we had 12 squadrons across the country."

He also flew a CF-104, "known as the Starfighter." Whiteley says they were really a beautiful airplane, but their role in Europe was for low-level flying. "And we did have accidents. Flying low-level, particularly in Europe, you encounter a lot of birds and things. If you're flying at 600 miles an hour and a four-pound bird hits you, it's the same as a 10-ton rock hitting your car. Next thing you know, your engine's gone."

From Trenton, Whiteley was sent to the training centre in Centralia, Ontario, as a "buck-line" instructor, which meant his jobs could change from flying to ground work. "I had four flying students at any one time, and I worked my butt off." While he was in Centralia, the Korean conflict was starting. Suddenly the air force was training a lot more pilots – "all the ones who had been turfed out were needed again" – and also a younger group.

He went to Gimli, Manitoba, in 1951, again instructing. From there to London, Ontario, on a ground job at an officers' school. Next, to Training Command Headquarters in the Air Training Division at Trenton.

"From there I went on CF-100s in the NORAD air defense system, which necessitated taking another course, at Cold Lake, Alberta. Before that I'd got into T-33s to learn to be back on jets; now at Cold Lake I was on CF-100s, and I took over a squadron in Ottawa."

At this point, his rank was Squadron Leader.

"I spent a couple of years working in conjunction with NORAD when they were worried about the hordes coming over from the North. It was run from the main centre in Colorado Springs, and there was also a centre in North Bay, Ontario.

The Russians posed the greatest threat at that time, "with their rockets and such."

"It was believed that if we were ever going to be attacked, it would be by the Russians. They'd be coming over by the shortest route, and their targets would be Ottawa or Washington. So these stations were set up at Comox, Cold Lake, North Bay, Ottawa, Montreal and Bagotville, Quebec. These squadrons, dispersed across the country, had to practice exercises during night and day. And so you see it was quite different from bush-type flying. A different ball game."

Whiteley was never called upon to attack, but "the boys on the east and west coasts, particularly the east coast, would be sent up to put trails on the Russian aircraft that would come over on their way to Cuba, things like that.

"You had your navigator and he used the radar. At that time we had people stationed right across the country operating the Mid-Canada Line, and farther north on the DEW Line. Those stations formed a net, and anything coming through would trigger it."

In 1959, Squadron Leader Whiteley, commander of Number 410 Fighter Squadron at Uplands, was awarded the Queen's Commendation for "courage, resolute action and flying skill" when control problems on a training flight in October, 1958, had prevented him from being able to turn the aircraft. The citation says, "He possibly saved the life of the observer as well as his own and a CF-100, which he would have been fully justified in abandoning."

From a three-year stint running a squadron in Ottawa, Whiteley attended staff college in Toronto to learn the rudiments of becoming a staff officer. Then he was sent to Portage La Prairie to take over and run the advanced flying school with T-33 jets. "Young fellows coming through would get training up to a certain level, then they came up to the T-33 jets and got their wings."

One of Bill Whiteley's finest moments was flying the CF-104 at twice the speed of sound (referred to as Mach 2), up to 1 500 miles per hour. "The CF-104 was the only airplane that could do it at the time."

He performed this feat twice at Cold Lake. "Everybody had to do it. There was no trick," Whiteley says. "It's just that very few people do it, percentage-wise, compared to the number of pilots."

Whiteley recalls that the wings on the CF-104 had steel leading edges that were sharp as knives. "They had to put guards on them when the airplane was on the ground, so if you hit them with your head you wouldn't get cut. But the ultimate restriction on speed, which we had to watch carefully, was determined by the temperature gauge. Ordinary metal can stand only so high a temperature and then it starts melting, shortly after Mach 2. That's why the space rockets are made of sophisticated metals."

Whiteley says there are no Canadian military aircraft that fly Mach 2 today. "Even the new fellows don't do Mach 2. They've got such sophisticated weaponry that they don't need the speed."

He says there isn't really much to experience when travelling that fast. He simply left Cold Lake northeast of Edmonton, and in moments he'd passed North Battleford. There was no sound, and he was very high – about 48 000 feet. He imagined he could see the curvature of the earth. The only way he could tell his speed was by the instruments and the distance he'd covered.

"The sensation of speed in the CF-104 is down at 50 feet, and that's where we usually flew them in Europe," Whiteley says. "At 600 mph at 50 feet things move fast! That's 1 000 feet a second! So in effect, you're contour-flying. That is the idea. If you run into cloud or something, you pull up to a safety height and go on radar – you've got your own ground map on radar. Then you're doing all kinds of things at the same time: the control column has maybe six buttons on it, for such things as radio transmitter, nose-wheel steering, aileron-elevator trim and bomb release."

Whiteley is proud of making it through the stringent training course and passing the medical to get on the CF-104. "Depending on your age – I was 45 by that time, in 1968, and they thought I was getting on – you had to go through the Institute of Aviation Medicine in Toronto, called IAM. They put me through numerous tests like the centrifuge, pressure chambers with explosive decompression, and the most extensive physical and psychological tests available to make sure, particularly when I was going overseas on the CF-104s, that I was physically fit. "

"After my CF-104 nuclear tour in Europe, I got sent back to Petawawa, Ontario, as Group Captain. We had just started integration of the three services, so my job was to work with the army, controlling all the army airplanes from the Lakehead east. Another station was scheduled to open in Calgary for the Lakehead west, but it never did come about.

"Then I got sent to headquarters in Ottawa to the Personnel office! Quite different again, but very interesting. And from there to Tokyo, as Military Attaché to the ambassador. Actually, I wore two hats: I was also Canadian 'rep' to United Nations in Korea.

"The Tokyo bit was quite nice and very different, for both my wife and I, as you can appreciate. We spent three years there."

Whiteley had one more assignment with the air force when he returned to Canada in 1973, as Director of Manpower Distribution in

Ottawa. That meant he was involved with the movement of 23 000 personnel annually.

When he looks back over his flying career to recall his "biggest thrill," Whiteley says, simply, "My first solo, in an open-cockpit Tiger Moth. I think most pilots think that.

"My buddies were the same way. We used to say, 'Imagine, they even *pay* us to do this!' We were making $1.10 a day!"

Another big thrill is also connected with home: "going back to that little village of Marshall with an airplane, and picking up my old dad and taking him flying. He'd be 70 then, and he'd never been in an airplane. I took him up to show him what the area looked like. It astounded him. He saw a friend of his combining north of town. 'That's Somers Beamish. Let's land!' We landed alongside the combine. Somers shut it down and came over to see us.

"I said, 'Somers, you've just got to have a look at your place from the air.' In he got. He'd never been up. He said, 'I've got to have one of these!' and he did. Mrs. Beamish, Mildred, who was in her late 40s and is now in her 80s, also learned to fly. They both had an airplane. So I feel I was a part of that, too! (Footnote 2).

"I feel the same way about the young kids I taught to fly in the air force who went on to great things – such as two-star generals."

Bill Whiteley says he is fortunate to have lived in that particular age. "When I look back to being a kid growing up in a little town, and I think of how things have changed, I have to put airplanes in the same perspective. Mach 2 sounds wonderful – but little old ladies get into a Concorde and fly from New York to London, and sometimes a portion of that trip is Mach 2! It's the only one that does it, the Concorde" (Footnote 3).

He feels optimistic about the future of flying, and he keeps active in the industry. Until 1992, Whiteley worked with the Air Cadets, giving lectures and courses to those on flying scholarships. "I've got lots of faith in the young people. These kids have a lot going for them."

But his advice is cautionary. "Let's be honest and say it's expensive to learn to fly. No question. In Dawson Creek we used to charge $10 an hour, and you could learn to fly for $120."

Today, achieving a licence is only the beginning, Whiteley says. "A graduate student tries to get on with an airline, but he's still got a lot of learning to do. Companies have no need for a young man like that, they'll take him a little later when he's got more hours under his belt.

"It was always a competition, between air force and airlines: the airline pilots made twice as much money as our air force pilots. I had four young fellows who left Number 104 Flying Operation to fly for Canadian Pacific Airlines. I met them when I was in Tokyo, flying

707s as third pilot. They didn't get to do much, but they had the moxie for all the jet stuff, and were biding their time and moving up. They're now captains."

The only way young people can get their time in, Whiteley says, is to go to some outlying area and get on with a little charter that is willing to take the chance and let them build up their time. Some might apply for flying instructor's jobs with a flying club to build hours.

But the worst time for a young pilot, Whiteley says, is when he or she is at that stage where "a little knowledge is a dangerous thing."

"We used to say, '50 hours is pretty dangerous. He's soloed. 500 hours is almost as bad. Now he's really got it aced.' Maybe he's got an instrument rating. By 5 000 hours, he may realize he knows a little bit, but he has to keep hitting the books. A person never quits learning."

Because of a medical problem, Bill Whiteley no longer has his pilot's licence, but he's intent on getting it back. "I think I can. I'd like to get mixed up in ultra-lites. I think that would be a real 'old man's' way to fly. I did it, as a matter of fact, in London, Ontario. A friend of mine has one."

He has accumulated a total of 8 690 flying hours, which he says by today's standards is nothing. "Some of my buddies have a lot more time. On post-war Maritime tours, they'd take off from the east coast of Canada and go to Ireland and back, nonstop. But if you're an instructor or a fighter pilot, you do it an hour at a time. Hours mean something, depending on who you talk to."

Bill and Eileen's daughter, Judy (Judith Ann) Patterson, lives at Red Lake, Ontario, "the Norseman capital of the world." The Whiteleys visit there three or four times a year, to see their daughter and her family and to see bush flying being done the old way.

Nostalgia aside, Whiteley will admit they were not all "glory days," especially for a pilot's family. "I was away a lot, both with the bush flying and the air force. It takes a particular type of woman to hang in there. Eileen was very supportive, and I suppose there were some days when it wasn't very good. She flew a little bit with me, and Judy did when she was a little tad in Dawson Creek; she'd get in and sit on my knee. But Eileen wasn't an enthusiastic pilot, let's put it that way.

"When we finally moved into this little house in Brentwood Bay she reminded me that it was our 29th house! So, that tells you something."

Whiteley belongs to the Air Force Officers Association of Vancouver Island (president in 1993 and 1994), a group that was formed in 1946 and is still going strong. He also belongs to No. 800 (Pacific) Wing RCAF Association which welcomes all ranks, and he acted as director of the Victoria air show for three years. "That was a lot of fun."

Bill Whiteley, Brentwood Bay, BC.
Photo: S. Matheson

Past and present mingle as the years go by: friends one has known can turn up again, and suddenly you're back to the day when you last saw each other, renewing the memories.

When the Whiteleys were moving to Victoria, his sister told him that Harry Wilford now lived there, too. Whiteley immediately looked up Harry and his wife, Hilda. Harry was going on 90 at the time, still spry and fit.

The first thing the old man said was, "Whatever happened to that box kite?"

One day, Whiteley took Wilford to the point by the sea to watch the kids flying kites."I'd give anything to make a kite and fly it again," the old man said wistfully.

"Why don't we, Harry? Do you think you can remember how to make a box kite?"

"Sure!" he said.

Whiteley got the materials, took them over to the well-stocked workshop at Wilford's place, and together they worked on the kite. They made a date to fly it the following Tuesday.

That Tuesday morning, Harry Wilford put his head down at the breakfast table, and died.

"It was a wonderful way to go," Whiteley says. "If I ever write a book, it's going to be titled, 'Between Two Kites.' And I'm going to say in it, 'This is the way it happened – and if it didn't, this is the way it *should* have happened . . . if it had.'

But before, or maybe after, he writes that book, Bill Whiteley has one last adventure to fulfil. He still intends to seek out Snuffy Johansen's mother lode, that lays in wait under a dry-bed waterfall, in a mountainous gorge that still guards its gold.

Footnote 1:

see: “Looking Beyond the Roads,” the Floyd Glass story herein.

Footnote 2:

see: “Queen of the Flying Farmers,” the Mildred Beamish story herein.

Footnote 3:

The Concorde was manufactured by Aerospacia/British Aerospace Aircraft, and launched in 1973. This French-Anglo supersonic (Mach 2.04) airliner holds 128-144 passengers, and has a range of 3 870 miles.

The Underwood Airship

Drive along Alberta's Highway #12. As you pass the village of Botha, 11 miles east of Stettler, you'll see a strange sight. Painted on the south end of a large Quonset-shaped arena is a . . . well, it's not a farm implement. It's not a modern vehicle of any kind. It *looks* like a flying saucer!

Farmers enjoy a joke as well as anyone, but their humor doesn't usually carry into fantasy. Not too often will they defend sightings of Unidentified Flying Objects. But this object is not "unidentified". It belongs here, right in this little farming village, because it was built many years ago by a local family and flew above the blue skies of Botha.

If you ask the right people, such as village administrator Josie Hunter, local historian George Kerl or artist Raymond Binder, who

Easily seen by travellers on Alberta Highway 12 between Stettler and Castor, this painting by Raymond Binder on the Village of Botha's arena depicts the wonderful Underwood flying machine. *Photo courtesy Village of Botha*

painted the picture, you will learn one of this country's best kept secrets: the story of the Amazing Underwood Flying Machine.

The flying object and its inventors should have qualified for a "first" in Canada's aviation history. But, it didn't happen quite that way.

The Underwood family was gifted with inventive minds. On arriving from England in 1640, they settled first in New York State and eventually moved west to Minnesota around 1870, where John K. Underwood and his wife started their family. Sons Elmer, George and Johny were born there.

In 1872, patriarch John K. patented the Underwood Disc Plough, and later invented stook sweeps and other mechanical devices. The family began to experiment in aviation after they'd moved to North Dakota. "The first tests were on a model using rubber bands to drive the prop, back in the 1890s," writes Howard Underwood, in a letter to the author. "They also made a prop and drove it with a steam engine that fastened to a scale, to test the pull that it could lift."

When the Klondike Gold Rush occurred in 1898, young Elmer headed north. Seven years later, Elmer came to Alberta and took a homestead a mile-and-a-half west of the Krugerville stopping house on an old trail west of Gadsby, near the present village of Botha. Other family members soon joined him, and so the Underwoods became part of Alberta's pioneer lineage.

Farming the prairie homestead land was a lot of work, but the boys took time out for their real love, the study of aviation. Every spare hour was spent studying the theory of flight, or working on and experimenting with machines. Johny's specialty was mathematical theory; Elmer's was craftsmanship; and George's contribution was his daring and constant encouragement.

When the Wright brothers' flying experiments hit the news in 1903 and 1904, the Underwoods' interest in aviation was sparked even more by these successes (Footnote 1). On December 17, 1903, Wilbur and Orville Wright made the world's first power-driven flight in a heavier-than-air machine. With Orville at the controls, the machine flew over Kitty Hawk, North Carolina, for a distance of 120 feet at an approximate speed of 6.8 mph.

On May 14, 1907, the Underwoods conducted tests using a rectangular eight-foot wide tailless kite. Success with this apparatus drove them to experiment with a larger 20-foot span kite. They stabilized their kite with a centre fin (jib) that ran from front to back. The first models used a 10-foot high fin (later refined to four feet).

The outer circle was made from long, sturdy, laminated fir-strips, which took on the property of wings. Of an elliptical shape, the structure was 42 feet wide and 26 feet long, prevailed over by the

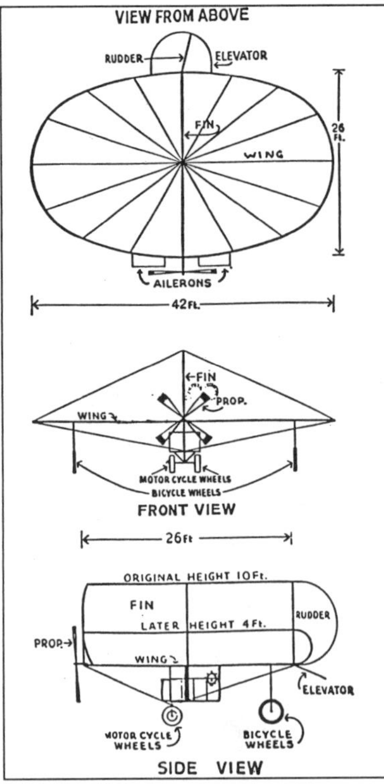

Diagram of the Underwood Airship. *Courtesy Village of Botha*

ten-foot vertical fin. Wire spokes fanned from a centre-post out to the laminated rim, like spokes on a bicycle wheel. Turn-buckles on each spoke allowed accurate adjustments.

The two front-control surfaces could be operated singly or together, and performed the function of ailerons. All lifting and control surfaces were covered with lightweight canvas, held in place by many lengths of cord. It weighed 450 pounds and had a lifting surface of 900 feet.

By mid-June, 1907, the Underwood brothers had perfected their "flying wing." News of their invention spread, and the brothers were invited to display the machine at the annual Stettler Exhibition.

Because it lacked wheels at that time, they mounted it onto a flat wooden stoneboat and pulled it behind a horse-drawn farm wagon over the rough 10-mile road to Stettler. The exhibit was an instant success, gaining rave reviews about "Alberta's Airship" from newspaper reporters in Toronto, Winnipeg and Edmonton.

But, the "airship" lacked one important component to bring it to the leading edge of aviation: an engine. Undaunted, the Underwoods tested it as one would a kite. They laid out 700 feet of quarter-inch rope along the ground, and tied one end to a sturdy fence post and the other to the nose of the craft. On August 10, 1907, the ship became airborne. The wing proved to be quite stable, and exerted a high degree of lift bolstered by the 20 mph prairie wind.

The brothers then tested it for weight-carrying capacity, laying five sacks of wheat, totalling about 350 pounds, onto the "cockpit platform." Up it went.

Twenty-two year old Johny then decided to go for a ride. After shortening the rope, he clambered aboard and was lifted some 10 feet into the air where he swayed about for 15 minutes, turning the craft this way and that. Thus, Johny Underwood became, in 1907 and under the blue skies of central Alberta, Canada's first aeronaut.

That same year, the Underwoods heard of Alexander Graham Bell's interest in aviation and his financing of The Aerial Experiment Association.

"My father used to correspond with Alex Graham Bell," writes Howard Underwood, "but all that material was lost in a house fire in 1924, along with many pictures of the plane."

The Underwood airship was fitted with bicycle and motorcycle wheels, attached so they could turn on a caster-designed fitting. This permitted them to manoeuvre the aircraft while it was on the ground. In the spring of 1908, the Underwoods procured a seven-horsepower motorcycle engine to propel their airship to even greater heights. Although the motor was coupled with a 10-foot diameter four-blade bamboo and canvas propeller, placed front and centre of the wing, the motor was just too small for the job. Coupled with an inefficient propeller, it was able to taxi at good speed but remained grounded.

The airstrip that the brothers prepared for the craft was another Canadian first. The perfectly smoothed and rolled earth measured 20 rods by 80 rods (330 feet by 1 320 feet) and ran beside a field of summer-fallow next to the Krugerville country road.

The Underwoods realized they required a more powerful engine. From the Curtiss Motorcycle company in Hammondsport, New York, they received a quotation of $1 300 for a (specified) eight-cylinder, 40-horsepower engine. That kind of money was out of the range of most prairie farmers, and the Underwoods were no exception.

Everyone who knew of the airship wanted it to work. A local member of parliament spoke about the Underwoods' predicament in Ottawa, and suggested a bill be passed that would allow any motor purchased in the United States to be imported to Canada duty-free. That idea hit the ground faster than the Underwoods' airship.

The Underwood Airship, taken in 1907.
Howard Underwood Collection

And so, while the Underwood machine

remained a glorified kite, they still had a lot of fun with it. At night when wind conditions were right, the brothers would mount lanterns beneath the craft and send it up for a flight. A stranger travelling the lonely road would be amazed to see lights bobbing eerily in the night sky, swinging and swaying with the wind.

But one day the fun, and the legends, came to an end. The rope that had previously been used to tether the craft had broken, and the brothers used in its stead some barbed wire. A fierce wind caused the wire to become tangled and the kite smashed to the ground, rolled over and played dead (Footnote 2).

No one had the heart to restore it. The novelty of the airship had worn off. Other – funded – experiments had allowed inventors to bypass the abilities of the Underwood craft. And so the brothers gathered up the remains of their machine and piled them beside the barn.

Around that time, 1908, John K., along with his sons George and Johny, moved back to the U.S., settling in Kansas. Elmer stayed, married and raised his family on the original homestead until 1915 when they bought another piece of land northwest of Botha.

In hindsight, the Underwood airship was an ingenious idea, designed by skilled, but underfinanced, inventors. Botha's local history book, *Botha Memories*, sums up the community's long-standing pride in the project:

> The flying models made by the Underwoods proved, beyond all doubts, that their design was airworthy, and later the stability and powerful lift which the full-sized machine exerted was demonstrated in many tests they conducted when flying it as a kite. It is frustrating to think that another thousand dollars might have put the Underwood brothers in the front ranks of the world's aerial pioneers (p. 91).

In 1979, two Edmonton schoolteachers, Gary Kozens and Bob Fix, became interested in the Underwoods' story. Kozens interviewed Johny Underwood, the last surviving inventor, at his home in California and came away amazed at the cleverness of the brothers and their invention.

"I'm intrigued with the Underwoods, because not one of those boys could have invented their airplane alone," said Kozens in an Edmonton *Journal* article dated March 3, 1985. "They had a collective genius and a great respect for each other's talents." Kozens and Fix agree that the Underwoods' inventions and experiments with flying machines have been sadly overlooked. "It's a tragic affair," said Kozens. "John is gone now, and the story is going to dry up."

Kozens and Fix set about to turn the course of those events. Taking time off work, they researched the design and capabilities of the aircraft, conducted interviews with people who had seen the craft and also visited Johny. Their goal was to rebuild a replica, and to make a video of the process. But, like their predecessors, funding became the object and the "second Underwood Airship" remained grounded.

The legend lives on, locally through "kitchen-table talk" in the Stettler area, during the annual Underwood Aviation Days sponsored by the Village of Botha, through the determination of people like Kozens and Fix, and by others who like to research old stories and write new ones (Footnote 3).

The Underwoods would have no objection to our retelling their story. That's what legends are for.

Footnote 1:

In 1899, the Wright brothers had begun their experiments with a five-foot biplane kite. In 1900 and 1901, they had graduated to ever-larger manned gliders. Then they began testing wing models, and discovered the effect of air pressure on curved surfaces. From that point on, they experimented with powered aircraft.

Footnote 2:

Gary Kozens, an aviation enthusiast from Edmonton, describes the last flight of the Underwood airship:

> "On that last fateful day, the wind abruptly stopped. John decided he was going to glide down, something he had done many times in the past. But the tether-line wrapped itself around a fence post and flipped the plane upside down. It came crashing down to earth" (Edmonton *Journal*, March 3, 1985).

Footnote 3:

Further stories on the Underwood Airship can be found in the following books & periodicals:

Ellis, Frank H., *Canada's Flying Heritage*. U. of T. Press, Toronto, 1954;

Myers, Patricia A., *Sky Riders, An Illustrated History of Aviation in Alberta, 1906-1945*, Fifth House Publishers/Friends of Reynolds-Alberta Museum Society, 1995; pp. 15, 16.

Botha Memories, "Underwood's Flying Machine," p. 90, 91; and "The Underwood Family," pp. 468-470.

Alberta History (Spring, 1995), "Alberta's First Airplane" by Hugh A. Dempsey, pp. 9-10.

Newspapers: Stettler *Independent* (August 27 and October 8, 1907; July 4, 1979; and July 25, 1984); and

Edmonton *Journal*, "Forgotten Riders of the Alberta Sky" by Damian Inwood, June 30, 1979; and "Flying saucer of Krugerville Corners" by Linda Goyette, March 3, 1985.

The Thin Edge of the Wedge

"Wildlife and people,
they act like they got a war on
- but it's kind of one-sided."
Excerpt from a Peace Country student's essay
titled, "What Wildlife Means to Me."

For most of his 84 years, Leo Rutledge has lived in the bush country of northern British Columbia. He's been a trapper, packer, outfitter, big-game guide, and more recently, an avowed environmentalist. Rutledge was instrumental in forming The Guide-Outfitters Association in British Columbia, and is author of *That Some May Follow, The History of Guide Outfitting in B.C.* (Footnote 1). An as-yet unpublished manuscript further details his experiences, and his views regarding past and current wilderness issues.

Leo Rutledge heading for the Peace River home cabin – but still three days to go – taken on the Clearwater River, 1945. *Leo Rutledge Collection*

"In my opinion, in the big-game outfitting business, if we'd never seen an airplane we'd have been a damned sight better off."

A strong statement, but Rutledge has no intention of backing down.

"We made just as much money before, and [aircraft] only caused more mechanization," he states. "One thing led to another. You get into aircraft, then you've got to get into fast communication –

you're into two-way radios so you can reach the world. You get an electrical power plant for a base camp; once you're into plug-ins, the whole thing gets more and more mechanized. The romance and the mystique are gone. And, as far as I was concerned, that's what it was all about."

Rutledge's hunting territory was located at the head of the Prophet and Muskwa rivers, southwest of Fort Nelson, B.C., on the Continental Divide. While he acknowledges that his view might be "a very old-fashioned way of looking at it," he maintains that as long as the outfitters used horses to pack long distances, the client enjoyed a lifetime experience.

"Now it's just a mechanized assembly line for the express purpose of killing – that's what it's all about – and the aircraft was the thin edge of the wedge. That's my opinion."

In the old days, it took 14 days for Rutledge to get his client to the head of the Prophet and Muskwa, and 14 days to come out again.

"Now, the outfitters fly their hunter in, along with his sophisticated artillery that he shoots with, the optical equipment and the whole bit," says Rutledge. "There's nothing he does that an eight-year-old boy or girl couldn't go out there and do with a few hours' training."

Outfitters in northern British Columbia didn't come into contact with aircraft until well after the war, in the late 1940s and early 1950s. Rutledge found himself "forced" into using aircraft more and more often.

Some of the outfitters started using aircraft on floats if they had lakes in their areas. This would eliminate the need to pack their clients in to the territory by horseback from the highway, allowing them to book shorter hunts than an outfitter whose territory lacked such access.

"These outfitters could offer just as good a hunt as I could for less money because it would involve less time," Rutledge says. "After all, it is a business, that's all there is to it. In order to compete and stay abreast of things I had to get into aircraft, too. But I had no lakes so I had to use wheel aircraft.

"I had to build a landing strip. I picked a place where it wouldn't be too much work because I didn't have any bulldozers, graders, or any machinery in there. I had four packhorses that I could hang harness on – they were just little Cayuses but they were harness-broke – and I hired Jimmy Anderson to fly in some harness and collars, double-trees, single-trees, various hardware, small things that could just be thrown out of the aircraft."

Jimmy Anderson lives at Mile 147 of the Alaska Highway (Pink Mountain), across the road from a 6 000 foot airstrip built during construction of the highway. He became the pilot Rutledge most often hired.

Jimmy "Midnight" Anderson, who acquired his nickname from his penchant and ability to fly at night, operated a Super Cub on wide "tundra" tires, and would take on jobs that were of little interest to more commercial pilots. As an bonus, he'd usually add a spirit of adventure to the job (Footnote 2).

Rutledge recalls that Anderson was a master at throwing cargo down in one pile. "He'd throw out so much, then zoom, he'd make another circle and throw out some more, and each pile would land just about one on top of the other."

Rutledge and his helpers made a small horse-drawn grader, and planned to use a three-horse slip to move the dirt, similar to the model once used to build railroads across Canada. The problem was getting this contraption into the airplane. When he and Jimmy finally managed that part of the job, they realized there was no hope of shutting the door.

"I had to sit underneath this big hunk of iron for the flight out to the territory," Rutledge says. "I couldn't see a thing, but when Jimmy suddenly cried, 'Now!' I pushed it out."

Amazingly, the huge piece of iron landed perfectly – along with the other hardware.

From there, Rutledge and his Indian helpers built an airstrip 1 900 feet long, wide open with no trees on either end.

"It was later used to land some pretty hot aircraft. The commercial flyers never complained about that strip. It was very successful."

Leo Rutledge, 1965. *Leo Rutledge Collection*

With the professional aviation companies, the guide-outfitters would have to set up their schedules to the hour, perhaps months ahead, Rutledge explains. "That's the way it had to be if it was going to function smoothly for me, for the air company, and for the clients. But during the off-season when we outfitters would go in to our camps to do some work, or to check our horses, we'd hire local pilots."

One year, it was very late in the season when Rutledge brought his hunting party out of the high country. They were still looking for a caribou. Although the weather was becoming cold, Rutledge knew there were lots of caribou on Klingzut Mountain. He hired Jimmy Anderson to fly his guide and a hunter out to the mountain in the morning, with arrangements to pick them up later that afternoon.

Then the weather "closed in," combined with early darkness. There was no sign of Jimmy returning with the guide and hunter, but Rutledge wasn't overly concerned. He knew his guide was capable and wouldn't just sit up there and freeze to death. They'd likely wait at the appointed spot, then head for timber and get a fire going. They could boil up some tea, eat the meagre supplies they'd brought, and try to get some sleep as they waited for rescue in the morning. "Supper won't amount to much, and they won't have the best sleep in the world, but nothing bad will happen to them," Rutledge thought.

"It turned into one hell of a night, snowing and blowing," Rutledge recalls. "It was bad enough on the relatively low area of the highway, but I knew it would be 10 times worse up on the mountain."

To Rutledge's amazement, he heard the drone of the Super Cub. It was Jimmy, flying back from the mountains with the hunter and guide aboard. Jimmy had felt badly about the men being stuck up on the mountain on such a night, and had decided he should at least make an attempt to pick them up.

"Jimmy had taken off, after he got himself hyped properly, and he brought them in!" Rutledge marvels.

The story contained its usual component of drama. Jimmy hadn't been able to shut off the engine for fear that the airplane would blow off the mountain.

"It was dark, a gale was blowing, and he'd landed right on top of the mountain. God knows how hard the wind was screeching up there! But he kept the plane sitting still with the motor wide open to hold it while they got in."

Rutledge is the first to agree that Jimmy "Midnight" Anderson has been blessed, when one considers the risks he's taken and the conditions under which he's flown. "But, he always did the right thing by me. I feel my life is better for knowing Jimmy," Rutledge says.

In the early days in the Peace River valley, most people ran horses wherever they felt like, stallions as well as mares. As settlers started to trickle in, they expected others to fence in their horses. Before that, if people had fields they fenced the horses out, but the new settlers couldn't see why they should have to fence their fields and let the horses run wild.

Rutledge decided it was time for him and his horses to move. He knew of a flat piece of land near the Prophet River, half-way between his home place of Hudson's Hope, B.C., and the Yukon. During the

Leo Rutledge on the upper Peace River, before the construction of the W.A.C. Bennett and Peace Canyon dams. *Leo Rutledge Collection*

early 1960s, the government was giving this land away "like popcorn." Rutledge applied for three sections, nearly 2 000 acres, that would give him a base. "Then I'd have a million unoccupied acres surrounding it, and I wouldn't have to fence."

He moved up his horses, and began to consider how he could fulfil his obligations to the government to make "improvements" that would give him title to the land.

The three-section area was fairly open, as "the Indians had run innumerable fires on it throughout the years." Rutledge brought in a small truckload of grass seed, hauling it in from the Alaska Highway by snowmobile during the winter. Then he made a deal with Jimmy Anderson to fly in.

They loaded as much seed as possible inside the plane, and took off. Rutledge sat in the back, throwing grass seed by hand out the window.

"When I finally ran out of seed, Jimmy and I agreed that we had the 2 000 acres pretty-well covered. The name of the game was to get title to the property through making improvements, so on the application form I stated that I'd just seeded 2 000 acres!

"It was all true, you understand," Rutledge smiles. "Whether anything grew or not didn't matter because the natural growth was there anyway. My statement seemed to satisfy the government. I got the title."

Rutledge moved between 75 and 100 head of horses up to this land, and built a kind of a "cowboy shack" to stay in when he was checking the horses, rounding them up and so on.

But that first winter turned out to be a tough one, and mid-season Rutledge decided he should make a trip to check on his horses. The easiest way was to travel by truck up to Mile 147, and hire Jimmy Anderson to fly him in.

"Oh, yeah," Jimmy said, "no problem. I can take you up."

Rutledge looked over at the little frozen Super Cub. The thermometer was hanging around 40 degrees below zero and the airplane was sitting outside. That didn't seem to bother Jimmy. He began immediately to tinker with the engine. The weather couldn't have been more cold and miserable, and the tinkering went on and on. He couldn't seem to get it started.

Rutledge was having second thoughts about flying under such conditions. "Forget it, Jimmy. I'll wheel up the highway and snowshoe in to where the horses are. It's only five or six miles off the highway."

Author Shirlee Smith Matheson and pilot Jimmy "Midnight" Anderson in his Piper Cherokee 6-300 at his home at Mile 147 Alaska Highway (Pink Mountain, B.C.), 1992. *Photo: Bill Matheson*

"Oh, no, we'll get 'er going," Jimmy insisted, and bent again to the task.

Again, Rutledge tried to talk him out of it. Besides the obvious hardship he was putting Jimmy through, Leo himself was becoming uneasy. "Supposing he gets this engine coughing – how safe is it going to be up there?" he wondered. "I've heard of air-locks – what about an ice-lock?"

But there was no stopping Jimmy. Rutledge had known that the way to get him to do something was to tell him it couldn't be done, and now he was stuck with it.

Finally Jimmy got the engine going. He jumped in, took off and went straight up, full bore. The plane kind of hovered for a second, flopped over, and vroom! screeched back down.

Jimmy got out and grinned over at Leo. "You think she'll make 'er alright?"

"Yeah. I guess you've shown me that it's airworthy," Rutledge said with a weak smile.

Their trip went smoothly. Jimmy landed on skis, and even had time to join Leo for a quick cup of coffee in the shack before the engine cooled. Then he took off in a cloud of frost and snow. Rutledge looked at the thermometer hanging outside the shack: 56 degrees below zero!

"There's only one Jimmy," Rutledge says, and adds in an understatement: "They threw the cast away when they made him."

At times, outfitters hired pilots to fly them over their territory so they could spot their horses from the air, but Rutledge says it was not always easy to find them. "In the overall, year in and year out, outfitters lose a hell of a pile of horses. They starve to death. Of course the wolves get quite a few, but these horses that run wild, they'll put up a pretty fair fight against wolves. The northern bush is not a natural environment for them, too tough, and the outfitters aren't there to watch them. Once the horses get snowed in it can be hard to get them out. Sometimes you *can't* get them out."

By hiring aircraft, the outfitters could drop protein blocks to the horses. "They're not much bigger than salt blocks and you can throw them out of the aircraft. They help somewhat. But you wouldn't believe the hundreds and hundreds of horses that starve to death in this country."

While Rutledge personally admires the dexterity of bush pilots and the ways that aviation has made remote areas more accessible, he also feels that the negative impact of aviation on the northern environment, and on the wildlife population, must be considered. In fact, Rutledge has observed and come to criticize many of the current practices.

"Aviation brings in customers more quickly, and the whole management system of big game has changed. The way it was before, we didn't kill very many animals because we were packing and travelling most of the time.

"You're probably quite aware that they shot 1 000 wolves out of helicopters here not long ago, out of Fort St. John and Fort Nelson." (Footnote 3).

Air transportation has a darker side, and controversy abounds as it does when culture, economy and ideologies collide.

Helicopters, Rutledge says, were the "flavor of the day" for such kills. Fixed-wing aircraft were used for scouting or spotting the animals, then helicopters came directly to the site. "They reduced the wolves, certainly, and the animals that the wolves would have eaten were available then for the outfitters' clients," Rutledge says. "That's what it was all about" (Footnote 4).

Rutledge scoffs at the term "wildlife management" used by government biologists to justify widespread distribution of poisons.

"First we had wolf bounties in British Columbia, where you killed them and got, I think, $10 per pelt. We used to bring them in to Fort St. John and they'd just throw the pelts into the fire. I saw that big pot-bellied wood stove glow red, burning up bountied wolf hides." Those were the days of the government's bounty binge (late 1940s, and 1950s): $1 for eagle heads, $10 or $20 for wolf hides, $40 for cougar, and so on, Rutledge says.

"Then they got into strychnine, and it's pretty fierce."

Sometimes the strychnine was dropped from aircraft, and other times outfitters or trappers applied it themselves, from the ground. "At one time, you could go into a drugstore and, so help me, tell the druggist that a pack-rat was the bane of your love life and walk out of there with enough strychnine to sterilize a township! I have some strychnine right here that I got under those conditions. I never used a single crystal of it, but I've got it.

"And then they got into a poison called 1080 [sodium fluoro-acetate]. It was supposedly selective to killing canines, the dog family only." In 1980, the British Columbia government sanctioned the use of the pesticide 1080 for a wolf-kill project (Footnote 5).

Past efforts of poisoning wolves were hampered by inadequate means of distributing poison baits, but this was overcome by the use of airplanes, helicopters and snowmobiles. The poisons used most commonly for destroying wolves were strychnine, cyanide, fluorine-acetate of barium and sodium fluoro-acetate (compound 1080) (Footnote 6).

"Then the Fish and Wildlife branch in British Columbia went hog-wild with the idea of poisoning from the air," Rutledge continues. "They bought horses from anybody who had horses they didn't want anymore, killed them, and pumped them full of this 1080 compound while the horses were still quivering. They used needles about 18 inches long – I think they were actually bacon needles, almost a quarter of an inch thick – to pump the meat full of this poison and then throw it out of airplanes. This is the Fish and Wildlife branch! This is *wildlife management!*

"The idea was, I suppose, to get the poison to percolate quickly through the meat," Rutledge continues. "Certainly the wolf population declined. I don't know how many horses they killed and poisoned here. I was talking to an old game warden along the Yellowhead who was part of it and he said in the 1950s they'd killed 75 head of horses and poisoned them, through the Chilkootin and Caribou, and north to Telegraph Creek."

Pilot Mike Thomas (now of LaRonge, Saskatchewan), recalls buffalo meat poisoned with 1080 being used for this purpose. "Because I was curious as to its effect, I would sometimes fly back over the drop sites several days later to see if I could spot kills," Thomas says. "I saw everything lying dead – marten, fisher, mink, squirrels, birds, you name it. Even some wolves" (Footnote 7).

At that point, Rutledge says, the environmentalists got hold of it, "and there was a hell of an uproar. The system was at least modified, and that's when they started shooting the wolves from the air. I believe they killed 996 over a fairly short period. The story hit the press in February, 1984. Before that, it was a hush-hush thing."

And "hit the press" it did. Print, radio and television media across Canada sent reporters up to Fort St. John and Fort Nelson to cover the "war on wolves." The government's plan was to kill up to 500 wolves in a 14 000 square kilometre (8 680 sq. miles) area in an effort to restore big game herds, which the branch said had been reduced by an over-population of wolves. B.C. environmentalist Paul Watson disagreed, saying the purpose of the kill was to turn the valley into an elk and stone sheep farm for hunters, thereby benefitting a local resort operator who catered to big-game hunters (Calgary *Herald*, Feb. 13/84).

The wolf-war came to a climax when Watson and his crew arrived to expose and hopefully stop the carnage through their "Project Wolf."

Watson planned to run interference ahead of the helicopter used by the Fish and Wildlife branch biologists, by scaring the wolves out of open areas and into cover before the hunters turned up. But, Watson was unable to buy aviation fuel at the Fort Nelson airport for his chartered twin-engined Piper Najavo airplane. Finally, orders came from Imperial Oil company's head office in Vancouver to "fill him up." The company spokesman was quoted as saying that while he sympathized with the local dealer's personal objection to Watson's campaign, it would be "totally inappropriate for the company to take a position on that" (Canadian Press, published in Calgary *Herald*, February 8, 1984). Fourteen wolves were killed the day the article was published.

Next, Watson and crew were refused accommodation at Fort Nelson hotels. Some crew members camped in the backyard of a local sympathizer, until they were finally allowed to book rooms in a hotel. Ironically, the hotel was owned by a hunter and businessman who also owned the ranch in the remote Kechika Valley where the government's wolf-kill team was camped (ibid).

Then came "engine trouble" with the airplanes and helicopters that Watson attempted to rent. Treks into the wilderness by the environmentalists were laughed at by locals, who said they were under-supplied and had totally underestimated the environment they were there to protect. Watson and his crew finally left the area on February 15, 1984, after mass media coverage had succeeded in exposing the violence associated not only with the actual kill, but also had unfortunately pitted neighbor against neighbor.

Leo Rutledge says that he lost all respect for the Fish and Wildlife branch in British Columbia over the wolf-kill programs of the 1970s and 1980s. He has little respect for outfitters, either, as far wildlife management goes. "It's dollar-controlled. That's the whole problem.

"They love the word 'harvesting'," Rutledge says. "Whenever anything is killed, legally, it's a harvest. But when wolves kill anything, it's a slaughter. Wolves slaughter, invariably. People never slaughter. And they *never* kill" (Footnote 8).

John P. Elliott (Regional Wildlife Biologist, Peace SubRegion, B.C. Environment), in a letter to the author dated May 10, 1995, defends his programs:

> For some ten years in the late 1970s and into the 1980s, this branch had a program which selectively (and humanely) removed specific wolves. In this area there are some 2 000 to 5 000 wolves producing some 2 000 to 5 000 pups per year, so you will realize that removal of some 100 per year had but very localized and short term effects. Regardless the change in ungulate survival was startling with chosen populations switching from decline to increase . . .
>
> The philosophical question was less clear. Some feel that with all the alteration of natural systems due to industrial activity, it is appropriate to have a few key capability areas which sustain higher numbers of animals (both prey species and the predator . . .) thus providing a better buffer against genetic loss. Others feel that man has already done enough damage through industrial activity and any further tinkering can only be negative. There is some merit to both views.

Some pilots will agree with Leo Rutledge that aviation was "the thin edge of the wedge" to put undue pressure on the ecosystem, and acknowledge their part in the complex drama. Working pilots, however, are often hesitant to shine a negative light on aviation's connection to such issues. But after retirement, or when they no longer depend on flying contracts, many pilots tell stories that corroborate Rutledge's views.

Most of Leo Rutledge's life has been spent working in the bush. It's given him ample time to observe nature's balance and consider how past knowledge could work with present practice to conserve our natural heritage. But can a person make a living by going back to the old ways? Can someone in a business such as guiding and outfitting hold onto the romance, the mystique and still make a dollar?

"You can't. That's the way it is. Aviation is the new system of doing things, and it's here to stay," Rutledge says. "The direction things are going in the new days may be interesting, but they'll sure be different.

"Unfortunately, 100 years ago British Columbia's game department went down the wrong path – and never left it. To it, there were two kinds of wildlife: the 'good' and the 'bad.' The bad were bad because they might kill the good ones before the 'sportsmen' of the day could."

Leo Rutledge himself is following new trails. He is knee-deep in attempts to develop a "Land and Resource Management Plan and Protected Areas Strategy" for Canada's northern Rockies. The plan hopes to protect the area by creation of a national park along the Rocky Mountains from the Peace to the Liard rivers, establish permanent protection for the Muskwa-Kechika region, and set aside the Redfern Lake area as a limited access tourist draw. This would place large tracts of land (a bit less than the Banff-Jasper National Parks combined) off-limits to industrial development, and tightly control against exploitation by tourism, logging, or oil and gas extraction methods such as the controversial "helicopter-portable" drilling.

In a position paper prepared by Rutledge on behalf of the LRMP, he states the case for implementing the plan:

"Following the game department's outlawed bounty and poison binges, the department became airborne, and again its 'vermin wars' were successful. Ably assisted by the gun clubs and the guiding industry's aircraft armada, the game department's helicopters gunned down a thousand wolves before being brought to earth and grounded by a B.C. Supreme Court ruling. In so many words, 'Enough is enough,' said Madam Justice Carol Huddart" (Footnote 9).

Rutledge lists other systems now being practiced (such as opening wolf-kill seasons and bag limits), and those being studied for future use (such as wolf sterilization, presumably by substance ingestion).

"So there you have the game department's sorry 100-year saga," Rutledge concludes, "and I have lived to see the last 70 years of it."

This is why he advocates the creation of a national park in Canada's northern Rockies where no sport hunting is allowed. "I simply refuse to believe that wildlife custodianship by bounties, poisons, aerial strafing, radio collaring, substance darting, netting, transplanting and general hell-raising, plus deliberately torching the countryside, is acceptable wildlife and wilderness custodianship," he says.

"While this may be [approved] by the game department, the guiding industry, the sport hunting fraternity, and all those striving so diligently to churn out shootables for the guns of autumn, it makes mockery of bio-diversity."

You can see that the northeast's land use issue is beginning to simmer, says Rutledge in a letter to the author dated April 10, 1995. "Like the wolf-kill programs, like the hydro-electric dam projects on the Peace River, it bodes to become a potboiler. Hope so. Perhaps the best story is yet to come."

Footnote 1:

Rutledge, Leo: *That Some May Follow, The History of Guide Outfitting in B.C.*, The Guide Outfitters Association of British Columbia, Box 759, 100 Mile House, B.C., VOK 2EO.

Footnote 2:

See *Flying the Frontiers, Vol. I*, Fifth House Publishers, Saskatoon, Sask., 1994, for story on Jimmy Anderson titled "The Jackpine Savage."

Footnote 3

Hummel, Monte, and Pettigrew, Sherry: *Wild Hunters, Predators in Peril,* Key Porter Books Limited, Toronto, 1991.

The authors state: "When wolf-control programs are intended to kill a large percentage, typically 60 to 80 percent of the wolf population in an entire region, then the impact can be more serious. In northeastern British Columbia, for example, a wolf-control program resulted in killing 1,000 wolves over five years in a specific area" (p. 111/112).

Footnote 4:

A number of authors whose interest lay in wildlife issues reflect Rutledge's observations. Naturalist Dick Dekker, in his book, *Wild Hunters, Adventures with wolves, foxes, eagles and falcons based on 25 years of field observation,* (Canadian Wolf Defenders, Edmonton, Alberta, 1985) discusses what he calls "the poison years."

> A new wave of wolf killings on wilderness lands began in the 1950s, and again the rationale seemed solid and above question: rabies was prevalent among northern canids and believed to pose a threat to humans. Aircraft were used for large-scale distribution of poison baits across the northwest.
>
> During the poison years, when wolves were destroyed on a large scale, populations of hoofed mammals built up and reached high levels, especially after a series of mild winters. Big game hunting for both subsistence and recreation greatly increased. Tourism was a growth industry. All across the northwest, licensed guides and outfitters opened fly-in hunting camps for wealthy clients from around the world. (p. 21)

Footnote 5:

An article released by Canadian Press (published in the Calgary *Herald* January 15, 1980) states:

> Approximately 200 wolves will be shot, trapped or poisoned this year to protect livestock, Environment Minister Steve Rogers said Tuesday. Rogers said he has ordered the fish and wildlife branch to reapply for a permit to use the pesticide 1080 under strict controls for predator control where hunting and trapping have failed.
>
> The Pesticide Control Appeal Board rejected an earlier ministry request, saying the application should be more specific as to where the poison would be used. A blanket permit originally was requested, Rogers said, because problems with predators, usually wolves and coyotes, can develop almost anywhere livestock is raised.

Dick Dekker *(Footnote 4 above)* describes the effects of compound 1080:

> Compound 1080 (sodium fluoro-acetate) pollutes every bit of the bait, as the poison is injected into the meat. It does not kill quickly. Mammals and birds that have eaten a lethal amount will have

time to slink away before dying a miserable death. If they are found and utilized by other predators and scavengers, which is nature's plan for the dead, they too may die, for the intestines remain toxic, with the poison concentrated in stomach contents. The trail of a dying animal becomes a trail of death if it has vomited frequently (ibid. p.26).

Footnote 6:

Mech, L. David, *The Wolf: The Ecology and Behaviour of an Endangered Species,* The Natural History Press, NY, 1970, p. 331.

Footnote 7:

Similar stories are revealed by author Barry Holstun Lopez in his book, *Of Wolves and Men* (Charles Scribner's Sons, New York, 1978) in his analysis of "the wolf war" that swept across North America.

> The final act of the wolf war in North America was staged in Canada in the 1950s. Between 1951 and 1961, 17 500 wolves were poisoned. In 1955, when most of the wolf range in northern Canada was covered with poison bait stations (some of them poisoned wolf carcasses) served by airplane, the take reached 2 000 animals a year. Some attempt was made to keep the baits in areas where they would not harm other wildlife. Nevertheless, in one area, from 1955 to 1959, 496 red fox, 105 arctic fox, and 385 wolverines were killed, along with 3 417 wolves (p. 194).

Footnote 8:

Rutledge's observations are substantiated by Dick Dekker's chapter (from his book, *Wild Hunters*) titled "The Poison Years" (see also *Footnote 7*).

Dekker states:

> [During] an intensive poison campaign to combat rabies that began in 1952 and lasted four years, the province of Alberta made the decision to exterminate all wild canids near settled areas. A fantastic amount of poison was distributed to trappers and landowners: 39 960 cyanide guns, 106 100 cyanide cartridges and 628 000 strychnine pellets. In addition, the number of "1080" bait stations expanded from 25 in 1953, to 800 in 1956. During a four-year period, an estimated 171 000 coyotes, 55 500 foxes and 5 200 wolves were destroyed (ibid., p. 24).

Lopez agrees with Dekker's statements. "In all that time," says Lopez, "exactly one rabid wolf was diagnosed, in 1952." (Lopez, p. 195).

Footnote 9:

> Madam Justice Carol Huddart on Monday (March 7/88) threw out government permits authorizing a wolf kill in northeastern British Columbia, saying the province gave too much discretionary power to a civil servant to apply laws regarding hunting animals from aircraft. . . . In Victoria, Environment Minister Bruce Strachan said he was surprised by the court ruling because the same permit has been used successfully for four years. He said that unless a new permit is written quickly and the weather remains cold, "this could really kill the program for this year."
>
> Vancouver (CP) – *Alaska Highway News*, March 8, 1988

A Bunch of the Boys Were Whooping It Up . . .

Robert Service was right. When the boys get together they whoop it up, even though Roy Staniland's Calgary home doesn't quite match the atmosphere of the Malamute Saloon, and the boys are, well, a bit more refined than Dangerous Dan McGrew and other Yukon gold seekers in Service's poems. But there's still the camaraderie, still the sense of seeking adventure, and, for the most part, of finding it.

Roy Staniland, Hal Rainforth and Bill Watts have all logged their time in the air. Where they differ is how they got into flying, where it took them and how they used their experiences to further their careers. All were Alberta-born and remained based in the province, flying various types of aircraft to all sorts of places.

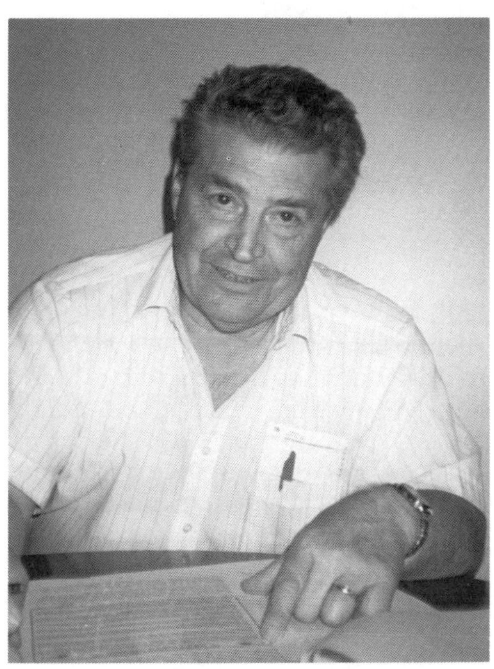

Roy Staniland, 1993. *Photo: S. Matheson*

Norman Roy Staniland "backed into" a flying career. "It's not something I thought I'd be doing for the rest of my life," he says. "For me, it was a happening – being in the right place at the right time. In the late 1940s there were a tremendous number of qualified ex-service people who'd had good training and certainly a lot more experience than I did. If I'd been competing head-to-head for a flying job, I'd never have gotten it."

Staniland was working as an apprentice movie-theatre projectionist for his family-owned Roxy Circuit Theatres at the time he got his private pilot's licence. He eventually became a specialist in charter and contract flying and engineering, with fixed and rotary-wing aircraft, mostly in remote areas. He worked for a number of companies, including (and being part-owner of) Associated Helicopters, Gateway Aviation, Western Aero Renters, and later became Flight Safety Officer and Helicopter Project Specialist for Petro-Canada.

Hal Rainforth, 1995. *Photo: S. Matheson*

Harold "Hal" Earl Rainforth was born in Lacombe on February 22, 1943. His childhood dream of becoming a pilot prompted him to get his private pilot's licence in Red Deer while finishing high school in Lacombe. He took an aircraft maintenance course at Southern Alberta Institute of Technology in Calgary, apprenticed as an engineer for Piper, then worked out of Fort St. John, B.C., first as an engineer and then as a pilot, to eventually become General Manager, Aviation, for Petro-Canada in Calgary.

William "Bill" James Watts developed an interest in aviation during his first airplane ride in an open-cockpit American Eagle in 1928. He got his chance to fly by joining the RCAF, first learning the basics of Aero Engineer mechanics, then being remustered to Air Crew, finally getting his wings at No. 7 Service Flying Training School at Fort Macleod through the British Commonwealth Air Training Plan. Following the war he got his commercial licence, but decided to move into the management side of aviation as assistant manager of the Calgary Airport. In 1951 he resigned to become a corporate pilot for Pacific Petroleums, which took him to the developing oil fields of Fort St. John and points north, as well as south into the United States.

In 1958, Watts returned to airport management, becoming General Manager of the Calgary International Airport and bringing its facilities into the "jet age". He still flies his own private aircraft, as well as maintaining involvement in Calgary's Aero Space Museum and the Calgary Transportation Authority's general aviation committee.

Bill Watts, 1994. *Photo: S. Matheson*

Right now the three pilots are discussing the phenomenon of "cabin fever", which hits many people after being cooped up in isolated conditions. This can also affect pilots who are away from home and are flying in unforgiving territory for long stretches of time. What happens when a pilot gets cabin fever, begins to act strangely, loses his nerve? How can you tell when it's happening to you? Or, if you're an employer, how can you tell when it's happening to one of your staff members?

From Staniland's personal knowledge, cabin fever was not uncommon when he was flying in the 1950s and '60s. For helicopter pilots, the summer working season was short and intense, but would give them the winter off if they didn't also fly fixed-wing. During the three-to-four month summer period, however, they were in the field seven days a week.

"When I was working in Operations with Associated Helicopters, we found that our best indicator of a pilot getting cabin fever was the engineer," Staniland says. "We'd send out a team of a pilot and an engineer with a helicopter, because there was a significant amount of maintenance required on the aircraft over the season."

The engineer might grumble to the base manager about the pilot: "He's cranky, sullen, not communicating. He's bitchy and owly, getting strange." Such symptoms were the first indicators of problems.

"If you waited until the customer complained, it was very often beyond on-site solution. They would have lost confidence in him, and you had to remove him from the job," Staniland says. "If the engineers reported problems – and we had the benefit of having all permanent employees rather than contractors – these people had vested interests in the job, the company and their own well-being so they would be very quick to let us know. Then something could be done.

"I think it was a credit to management that they didn't look on this as a totally negative thing. They didn't hold it against the pilot, but gave him an opportunity for 'R and R' [rest and recreation]."

The employer would call in the pilot and ask discreet questions. It might be discovered that there were problems at home and they had begun to play on the pilot's mind. Fatigue could be another factor, from working long days during the North's almost 24-hour daylight. "Those are very significant factors and have probably been unidentified reasons why certain accidents, or non-performance, actually came about on the job.

"When you're in the field like that, fatigue is not readily acknowledged," Staniland says. "Most pilots would rather be flying than sitting around in a hot tent fighting bugs. So, from a stress level, depending on the type of work you're doing, sometimes you felt you were better off flying."

Rainforth agrees with this diagnosis. "There are two kinds of fatigue: mental and physical. Mental fatigue certainly can be a factor. One guy I knew who lost his nerve was running a Twin Otter. It first started, as I think back, when he was sent away from our home base, and he resented the move. We had a policy of two pilots per plane, and he didn't want another pilot with him.

"He didn't like the fact that we did a fair amount of training, every six months for sure and definitely before he did his instrument rides [Transport Canada flight tests] every year. He was very nervous about his instrument rides and he was performing worse and worse."

Then the pilot started having medical problems, such as ulcers.

"Like Roy said, the engineer let us know that there was some strange behavior going on. This pilot seemed to always have a tire go flat on the airplane. The crew would fill it up, or go out early in the morning to make sure the tires were good, then they'd go over to the coffee shop. One day they came back to the aircraft earlier than usual and caught the pilot letting the air out of his own tires! I don't know what he thought he'd prove. It was just irrational, because the plane was still going to go flying."

"That happened in the war a lot, too," Watts states, "where pilots had done a number of tours, and had been decorated with DFCs [Distinguished Flying Crosses] and so on. They'd finally reach the stage where they could not make one more trip and had to be rested."

This kind of behavior can embarrass the pilot who feels he's let down the gang. "You feel your image is shot," Rainforth says. "Pilots have a lot of macho image!"

Luckily, these problems often manifested themselves on the ground, seldom in the air.

"If you lost it in the air, panic would get you," Rainforth states. "But there's no special magic for flying. People think you've got to have good nerves, but that's not the case. If you don't have confidence, then you shouldn't be in the air in the first place. If you have confidence, you're not really going to be too uptight about the airplane."

Safety is a subject that is drummed into pilots' heads from their first day of ground school training. All three pilots admit, however, that they pulled some rather risky manoeuvres when they were younger, when nerves were made of steel and adventure was craved.

Watts says that the old World War II pilots who later became inspectors for the Department of Transport had a tendency to be more sympathetic to a pilot, and let him get away with some fairly flagrant violations. "Today, a lot of the inspectors are recent ex-air force. They're more militarily trained, more inclined to really throw the book at you."

Rainforth laments that the flying business has matured to a point where at times these regulations are counter-productive. "You have to spend a three-foot pile of money for a three-foot pile of safety, and then you've got to spend another three feet of money on top of that to get another inch of safety. Diminishing returns come in. We're getting so much stuff legislated.

"If you're a large corporation, you're going to meet up with the term, 'due diligence', to where it gets beyond reason. Suddenly you can't just go and get the job done."

He cites an example of a pilot on a trip with a G-1 (a 15-passenger turbo-prop Grumman Gulfstream) which had two fire warning systems on each engine. Every three or four months, one fire system would send out a false alarm; they'd shut down the engine and discharge the extinguisher, following the correct procedure. But when the airplane was on the ground and engineers tested it, the system always worked properly.

A pilot was en route to Norman Wells when the fire alarm sounded. He landed in Edmonton, the airplane was given an inspection on the ground and there was definitely no fire. He phoned Rainforth, asking what he should do (this type of call usually went to the chief pilot, but he was away at the time).

"What do *you* think you should do?" Rainforth asked.

"I think I should finish the trip. I've got another, stand-by, fire alarm system."

"That's what I would do – but I'm not going to ask you to do it. It's your choice – and I'll back you all the way."

Rainforth says it would have cost the company $13 000 and several hours to bring another airplane in to finish the trip. "But the decision to go on wasn't made just to save dollars. I thought, let's be real about this. The system had failed before they'd landed in Edmonton – they were landing there anyway; they'd made an inspection, and there was no fire. There was a stand-by system. So, he went on to Norman Wells and back.

"When the chief pilot and training pilot got hold of that, they jumped the guy. I said, 'No, he asked me and I gave him permission.' They kept giving me hell for many, many months. But somewhere there has to be a balance between what's real and what isn't."

Rainforth stresses that he is not talking about violations. "In the old days a pilot had freedom to fly using his judgement, and nobody knew better than the guy sitting in the seat just what his situation was. Nowadays it's got to the point where the airlines have operations manuals, and companies have operations and procedures manuals, and these must all be followed.

"If it made common sense to do it a little differently, you couldn't because you've got a copilot who's with the airline, unionized, and he's going to fink on you. You've got all these procedures in place that were designed by people sitting in an office – not in a cockpit. I'm not saying it's not necessary to have rules – if you've got 1 500 pilots there has to be a set-up for the weakest link – but to take away the ability for a person to use his or her own judgement sometimes takes away the ability to be cost-effective, too."

"Well, you know the three biggest lines," Bill Watts says. "'The cheque is in the mail,' 'Of course I'll respect you in the morning' and" – he pauses for effect – "'I'm from the Department of Transport and I'm here to help you!'" The pilots laugh, knowing how the two-edged sword of DOT (Department of Transport) regulations affects all people involved in aviation, whether they're a single bush operator, or a corporation.

"Yeah," says Rainforth with a smile, "except that the DOT don't make it out to the bush very often!"

Roy Staniland went from "show biz" to flying in one easy step. He was born in Edmonton on August 4, 1928, and grew up in the farming community of Barrhead, north of Edmonton. "My father was in the lumber business. He later had hotels in Camrose, Blackfalds, and Lacombe, and followed that by getting into the motion picture exhibiting business with theatres in Athabasca, Barrhead, Westlock, Edmonton, Leduc, Wetaskiwin and Red Deer."

One day a friend of Staniland's, Frank Holton, came back home to Westlock from his stint in the air force. Although Staniland had been too young to join up himself, he was thrilled by his friend's tales of flying Beaufighters in Burma.

"We teamed up and ultimately decided we could make a few dollars by buying a little airplane, so we bought a Piper J-3 Cub (CF-DCX)." Frank taught him to fly, although Staniland wasn't licensed at that time – "I didn't need a licence!" he laughs, "but I had to formalize it before long to keep the DOT off my tail."

He got his licence through Associated Airways Limited in Edmonton, in whose hangar they kept the J-3.

During 1947 and 1948 they flew to local fairs doing barnstorming and passenger hauls. "We'd go to Westlock or Athabasca and make arrangements to get some fuel from the Imperial Oil agent. If the weather was good, we'd fly passengers. One of us would go out and sell seats and the other would fly them around. We usually ended up paying for our gas and food, so to me it was a great time-builder.

"Frank ultimately got married. Because he then had to make an honest living, I ended up acquiring the airplane," Staniland says. "I'd lease it out once in a while, and I'd also fly it myself."

Staniland took flight aerobatics in 1948 from Al Laing, a former Battle of Britain pilot, on an old Tiger Moth and a Cornell out of the Edmonton Flying Club. "He put me through all the traditional routines. With a Tiger Moth, if you went into a roll and inverted it the engine would flutter. You'd have to come around again, get it started and go. The problems with both the Tiger and Cornell were that their rates of climb were so slow, you spent more time getting up to your altitude than doing the aerobatics. The Harvard changed that, with its power improvement."

Also while building up his time Staniland did a lot of timber-cruising in the Swan Hills and Fort Assiniboine areas. Very often there would be floods on the Freeman and the Athabasca rivers which meant the ferries were inoperable. Staniland was hired to air-drop food and supplies. The men said they were in need of food, supplies for the mill equipment – and snuff! They emphasized, "If you can't bring anything else, make sure you bring the snuff!"

Staniland recalls that it was a mixed blessing to get a larger airplane, because that meant he had to load and unload more freight. Boxes of snuff turned to machines, drill-bits, bags of cement and cases of canned goods, but he got into the business of commercial flying nevertheless.

Roy Staniland returning from timber cruising, Swan Hills, AB, in Piper Cub CF-DCX, 1947. *Roy Staniland Collection*

"Every once in a while, Associated Airways would run short of a pilot. Because I kept my airplane there and they'd taught me to fly, they would ask me to do the odd trip for them. It gave me a little money and the chance to fly different types of airplanes," Staniland says. "They were pretty good at checking me out on all the new equipment they had, as I became experienced enough and competent to fly. That worked out very well for me."

When he acquired his commercial licence, he came to the attention of the "movers and shakers" of Edmonton's aviation industry. In 1950 he was approached by Tommy Fox, pilot and owner of Associated Airways. "What are you going to do for a living, Roy? Are you going to fly for us, or are you going to keep playing around?"

Staniland decided to give commercial flying a try. The company based him in Edmonton, with duty tours to places like Fort Smith and Yellowknife, and checked him out on more equipment.

Hal Rainforth, having earned his private pilot's licence in 1961, the year he graduated from grade 12, followed that by attending technical school in Calgary to take a two-year course in Aircraft Maintenance. His first job was with Waskasoo Aviation, based at the little airport between Red Deer and Sylvan Lake in central Alberta. He continued to fly whenever he got the chance.

He next became an apprentice engineer for the Piper dealer in Calgary. "In those days there was lots going on, you could get all kinds of jobs." During the latter part of 1963 and in 1964, he worked for Trans Aircraft and prepared for his commercial licence.

Rainforth married Joan Klassen in 1965. Things were not easy, financially, for the young couple. "You spend a lot of time being broke if you want to be a pilot. I was employed all the time but we didn't have much money."

He hadn't quite finished his commercial flying course when he was offered a job in Fort St. John, B.C., as an engineer for Jim Burrows of Executive Air Services. "He had an Aztec, a Cessna 206, and a Dornier aircraft that he leased from Don Hamilton. I wanted to fly and he promised me I'd get in a bunch of flying hours up there, but I ended up working as an engineer – a 24-hour-a-day job.

"When winter came there was no heat in the hangar. It was colder than outside and my fingers stuck to everything. When that old hangar burned down I was delighted to see it go."

Rainforth completed requirements for his commercial pilot's licence with Fort St. John Aviation while working full-time as an engineer. "But Burrows never did let me fly airplanes because there was too much maintenance to do. He needed three engineers, not one."

Finally Rainforth got a chance to come back to Red Deer to work for Pat Johnson, owner of Johnson Air Services. His first job was flying fishermen and hunters north of Hinton for a guide and outfitter, which he enjoyed immensely.

"It was beautiful. I'd land with the Stinson on wheels at a forestry strip in the area of Grande Cache. There was no town at the time, and there were wild horses up there."

When Johnson Air Services decided to buy out Waskasoo Aviation, they were lacking an engineer. Rainforth was asked to fill this position. Back to maintenance. "Every once in a while I'd get depressed and I'd fly down the river, go someplace and have lunch, and come home. Then I'd be able to work for the rest of the week."

At that point, he also got his instructor's rating. When he finished his test in Calgary, he was so elated that he flew back to Clive and "shot up the family farm," (meaning he flew low over the farmyard). "Well, I was just celebrating a little bit. I buzzed my dad's place, just fooling around."

The only ones not impressed with the local hero were the chickens.

Bill Watts laughs. "That's the first thing you'd do when you got your licence in the air force, you would go 'shoot up' someone's farm. But you'd look back to see how you were doing, then sometimes stall, and that would be it."

"A lot of them killed themselves that way," Staniland adds.

"I'd go through, then pull straight up, kick it over and turn back," Rainforth says. "Actually, the way the Stinson worked, you came back at 90-degrees, so you were continuously doing a clover-leaf."

"Don't forget, Hal, you'd done crop spraying too, so you knew how to operate it," Staniland clarifies.

"No, I did crop spraying after that!" Rainforth says.

For one summer, Rainforth crop-sprayed for Evans Air at Stettler. "That was a real hoot, a lot of fun. In a little Super Cub I could leave the doors open when I was flying, and smell the trees and the flowers as I was going along."

"And the chemicals," Watts adds.

"Yes. But with everything open you really didn't get the chemicals on you unless it was calm and there was no breeze. When you came on your pass-back you'd get some of the spray that you'd put out the time before.

"It was a lot of fun, going over the country doing that work," Rainforth recalls. "Power lines were easier to fly under than they were to fly over. You just had to be high enough to miss the fence – that gave you a reference. If you went over the Power lines you didn't really have a reference – and you couldn't afford to be too high above them because then you wasted too much field trying to get down."

The spraying job began around five o'clock in the morning, ceased during the hot mid-day hours, and recommenced in the evening. "But," Rainforth laughs, "you didn't get a lot of sleep. If you'd been spraying some hilly fields, you'd dream at night that you were up there. The bed would move up and down and you could see the rows of grain going under your wheels! All day long, and all night long!"

Bill Watts was born in Calgary on June 13, 1914, and grew up in the city. Following his momentous airplane ride in the American Eagle biplane, he continued to pay for rides in de Havilland Puss Moths, Cirrus Moths, Stinsons and Curtiss Robins – at the going rate of one cent per pound of the passenger's weight – when pilots would come to town for air shows. The young man's thrill-seeking spirit was fed by riding his 1928 Indian Scout motorcycle.

When war was declared in 1939, Watts joined the RCAF as an aero-engineer mechanic. In January, 1941, Bill married Ethel Mitchell from Drumheller (who passed away in 1974). While in the service, Watts vowed to become a pilot. He took his elementary flying training at Abbotsford, B.C., where Floyd Glass was the chief flying instructor, and in April, 1944, he received his wings. He then worked as staff pilot at Number 1 Central Navigation School at Rivers, Manitoba. Following his discharge from the RCAF in October, 1945, he obtained his commercial pilot's licence, which he still holds.

The Calgary International Airport had been opened at its present site in 1939 with the advent of trans-continental passenger service. At the start of the war, the Department of Transport took over airport management from the city. On December 10th, 1945, Bill Watts started working as Airport Attendant Grade II, for airport manager Cyril Huntley (and later, George Craig). Neither Watts nor Craig knew much about airport management so they learned by asking questions and then by doing the job. They "grew" with the airport, when the first flying schools, as well as increased commercial and corporate aviation, began in earnest after the war.

Flying Officer Bill Watts, in a Mark V Anson at Central Navigation School, Rivers, MB, 1944.
Bill Watts Collection

In 1949, Craig and Watts convinced the City of Calgary to take back the airport from the DOT. The U.S. Air Force had operated a base on the west side of the airport for refuelling and making minor repairs to aircraft being transported to Russia on a lend-lease basis. When they left the site, they donated a huge concrete ramp to the city. Craig and Watts took advantage of this ramp by relocating the terminal to the west side, and joining the building to abandoned USAF barracks. This terminal, known as the "Tarpaper Shack," served from 1949 to 1956. They also supervised the construction of a 6 000-foot runway (16/34) (Footnote 1), with a parallel taxi-way on the west side leading to the concrete ramp. In 1950, Runway 07/25 was constructed, also 6 000-feet long.

Watts resigned from the airport in 1951 to go flying again, this time with Pacific Petroleums. He flew their Lockheed Lodestar, Lockheed 12, Cessna 180 and 195, and Stinson Reliant, throughout Canada and the U.S.A. He also flew the company president, Frank McMahon, into the Flathead Valley north of the U.S. border west of Waterton Lakes when they found surface indications of oil. A strip was cut out of the forest, and supplies were flown in with the Cessna 195. In winter, there would often be snow on the isolated runway and he couldn't land. "It was a difficult way to make a living," Watts says. "We had to be careful because we were landing into the mountains, and taking off in the opposite direction, with a steep turn."

Roy Staniland had started working "as a permanent fixture" for Associated Airways in 1950. Two years later, the company asked if he would like to fly helicopters. He jumped at the chance. "I thought I'd be a bigger fish in a small pond, because nobody had a lot of helicopter experience and there would be more opportunities.

"I did a familiarization in 1952 and then went back flying fixed-wing again. In the fall of 1953, when I'd finished flying fixed-wing for the season, I got the endorsement on the helicopter." He continued to wear two hats because of the shortness of the helicopter season. When it concluded, he would go back to flying fixed-wing. This system allowed the company to maintain a permanent staff.

"Most helicopter companies had a core group of people, and then they hired pilots and engineers on a seasonal basis. We hired a number of American helicopter pilots who were coming out of the Korean war at that time. They contributed considerable expertise to the company's operations, because there wasn't a very elaborate training course. One of the instruction books I had on learning to fly the helicopter said, under Controls, 'This section is deliberately brief as it only serves to confuse the pilot.'"

Staniland trained on the early (1948) Bell 47D model, "the old original 178-horsepower, the kind you see in *M.A.S.H.*

"I think we had to have a minimum of 1 500 flying hours before we could train on helicopters. I didn't 'buy' my training, I just agreed to stay working for the company for three years and they underwrote the costs."

There is quite a difference between flying fixed-wing aircraft and flying helicopters, Staniland says, and pilots must realize they can't already fly them before they take the specialized instruction course.

"Helicopters are like hookers," Rainforth interjects. "They have no visible means of support."

Everyone laughs, but Staniland agrees with the summation.

"When you start flying helicopters, you've got a little ego that says, 'Aw, it's just another flying machine. If I really had to, I could probably fly this thing.' Well, it takes you an hour to realize you can't, that you'd kill yourself."

Staniland says it's far easier to fly helicopters today, with their hydraulic-assisted flight controls and correlated throttle-power inputs, than it was then. "You first had to learn to coordinate the delayed response in the control system," he says. With helicopters, there is a cyclic control which governs the plane of disk rotation, and the movement always comes 90 degrees in the direction of rotation from the control input.

"In order to move ahead, you have to move the stick forward, which unbalances the rotor and tilts the rotor disk in that direction." In moving forward from the stationary hover, part of what is holding you up is now also pulling you ahead.

"You've got to crank on more power to keep from settling back to earth, so you're always trying to bring the system into equilibrium," Staniland explains. "It requires a lot of throttle twisting and pitch pumping – decreasing and increasing the main rotor pitch."

Rainforth, who doesn't fly helicopters himself but has chartered and travelled in lots of them, agrees. "You don't get an itch on your nose, because you can't let go of the controls!"

"That's right!" Staniland says. "They used to say, if you want to send your girlfriend up for an airplane ride, do it in a helicopter. The pilot has both feet and both hands busy, so she's safe!

"But," he adds, "keep the helicopter in sight, because it could easily land in some private out-of-the-way spot!"

The pilots laugh at the legendary jokes.

Landing helicopters is different from fixed-wing, too, Staniland continues, on a more serious note. "The first time you see the airspeed indicator drop below 65 or 75 miles an hour, you get a little twitchy, because airplanes stall at that point. But in a helicopter, you go through a complete approach down to zero (Footnote 2).

According to Staniland, the best thing to happen with helicopters was the arrival of turbine engines. Their fuel-control governors relieved the pilot of the demanding throttle-pitch correlation. Further, hydraulic controls reduced the physical efforts once needed to control the machines.

"Someone told me that the only reason helicopters fly is that the earth rejects them!" Staniland says. Then he adds with a laugh, "That guy had to be a fixed-wing driver!"

"I look back with a great deal of pleasure at having been part of a technology that was at its commercial beginning," Staniland says. "If you were then to evaluate the helicopter on a basis of safety, performance and reliability, it would never have been hired. But, because it could do something that nothing else could do, people were tolerant. They paid the price and accepted the aircraft's limitations. The accident statistics were actually very good, considering the unknown aspects" (Footnote 3).

Staniland quickly learned the idiosyncrasies of helicopters. "If you take the power off, you can control it like a bicycle, by leaning," he says. "When you're in auto-rotation, the air's coming up through the rotor system rather than coming down through the top. *As long as you keep up your forward speed* you can guide it wherever you want to."

But, as an example of the experimental stage of helicopters at the time, Staniland recalls working out of Norman Wells in 1956, doing a long traverse with the Geological Survey of Canada. They were setting out fly camps – two-man camps complete with equipment and food. When they moved the camp from Norman Wells to a lake in the Yukon, the traverse was 250 miles from old to new campsite. At that time, Army Signals Corps provided the only communication, aside from the mail flights coming in by Canadian Pacific Airlines.

Following his third 'set-out', Staniland felt a vibration and suddenly the tail rotor let go. The shaft sheared and he found himself going the opposite way of the rotor. The machine turned half-way round before he could shut it down.

"I had to take the power off even though I had engine power to the main rotor, but without an anti-torque rotor I couldn't use it because I'd spin. I landed without any damage to the aircraft but I could see we were in trouble. It wasn't something I could fix. I couldn't carve a prop and a shaft out of a piece of wood! There was no wood there to speak of, anyway."

Their only communication system was a little hand-held portable VHF (Very High Frequency) radio. When he sighted the search aircraft, he reported their location and was informed that PWA's (Pacific Western Airlines) contract Beaver would be in to pick them up at a small lake 10 miles away.

They walked out to meet the Beaver at the rendezvous point and were transported back to base. There, a number of messages awaited them. One bulletin, communicated through the Army Signals Corps, said that certain helicopter tail rotor gearbox drive hubs needed to be inspected. Those manufactured between certain serial numbers had machining faults. Sure enough, the hub shaft on their helicopter fell into that group. "Had we received that message a day earlier, we'd have known about this problem. Every time you had a failure, particularly in those early years, Bell was on top of things. They wanted to see the old part, or at least a description of the problem, and they asked us to give the parts regular inspections in addition to mandatory requirements. We became sort of field-testing participants."

On another occasion, Staniland was transporting Gulf Oil geologist Hans Knipping. They were flying low down the Steep Bank River, a tributary to the Athabasca River north of Fort McMurray, so Knipping could look at some outcroppings. Wherever the small meandering river followed a bend, there was usually a little gravel spit where they could land when the water was down.

"This one time, I went to add power and nothing came. I was downwind and had no room to turn, but I was able to put the aircraft down on a spit."

To prevent overshooting their only landing spot, a sharp flare at low altitude was required. Staniland wasn't able to get the helicopter completely level before touchdown, and the uneven landing caused the main blades to flap and flex. One of the main rotor blades contacted the aft section of the tail rotor drive, and the throttle linkage became disconnected. They would have to bring in a new set of rotor blades and a drive shaft. They set out to walk to the Athabasca River.

"The ice on the Athabasca, as with most major rivers, had pushed all the willows down flat along the riverbanks," Staniland recalls. "You couldn't walk *on* it and you could hardly walk *through* it, you got hung up, so it was a devil of a walk. When we finally got to the river it was pitch black out, so we decided to camp on the shore for the night. We took shelter behind a big log and started a fire with the driftwood."

In the middle of the night they heard the sound of an engine coming from the river, and then the running lights of a tug and a barge came into view.

"It pays to know some survival skills, like SOS signals," Staniland said to Knipping. He beefed up their fire, took off his jacket and started flashing SOS in Morse code by the light of the fire.

The engines quickened toward them. "See, it pays to know this!" Staniland said wisely.

Suddenly from out of the darkness a voice yelled, "Where do you want it?"

"Want what?"

"This Cat!"

It turned out that the tugboat captain had been running up and down the river searching for a location to dump off a Cat he'd brought up for a seismic outfit.

"Did you get my SOS?" Staniland asked.

"What SOS?" was the old captain's response.

Knipping laughed – and that ended Staniland's reliance on Boy Scout methods.

"The captain, thinking we were the crew waiting for the Cat, had pushed the barge right up onto the shore and got stuck. Now he couldn't off-load the Cat – and he had the extra weight of two more people on board. Not a happy rescuer. He spent a long time backwashing, trying to free up the barge."

In the early morning, the air force search and rescue Canso flew out to find them. They let the Army Signals Corps know they'd been rescued, and then travelled back to Fort McMurray on the barge. Staniland went back later for the helicopter, accompanied by engineer Neill Murphy. The air force S-55 took them to a landing site nearby, and they had to trek through the bush again, this time carrying a new set of rotor blades and another drive shaft.

That was just one of the times Roy Staniland was reported missing.

Staniland and his wife Kathy (Kathleen Byers from Ponoka, whom Roy had married in 1955) were living in Edmonton, and had one baby and were expecting a second. The day Roy had gone down, Kathy received the dreaded phone call. "Don't worry, Kathy, but Roy's missing." She did worry – for 18 hours – before being informed that her husband had been found.

In 1957, Pacific Western Airlines bought out Associated Airways. The employees had to decide whether to fly fixed-wing for Pacific Western, or stay with the independent helicopter group. Some, like Staniland who had more experience on helicopters, decided to stay (although he also did some flying for PWA for a couple of years "on demand" while PWA was restaffing).

"At that time we had a contract with the Government of Alberta for forestry work," Staniland says. "Associated Helicopters wanted us to keep our fixed-wing proficiency so we could fly both the government's fixed-wing aircraft and their helicopters."

Fire-bombing of forest fires became an especially interesting part of Staniland's work.

"On helicopters, within that four-month period we would fly anywhere from 400 to 550 hours, especially when we got on with Forestry and they extended the season," Staniland explains. "When you got on fires you might fly 20 hours in two days."

The difference in fire-bombing with helicopters compared to fixed-wing was mainly that the pilot had more control, and a much shorter turnaround so he could complete a cycle more quickly. This cycle included water pickup, transport, approach to the target hot-shot, the drop, and a return for another pickup. With a helicopter, water could be picked up from nearby small ponds and streams that might be unattainable to fixed-wing.

"You had to watch for other aircraft, you had smoke to be concerned with – then you had to get back to your pickup point, which you hoped was fairly close by. The pickup itself was a challenging situation, especially from shallow lakes or streams. You had to come in and put the bucket down easy so you didn't damage it. If it was a shallow spot, you had to drag the bucket to fill it; if you had deep water you could let the bucket sink. Some buckets opened from the bottom, and the doors closed when you lifted up" (Footnote 4).

Staniland feels that the job wasn't particularly dangerous "if you stayed within the limits of the aircraft and yourself. You had to recognize when fatigue was affecting you. I always worked on the premise that there were three parts to an accident: maintenance of the aircraft, flying of the aircraft and the company's supervision – not necessarily in that order.

"The customer had a responsibility to be honest about the job when talking about it and hiring for it. He had to be willing to pay for the right aircraft so we weren't operating on the thin margin. And he was expected to provide proper accommodation and relief, if you wanted to call it that."

All three pilots agree that the customer might think he had no input into an accident, but that wasn't so. "When you asked for a certain landing area, or an airstrip for fixed-wing, they might say, 'Oh yeah, we've cleaned off an airstrip.' You'd get in and find that it was 500 feet shorter than it was supposed to be, they hadn't spent the extra money for drainage of the darn thing, and they'd left piles of rocks and roots and ruts! And it was something that the airplane operator couldn't do anything about."

Proper drainage of the strip is an aspect that's especially important, but seldom mentioned. If the strip is not paved or gravelled, just dirt scraped off by a bulldozer, it can become a quagmire. If proper drainage facilities are made, and nobody uses the strip until it has dried after a rain, even an earth-strip will stay in good shape.

"A bad time is in the spring when the ground starts to thaw," Rainforth says. "Underneath, everything is frozen solid. Then you get a warm day and you get this 'baby shit' on top and it's really slick. You've got absolutely no brakes, you're just sliding all over."

"And you don't know that, 'til you land," Staniland adds.

Staniland likes flying with floats. "They don't alter the characteristics of the aircraft too much, but you have to learn to 'sail', especially in a single-engine airplane. You haven't got much fin and rudder area, and you can only tack a certain amount; you shut the power down when you're trying to pull into a dock area. But the trick is how to get the darn thing there, working with the wind!

"The nicest situation is when you have a twin-engine airplane – like the Twin Otter – and you've got two engines to turn you, in addition to the reversible props."

Rainforth agrees. "When you're on the river with floats you've got to be going quite fast for your water rudders to be effective. If you're ever stupid enough to let yourself go downstream in a small fast-flowing river, you've got to be moving along so quickly for the water rudders to be effective that you're going to tip your airplane over when you're turning.

"Another thing when flying with floats is being able to see where the water surface is. Sometimes you can't tell."

The three pilots all mention a further conundrum: when do you put floats on your airplane and when do you take them off? Rainforth recalls situations in places like Fort Simpson, when the trappers wanted to go out as late as possible so they'd charter a plane to fly them out *just* before freeze-up. At this late date, thin layers of ice could form at certain times (like in the morning), which could pierce the floats.

"Wait too long, and then they have an even longer wait until it freezes so we can land on top of the ice with skis," Rainforth says. "There's this dicey period between open water and ice, in both spring and fall.

"Also, in the spring the ice will candle, or be mushy and you can fall through. You get a dangerous period both times, and you're often pressed really hard by the customer to go anyway."

Staniland adds to the list of concerns. "Sometimes the trip is okay, and the customer wants to stay overnight. You get up in the morning and it's all frozen and you've got to knock yourself out of the ice.

"In the spring of the year, when things clean off nicely, you can go on wheels because you've got clear ice. But other times you can end up with overflow conditions and you drop through! It's hard to win."

By the close of the 1960s, Hal Rainforth had finished his apprenticeship in more ways than one: he'd obtained his licenses, he'd taken on miserable jobs servicing airplanes in cold hangars, and he'd flown airplanes from rig sites in the Peace River country of British Columbia to the grain fields of central Alberta. His next employer after Pat Johnson in Red Deer was Bev Hughes at Hughes Air in Ponoka, where for 10 months he did maintenance on the airplanes as well as instructing, and running satellite schools in Camrose and Hanna. "That's the problem of having both licenses; it means you work all the time."

Next, he was hired as a copilot in 1968 by Al Potter of Hudson's Bay Oil and Gas, which Rainforth considers "the break of the century, flying the most beautiful DC-3 (CF-HSX) you ever saw." For this job, the Rainforths moved to Edmonton. "I had 1 700 hours total time then, most of it instructing. We flew out of Edmonton to Drayton Valley, up to Zama Lake, all those kinds of places. It was a wonderful airplane. I really spit-and-polished it. You could comb your hair from the reflection off the panels inside."

After 10 months, the company changed presidents and also changed their attitude about airplanes. "I got laid off, and the Edmonton base manager, Bill Granley, quit."

In 1969, Granley became manager for Bob Keen of Keen Industries at Fort Nelson, B.C. Granley called on Rainforth to maintain and fly their DC-3. The company bought out Arctic Air at Fort Simpson, and at one time owned 13 airplanes.

Hal Rainforth resting on one of several dozen loads of dynamite used to blow the sump at Stokes Point on the Beaufort Sea, 1973-4.
Hal Rainforth Collection

When Granley took over Arctic Air in Fort Simpson, and Executive Air (Jim Burrow's operation) in Fort St. John, Rainforth became the Fort Nelson manager. "That two years was probably the most interesting flying I ever did," Rainforth says. "I ran a DC-3 supplying road camps. The Stewart-Cassiar Highway was being built, so we were flying all the way across the mountains, over the most beautiful piece of earth you ever saw. I was making five trips a week and when the weather was good I'd do two a day, so we're talking lots of hours. And on each trip, the scenery was more beautiful than I'd remembered it from before."

One of his jobs involved flying to Bob Quinn Lake near the Alaska border and landing on a wide part of the road. A railroad was being built as well as the highway, north from Fort St. James, so he would fly to Bulkley House, which was further south into more open country. Rainforth was entranced by what he saw from the cockpit as he made twice-daily trips. He compared it to sitting in an armchair watching a National Geographic program, showing mountains, rivers and 40-mile long glaciers.

"When you go through the Rocky Mountain range west of Fort Nelson, there's an area just like a moonscape. Past that, and down, are the Tuchodi Lakes and different scenery completely. Then comes flatter country toward Fort Nelson. It was absolutely incredible stuff. It made quite an impression on me."

Rainforth also admired the view as he flew out of Stewart on B.C.'s west coast, even though the loads of dynamite he carried could have blown it all to smithereens. "One time we nearly had to start throwing dynamite overboard because the valley was coming up faster than the darn airplane. My copilot was luckily very good at reading maps. You can't afford to get jammed into a valley where you can't turn around, and when you're flying under the weather."

Rainforth says it's not dangerous to fly dynamite, but the caps are very dangerous. It is a "no-no" to carry caps and dynamite in the same load. The pilots were also instructed to not carry E-cord on the same load with either dynamite or caps.

"Although the dynamite itself is not dangerous, the airport manager at Terrace would make us load over on the far side of the airport," Rainforth says. "The truth is, we had enough dynamite that if it went off there'd be no airport left anyway! We were hauling 7 000 or 8 000 pounds at a shot."

Even though he was flying aircraft he loved, in country of incomparable beauty, when Rainforth was offered a job with Pacific Petroleums in Calgary he had no choice, career-wise, but take it. "I hated to give up that kind of flying, but I was working all the time and certainly there was no married life. I was living in a hotel in Dawson Creek more than I was at home in Fort Nelson.

"So, I came to Calgary to fly for Pacific Petroleums. The company had bought a Twin Otter and were looking for someone with Arctic experience to fly it."

During the next two years he found himself back in familiar territory, but he was also able to explore some entirely new areas. "The first job was out of Norman Wells, but they had actually bought the airplane for a project out of Inuvik. They had drilling operations down by Fort McPherson, and on the Beaufort Sea by Kay Point and Herschel Island. I would land on the beach. We had a lot of work there."

Rainforth was also flying out of Calgary. "At that time we had an Aero Commander, a Twin Otter and an Aztec, and then I started flying the jet (Hawker Siddeley 125/400) two or three years later. I would spend three weeks up on Baille Hamilton Island flying across the magnetic North Pole – and then come to Calgary, get into the jet and fly to Palm Springs."

In 1958, Bill Watts returned to the airport, this time as the manager, succeeding George Craig on his retirement. The airport was now operated from Canada's first modern terminal building, built in 1956. Bill Watts's job became busier each year. He oversaw many major improvements: the extension of Runway 16/34 to 12 675 feet (making

Bill Watts, Calgary Airport Manager, standing on apron in front of terminal building under construction, 1977. *Photo: Calgary Herald*

it the longest commercial runway in Canada), as well as construction of a second major runway (10/28). Zoning regulations were set for all runways so they didn't encroach on Calgary's new suburban developments.

By 1973, the airport was anticipated to be Canada's finest with a new $57.7 million terminal planned, which was touted as a prototype. The previous year, the airport had served 1.6 million passengers, and Watts's job entailed involvement in everything from construction plans for the new terminal, cargo, passenger and baggage handling, to personnel who worked directly for the airport, concessionaires and tenants. The new terminal building opened in 1977, and is still a top-notch facility. Watts successfully managed this large, and increasingly important, airport until he retired in 1979.

His northern flying became just a memory – although always remaining a fond one.

Roy Staniland's career was likewise moving ahead, with the wholly-owned subsidiary of Associated Helicopters.

"They picked certain key people for whom they wanted to provide incentive to stay, and allowed us to take an equity position in the company," Staniland says. "I think there were five of us who had equity, besides the original shareholders who were Tommy Fox, Vern Simmonds and Rex Kaufman. The company paid out dividends, so we were getting some reward even beyond our paycheques."

Staniland explains that up to 1980 he was one of the principals of Associated Helicopters, and was responsible for all their marketing and consulting services. This included doing small consulting jobs for various companies who were getting into new areas of expertise. One of these areas was moving drilling rigs. "I worked with various drilling companies, breaking up their packages, moving parts with slings under the helicopters, determining what aircraft could do which job. Oh, that was a challenge. I thoroughly enjoyed it."

"It was dangerous," Rainforth adds.

"It was a challenge," Staniland emphasizes. "Helicopters are very effective for moving things."

Staniland's work with Associated Helicopters took place mainly in Canada. "We made a few bids for overseas work, but the company always had the attitude of 'Let's do the job we can do, well. Let's get better rather than try to get bigger.' Companies were mushrooming all around us, but we were able to maintain permanent employment.

Bell 206B helicopters during seismic operations in the Alberta foothills, 1970s. *Roy Staniland Collection*

We got to know our equipment extremely well, and we came to be recognized for accurate job estimates.

"I did a lot of innovative work when I moved from Operations to Job Development and Marketing. They're all tied in. Marketing isn't just putting an ad in the paper; it has to have a technical side so you can provide information to the people seeking the product."

"Some of them don't know what product they need until they get an expert in to tell them," Rainforth says.

"That's right," Staniland agrees. "But I don't like the word, 'expert'. An 'ex' is a has-been, and a 'spurt' is a drip under pressure!"

The company was sold to Neonex in 1969 (and later to Okanagan Helicopters). "We continued to operate it, still known as Associated Helicopters, on behalf of the new owners. I stayed with them until I retired in 1980, to go with Petro-Canada."

Staniland has many good things to say about Associated Helicopters, where the same core group of people stayed for over 28 years.

Rainforth agrees. "They were the best people to charter. You knew what you were getting."

The conversation turns to experiences shared by all three pilots when they flew in the North.

One such job was transporting corpses wrapped in tarpaulins. "Everybody gets to do that," says Rainforth, who remembers an "inordinate" number of corpses being flown out of Fort Simpson during his time there. "I don't know what was going on, maybe it was just a normal attrition rate for a community like that, but it seemed that after every Saturday-night stomp there'd be somebody taking a body-bag over to Hay River the next day for an autopsy."

It also seemed strange that nearly every corpse required an autopsy. "According to the RCMP, one we took over had supposedly died of pneumonia – but when they took him out of the bag in the morgue they found he'd been hit on the head," Rainforth says. "We also had one that bent in the Aztec [airplane] when we were going across. We took out the seats, leaving a spar, and stretched him out. Then the plane warmed up and we had trouble getting him out. He wasn't quite the right shape to get through the door."

Staniland recalls hauling a "high-ranking" combination cargo of two dead people and a team of very alive dogs, in a Barkley-Grow on skis. "I'll tell you, that was not a trip I'd want to repeat. We had to go to a remote cabin quite far north of Peerless Lake. The guide was supposed to show us the way when we got to the edge of my map. He was standing between me and the RCMP, sort of looking around. I waited for some sort of recognition in his eyes. When I had only 10

Typical mail flight of the 1950s. Pilot Roy Staniland with Barkley-Grow Yukon Queen at Pelican Portage, Athabasca River. *Roy Staniland Collection*

minutes to go before I'd have to turn around, and I'd nearly lost confidence in him, all of a sudden he saw something he recognized.

"I got down, and dropped off him and the RCMP officer as close to the cabin as I could. When they reached the cabin, they found two people dead – murder-suicide. They had to bring them back out to the airplane by dog team."

Staniland says that carrying dogs in the airplane was not very nice in most cases – the half-wild dogs often became quarrelsome or sick. This time the dogs had a reason for being unhappy, and he felt sorry for both the dogs and the people back in the cabin of the airplane. The Barkley-Grow had a door so the pilot could separate himself, and he could get a window open.

Rainforth was told of a situation endured by pilot Clare Carrothers, when he was hired to fly an Indian man and his dogs in a Cessna 185 on floats. "The man had to keep beating the dogs away from Clare while they were travelling. When they stopped and opened the door all the dogs piled out, on leashes. One went tearing over on the wrong side of the float and fell into the water, underneath the float. The leash wasn't long enough to let him come up the other side. They had to really scramble to get the beast out, snapping and snarling, before he drowned."

Cats can also present a problem, as they did to a pilot who was transporting a nurse and her pet from Fort Smith. The story goes, Rainforth says, that the cat got nervous in the Norseman, started jumping around and ended up on the pilot's head, clinging on with its claws for dear life. The pilot reached over, put the side window down, and dragged the cat off with the claws leaving skid-marks across his scalp. Then he flung it out the window.

"I wonder if it landed on its feet?" Bill Watts says, contemplatively.

"It had lots of time to get lined up," Staniland estimates.

In the 1950s, Staniland accepted a flying contract with the Department of Health and Welfare to fly their tuberculosis x-ray party to remote settlements. The team included an x-ray technician, a nurse and/or a doctor, often an RCMP officer, and a missionary to act as an interpreter. They would fly into communities, x-ray residents, then take the tests back to the Charles Camsell Hospital in Edmonton to determine which cases were active. Six weeks later they'd return with the RCMP or another person in authority, to round up the people who had to come back to the city for treatment.

Many of the natives used several names: their registered name, their local name and an Indian name. If they didn't want to come out for treatment, they simply couldn't be identified.

"To my recollection, we took out mostly young people," Staniland says. "But the ones that got my heartstrings were the children."

Rainforth had similar experiences in having to separate families, in the 1970s when one of his jobs involved taking northern children to and from residential schools.

"In the fall we'd go out to collect the kids and take them in to the central boarding schools, and that's where they'd stay until the next spring. I mostly transported them from Fort Liard up to the school at Fort Simpson; when the kids got a little older they would go to Yellowknife. The older ones would actually be quite excited about going back to see all their friends, but it was hard on the little guys for their first year. They knew we were taking them away from their parents and they wouldn't be coming back for the entire school year.

"A lot of Indians used to hit the river and take their kids with them about the time they knew the plane would be coming, when school would be starting. They'd disappear, get scarce for a while. I don't blame them, you know."

"I don't either," Staniland adds.

"Their culture didn't put a lot of value on the education they were getting, and here you were coming to take their kids?" Rainforth says. "I'd be inclined to do a little shooting."

There are varying opinions regarding the need for a residential school system for northern students. Other cultures were encroaching, and education – learning to speak, read and write in English and understand mathematics – was considered important if the residents were going to be part of the new economy. They couldn't attend school from the trapline – so what was the answer?

"Oh, the answer was what the schools were doing," Rainforth concedes. "It's just that to some of those people there was no value to it, and it was just sad."

Staniland recalls one of the experiences that "really got to me."

"On one trip I went to a lake to take a girl back from the hospital and pick up two little boys. This was before the development in Rainbow Lake but it was in that area. This girl, who was around 14 at the time, had been in the Charles Camsell Hospital in Edmonton for probably five years. She had lived with white sheets, had eaten hospital food, had learned to read and write, and now she was back – a stranger in her own culture. As a consequence, this poor girl didn't have a hope.

"My criticism was, *there was no follow-through*. If you're going to train them they should be provided with some employment, either at the Hudson's Bay post or the missions, or some place where they could utilize their training, perhaps become teachers in their own right. But they were just dropped off!

"At the time when this girl could have become a contributor to her own culture through trapping, tanning, whatever skills were expected of the girls, she was almost useless. So you can expect that she'd be ostracized almost, maybe come down with TB again, or probably be pregnant before too long. And what have you done? You haven't done her a favor at all.

"But unfortunately, any society in transition is going to bleed."

Bush flying in the North has changed, too, says Staniland, in the sense that there are now more facilities. But people still get lost, and search and rescue operations must be put into action.

Search programs vary, depending on whether they are operated by individual bush pilots, charter companies or the air force. "When the air force comes in they have a structured system and they try to get everybody to work together," Staniland says. "Where the locals are very effective is in knowing the individual pilot who's gone down."

"They know his habits," Watts says.

"And they know the area," Rainforth adds. "We've had company people who were flying their own airplanes and got lost; their families have asked us to put planes in the search, which we've done. But the air force doesn't necessarily want us around."

"They may want us around, but under their direction," Staniland says. "Any Search Master who knows there's a good local group of commercial people will reach out to them, and to a degree will let them have their heads. But as far as the air force is concerned, and rightly so I guess, they've got to search a certain way. The locals might say, 'No, he'd never be there but he could very easily be over here, because these are the conditions that he would have run into.' You find a lot of people out of the traditional search area because they had more fuel and could travel greater distances to go around weather, or to reorient themselves after being lost."

"The equipment is more reliable now," Rainforth says. "In those days, pilots were prepared to land and wait out a storm, whereas now it's unusual and they aren't quite as aware as they used to be."

"There is some good bush flying still going on, though," Bill Watts interjects.

"Oh yes," Staniland agrees, "but it's not the industry it once was. That industry has now evolved to IFR (Instrument Flight Rules) operation, scheduled runs, and there are more facilities. I think genuine bush flying is a bit like the steam engine: there will always be some part of it out there, but it's not the dominant sector of the industry that it once was.

"When flying through the North in a bush pilot mode, you looked to the Hudson's Bay posts and to the missions," Staniland adds. "They were sort of your 'islands in the sky', because you knew you could get sustenance, and there would often be fuel.

"The Oblate Brothers were great at helping me bed the airplane down, getting it started in the morning and helping me load. They always had something for me to eat. I also enjoyed going in to the Anglican Mission in Aklavik. There was always good discussion – just philosophical if you wanted it.

"The Hudson's Bay post used to employ a lot of people from the old country, who were desperately searching for somebody to talk to. Gosh, they'd chew your ear off all night."

Staniland's wife, Kathy, experienced the other side of bush flying: staying home and looking after everything from the children to the finances, to everyday chores – and trying not to think about her husband flying God-knows-where and in what conditions.

"I think over our first 20 years of married life, we hardly lived together," Kathy recalls. "I spent a few years in Edmonton, but most in Calgary. I raised the first five kids pretty well by myself."

The first five?

Kathy laughs. "We had six altogether. Roy didn't see Terri Lynn, the third one, until she was eight weeks old."

Staniland acknowledges that there was no compassionate leave if you were on a job and your wife was having a baby. It just wasn't considered as an excuse to come home.

Kathy never lived in the bush camps, and she took only a few flights with Roy. One was to Wabasca in northern Alberta, in the Barkley-Grow, in 1954. "I played pool with [Oblate] Brother Bossé while Roy flew to the outlying posts to collect the mail."

She also flew with him several times in helicopters, and once in his Bonanza, but that experience nearly ruined her ears. "He didn't tell me I had to swallow and all those things.

"We wives spent a lot of time alone, usually from April through to September or October. It was a way of life and we accepted it."

Someone asks Kathy Staniland what aviation means to her. Rainforth quickly offers an answer: "It kept Roy out of her hair all those years!" She laughs, and the question is rephrased: Would she advise her daughters to marry pilots?

"No!" Kathy replies. "I used to say I'd never marry a doctor because he was never home, and then I ended up marrying a pilot!"

Staniland admits that there were "field periods" inherent in much of the work, both with flying fixed-wing and helicopter. "It lasted much longer with helicopters – you could be out for three or four months. You were psyched up for it, you had your bag packed. But what would seem worse was when you were on your way home and you'd get a wire that said, 'You've got two more weeks' work at Steen River.' That two weeks looked longer than the four months, because you'd been all ready to go home!"

Sometimes, because of long periods of time spent away from home and "civilization", a bush mentality developed.

"You'd put your dirty laundry in the bottom of the bag and just use the top stuff. Then, when you'd get this extra two weeks work, you had to start recycling so you went down to the bottom of the bag again!" Staniland laughs.

"On the way home, we'd stop in some place like Fort St. John or Dawson Creek to get to a washing machine and try to clean everything up. I'd think I'd done such a great job getting everything all washed, until I'd roll into Edmonton. Kathy would come to pick me up and, well, she didn't actually hold her nose but she'd leave the window open on the car on the way home!"

Rainforth adds that if there were women in camp the men tended to keep themselves, and their laundry, in better shape. "That makes quite a difference. If the cooks or whoever are women, the whole scene changes."

This brings the conversation to the subject of female flyers. "I hired a woman pilot a few years ago," Rainforth says. "You know where most of the resistance came from? The guys' wives."

"That's right – I remember that," Staniland says.

"They're all travelling together and staying in hotels, on expense accounts and stuff, and the wives back home get pretty uptight."

So the families stayed home, and listened to all the stories – of camp antics, wild blizzards, malfunctioning motors, difficult passengers (two- and four-legged) and impossible loads.

The loading requirements illustrate the irony of pilots who think they're being promoted when they get to a bigger airplane. "The trouble is, they don't give you any more help, so you end up working harder!" Rainforth says.

Staniland agrees, stating that at the main base you usually had someone to help you load, depending on the type of airplane. "Gas drums were tough to handle, but you learned little tricks about how to load things and how not to. Floats made it tough because you had to get the freight from the float to the dock, and you couldn't get the airplane to sit still in the water."

Rainforth would use a ramp to load 45-gallon drums of fuel. "I'd take a shim, push the barrel up, get the shim under it. We used to fuel up from 10-gallon kegs all the time."

"If somebody was helping, you could always tell if they'd never done it before," Staniland says. "They'd pick up the whole keg and hold it, with the spout down, to fill a pail. That meant they were holding up a 90 or 100 pound keg. After a while you learned to get a pail that was just the right height, and leave the keg on the ground. You'd put the pail underneath it, rest the bung of the drum on the rim of the pail and tilt the barrel over, lifting up the back end.

"Without such tricks," says Staniland, "you're good for about two barrels."

The worst kind of load, says Rainforth, is one he sometimes had to take in the DC-3: blades for Caterpillar tractors. "They're 3/4-inch thick, 18 or 24 inches wide, and eight feet long. They lay right flat. I don't know what they weighed but they really, really, were mean. You couldn't get underneath to lift them off, and you couldn't tie them properly. I'd do my own tying if I could. One time they loaded my DC-3 with a bunch of those blades underneath a pile of groceries. I knew when I was taxiing it was heavy. When we got airborne and over the mountains into some cloud, we weren't just flying VFR (Visual Flight Rules). I couldn't maintain enough altitude to be safe . . . it was just by the grace of God."

One would think that if there was an accident the customer who'd overloaded the airplane could be charged, but such an infraction was seldom – if ever – reported. "No," Rainforth says, "I'd have got hung with that."

Bill Watts agrees. "I think that Transport Canada closed their eyes to that sort of thing, to a certain extent, up North, because they couldn't monitor it all the time."

Staniland says that the oil field was particularly bad for dumping excessive loads into an airplane. Watts agrees. "I was always overloaded in that Cessna 195, taking up all sorts of gear. But with the Mark V Anson, you could overload it and get away with it."

"Like a DC-3, it has a tremendous capability for taking more than it should," Staniland concurs. "They do it for fun, you know, some of these guys. They have the attitude, 'Aw, let's make this guy work for his living!'"

"But," he adds, "with some early airplanes that were licensed to operate in the North, you couldn't make any money with them unless you overloaded them."

A common load when hauling for oil companies was "shock subs" and test equipment that goes down drill holes. "These round pipes can be anywhere from six feet to 20-some feet long, and they weigh about 110 pounds a foot," Rainforth explains. "They're very, very difficult. It's quite hard to get the long ones in the door, and they're mean to handle because they're so heavy. But they're still not as bad as those blades for graders."

Leaking oil was another non-favorite situation. "It was messy," Rainforth says. "But you had to be really careful with batteries, stuff like that, where acid can leak and cause corrosion.

"We often had to haul dangerous goods, too. The production department would send out samples. If the bottles leaked we might be exposed to hydrogen sulfide. It wasn't hard to handle, just dangerous to breathe."

Staniland picks up the list. "Sometimes you'd get to a site and find two extra people expecting to board. Are you going to leave them? They're not set up to camp or anything. The weather's going bad, you know you can't make another trip that day. What are you going to do? Drop some freight and take the people? Who's going to pay for the extra trip? Or do you just overload?"

"I think that today, pilots and certainly inspectors are a little more vigilant," Watts says. "The pilot knows he can get a licence suspension or a fine."

Staniland agrees. "One of the things we tried to get across to the customer was that they weren't doing any favors to the pilot, themselves, or the charter company, by doing anything illegal. There's a lot more discipline in the flying end of it now than there was at that time, and more consciousness of it on the part of the customer."

"But," adds Rainforth, "there are still some customers who will sacrifice everything for a buck. The bigger companies don't dare. I pay Roy good money now to do inspections on the charter operators, and overloading is one of the very things he looks for, to make sure they're not doing it."

"It takes one to find one!" Staniland laughs.

It was inevitable that these three pilots meet. Rainforth got to know Watts just before he began flying for Pacific Petroleums through Watt's position of airport manager in Calgary – "and a very, very well-known airport manager!" Rainforth emphasizes. "Bill was so well-liked. Everybody knew him."

Watts is modest about this comment. "I got more fun from going into the hangar and talking airplanes than I did running the airport!" he laughs.

Bill Watt's Cessna 180 C-GAPM (**C**anada's **G**reatest **A**irport **M**anager). *Photo by current owner Rick Lowcay.*

"And that did more to make the airport run smoothly than anything else," says Rainforth.

Rainforth and Staniland met a little later on. Rainforth started working for Pacific Petroleums in November, 1971. In 1979 Petro-Canada bought out Pacific Petroleums, and then began to amalgamate flight departments of the newly-acquired companies.

Gordon Davis, then aviation manager for Petro-Canada and Rainforth's predecessor, hired Roy Staniland as their helicopter specialist. In 1980, Rainforth took over the company's aviation department.

From starting as a pilot-engineer with the company, Rainforth now found himself in administration, "flying a desk."

"That took all the fun out of it," he says.

When Petro-Canada began to take over other flight departments, it wasn't down-sizing that was required as much as building up the new structure. "I guess I'm not such a nice guy, because they gave me the job of doing some very hard things," Rainforth says. "It was very difficult. I had to do a lot of firing and laying-off of people. At the same time as that was going on, we were growing."

Staniland sympathizes with Rainforth's position. "It feels like you don't have control, especially after you've come from a hands-on environment where you could speak personally about all that was going on, and make confident judgement calls."

"In a situation like that," Rainforth continues, "the manager gets so swamped with paperwork that it becomes difficult for him to keep in touch. I was initially in a good position to see what was going on. I knew what had to be done, and I just got on with doing it.

"But after you get things cleaned up, the issues become less black-and-white and more grey. We had 53 people and nine airplanes with a tenth on order. From three bases we expanded to five. It all came together at the same time, in 1981, and it was an incredible mess."

Coupled with personnel shifts, the company had jobs going on world-wide. The original bases were in Fort Nelson, Fort St. John and Calgary; then bases were opened in Ottawa and Toronto.

When Rainforth took over aviation management in 1980, Petro-Canada was spending $10 million a year on helicopter charters, mostly in Newfoundland. Recognizing Roy Staniland's talents, Rainforth began to send him all over the place. One job was to Newfoundland to oversee helicopter service to the offshore oil rigs. He also sent him to Papua, New Guinea, to Botswana, Tanzania, and Ecuador ("We did a video of the Petro-Canada operation in Ecuador. We had the two Pumas down there").

The international work was challenging. Staniland explains his role in it: "Petro-Canada's original mandate was to be a catalyst for development. The federal government wanted the company to represent Canada when dealing with foreign governments on petroleum issues. In the process they set up a company called Petro-Canada International Corporation to work alongside of CIDA (Canadian International Development Agency). They used Canadian and World Bank money and so on to develop projects in third world countries. The benefit to Petro-Canada was that it would provide the expertise, and arrange for Canadian content and technology transfer as much as was practical, in these aid programs. That way we got some of our aid money back into Canada."

Rainforth continues: "The idea was to help third world countries become self-sufficient in oil so they didn't have to buy it, because their economies were really bad."

In these foreign countries, Canadians were usually seen as "no threat", and Staniland says that was one of the reasons why a lot of companies provided services from Canada. "We were 'politically acceptable'. I'm not sure we've enhanced our reputation much in the last while, but we're still not considered a threat. We're not overpowering anybody."

Staniland looked after a number of areas. "Helicopter specialty was really my key position, but it also was broader in that I looked after aviation safety and operational performance, as a total package."

"And logistics on how we operated," Rainforth adds. "We had no helicopters of our own."

"No, but we leased machines as required on casual, long- and short-term contracts," Staniland recalls, "so I was trying to service our various operating groups within Petro-Canada. I looked after things like mission analyses, aircraft type selection, preparing and qualifying bidders' lists, input to contract preparation and negotiation, on-site start-up and management, developing operating guidelines, safety, accident investigation, and program review after completion to identify improvement strategies." Staniland stops for breath.

"That's what the job was, and why I got involved in these things. It was very rewarding, and very stimulating."

Rainforth says that the company "had things going on all over." They had offices in Ecuador, did work in Venezuela, drilled wells in Columbia, had offices and people in Islamabad, Pakistan and in Burma that serviced their drilling program there. They also worked in Vietnam and drilled some wells in Botswana, Senegal, Tanzania and New Guinea.

Sometimes this work entailed adopting – or accepting – strange customs. "We ended up once in a Nomad camp in Mauritania (French West Africa) on the desert," Rainforth says. "We were the first outsiders that the chief had ever had in his tent. All his wives sat in a certain order and made tea. They do three levels of tea, and that's how you know when it's time to leave.

"But anyway, they brought a goat over to the side of the tent, and right in front of us they cut its throat and opened it up. To them, a delicacy is the lining of the chest cavity, so they peeled this and gave

Hal Rainforth with a Hawker Siddely HS125-700 in the Sahara Desert, Ghardaia, Algeria, on a May, 1980, trip with then-Energy Minister Marc Lalonde.
Hal Rainforth Collection

it to us, with great pride and ceremony, to eat with them. They poured the goat milk into a tray and passed it around. It had been kept cool by being buried in the sand.

"Reg Spencer and I just about woofed our cookies, but we had to go along with it. These people do not understand different cultures, and offend easily. It was rather ironic: we were in Africa to assess how to best provide famine relief, and they were giving us food that we didn't want to eat."

Before the company began working in Africa, they did research into the country's historical and political situation and sent out security briefs to the crew. That didn't preclude them from being caught in some unexpected high-action scenes.

They were drilling offshore of Senegal (a United Nations country that gained its independence in 1960, located in West Africa) on the river delta. One day a car – with flags flying high – drove to the site and asked to see the drilling manager. Inside was the general, head of the military. He said there was a territorial dispute over the oil and he asked the manager for permission to go out and intercept a gunboat that had been seen heading for Petro-Canada's drill ship.

"Guinea Bissau, next to Senegal, had three MIG fighters that the Communists [Russians] had given them. Two of them were buzzing our rig and scaring heck out of everybody," Rainforth says. "But, considering the military expertise of these countries, if they were trying to kill you, you were probably pretty safe – but they sure could get you by accident!

"These guys began buzzing the rig and they burned a lot of fuel flying so low. When they finally headed back home they ran out of fuel, crashed and killed their ace pilot – wiped out two-thirds of their air force."

Staniland's actual flying work also diminished as administrative duties took over – a common occurrence with pilots who climb the corporate ladder.

"I'd go out and do check rides, fly with the people to assess their professionalism, but as far as having to carry a flight role, I didn't do that any more. I deliberately excluded that from my job because I knew what would happen: I'd get tied to a flying job and wouldn't be doing the job I was hired for."

Bill Watts notes – also from experience – that the sad fact is, "you can't fly and still run the operation."

Rainforth couldn't agree more. "It was against my nature to have to clean out our department, to let people go. But running the business right was also part of my nature. The cut-backs began, voluntary and involuntary, in 1983, and again in 1986. We survived the 1989 cutbacks. I did a lot of dancing for the board of directors. In 1992 we sold our Canadair Challenger and again I had to lay off people. In July, 1993, we sold our Falcon 50, a three-engine corporate airplane. We've got no jets left."

The company's aviation department is now cut to a dozen people and two aircraft: a Grumman Gulfstream I, and a de Havilland Twin Otter. "That's it."

Roy Staniland was a casualty of the 1986 lay-offs but continued to serve Petro-Canada on an "as-required" basis, providing helicopter expertise and doing safety audits on charter companies.

One of Staniland's favorite fixed-wing aircraft was the Barkley-Grow. "They have a tremendous history throughout the North," he says. "The Yukon Queen (CF-BLV) was a Barkley-Grow. The Yukon King (CF-BMG) was a Barkley-Grow. They were run by Leigh Brintnell's Mackenzie Air Service and Grant McConachie's Yukon Southern Air Transport, and both became part of Canadian Pacific Airlines' fleet. I got all my experience on them – approximately 1 000 hours – with Associated Airways in 1950 to 1958. They bought the three remaining Barkley-Grows from Canadian Pacific Airways in 1949" (Footnote 5).

"I'll start this story and then Roy will likely pick up on it," Bill Watts says, smiling. "Roy flew Barkley-Grows [CF-BLV, BQM and BMW] for Associated Airways for quite some time, and then he got into helicopters, but he never forgot the Barkley-Grow. He was in Montreal in

1977 when he discovered his old Barkley-Grow [CF-BQM] abandoned, on floats, pulled up on the banks of Riviere du Prairie south of Laval."

He tried to persuade the owner of this wreck to donate it to a museum, but the owner elected to sell it. So Staniland bought it, "for more than I should have paid."

"Now he had to get it back to Calgary," Watts continues. "He got two of his friends, Art Bell and [the late] Jim Dick, to go down there, with Roy underwriting all the costs, and bring the relic into condition to fly it back."

Roy picks up the story: "Art Bell had just retired, he was my old chief pilot and had checked me out on this Barkley, I think. When PWA got rid of their 707s, instead of requalifying on 737s Art had only six months to go so they paid him out. He phoned me and said, 'I understand that you're restoring the Barkley. How would you like some help?' I said, 'Oh God! Yes, please!' So he came down and he worked his butt off, because he knew this airplane as well as anyone.

"Art and Jim had worked together, so it was kind of like three old buddies, and I was the kid who was the catalyst for putting this thing together. I was happy to be the go-fer! They knew what they were doing, even if I didn't," says Roy.

They first had to pull the cylinders off the engine to ensure there was no internal rust, to satisfy airworthiness requirements for the ferry permit to bring it back. This work took a month.

Staniland recalls his most anxious time, especially after he'd sunk a lot of money into the project, was when he'd wake up about 4:30 or 5:00 in the morning, thinking, "What if we find critical corrosion? What if we find a problem we can't solve?" He would have to write it off – and it would cost him more money just to get rid of it.

When the men finished work on the airplane, they did a test flight and everything looked good. The only thing that went wrong was a broken primer line, but, as they could prime each cylinder separately, they just pinched it off as it wasn't needed anyway. The airplane ran like a charm.

Watts continues the story, barely able to keep from laughing. "They got that darn thing to where Transport Canada, in their 'wisdom', gave them a ferry permit to bring it back all the way from Montreal on floats, flying from lake to lake, to land at Chestermere Lake."

The adventure of ferrying a vintage airplane 2 500 miles across Canada in 17.5 hours, was one nostalgic trip.

"The real challenge was, the potential for failure was far greater than the potential for success," Staniland explains.

That, says Watts, is an understatement. "When he got that airplane back and an inspection was done on it through Tubby Jarrett, who was a qualified air engineer, he just said, 'I think we should bow down to these people because they are still living . . .'"

Staniland defends his love for the old aircraft. "I took Kathy for her first airplane ride in that particular airplane!"

Kathy Staniland still shakes her head over the episode. "When we went out to see it at Chestermere Lake, the floats were so full of holes that they'd had to stuff them with rubber balls and bath-tub stoppers!"

Staniland laughs. "The main requirements in motels we stayed at was, did they have sinks with rubber plugs? Could we take them out to replace the ones that blew off last night?"

Watts recalls that the aircraft was a horrible-looking monstrosity. "Someone had painted it a purple color, and the paint was all peeling off.

"We had to take that thing out of the water from Chestermere Lake, put it on a trailer, and bring it in to the museum," Watts says. "Roy had to taxi the airplane from the far end of the lake to load it with the crane, so I went down with him. He started it up and we were taxiing around the lake and suddenly we were on the step [of the floats], like he was going to do a final circuit. Entirely illegal, as the ferry permit had expired! Then he chopped the power and settled back in the water – so I never got my ride in a Barkley-Grow. But . . . maybe I did! There could well have been some free air between the floats and the water!"

Last stage of the journey for Barkley-Grow CF-BQM, hauled by trailer from Chestermere Lake to Dome Hangar at Calgary Airport. *Roy Staniland Collection*

We will never know for sure, and Roy isn't saying.

"When we finally got it off Chestermere Lake and brought it back to the Calgary International Airport and set it out on the field, even Roy didn't quite know what he was going to do with it," Watts says.

"I didn't know what I'd got myself involved in," Staniland admits.

Amidst the shared laughter, Staniland still defends his expensive and time-consuming personal mission. But Rainforth's and others' congratulations for doing it for benevolent reasons – eventually donating the old Barkley-Grow to Calgary's Aero Space Museum – somewhat softens the memory of money and time spent.

Watts also lauds Staniland's effort. "That airplane is the only one of its kind in the world!"

"In flyable condition," Staniland qualifies.

Although Staniland wanted to continue to fly it after they got back, he couldn't because it had been given only a ferry permit. "We thought we'd get it licensed in short order, but I'd been away a long time and had a lot of work to catch up on, so I didn't have time to devote to it. And we kept finding more things that had to be done."

"When we finally got the Aero Space Museum going, we took the Barkley-Grow and did the restoration," Watts says. "I'd say the aircraft is worth about $75 000 now."

For all its cost in time and money, and its ugliness when found on the banks of the river, the old airplane is now enjoying the prestige of being the only flyable Barkley-Grow in the world today. And the three who made it thus can take pride in that fact.

All pilots enjoy reminiscing about their flying days, and what aviation has done for them.

"It's been fun," says Hal Rainforth. "I really enjoyed flying the DC-3 from Dawson Creek over to the Alaska Panhandle. So much of the time I was looking at country that man had perhaps never set foot on before, or very few had ever been through. I saw huge herds of caribou and stuff.

"Each phase of my career has been totally exciting, even the last phase where we made deals. Then I got buried in the mundane paperwork of day-to-day operations. Now that we're down-sizing, I'm going to be flying again."

Hal Rainforth has over 10 000 flying hours, on 65 types of aircraft.

"The most exciting years of my life were the war – coming out of the Depression and having a job when I joined the air force," Bill Watts says. "They paid me, gave me food, clothed me – and put me into aviation.

Douglas DC-3 at Stewart, BC, getting a load of dynamite for construction on the Stewart-Cassiar road. *Hal Rainforth Collection*

"We used to fly without really knowing too much about what we were getting into, so it didn't worry us. But with the equipment they now have, they point out all the dangers, and sometimes you're afraid to even get into the air!"

Bill Watts has 8 000 flying hours. He presently co-owns a Piper Arrow PA28 200 (C-GVML) with Trudy Armstrong, widow of Neil Armstrong (Footnote 6).

Once, during the course of conversation with a pilot from Federal Air Express, Watts mentioned he'd been flying since 1943 and hadn't flown a jet aircraft. "It's a piece of cake," the pilot said. "You fellows who flew the piston engines are the ones who flew the airplanes. To fly a 727 you sit there, open the taps and let it go. At a certain altitude you pull it back a little bit, climb to 25 000 or 30 000 feet, then sit and pick your nose for four or five hours."

"That's right," Rainforth laughs. "It's like flying a video game. You can engage the auto-pilot, then you don't even have to fly it. Every time I take off in a jet I wonder what I've forgotten, because I haven't done anything!"

"The real work now is in aircraft and systems knowledge, training, simulator exercises, flight planning and procedures," Staniland says. "There's lots to do, but the physical flying is the easiest."

The mood turns pensive. "It was a privilege to be able to sit in all those airplanes, and view the different areas of God's creation," Rainforth says. "In the Arctic when you were flying, you were a vital part of the community. They gave us pilots flu shots because we were needed so badly. There's a sense of worth when you're of value in the system."

Staniland agrees. "You feel you're making a contribution that other people acknowledge and respect. The primary thing is the enjoyment of doing it right."

"The pilot has to impart confidence to the people who are flying with him," Watts adds. "He must show a cool, calm demeanor."

"Yes, and a problem I run into as a manager these years is exactly what you just said," Rainforth states. "We were carrying prime ministers, energy ministers, presidents of other countries. These people would walk up and look over the crew, and they'd need to immediately develop confidence.

"The heads of corporations are powerful people, and they're used to being in control. When they're in the back of the airplane they aren't in control, so they desperately want to believe that the pilots up front are the best in the world."

Nowadays, individual rights might interfere with company policies such as dress codes.

"What do you do when you have a young kid on staff who decides to get his hair permed? Or grows it out and ties it in a ponytail? You can't tell him to cut his hair, or not to get a perm!" Rainforth says. "He looks ridiculous standing there in front of a jet airplane – and you've got the president of Mexico getting on board. The customer doesn't have the same confidence in a guy piloting the airplane when he looks like that."

Staniland laughs. "Oh, the problems of an aviation manager!" But Rainforth is serious. "I've had that happen. You have to be so careful who you hire. The guy with the ponytail could be the finest pilot on the face of God's earth, but in the corporate world he can't wear a ponytail when he flies an airplane, and maintain the image that these people want to see. Pilot work is mostly black and white: it's right or wrong. So, where you want standard procedures, you want people who are very orthodox."

Rules, regulations, standardized procedures. Where have the old fun days of flying gone?

"They don't let you fly down the river between the banks just because it's a nice afternoon and you might enjoy it," Rainforth laments.

"What you're saying is, we got the good years out of aviation," Watts concludes.

"Yes," Staniland says, "that's right. We had the good times."

He stands up and goes to the cupboard.

"I think a good drink of Scotch should bring this evening to a close quite nicely!" he says.

Good idea . . . but did the Malamute Saloon serve Glenfiddich?

Epilogue

Roy Staniland died on June 4, 1995, following a brave fight with cancer. Family members, along with many friends, "celebrated his life" at a service held in Calgary on June 10, by singing "What a Wonderful World," and recalling many "Roy" stories from over the years.

Footnote 1:

The numbers that designate a runway indicate magnetic compass headings. The directions of runway 16/34 are: 160 degrees south (16) and 340 degrees north (34).

Footnote 2:

Roy Staniland continues his explanation of the difference in landing helicopters compared with fixed-wing aircraft:

"With the correlated system, as you pull up on the collective control to which the twist grip throttle is attached, you're increasing the pitch of the blades. You also have to add more throttle to keep the r.p.m. stabilized because it's all predicated on flying the rotors at a certain rotational speed. When you come off, to unload the rotor you have to take throttle off.

"The throttle control is similar to that of a motorcycle. You can rig the helicopter so you can just lift up and push down on the collective control, but that's only valid for a certain weight and temperature. If you're less weight, you've got to take the throttle off even when you're coming up; if you've got more weight, you have to keep adding throttle in there – a more natural response."

As a result, the pilot often rigged the controls. If he was flying the same machine for a long time, he would "tweak it" in a number of ways until he felt comfortable.

"One of the real problems in cold weather came with the early cyclic control system. They had what was called an 'irreversible', a flat round friction-adjustable disk in the mechanical control system which was graphite-lubricated. You always carried in your pocket two 3/8-inch wrenches, which you used to tighten this control so it reduced the feedback. The aerodynamic forces at work can give you a lot of strong and rough feedback into the stick."

Footnote 3:

Roy Staniland reminisces about the early days of helicopter flying, and why its history is relatively accident-free:

"You could go only 65-to-75 miles an hour, and very seldom did people get killed in helicopters," Staniland says. "The machine usually developed a vibration indicating there was a problem of some sort. Depending on the speed of the vibration, you could isolate where it was. The fan, the tail rotor drive-shaft, the tail rotor, and the main rotor all ran at different speeds, so if you had a very high frequency vibration, you knew it was tail rotor or fan drive. Usually those things would give some warning, and you prepared to land. You flew with the idea that, 'If I have to go down, I can land here, or here.'"

Over the years, the statistics got better and better, Staniland adds, and he felt good about being part of a technology that every year showed improvements.

Footnote 4:

The size of bucket a helicopter can carry depends on the size of the aircraft. "With the small Bell 206s, Hughes 500s and Astars, we'd be carrying up to 1 000 pounds of water," Staniland says. "In the 204s, we'd be carrying up to 3 000 pounds of water. Firefighting buckets came in a variety of configurations, some rigid, some collapsible. Sometimes the tanks were built right into the aircraft. The bucket style allowed any helicopter with a cargo hook to be used, while a purpose-built type bucket restricted the use of the aircraft.

Footnote 5:

The Barkley-Grow T8P-1 (Transport eight-passenger, 1st model) is considered to be one of the most obscure bush airplanes in Canada's flying history. Of the 11 airplanes manufactured in 1939 by the Detroit-based Barkley-Grow Corporation, seven were used in Canada. They were a twin-engine all-metal eight-passenger monoplane. Their unique low-wing style was built in three sections and featured a series of V-shaped stringers, or spars, running lengthwise along the top of the wing, and a similar set of inverted stringers running along the bottom; the stringers were joined at the apexes to form an X. Called "multi-spar," there were no conventional ribs in the main-wing panels.

Footnote 6:

Neil Armstrong died on November 23, 1994, along with his son, pilot Corcoran (Corky) Armstrong, first officer Eirik Odegaard, and Dale Fredlund, when their Twin-Otter hit an iceberg in Antarctica.

Looking Beyond the Roads

"Do you make any money at this writing business?" is the first question Floyd Glass asks as we sit down to talk. "How much?"

"More than I'd win at the track," I say, and he laughs.

That matter dealt with, Glass becomes interested in my research, the recording equipment I'm using, the whole system of selecting and interviewing subjects. The man is interested – as well interesting. Although he says he's now retired, the engine is still in prime condition and he's flying high.

Floyd Robert Glass was born in Kerrobert, Saskatchewan, on March 21, 1916. He grew up on a farm, and attended school in Kerrobert up to and including grade 11. His father had a dairy farm with a good-sized herd, but the drought chased him from the prairies to Prince Albert where he began operating a creamery. Floyd finished high school in Prince Albert. Planning to follow in the family business, he took courses in dairy management at the Ontario Agricultural College in Guelph, and returned home to work his way up with Glass Dairies Limited.

"I was always interested in flying from when I was a young fellow," Glass says. "When an instructor arrived at the Prince Albert Airport – there was just a field, no buildings at all – from the Saskatoon Flying Club to give lessons, I signed up. I got my private licence in 1938."

Following a series of lessons, the instructor and his airplane went back to Saskatoon and Glass thought that was the last he'd see of them. A short time later, however, he received a call from Andy Madore, the chief flying instructor, asking Floyd if he would like to buy the airplane that he'd trained on, an old Avro Avian.

"How much?"

"Four hundred fifty dollars."

"Why do you want to sell it?"

"The students keep doing hard landings with it. The under-gear isn't very strong and it folds up," the instructor said. "But it's a good little aircraft."

"Sure, I can scrape up $450." Glass bought it and immediately removed and reinforced the under-gear. Thereafter, the airplane proved quite reliable.

So there he was with a private licence and a little open-cockpit airplane. It was fun, but he wasn't anxious to carry all the costs.

"I had two friends who also had started to fly in Saskatoon. When I bought the airplane I shared it with them so they could build up their time. We jointly covered the expenses on operating the aircraft."

Glass got his commercial licence in the late fall of 1939. When war was declared, each commercial pilot in Canada received a telegram from the federal Department of National Defence, asking them to join the air force as a "volunteer", take an instructor's course, and then be given "leave" from the air force to teach at civilian-operated schools being set up under the British Commonwealth Air Training Plan. The 28-week course was developed to teach elementary flight at 22 bases across Canada; the goal was to train 6 000 pilots per year from the British Commonwealth countries for active overseas duty. In fact, more than 131 000 aircrew graduates received training under this plan, including pilots, flight engineers, navigators, bomb aimers, wireless operators and air gunners.

"The three of us who had trained on my old airplane went to Trenton and took the instructor's course," Glass says. "Then we three were selected to stay for another month and learn to instruct students on the Link trainer, which was used for instrument training."

Glass has what he calls the "air force equivalent" of IFR (Instrument Flight Rules) certification. "It was a preliminary so the students would have some idea of how to fly 'under the hood', for their final tests." The term "under the hood" basically means being prevented from seeing outside the airplane, so one must learn to fly by relying completely on instruments. "We learned to fly compass headings safely and maintain a steady course, do turns, climbs and descents. Then we had to recover from spins under the hood, which was a little hair-raising at first."

In June, 1940, Glass began teaching at Number 6 Elementary Flying Training School in Prince Albert – in fact, from the same hangar from which he now operates his flying service. Approximately 30 instructors were there to start with, Glass says, and they put through "hundreds and hundreds" of students.

"It was tough on the young students because they had so little time. We turned them out ready to go to Service Flying Training School in about 30 hours, that was all. They got another 30 or 40 hours in service school, then were sent overseas. They were put onto a Miles Master [single engine aircraft] or some other type for a little training, then they went right on to either fighters or bombers. They were very inexperienced people – but the pressure was on to turn out pilots."

The instructors kept track of some of their graduates, anxious to know how they fared. "We struck up a friendship with a lot of them and we'd get letters back. Sometimes we'd get notices that they weren't going to come back."

Glass instructed at Prince Albert for about 18 months, into the fall of 1941. The work was hard, demanding six to eight hours of daily instruction followed by additional four- or five-hour shifts at night running the Link trainers. The instructors were young, and they were just as anxious as their students to get active postings.

"We wanted to get overseas where the action was, as young men think those kind of things. Because we were restless and complaining, they said, 'Well, come on back into the air force!'"

They were sent to Montreal for aircraft recognition and drill training, machine-gun training and "everything that goes with being in a fighter or bomber airplane." Glass recalls that aircraft recognition was one of the big items. "We had to know every aircraft type that was being used by enemies and allies. I'm sure there were 40 or 50 that we had to recognize, instantly, in clear or cloud, and going fast."

From there, they attended service schools to get their wings. Glass was sent to Dunville, Ontario, where he discovered that some of the instructors were men he'd taught to fly in the elementary school! They flew Harvards and Twins, usually Ansons or Cessna Cranes. But, his desire to see action got stalled.

"Just as we were finishing our course, they said that since they'd pulled us out of the service schools a whole batch of the new inexperienced instructors were having all kinds of accidents. Students were being killed – they'd had several right here in this field. They said, 'We're going to send you back to instruct in the schools – and now that you're in the air force, you'll go where we tell you to go!' So that's what happened."

Glass told them he'd go anywhere except back to Prince Albert. That was home, and he wanted to see the world! He was sent to Arnprior, about 60 miles west of Ottawa, where he taught pilots to be instructors. But again, he became bored.

"There was so little to do. We'd go up and run through the particular 'patter' that we were using for instructing. We'd do this with two students, they'd go up and practice with each other, then we had to go back up and see how they were doing.

"It got so monotonous that finally I went to the commanding officer, the chief instructor, Russ Bannock, and I said, 'Russ, I just can't take this. There's so little to do, and too much drinking goes on in the bar, not that I'm not a drinker, but I'd like to get a posting overseas.'"

"Well," said Bannock, "so would I."

Glass stuck to his guns. "If there's nothing coming soon for overseas, I'd just as soon get another posting in Canada."

Bannock called him in a few days later. "We have a posting for you in Abbotsford, B.C., if you want it. A new school is opening up."

"I'll take that."

Glass received a letter from Bannock later on, saying that he'd gone overseas and was flying Mosquitos and enjoying it very much. He even detailed some of the trips. Glass says that after the war, Bannock became president of de Havilland Aircraft of Canada Limited, then started his own business, Bannock AeroSpace.

In Abbotsford, Glass was in charge of one of the sections of flight training; from there he was sent to Trenton, Ontario, to take an officer's administration course. "I found it to be very interesting, because the history of air force law was based on the original British Navy laws, and for every law there is a story behind how it came into effect. The old fellow who was teaching us was a retired lawyer and was very knowledgeable; he would tell stories about the punishment for certain infractions and so on."

Following that, Glass returned to Abbotsford. It was the fall of 1944 and the war was slowing down, so they began to close some of the stations. They sent Glass back to Prince Albert for a few weeks, then to Gimli, Manitoba. In January, 1945, he was released from the air force. "And that was the end of my military experience."

Back to Glass Dairies Limited. Just as he arrived home, however, he heard a radio announcement: the Saskatchewan government's Department of Natural Resources had just bought an airplane, and were looking for a pilot to fly it and do natural resources work. This sounded very interesting to Glass, who immediately went to Regina to check it out. "There was quite a line-up of fellows, all ex-air force, but I was interviewed. The next day I got a phone call from the minister. 'You're hired. Go down and get that airplane'."

They had bought a standard Waco (CF-AZQ) from M&C Aviation.

"There were only three field officers working in Natural Resources in all northern Saskatchewan, outside of the Prince Albert area," Glass says, "so I was made superintendent after six months. By this time I'd covered all the North, flying the Waco, and had seen the problems first-hand. And there were lots of problems."

The first airplane purchased by the Saskatchewan DNR, a Waco CF-AZQ.
Floyd Glass Collection

The government was seriously concerned about Saskatchewan's freshwater fishing industry. Glass explains that the lakes had been designated as either 'A' or 'B'. Fish in the 'A' lakes had "minimal" infestation of wormy little cysts; fish in 'B' lakes were more highly infested and could not be sold for export.

"There were lots of 'B' lakes in northern Saskatchewan, so many fishermen were taking 'B' lake fish and putting an 'A' lake stamp on them – they'd made a deal with one or two of our field officers – and shipping them out as 'A' lake fish. Most of these whitefish were exported to Chicago and New York, and once they hit the American border they were rejected. Carloads of fish were being turned back, and the government was being held responsible because they were in charge of the licensing of these fishermen and so on.

"That was one of my projects that first winter, going around straightening up this matter. I caught all kinds of shenanigans, such as switching tags.

"That spring we hired a couple of experts and dropped them at the lakes. They set their nets, and we candled these fish, tested them and counted the cysts. Then we reclassified the lake as 'A' or 'B'."

Glass also flew directly in to the lake where the men were fishing. When they had their fish loaded in boxes he would check the tags on the boxes. He was amazed to discover that, although the lake where these fish were caught – right where he stood inspecting the boxes – was a 'B' lake, the boxes were all tagged 'A'. He stood looking at the fishermen, then down at the boxes, knowing that the wrong word said at the right time could have him staring down the barrel of a gun.

"It was sorrowful because it was these guys' living, but I had to explain to them what was happening. I said, 'This just can't go on!'"

Glass did receive a number of threats, but none that scared him, except from one trapper up in the Reindeer Lake area. "I backed out of his tent with a gun pointing right at me. But, within two years we had the problem cleaned up."

Testing fish was just one of his tasks. He also checked mineral licensing and forestry operations, taking one of the senior managers or superintendents with him to the site.

At this time, the provincial CCF (Co-operative Commonwealth Federation) government had started a number of Crown corporations. One was the Saskatchewan Fur Marketing Service. The Minister of Natural Resources, Joseph Phelps, phoned Glass with an announcement about this latest plan.

"I want you to go to the private buyers, and tell them all their furs have to come into the Saskatchewan Fur Marketing Service in Regina."

"That's a big order!" Glass said. "I'm going to have a lot of trouble doing that."

The two debated the problem, and Glass worked it down so instead of "all fur," he need only be concerned with beaver and muskrat pelts.

"The service was reasonably successful," Glass recalls, "except for the static we got from fur buyers, and from many trappers who shipped their fur out to Robinson's fur-buying company in Winnipeg or some place else. I got into some very serious arguments with private fur buyers in the country here. There were bitter feelings over it."

Not only did Glass have to state the case on behalf of the government to angry fur buyers and trappers, but he had to communicate it to people who spoke languages other than English, mainly Cree, Chipewyan, or French. Although he hadn't enough knowledge of these languages to be conversant, "we understood one another most of the time. There was no question about it."

He also had to keep tabs on sawmill and logging operations in the area on behalf of the newly-established Timber Marketing Board.

"Most of it was in the Prince Albert area. There were a few sawmills in the North like in Cumberland House, LaRonge, and two or three going where they cut some lumber at Stony Rapids and Sandy Bay.

"Then a whole new program was inaugurated by the government for developing the North. They built schools, and the federal government built several outpost hospitals, so I was very involved in providing transportation to these, and also doing Natural Resources work."

In 1947 Glass took Saskatchewan Premier Tommy Douglas, and the Department of Natural Resources minister Joseph Phelps, on several flights throughout northern Saskatchewan, to help them formulate a plan to integrate the North with the rest of the province. Glass feels that it was farsighted of Douglas and Phelps to put such a plan into motion at that time.

"On the first trip, we stopped in several places and they asked the people, 'What has to be done to develop the North?" At this point uranium had been found in what was to become Uranium City. All of a sudden there was great interest; prospectors were starting to pour into the province. The provincial government set up the Prospectors' Assistance Plan where they conducted schools for would-be prospectors, although they didn't have to know too much about minerals – all they used was a Geiger counter.

"I was given a pretty free hand. We had to acquire more airplanes because we had the fishing operation, and then the uranium operation. So, on behalf of the government, I bought several airplanes including a Norseman. I even put four Tiger Moths on pontoons. We used them for patrols in forest fire detection work, and flying people in to test the lakes for fishing and so on. I also hired more pilots, a number of the ex-air force fellows I'd known who were experienced flyers, such as Lefty McLeod, Fred McLellan, Harry Paul and Stewart Millar."

Then Premier Douglas and Minister Phelps asked Glass what he thought should be done to get things moving.

"We have to get air transportation for people," was Glass's answer. "There is none except for M&C Aviation in Prince Albert, and they're financially in trouble. Unless we provide transportation there's going to be a real bottleneck in moving people around, especially in the mining business that's starting." He suggested that the government form a company. Glass was then called to Regina to present his ideas to various government officials.

"I outlined a plan for servicing the North with scheduled flights, and then establishing charter bases at Prince Albert and LaRonge which were the main key points at that time," Glass recalls. "They sent me to Ottawa, and I had an hour's meeting with C.D. Howe, then Minster of Transport. One of the government people, Don Black, came with me. I told Mr. Howe details of the plan and showed him a map. He said, 'Young man, that looks pretty interesting! I hate that government back there, but you'll get a licence – go ahead and apply for

Floyd Glass with the first pilots hired to fly with Saskatchewan Government Airways: Lefty McLeod, Fred McLellan, Harry Paul and Stewart Millar. *Floyd Glass Collection*

it.' So we got a licence and formed Saskatchewan Government Airways."

This was a "first" in Canada, to have a province owning a commercial airway. "Ontario Provincial Air Service had a big service for many years, but it was strictly for government work, forestry mostly."

Minister C.D. Howe had advised Glass and his delegation to "talk your government into buying out M&C Aviation." Glass reported this advice to the Saskatchewan government officials in Regina, who agreed, and told him to "go up and buy them out."

He began to negotiate a sale price with M&C Aviation. Of the two owners, Angus Campbell had died during the war, and Dick Mayson lived in his home country of England. A sale price was negotiated over the telephone for four airplanes, two Norseman and two Wacos, which Glass planned to put into charter service.

Glass says he didn't encounter any bitterness on the part of the private sector over the government moving in on them. "No one else could afford to get in. It was right after the war and everybody was broke. M&C Aviation was in financial trouble, there was no question about it. It was just the right time. So that's the story of how we got Saskatchewan Government Airways going."

Almost simultaneous with these negotiations, a fire broke out on August 1, 1947, in the Saskatchewan Government Airways hangar down by the river in Prince Albert. "I was coming in from the North next morning. From about 80 miles away I could see this tremendous black smoke coming from Prince Albert," Glass says. "When I got here I discovered that the hangar had caught fire. We think it was spontaneous combustion, we never had any indication it was otherwise." They lost four aircraft: an Anson, two Tiger Moths and a Norseman, plus radio equipment.

On August 15, 1947, Floyd Glass was made manager of Saskatchewan Government Airways, and on September 8 the company started its first scheduled flights to the North.

"1947 was a busy year. The Saskatchewan Government Airways was formed as a Crown corporation. The hangar burned. We made a deal to buy out the M&C Aviation company; we took over their hangar, their staff, all their maintenance, and started the commercial-flying service. Then we commenced the scheduled service. We were working off the river here [in Prince Albert] with a Norseman and would go to LaRonge. Then we made four separate routes into the North, which included all the settlements in northern Saskatchewan, giving them the first regular service that many had ever had.

"I went to the post office people and got mail service going into all these places – they weren't any great shakes as money-makers, the mail contracts, but they did help. Then the natives began to order things by catalogue, and we had all sorts of cargo."

They also had to contend with an influx of people attracted by the work in uranium and geology exploration and mining.

"There were literally hundreds of prospectors and companies in northern Saskatchewan, who were finding indications of radio-active ore in a number of places where there are mines even today. Eldorado was the first one to develop a producing mine near the old Goldfields site. Once that was confirmed as a development the government decided they should build an orderly town instead of just harum-scarum. I had the assistant minister of Natural Resources with me and we picked the site for Uranium City. There was nothing there but it was a suitable location, a nice sloping hill on a good lake for water and everything else."

As time went on, Saskatchewan Government Airways changed its name to AirSask. Also at that time, AirSask and Floyd Glass parted company.

"I left in June, 1950, and the assistant manager, a friend of mine, Scotty McLeod, became the manager."

Glass decided this was a good time to check out the country, to see what was going on in aviation. He ventured to the west coast and ended up flying for two years with Queen Charlotte Airlines, based out of Vancouver and Prince Rupert. He also became the airline's emissary to settle a bitter conflict.

The company flew to two places: Kemano, site of the hydro-electric generating station where they'd tunnelled through the mountains to lakes inland created by the dammed Nechako River; and Kitimat, the destination of Kemano's power, where the Alcan aluminum smelters were located.

"Queen Charlotte Airlines had had a serious accident with one of the Cansos before I got there, so the airline was forbidden to go back into Kitimat."

When Glass had been flying with the airline about 18 months, Jim Spilsbury, the manager, asked him to find out, during a trip to Prince Rupert, if there was any way that Queen Charlotte Airlines could get back into Kitimat. He warned Glass that he might be met with a shotgun if he landed at their dock. Glass phoned Mr. Whitey, the manager, and introduced himself. "I'm calling from Prince Rupert. I wonder if I could have a few words with you?" A strong response followed. Finally Whitey said, "Okay, come up and have dinner with me."

"I went to Kitimat," Glass recalls, "and he was a real tough guy. We had a long visit. When I left there that day, I had permission for Queen Charlotte Airlines to start flying into Kitimat again.

"Mr. Spilsbury wouldn't believe me when I told him. I said, 'You send your Canso up there tomorrow and they'll give you a load out.' They did, and we were in from then on."

By June, 1954, Glass had had enough of west coast flying. He decided to come back to Saskatchewan and take on the challenge of starting an air company in competition with Saskatchewan Government Airways.

"We had to have an Air Transport Board hearing and prove our reasoning for another airline. In the fall of 1954 the hearing was held in Prince Albert, and in January of 1955 we got charter base licenses for Prince Albert and LaRonge," Glass says. "I said I wouldn't go into scheduled service, just strictly charter-based, because I figured that's where the money would be. The business was called Athabaska Airways Ltd."

He picked the name because he reasoned that the many mining companies, and people working in the area where uranium was being found on Lake Athabasca, would remember it. He looked up the history of the name Athabasc(k)a and found it had been spelled both ways over the years, so he stuck with the "k" (Footnote 1).

To get his airline going, Glass raised some money himself and borrowed $4 000 to buy the company's first airplane, a brand-new Cessna 180 (CF-HZE).

"Then it just took off," he says. "We started in February, 1955. I bought the second airplane – another Cessna 180 (CF-IEA), on floats and skis – within a couple of months. By this time I had some financing arrangements set up – I didn't have the money myself – but we got the two machines going that summer."

They hauled tourists and mining people, and quite surprisingly, gravel.

"The federal government was building the Mid-Canada Line, a dual [parallel] radar line. Stations were being established every 35 miles, from Quebec across northern regions of Ontario, Manitoba, Saskatchewan, Alberta and up into the Yukon," Glass explains (Footnote 2). "As an aircraft entered and passed through these lines, its direction and speed were recorded. Once it got established, we had to report in on radio.

"There were three diesel power plants in each station, and they had to rest on concrete footings. At most of the places they could find gravel, except for one site west of LaRonge. When they asked me if I could haul gravel, I said, 'Sure! We'll haul anything.'"

The gravel was put up in 80-pound bags so it could be more easily handled and piled. Athabaska Airways started moving the bags between charter flights as time allowed.

"We moved tons and tons, one other pilot and myself. By this time I had written my engineer's licence, so I did my own servicing as well as flying, loading and off-loading. We had one secretary in the office, with bases in Prince Albert and LaRonge."

By late summer of 1955, Glass bought another Cessna 180. He was now able to pay cash for each aircraft. "We built up three 180s the first year, then I bought a couple more so we had five 180s going by the second year."

He stayed with the Cessna 180s for several reasons. "You can't get along with more than one type of an airplane if you want to go into that kind of a business. If you've got one Cessna 180 and something else, you're going to have a breakdown some day and what do you do? I learned that you have to have multiple airplanes of a type."

He also felt the Cessna 180 was a terrific new modern airplane that could perform well on floats or skis. "A light airplane like that had never been heard of in bush work. We did things like taking 16 sheets of 1/4-inch plywood, putting them all together with two clamps, laying them on the spreader bars between the floats, roping them down, and flying them in to some area where an outfitter wanted to build cabins."

There wasn't much time for rest, especially during the months from May to August. Glass's personal life was going through as many changes as his professional life. His first marriage, to Helen, broke up in 1957. They have one daughter, Susan, who now lives in Winnipeg.

Glass married again, in 1960, to Mamie, a pathologist who kept her professional name of Dr. Bailey. They have four children: Carol, Jim, Barrie and Daniel.

Meanwhile, Glass was steadily building Athabaska Airways based on his five Cessnas. Then he acquired his first twin, a Cessna 310, from a salvage operation.

"It came from the United States, going to Stony Rapids, Saskatchewan, on a fishing trip. The aircraft had taken off from LaRonge but didn't really have a flight plan filed. The pilot had spoken to one of our people, mentioning they were going to Stony Rapids and would be back in five or six days. When they didn't return, the young fellow they'd spoken to reported it. We sounded the alarm although we didn't have very much information on them. The air force put on a search and rescue, and we went looking, too."

The air force from Cold Lake was conducting low-level flying exercises in the area. About five days after the airplane had been reported missing, one of their pilots thought he saw the outline of a submerged airplane in one of the lakes they'd passed over. Athabaska Airways was notified of the location. They contacted officials, and flew to the site.

"First we saw about two feet of the tail sticking out of the water. And here was this pilot sitting on the shore, with three dead bodies of his passengers," Glass says. "What happened was, he realized he'd missed Stony Rapids and had better turn around and go back, but he didn't have enough fuel to get back and he didn't know where he was by this time. He told the passengers, an elderly fellow and a younger couple, that he was going to pick a shallow lake and ditch the airplane. They had put on all their heavy clothes and boots because they were going to be in the bush. Well, that was the worst thing in the world to do!

"He landed with wheels up and everything, got stopped and opened the door and the three passengers got out. It was a real smooth landing – as a matter of fact, there was hardly any damage to the airplane except from water, and two of the cowlings had torn off the bottom, that's all. They were only 100 feet from shore. They all started swimming. He took off after them, and passed them. When he got to shore he turned around and they were all gone. Drowned. They later had drifted in to shore.

"When we got in there and started talking to him, he was babbling and in poor shape. We flew him out, and sent another plane in to pick up the bodies."

The insurance company later put the aircraft up for sale and Glass put in a successful bid.

To salvage the aircraft, he took in a couple of men, four tractor tire tubes and an air bottle to blow up the tubes. They cut poles to make platforms for each tube, and floated them on the water above the engines. He hired a diver to go down and tell them where to hook onto the engine mounts. They lifted the airplane to the bottom of the floating platforms with winches, then let it drift down to the east end of the lake where there was a nice gravel bottom. They set it down in the shallow water and removed the floating platforms. With two gin-poles leaning out over the water, they used the same winches to lift the aircraft. They got inside, lowered the wheels, set them on a couple of sheets of plywood and pulled the aircraft up on shore.

Floyd Glass (2nd from left) and crew during the salvage of the C-310.
Floyd Glass Collection

The next job was stripping out the engines and taking them in to be overhauled. They returned in December when there were 10 inches of ice on the lake, and installed the engines and enough instruments to fly it out.

"That was our first Twin," Glass says.

He paid $3 200 for the aircraft and about $10 000 to overhaul it. He estimates it was worth, at that time, $70 000 to $80 000.

"I ended up buying six Cessna 310s after that," Glass says. "We still have some of them. We were the first to have light twins like that in the country, and they caught on quite well."

Meadow Lake Air Service was owned by a contractor in Meadow Lake, Saskatchewan. One day Glass received a call from his bank manager in Saskatoon. "Do you want to buy another airline? Meadow Lake Air Service isn't making any money and the contractor who owns it is too busy to be looking after it."

"Maybe we can make a deal," Glass said, and went to look over the situation.

He ended up buying four airplanes (two Cessna 180s and two 195s). He promptly sold three of the airplanes, which reimbursed the money he'd paid for the whole shebang – and ended up with a good Cessna 180, free and clear. He hired Maurice Gran, who was a pilot and had been managing the company, and moved the operation up to Buffalo Narrows, adding two more 180s.

"Maurice did a real good job for us. His wife also managed the base as dispatcher and bookkeeper," Glass says.

Later, he folded the company into Athabaska Airways. "I had the advice of a good chartered accountant in Saskatoon. When it was all wound up I put about $35 000 in my pocket clear, and that was the end of Meadow Lake Air Service."

Athabaska Airways had expanded rapidly. By 1959, the company had acquired eight airplanes, including Cessna 310s and 180s, and Beavers. In 1960, they acquired a Cessna dealership. The Cessna company was developing a number of different types of aircraft, private models and also some excellent commercial types, such as the 185 and 206. This venture also became successful, as a strong economy gave people with a little money the opportunity to buy an airplane at a reasonable price. They sold some 80 aircraft.

In 1961, the company brought one of the first helicopters into Saskatchewan.

"I went to the Saskatchewan government's Forestry people – I was in opposition to Saskatchewan Government Airways but I still had some friends amongst the people running Natural Resources – and found they'd had two helicopters coming in to Saskatchewan for two years from Calgary to do forestry patrol work and some fire-suppression work. I said, 'If we go into the helicopter business, will we be given some consideration for this contract?' and they said, 'Sure.'

"Once we got a licence – and it was easy to get a licence at that time – I went to Toronto and bought a Bell 47G2."

Glass bought one and leased one, and got the contract on a year-to-year basis. This deal went on for two years. "Then Saskatchewan

Government Airways decided that if I was in it, they should get in it, too. At that time there was a change of government – that's when the Thatcher government got in [1964], so they squashed that right away."

Frustrated with the contract's instability, Glass again approached government officials. "This business of a contract for two months' work each year for two helicopters is crazy," he said. "I can't make any money and I never know from year to year whether we'll be in the business or not."

He then approached the Minister of Natural Resources. "This has to change for any kind of a business to be built," he said, "and also so you can depend on the machine. Issue a four-year contract for three or four machines. You can put it out to tender – at least the successful bidder will know there's a four-year contract."

The government saw his point and put out the tender. Athabaska Airways got the four-year contract, which was renewed several times. By that time Glass was into bigger helicopters, which he also flew himself as he was by now licensed for both fixed-wing and rotary.

The company continued to grow, establishing bases at Buffalo Narrows (dating from the purchase of Meadow Lake Air Service) and LaRonge, followed by bases at Points North (which they kept for just three years), and at Stony Rapids. "I always wanted to get into a base up there because of the name of Athabaska Airways," Glass says. "Stony Rapids is right on the eastern shore of Lake Athabasca."

In the late 1980s bush-flying work started to die out. With a hefty stock of airplanes that might soon be sitting around, Glass discussed plans with his son, Jim, and other management staff, of how they might work around the recession. They decided to look into starting a "sked" run.

Time Air had scheduled flights running the length of the province. Glass explains that "the original owners of Norcanair sold out to Albert Ethier and he sold it to Time Air, or PWA, which became part of Canadian Airlines."

Glass went to see the president of Time Air in Lethbridge. "We're planning to start a scheduled air service in opposition to you people," he announced. "We're a Saskatchewan outfit so we'll have a little bit of an advantage there." He stopped to let that sink in. "But maybe you'd like to get out of the business," he added. "If so, and if we can work something out, fine."

"No, we're staying," was the firm response.

So Athabaska Airways started up a sked on their own. "We started getting some real nice loads on a 10-passenger type of airplane, with Cessna 404s," Glass says. "Within a year Time Air called me. 'We'll

Ready to depart in a Beech 18 CF-IMC. *Floyd Glass Collection*

make a deal with you. We've decided to get out of the scheduled business in northern Saskatchewan.'

"We didn't have to pay anything for it, it was a working arrangement, directing passengers and so on," Glass says. "They withdrew from all the northern run, but they still did some charters into the mines with their jet. I kind of turned that over to my son, Jim [presently general manager for Athabaska Airways], and he's been working very closely with them on the schedule business the last few years. It's going pretty good."

The extra business necessitated buying a bigger airplane. The company bought a 19-passenger Beechcraft 1900, brand-new from Beechcraft's factory in Wichita, Kansas. "Four Million bucks apiece. We now have two of them," Glass says.

Acquiring aircraft and business contracts is one thing, but acquiring staff is another. When hiring pilots and engineers, Glass looks first for experience, "if you can get it."

"At one time, pilots were awfully hard to get. We had to take young fellows and break them in. We've had some mishaps, no question about it, but usually due to inexperience nine times out of 10."

He also seeks pilots with good mechanical ability, although this might not mean one person should have both engineer's and pilot's licenses.

"Not necessarily, but that helps. But then you can get an unhappy fellow if you've got him on engineering work and he wants to be flying, so we found that isn't too good a combination. They should at least have mechanical ability, and a feel for machines."

Survival skills are also important. "They've got to have a lot of savvy, preferably a knowledge of the North. If they haven't, we put them on as passengers to Stony Rapids where they can fly with experienced pilots in a Twin Otter and so on. Most of them eventually will make it, but some are never happy with the North."

A common practice is a pilot coming to an airline like Athabaska to gain hours, then moving on. "Practically all of them do that," Glass says. "Since we started, more than 100 men have gone through our organization who are with major airlines today – Air Canada, Canadian, or some of the American airlines. They get good experience."

When hiring an engineer, the qualifications Glass looks for are "fellows who are experienced and are steady." He says that Athabaska Airways has an excellent engineering staff with lots of experience behind it.

"We've trained many engineers ourselves, but the rules are getting tougher now. Most of the young fellows who want to become aircraft engineers are required to go to a technical school for two years, then apprentice for two years. It's a good thing, we can see the advantage, and they keep modern."

He explains the work that he and his 100-plus staff have done to achieve a high standard of operation. "We've gone along with all the new regulations from the Department of Transport, and have instituted our own inspection systems, that they approved of. It took some time to set up the operations manuals and so on. On the flying, we have our own check pilots now. We have a training pilot who trains our people and gives periodic training from year to year. We do our own flight tests as well. The DOT (Department of Transport) just comes in and does spot checks on our training and our pilots."

With regard to hiring female pilots, Glass has some reservations considering the kind of work his company offers. "We've had four or five over the years who were good, but we had to limit the type of work they did in connection with the flying, like handling 45-gallon drums that could weigh 450 pounds. One woman said, 'You can't hold that against me.' I said, 'Let me see you load that 45-gallon drum on that Beaver that you want to fly!' She turned around and called a couple of guys standing there, 'Come and give me a hand!' I said, 'That's fine, but if you're off in the bush, and alone, it doesn't work.' There's a lot of freight involved in bush work."

He hasn't hired any female pilots for sked runs yet, "but that may come, and they'd be okay. There isn't any reason why they can't be just as good a pilot as a man, when it comes to knowledge of flying the airplane and weather systems."

The success or failure of a company can be heavily influenced by the personnel on its payroll, and employees' talents as well as their personalities are integral to creating a positive work place.

"You must have employees who have in mind that they've got to be part of the success of the business. If they're not, if they're a griper or they're unhappy, you have to get rid of them. Attitude! We have an excellent staff of both pilots and engineers."

Motivation is a key word, and Glass says Athabaska Airways operated an award system "when we were making lots of money."

Athabaska Airways radio shop and staff. *Floyd Glass Collection*

"We used to give them extra bonuses every year, $100 000 and $200 000 at a time to a staff smaller than this one. We're not doing it now because we're not making that kind of profit. But we've never missed a pay cheque for anybody here."

With trapping becoming very limited, mining development being reduced, and roads being pushed through to remote settlements, bush-flying work is declining at a rapid rate. Tourist camp outfitters are still going well, but they are just summer operations.

Glass cites an example at the Buffalo Narrows base, where they used to have three or four airplanes. "Two settlements, Pataunak and Dillon Lake, had no roads in and they were our main customers. Once roads were built our business died immediately, so we closed the base.

"I can't see any immediate new developments," Glass says, "but again, we're looking further north, 'beyond the roads'."

When the company started buying Twin Otter turbine aircraft, they had three. Although the planes were kept busy in the summer months, there wasn't much for them to do in the winter, so Glass got busy. He drummed up some 90-day contracts in the Arctic Islands, running from the Banks Island base of operation to Prince Patrick Island and to Victoria Island. He also had a Twin Mitsubishi aircraft working out of Resolute on Cornwallis Island as a stand-by machine for a drilling outfit. They spent three winters working in the Arctic islands on contracts for seismograph crews, until work there slowed, too.

"That was a successful operation, a good fill-in for the winter months."

The company has downsized its inventory considerably, and may do more. "When you're only getting 300 or 400 revenue hours a year on an airplane, it's not enough. A good or break-even average is at least 500 hours. We used to put in over 1 000 hours per year on our

Athabaska Airways' S55T helicopters. *Floyd Glass Collection*

bush planes." Their fleet presently consists of about 30 airplanes, as well as 10 helicopters, and some other aircraft such as a single Otter which they lease.

If Floyd Glass was asked to make a statement about aviation, the first thing that comes to his mind is, "We have too much regulation." He adds that while much of it may be necessary, he thinks it's overdone. "However, we have to live with it."

He feels that his company has bent over backwards to work with the Ministry of Transport's system. "You can't work against them, no! We find that it pays to work with them, and we're prepared to do it. They tell us we're the largest operation in their district, and that includes the Ontario Lakehead, Manitoba and Saskatchewan."

Glass has two other companies in Prince Albert, and his family members are shareholders. "We're building those up as well." He also took over his father's farms consisting of about 2 000 acres of land just west of Prince Albert, with 200 head of beef cattle.

Floyd Glass's latest personal acquisition is a development in the Bahamas. "I bought an island down there. Whale Cay."

He has a Cessna 310 of his own, in which he flies back and forth to his island paradise. The 800-acre island is long and narrow, with fantastic beaches and marvellous fishing, and it's all his.

"The island was originally owned by a wealthy English woman named Betty Carstairs," Glass says. "She was a speedboat racer, and I mean big speedboats; I've got pictures of her when they were trying to break the 100 mph record with boats. She bought Whale Cay in the Bahamas and developed it into a private island estate. She built a beautiful big home we call the Great House, and that's where I stay now when I go down."

So, how did a Saskatchewan pilot come to acquire this Bahamian island estate?

To begin with, Glass read an article in COPA (Canadian Owners and Pilots Association) magazine written by a Toronto realtor named Bill Penny. He had bought this island from Carstairs and was developing it. He'd built an airstrip on it, and was inviting people to come down for a couple of days as his guests, and look at buying a lot. Floyd Glass went down and bought two lots.

On hearing of the developer's plans for the island, Glass said, "If ever you want a partner here, and if I can afford it, I wouldn't mind getting in on it." And so a deal was struck.

"It turned out Penny was an ex-air force pilot during the war, so we became friends," Glass says. "I bought a quarter-interest in the development. Then he took sick from cancer he'd had before, and died. That's when I discovered he had a mortgage on it and he hadn't paid very much on it. I either had to walk away and take my loss, or dig in and see if I could get clear title to the island. I made an offer to Carstairs' lawyers in Nassau, which was accepted, so I went to a bank here in Prince Albert. 'Do you want to stake me to an island in the Bahamas?' They said, 'Sure, if you put up some collateral!' I think I put up a Twin Otter.

"I had to go through a few court proceedings to get clear title. There were a couple of questionable lawyers involved, one in Toronto and one in the Bahamas, and I had to get rid of them. There were some other complications, but I got clear title and carried on the development, but not to the same extent."

A commercial developer has since expressed interest in furthering the project. If that goes ahead, Glass will just keep his original two lots. Unfortunately, that doesn't include the Great House, which he describes as "a fabulous two-storey place." Glass flies back and forth to the island in his Cessna 310, each trip adding another 30 hours of flying time. He estimates he flies about 200 hours a year now, a far cry from when he practically lived in the cockpit. Glass has "somewhere over 30 000 hours" flying to his credit, mostly gained by short jobs.

Floyd Glass, 1993. *Photo: S. Matheson*

He still makes trips to the company's operational bases in the North, and sometimes flies to Calgary or Winnipeg. "I keep fairly active, but I don't do any commercial flying." He is semi-retired from the business, just retaining involvement with "major items".

He has time now to reflect on decisions he had to make over the years – accommodating ever-changing rules and regulations, swings of economy, and opportunities that suddenly rose or fell. It is obvious, from the success of Athabaska Airways, that most of Floyd Glass's decisions were sound.

"Yeah, maybe," he says pensively. "But I think we had a lot of good breaks, too."

Footnote 1:

Athabasc(k)a is the name of one of the chief North American linguistic families which covered most of northwest Canada and much of the southwest United States, as well as many isolated groups in California, and including Navajo and Apache.

Footnote 2:

The all-Canadian Mid-Canada Line consisted of a mostly-unmanned radar warning system at 55 degrees North. It was considered by the St. Laurent (Liberal) government to be cheaper than an Arctic chain, and would not involve American presence on Canadian soil, as did the DEW Line. Ninety-eight Mid-Canada stations were built by 1957 at a total cost of $250 Million. The Mid-Canada Line was phased out in 1965 when more sophisticated systems took over (*Canadian Encyclopedia*, p. 639-40).

Apesis Muskwa (Little Bear)

Raymond Sinotte, known as "Muskwa," earned his nickname the hard way – in a direct encounter with a bear.

His father, Henry, a French-Canadian trapper from the Gaspé area, and his mother, Agnes, a French Sioux Indian woman from eastern Canada, ran a trapline at McTavish Lake, 90 miles north of LaRonge, Saskatchewan. When Ray was two years old, he accompanied his family on spring trapping. One sunny day he was playing outside with a little wooden horse that his sister had given him for Christmas, when the toy went rolling down the hill. Ray went after it, and rolled right to the feet of a big sow cinnamon bear with three cubs.

"She pounded the hell out of me, and buried me in the muskeg," Sinotte says. "My sister, Annette, was watching and saw where the bear buried me. The little cubs ran away and the mother bear went to look after them – I imagine she was going to come back and dig me up later – but my sister dug me up first and took me to the cabin.

"An airplane came in about 10 days later and flew me to the nursing station at LaRonge. I was pretty badly mauled. When we got back home, the Indian people named me *Apesis Muskwa*. That's 'little bear' in Cree."

Ray Sinotte was born in LaRonge, Saskatchewan, on May 1, 1946. His father worked as a trapper, commercial fisherman and guide. Sinotte attended school in LaRonge where a friend got him interested in aircraft engineering. He took a three-year apprenticeship with Sas-

La Ronge, SK, taken from a Twin Otter, 1993. *Photo: S. Matheson*

katchewan Government Airways.

"We did an 'everyday apprenticeship,' learning from the other engineers – you know, sweeping floors, emptying the crapper, things like that," Sinotte laughs. "Actually, we did. They didn't have running water at the SGA hangar. When I first started, I had to dump that toilet every day. And wash the bellies of the airplanes. I never touched a wrench for five months.

"After a while we did cylinder and magneto changes – but the first thing I ever did was change spark plugs when I wasn't supposed to! Neil McLeod, an old Scotsman, left one night. He always drank Scotch so he took off to the bar, and when he came back I was changing spark plugs because one of the other engineers had told me to. McLeod bawled me out. Then he said, 'Now you get back down there and clean that airplane belly!' So I had to go back to cleaning for a while."

In 1965, Sinotte wrote his test in the LaRonge Motor Inn – "they brought the exams up here" – and earned his engineer's licence. In 1968, he took a three-week training course in Toronto on Twin Otter turbine engines.

He stayed working for 10 years in LaRonge as chief engineer for LaRonge Aviation, then he moved to Edmonton to work for Mackenzie Air (an off-shoot of LaRonge Aviation). When their hangar had expanded to include DC-3s, F-27s and a Lear jet, Sinotte wrote for the licence endorsements to work on these aircraft engines. "I really enjoyed the turbine work. It's not modern today, but it was in 1968 when I first started. Most of the Twin Otters are 25 years old now."

Turbines, he says, are a lot more challenging than the old piston engines. "You're not allowed to take piston engines right apart. But you can split the turbine engines at the C-flange [located between the 'hot' section or rear part of the engine where the exhaust comes out, and the 'cold' section on the front end where the compressor is located], redo the compressor turbine wheel, and replace segments. We did that a lot."

Engines have a 'life expectancy', just like anything else, Sinotte explains. "Some engines can run 1 800 hours and then it's mandatory that they be overhauled in an approved overhaul shop, perhaps in Winnipeg or Oklahoma. They come back and we simply do the engine change. If you're in a remote location and you have an external problem with a cylinder or a magneto, things like that, with our licence we can do anything to the engine except split the case – that is, the main case and the crankshaft and the camshaft. But we can change all the other components, and sign it out for flight."

As far as the airframe work is concerned, engineering licenses are much the same. "We're called engineers but we do a little of everything, including electrical work, engines and airframe work. We can take an Otter, dismantle it, have 1 000 pieces on the floor, inspect all those pieces, put it back together and sign it out."

In addition to his enjoyment of repairing and maintaining turbine engines, Sinotte also welcomes electrical work. "I always enjoyed working on electrical problems – not that I was really great at it, but I'd usually spend a little extra time. Electrical takes a lot of patience. You have to trace everything down, go through wiring diagrams. A lot of engineers have difficulty with the electrical."

Combined with the challenges of the work, however, engineers say there is often somebody behind you breathing down your neck, demanding to know, "When's that airplane going to be ready?"

They must also make repairs in less than ideal conditions, such as when the airplane breaks down in 60-below (Fahrenheit degree) weather. "Well, you've just got to fix it, no way around it. You have to get the big Herman-Nelson heater out and do it, in any conditions."

At times, the companies Sinotte worked for had contracts with oil companies, to provide air transportation of supplies and personnel to their northern rig sites and also for emergency purposes, so the aircraft had to be always ready to go. "There weren't many times when we were down for more than five or six hours," he says. "As soon as something happened, we had to get right on it. There were no hangars out there, you were always in the wind, no trees. And you got pushed to speed it up. Lots!"

One thing Sinotte is adamant about: he will not be hurried, even when people are saying, "Let's go!"

"You don't let it go if it's not airworthy. You have to get skin about that thick!" He indicates the space of an inch with thumb and forefinger, and laughs.

"At times you have to piece things together to salvage the aircraft and fly it home. You wouldn't fly like that with passengers," he adds, "but you can beef it up with birch poles or whatever in an emergency. I've had to do that a few times."

Sinotte worked in Edmonton for a year and while he liked the work he didn't like the big city, so he moved back to LaRonge. He stayed with LaRonge Aviation for three years, then became chief engineer for Athabaska Airways.

"After a year-and-a-half I got really tired of it, so I went teaching for a while at LaRonge College here, and Creighton College [at Creighton, Saskatchewan, about 90 miles southeast of LaRonge]. I taught courses in bush work, chain-saw maintenance and operation, operation of logging skidders and forwarders [equipment used to haul logs through the bush to load onto trucks], and also taught a few small aircraft training courses."

A passenger disembarks from a Twin Otter, assisted by co-pilot Burk Thacher, at Nordstrum Lake, SK, 1993.
Photo: S. Matheson

Sinotte enjoys teaching. "One course was really good, Women in Trades. We had a lot of fun. Twelve women. I taught them minor things of working on aircraft engines and airframe."

He feels that women make great mechanics. "I'd say they were a lot more meticulous than some guys I've worked with, not to say that all guys are sloppy but I found that the women took a lot of time and care to make sure everything was good."

Although it's not common for women to pursue this trade, Sinotte says he knows quite a few who have. (He has worked with three female engineers so far.)

One would assume that people with both an engineering ticket and a pilot's licence would be worth their weight in gold in remote locations. Sinotte acquired his private pilot's licence in 1970, but never went on to get a commercial licence. "I've probably flown no more than 1 000 hours. I wanted to know how to fly just to know how to do it. Part of survival." Sinotte estimates that there are only about four double-licensed pilot-engineers in LaRonge (compared to approximately 40, including seasonal, with just pilot's licenses, and 30 holding just engineer's licenses).

Sinotte often flew as part of a pilot-engineer team, especially in the Arctic with LaRonge Aviation.

"The pilots usually help us when we're fixing the aircraft, and then we help them with flying. Some of the trips in the Arctic were three or four hours long, without stopping. The engineer usually takes over the flying so the pilot can sleep for a while."

But there were times when he and the pilot had a difference of opinion that resulted in a stand-off – in the middle of nowhere when mutual dependence was of prime importance.

"One night we were changing a fuel control unit on the Twin Otter and it was blowing terrible out, it must have been 45 below with a 30-mile-an-hour wind. We tried to set up a big heavy plastic shelter around the aircraft. We finally got it up and had a Herman-Nelson heater blowing inside there. The pilot was standing right in front of a big hole in the plastic, and he got mad, kicked the ladder out into the snow, said he wasn't going to help. He took off, and I finished the aircraft about three o'clock in the morning, all by myself. Then he woke me up at six a.m. to go on a flight with him.

"I refused to go. I thought, 'To heck with you, mister. If you aren't going to help me, I'm not going to help you.' I didn't fly with him for a whole week after that. Two guys fighting in the middle of the Arctic!" Sinotte shakes his head at the memory.

"It gets that way sometimes. You get on each other's nerves after being there so long. A lot of our stints were for five or six weeks at a time with the same guy, the two of us as partners."

Sinotte has often been called upon to make repairs using only the materials at hand.

"One time I was out on my dad's trapline when he was guiding caribou hunters. The hunters came in with a Beaver, went to turn and smashed into a tree on the shore, damaging the left wing. They sent someone to bring me out to help them. They told me it was just the leading edge skin that was damaged, so I repaired that.

"It was getting dark and we were just about ready to take off when Bob McNabb, who was flying us back, got on the ladder at the end of the wing, put out his hand – and moved the wing back and forth! The whole rear fitting was broken out of the fuselage! I'd never noticed it because I was in such a hurry, but I should have checked it."

Sinotte went back to his dad's cabin, and asked him if he had any steel he could use.

"No!" the old Frenchman replied. "I haven't got anything!"

Then he got talking to one of his tourists in the camp, so Ray ran outside, turned over one his dad's old sleighs and ripped off a piece of the metal runner. He cut it with a hacksaw, brought it inside and shoved it into the stove.

"What have you got there?" his father asked.

"Ah!" Ray said, "just a little piece to repair the airplane."

"Oh."

When the metal strip was red hot, Ray took it out with vice-grips and bent it between the legs of the stove. When it was curved to the angle he wanted he threw it into the snow to cool it off, then drilled and bolted it onto the wing fitting and through the fuselage. Because it was getting dark they left off the fairings and everything else, and flew home like that.

"It was good and solid," Sinotte says.

That was the last time he ever took anyone else's "accident report" for granted.

De Havilland Twin Otter DHC-6, one of Ray Sinotte's favorite aircraft.
Courtesy Canadian Wings, October, 1965, A. LeGuilloux publishing editor

Sometimes engineers hesitate to do such quick repairs because they will later discover the operator has flown for several weeks, or even months, still using the emergency restoration.

The wing repair wasn't, however, his last "bush" job.

"LaRonge Aviation was the first to go into the Arctic from this area," Sinotte recalls. "We landed on Cornwall Island north of Resolute Bay one afternoon, in our Twin Otter (CF-WTE – Footnote 1). The pilots went out to do a quick flight to haul some stuff from another place. I was setting up the radio so I could talk to these guys when the camp manager said, 'You might as well shut that down. You don't need the radio anymore. They've just crashed.' Oh Jesus, I was thinking about my buddies! I didn't know how bad it was."

A helicopter was sent to pick them up. Luckily they were uninjured. Sinotte went the next day to assess the damage. The aircraft had landed in a dry river-bed where rocks had been hidden to the pilot's view by built-up snow. "It wasn't really their fault – they landed and sunk in the snow and then hit this big rock," Sinotte says. "They knocked off the nose gear. It came right back and knocked out one fuel cell and the leg fairings along one side. We ordered parts from Edmonton, which took a week."

When the parts came in, they left on a dark stormy night to repair the Twin Otter out on the lonely river-bed, southeast of their camp on Cornwall Island. Sinotte brought a supply of tools, parts, and an electric drill that operated, along with their lights, from a little generator.

"The pilots helped me do the repairs out there, so that was good. A crazy experience, though. We started pulling off the nose gear. I was in such a hurry that I forgot to release the air in the nose oleo strut [a nose-gear shock that operates on oil and air, and acts like a shock absorber for landing]. If you don't release the air pressure it's just like a big cannon going off.

"Jim Fournier [a pilot-engineer with LaRonge Aviation] and I had this big bar and were pulling off a nut; it was coming but it was really tight with all the pressure on it. Jim was looking up and I gave it the last wallop, and man it just blew! Hydraulic fluid all over.

"It drove Jim's mitt right into the ice, with his hand still in it. Oh, man, that was wicked. He was screaming and hollering at me, trying to get his hand out. I was trying to lift the oleo to get it off his hand because I figured he'd broken his fingers or torn his hand off."

Jim's hand fortunately wasn't damaged, and they were able to continue with the repairs. "We went ahead and replaced that whole nose-gear casting. Everything was broken in there, in the area we call Station 60." (Each section of an airplane is marked off in stations, on the drawings. Station 60 is where the nose wheel attaches on a Twin Otter, just forward of the cockpit.)

Because the entire bulkhead was ripped out, Sinotte made big clamps with steel struts coming back to the bulkhead to hold on the nose gear.

"We bolted it in temporarily just to fly home. That was a real job, oh man! It was nearly 50 below that time. It took us two days and two nights, and we finally flew out in the dark. We got a little tractor out to make a runway, and some people from the camp set up flarepots; we took off from there and headed for home. I couldn't close up everything in the nose wheel area, and it was really drafty. We took the engine tents, the tarps that we'd put on overnight, and draped them over our legs in the cockpit. Oh, it was cold!"

After that, the repairs had to be redone properly – everything torn out again and replaced: the bulkhead, and all the hydraulic fittings for the steering. But, they did that repair in a warm hangar.

Sinotte had another experience in the Arctic, flying out of Sachs Harbour, that he wouldn't care to repeat.

"We got lost," he says simply.

Sinotte and a pilot were flying in a Twin Otter in November when the temperature was cold but the sea was free of ice. They lost all radio contact because ice built up on the antennas, and also on the aircraft.

"We lost everything – we couldn't pick up the radio beacon from Sachs Harbour on the southwest end of Banks Island. We missed our destination of Johnson Point [located about 150 miles north of Sachs Harbour on the east side of Banks island]. The island kind of curves around so it was easy to miss. We were starting to run out of fuel, and I knew we were off-course over the ocean, I could just tell. I convinced the pilot to head back toward land."

The pilot would eventually have turned back, Sinotte says, but it made him nervous watching the "low level" fuel lights flash. They were down to their last 15 minutes of fuel, flying off-course over the ocean, and on wheels, not floats!

A little further to the north lay M'Clure Strait. "It goes kind of parallel to the top end of Banks Island, so if we had turned left over that water we'd never have got to any land. We'd have ended up in Japan!"

At that point there was only a bit of daylight left, and it was snowing very hard.

Because the pilot was concentrating on flying instruments, he told Sinotte, "You keep an eye out that left-hand window. Tell me when you see the breakers on shore."

It was nearly impossible to tell where the shore started, because of the similarity between the dark color of the land where the snow had blown off and the open water of the sea. Just as darkness fell, Sinotte managed to pick out the shore. He tapped the pilot on the shoulder and down they went.

"Throw this thing in reverse right away when we hit!" Sinotte yelled.

The pilot reversed the props and applied the brakes, so the aircraft slowed immediately.

"We didn't know what we were landing on, and it was really a rocky shoreline," Sinotte explains. "We were lucky there weren't big boulders, just stones. We landed uphill, which was lucky too, because it slowed us down a little more."

They stayed in the aircraft overnight, wrapped in three-star eiderdown sleeping bags. They had some food from the ration kit, and also a bucket of Kentucky Fried Chicken they'd bought in Yellowknife, "so the pilot and I were chewing on this chicken."

At first light Sinotte, ever the trapper, went outside to set snares.

"I knew we had to have something to eat, and I couldn't eat that old bugger!" Sinotte laughs. "I probably would have after a month or so, though! But I went out to set snares for Arctic hare and foxes, whatever we could catch.

"I walked ahead of the airplane about 200 yards and here's this cliff – straight down 150 feet to the sea! Man, if we hadn't stopped so quickly we'd have been dead! They would never have found us. We'd have been right in the drink."

The airplane had enough fuel left to run the engines, and the pilot finally got a fix with the ADF (automatic direction finder) on Mould Bay and Isachsen, and was able to figure out the coordinates of their location at the north end of Banks Island at Mercy Bay. When they finally got the HF (high frequency) radios running they radioed Inuvik and another Twin Otter was sent to pick them up, landing right beside them.

The rescue plane got plenty of warning about the cliff.

They had been down for the entire night, and were picked up about three o'clock the next afternoon. "We were really lucky," Sinotte says.

"It was crazy sometimes, up there. The Arctic is tough on animals, people and equipment." He much prefers flying in his home territory of northern Saskatchewan. "I spent five winters in the Arctic and that was enough. We'd go up for five or six weeks at a time, then someone else would come on rotation to take our place. We'd be stationed anywhere the rigs were: Prince Patrick Island, Resolute Bay on Cornwallis Island, Cornwall Island, or even up the west coast of Greenland to Thule, or Rankin Inlet on the western coast of Hudson's Bay. Then we'd come back and work in the shop here in LaRonge. Much better."

He has witnessed a number of changes in the North, concerning nearly all the industries familiar to him. "The aircraft business has been declining steadily since the mid-1970s because of roads going in. And the trapping business has gone way down because of all the Greenpeace hollering and screaming, I think. Trappers' livelihoods have disappeared. It's not worth going out trapping anymore.

"These people have been forced to find different occupations. Some have gone into commercial fishing, but the majority of them are just on welfare, social assistance," Sinotte says.

Commercial fishing, too, has suffered and a number of lakes have been shut down because of over-fishing. Quotas have been established on some lakes, "until it hardly pays a fisherman to go in." It's costly to get there, and costly to get the fish out.

"See, you have to fly your fish out, or take them out by snow machine," Sinotte says. "A lot of times you barely break even."

He is not optimistic about the future of bush flying, either.

"I think it's really going to go down more. A lot of people are building runways at tourist camps, so they don't need float planes. They just fly into their own airstrips."

Another interesting factor, he says, is that soon there won't be any more working bush planes. "They quit building Beavers and Otters a long time ago, they quit building Twin Otters about five years ago. Nobody is building a bush plane anymore."

These airplanes have a life expectancy. "When a Twin Otter, for example, gets to 25 000 hours you may as well throw it in the trash, because the wings are 'lifed-out', time-expired, and can't be rebuilt," Sinotte says. "Nobody's building wings for them. After 30 000 hours, Beaver wings are 'lifed-out', and you can't rebuild them. You can't use them again and you can't rebuild them. They're done."

Repair of vintage aircraft is usually done as a hobby, and an expensive one at that, because a lot of the parts must be remanufactured. If you wanted to buy a pair of wings for a Twin Otter, what would it cost? "First of all, nobody's building them," Sinotte says. "To manufacture some would be nearly the same price as you used to pay for a brand new Twin Otter, or a used Twin Otter in good condition."

Ray Sinotte, LaRonge, SK, 1993.
Photo: S. Matheson

Sinotte says he isn't interested in getting into the business of salvaging, repairing and reselling aircraft. "If I was a younger fellow I would, but I've had almost 30 years in it, and I'm tired. I'm tired of scratching around the bush. I like the bush, I love it, but like the work itself it really tells on you after a while."

He would consider taking a job again in a city, but only

if he could live in a small town close by, "like work in Saskatoon and live in Warman or some place. I would do that."

But job scarcity is another factor. Even with his experience and qualifications, which should make him a valuable employee, he says "there are a lot of 'valuable' engineers around, with experience."

In the past, there was great demand for aircraft engineers. Anybody who had a licence had a job, and he or she could state their price. Anyone who was both a pilot and engineer had "licenses to print money," but that hasn't been the case in the last few years. Following his teaching stint at LaRonge and Creighton colleges in the late 1980s, Sinotte "just freelanced," working for LaRonge Aviation again until he and three others were laid off in August of 1992 because of lack of business. In the summer of 1993, Sinotte checked the computer job board of Canada Manpower, and found one engineering job open in all of Canada – for a helicopter engineer in Yellowknife.

Ray says he hasn't advised his two sons to get into aviation. His father, likewise, couldn't advise him to be a trapper, and Sinotte feels that the time has also passed for his trade to be viable for his sons.

He still has his father's trapline 90 miles north of LaRonge, but his career is again focused on teaching. Employed by Northern Lights School Division as an instructor for small engine repair courses and in charge of technical programs for Continuing Education, his territory still covers the North, from Prince Albert up to Pelican Narrows, Buffalo Narrows, and Creighton.

"Muskwa" is using his skills any way he can to stay in his beloved north country, where the legacies of his ancestors make up Canada's unique heritage.

Footnote 1:

CF-WTE was one of the first Twin Otters in service with Wardair in 1968. This aircraft is still in service at LaRonge (in 1995), operated by LaRonge Aviation.

Too Much Hurry

"I've always considered 13 to be my lucky number," says Short Tompkins. "I was born on the 13th day of the month, I drove truck number 13 on the first haul over the Alaska Highway, and I've owned 13 airplanes."

Considering his adventures – and misadventures – he's lucky to be able to count those 13s. Tompkins readily admits he's used up more lives than the proverbial cat, while striking out in new directions from finance to flying.

Short Tompkins' given name is Arthur, "but my mother and my wife are the only ones who ever called me that. When I was four or five years old, I was nicknamed Short by a cowboy we used to have at the ranch at Halfway River. I don't know how he hung it on me, but it stuck, partly because I never did like Arthur. In school they used to call me King Arthur, they pulled my leg about that."

No one ever called this human dynamo "King Short."

Short was born in Pouce Coupe, B.C., on October 13, 1924 to Emily and Philip Tompkins, who was known to be a forceful and domineering patriarch. There were initially seven Tompkins children, and all were taught the meaning of hard work from an early age. The family owned a ranch situated at the mouth of the Halfway River, "half-way" between Fort St. John and Hudson's Hope, B.C.

Short became interested in flying from an early age when an airplane went down on the Halfway River above the ranch. After it had been repaired, the Tompkins did some work preparing a landing strip at the ranch and Short got to know the pilot and crew.

When World War II was declared, Short's plan to join the air force and learn to fly was stymied by his young age and lack of education, as he hadn't reached the required enlistment age of 18 and had just completed grade 10 at the time. Later on, the air force relaxed its education standard. Short reapplied and was put on a waiting list. "I was close to the last number when the air force filled their ranks toward the end of the war. So I joined the army in late 1944, because I wanted to get into the war."

He, along with another Fort St. John lad, Jimmy Anderson, trained at Shiloh, Manitoba. "There were three different areas of training at Shiloh: infantry, artillery and paratroopers. Jimmy was in the infantry and I was in the artillery training as an anti-tank gunner."

By the time Tompkins was placed on overseas "draft" leave, the war in Europe had ended. He volunteered for the Pacific, but that confrontation concluded before his unit was ready.

"The army used a point system for discharge," he says. "They kept the younger recruits, who hadn't enough points to get out, around doing chores. I took an opportunity to get into the Provost Corps, the military police force of the Canadian Army. I thought it would be good experience."

He was sent to the base at Petawawa, Ontario, for his last six months of duty. On receiving his discharge in April, 1946, he returned home.

"I was always interested in heavy equipment. I talked my father into supporting that, and we went to Alberta and bought a crawler tractor. That was the beginning of what we later built into a very large, successful, contracting business in the oil fields here, called Tompkins Contracting Limited."

In the spring of 1951 Short married Audrey Waite, who was born in Fort St. John and had grown up in the farming district of Montney. Short and Audrey proved to be a hard-working team. Immediately after their wedding, Audrey accompanied Short on a job at Eureka River east of Fort St. John in the Hines Creek area, she doing the cooking and he supervising the work of two Cats. Audrey also went with her husband to the next job on the Alaska Highway south of Fort Nelson, building roads for some of the first oil rigs to come into the country. The work of Tompkins Contracting at that time involved mainly construction of access roads for rigs and seismic operations, and well-sites.

This backbreaking joint effort continued for four years, until the spring of 1955. By this time the couple had two children, daughter Rae and son Russell (and later, Jill and Michael), who would soon be getting ready to go to school. Audrey said, "That's enough," so Short continued alone, doing jobs that took him away from home much more than he liked.

In the meantime, changes were coming to the North Peace area. Pen Powell had started flying and Short began hiring him to make trips for the company. It didn't take long to see how essential an airplane could be to his business, and it would also give him a lot more time at home.

"In 1959, during break-up when bush work was shut down for a while, we took the kids to Edmonton for Easter and I went to work getting my pilot's licence at the Edmonton Flying Club," Tompkins says. "It cost only $200 in cash, after the $100 subsidy from the federal government. I spent 29 hours training on Fleet Canucks, real sturdy airplanes, with the standard gear like tail-draggers [with a wheel on the tail]. They had an 80-horse and a 95-horse. I had my licence in two weeks."

Following the training course, Tompkins returned to Fort St. John. During the summer he increased his hours on the local flying club's aircraft. Short's enthusiasm for flying led him to try anything and everything. "Jed Woolley, a good friend of mine, was going for his licence, and he and I used to go up to the club. They had a Fleet Canuck with dual controls, and Jed and I loved to spin that thing. We'd go up to 6 000 feet, kick it loose and spin it as far as we could, to see who would chicken out first.

"We'd pull it up and stall it, then go on a downward spiral.

"It looked like the ground was going 'round and 'round. If you applied the opposite rudder to the way it was turning, and put a little bit of forward pressure on the stick, it would come out of the spin. But if you applied the other rudder, it would just keep spinning. Try to pull back on it, it would just spin. Whoever would bring it out of the spin first – the one who applied the opposite rudder first – was the one who chickened out."

The fast rate at which the airplane fell made waiting the other out quite dangerous. Short's son, Russell, who has held a commercial pilot's licence since 1971, explains: "An aircraft close to the ground doesn't have much chance of recovering because it takes about 500 feet to recover from the spin. The minimum you could recover is about 300 feet, but you'd have to have everything just perfect."

Short denies this was a risky game. "That's one of the things instructors used to do, take us up and stall the aircraft, and make us bring it out of a spin. If you get rigor mortis and do the wrong thing, why you'll continue to spin right into the ground! Some people will mistakenly jam both feet on the rudders and grab the stick and pull it into their belly!

"But anyway, that's just one of my memories of how I was improving my hours that summer."

The Fort St. John Flying Club's Tri-Pacer met with a bit of an accident at Short's hands, but he maintains that he "didn't really put it into the bush – I just had a short landing with it."

The incident occurred when he was doing an approach to a fairly small airstrip north of Beatton River airport. Although by this time he owned a Super Cub, he needed a larger airplane to haul some Cat parts to a work site. His passenger was Bud Woodruff, the DOT

(Department of Transport) radio operator at the airport who had married Audrey's sister, "so was some kind of a shirt-tail relative."

Short flew over the strip to take a look at it, and set up for an approach. The only blame he will take for the mishap that followed is that he'd missed doing one of the ground checks before leaving Fort St. John. He hadn't checked the aircraft's idle. "That's one of the things that is part of your 'run-up'. You should bring the throttle all the way back to see if the aircraft will still idle. I hadn't done that."

He started the approach, brought the throttle all the way back, and the engine quit. The prop was still windmilling so their approach was fine, but he needed some power to get onto the strip. "I applied what I thought would be a little bit of power and nothing happened – so we settled down in a bit of brush at the approach to the strip. Did some damage to the aircraft. It knocked the gear out from under it." Then he adds defensively, "But it didn't go over on its back!"

It cost Short $3 700 to haul the aircraft out and repair it. Hudson's Hope pilot and old friend, Pen Powell, recalls the incident. "He blamed the airplane. Said the wings were too short," Powell laughs.

On October 30, 1959, Tompkins bought a Super Cub (CF-LKR) from Stan Reynolds in Wetaskiwin, Alberta, and flew it to Whitecourt the first day. "I see from my log book that I had a total of 63.38 hours then," he says. "It was dark by the time I got to Whitecourt, so I overnighted there. The next morning I was anxious to get going because the days were getting short, so I left before daylight. That's when I gave myself one of my first weather scares. It was just barely getting daylight when I started running into wisps of cloud in the Fox Creek area, so I got down real low. The clouds were almost in the trees.

"I scared myself pretty good before I got to Fox Creek. I hadn't enough hours to be familiar with the Super Cub. I was alone, and I didn't stop until I got home. The airplane then became 'my legs'."

Son Russell remembers spending "lots of hours in the Super Cub when I was about six years old – Mom, Rae and me – flying around with Dad while he was practising the instruments."

"The Super Cub was a great little airplane," Short says. "For three years I flew that thing, before I got careless and stalled it."

The Super Cub came to its end during a moose-hunting trip to Bear Flats, about 20 miles from Fort St. John. Russell and a family friend, Don Watson, were in the airplane with Short as they headed to a little airstrip at the Halfway Ranch that had been cleared the year before. When Short made his circuit over the strip he happened to spot two moose grazing alongside the runway.

"I paid a little too much attention to those moose when I was doing my turn on final, and I was quite low. I stalled it, and ran into the bush."

Russell, then nine, recalls the accident. "I was riding in the baggage compartment, and Uncle Don was ahead of me. One wing hit a big old snag of a dead tree and dragged us down." The airplane flipped around the snag before smashing into the bush.

"I was at full power trying to do a recovery when it hit the ground," Short says. "Probably if I'd had another 50 feet I might have made it because an aircraft, when it stalls, goes nose down. When we hit the ground we didn't hit head-on. You might say it was just starting to come out."

Russell agrees. "We probably would have come out except for that one tree."

"But that was the end of the airplane," Short concludes mournfully.

Injuries to the passengers were less extensive than they might have been. Short broke some teeth and Don Watson injured his shoulder.

"I was still flying that Super Cub when I quit keeping log, January 18, 1962. By that time I had 1 931 hours," Short says.

The Super Cub had been used extensively to support their work, moving men, and supplies which included everything from groceries to awkward steel parts. Although the cargo wasn't weighed, Short says "you were very much aware of your weights."

Russell adds, "But the thing is, nobody ever weighed it. Lots of times they say legal specification of an airplane is this much; well, you can overload it. Most people do. You always try to get your heavy stuff closer to the front, the centre of balance, and the lighter stuff in the back."

Russell has no recollection of cargo ever being tied down. "Lots of groceries hit me in the head."

Short Tompkins on one of the 13 aircraft he has owned, Aiken Lake, 100 miles NW of Finlay Forks, 1970s. Preparing to fly home on one magneto, since no repairs were possible. *Short Tompkins Collection*

Daughter Jill recalls one trip where she fell asleep lying across the two back seats of the Super Cub, when they hit some rough weather in the mountains. "Dad's toolbox was on the floor. We hit an air pocket, the toolbox lid opened, the tools came up and flipped in front of my face, then crashed back into the box and the lid closed again. I sat up and paid attention for a while."

Tompkins' flights into remote areas, while setting up or maintaining camps, brought about situations that required quick thinking and a lot of ingenuity.

"Throughout my early years of flying I scared myself many times, flying after dark and pushing weather," Short admits. "I particularly remember one night at Fort Nelson leaving our airstrip to go and look for some trucks. When I got off the ground I realized that it was a very black night. Once airborne it was clear weather, but I wished a thousand times before that trip was finished that I was back on the ground."

"I can tell you a story," Russell volunteers. "When I was 13 we went out to a Cat camp at Hay River with [Fort St. John pilot, now deceased] Al Henderson's Super Cub. The Cats had cleared a narrow strip, sort of widened out a line a little bit on a small hill. When Dad flew over he glanced at the strip and it looked plenty long enough.

"We landed, and when we broke over the hill we saw they had piled all the brush at one end – he'd thought it was part of the strip – so he locked the brakes up. We skidded along and flattened a tire. The aircraft went up on its nose and damaged the propeller."

Short explains what happened: "Those oversized 'tundra' tires we were using would sometimes turn on the hubs. If they did that, the valve stems would get pulled out and the tires would go flat. With full brakes on it turned the one tire, pulling the valve stem out of the tube."

"There was a Bombardier [snowmobile] at the site so we took a tire off it and jerry-rigged it onto the airplane," Russell continues. "A Bombardier tire is about two-and-a-half feet high compared to the other tire about three feet high. Then we pulled off the prop, got a sledgehammer and straightened it out, and took off.

"I remember how scared I was when we were flying back to town. When we landed at Fort Nelson, the airplane was on a real tilt because we've got a big high fat tundra tire on one side, then a little skinny Bombardier tire on the other side. The flight services guy was peering out the window at us!"

"It was interesting," Short acknowledges.

Another successful ad-hoc repair took place in the Northwest Territories. "I was taking a cross spring for a D-7 into a place called Dogface Lake," Short says. "They told me over the radio that they had a strip ready for me, but I hadn't yet seen it. I was flying the [Cessna] 180 on wheel-skis. I'd say I was 100% overloaded with this spring, and the way the spring was shaped, the C of G [Centre of Gravity] was way back.

"Getting out of here was okay but I knew if I went into a rough strip I'd have a hard time keeping the tail up, which is one of the things you need to do on a rough strip.

"I managed to land okay, but the strip was really bad. The pounding the tail wheel took on these humps broke the hollow steel rod that comes out of the back fuselage and holds on the tail wheel. Of course there was no way I was going to sit out in the bush and holler for help.

"With a cutting torch we removed the two parts of the rod that were bent, cut a willow branch, drove it inside the steel tube, and away I went. I was able to get home with it."

Awkward and overweight cargo seems to be the nemesis of many pilots, but Tompkins' situation was a little different.

"The thing is, with Dad, nobody ever *asked* him to haul difficult loads," Russell says. "He was the boss! He was hauling all his own stuff."

"Everything we were doing, we were doing to get our job done," is Short's rationalization. "That is one of the reasons we got the aircraft – it gave us a jump on the other contractors. We'd be able to look at the work ahead of time and then support it after we got going. That gave us a big edge. An oil company might phone us from Calgary and give us a coordinate on a map where they wanted to go. We'd go have a look at it, then tell them it would take so many work days."

"When you're bidding [this type of] work," says Russell, "they always say 'if you fly high, you bid low – if you fly low, you bid high.' Which means, if you're flying high you bid low because it all looks good from high up in the air. If you fly low, you bid high because then you can see what actually has to be done."

Helicopters were not commonly used for northern bush work in the 1960s, Tompkins says, and fixed-wing aircraft were just beginning to be used extensively. "Companies that did some of the original northern development work would call us. A lot of the work we got was on the basis of, you might say, our own expertise and knowledge. And also the fact that we had aircraft and knew what we were talking about, so we could advise them."

In many ways, the airplane made Tompkins Contracting Limited the success it was.

"The summer of 1962, a microwave line was built through to Alaska," Short says. "RCA Victor were the supervising engineers of the job. Myself and a fellow named Don Gordon from Fort Nelson formed a joint venture and we did some of the sites for RCA Victor. The job superintendent was a Turk – I've forgotten his full name but we called him 'Souli' – who said he'd been a pilot during World War II for the Turkish air force. He said he had 7 000 hours, and he always wanted to fly my Super Cub. I'd let him fly it but I'd be in the back seat – a Super Cub has dual controls. The first time I had him up front flying he rounded out – started doing his landing – 50 feet above the ground! If I hadn't been in the back seat to correct him, he would have stalled it 50 feet in the air. After that I always called him 'Fifty-Foot Souli.'

"But that was an example of where the aircraft helped us with work like that, even along the highway. Souli was so intrigued with my Super Cub that he gave me all the work I wanted to do."

Tompkins considers a pilot's sense of navigation to be of prime importance, especially when working in remote bush areas. "It's everything. If you didn't have a good sense of east, west, north and south it would be hopeless. That's something I always had, a good sense of direction. It was hard to get me lost on the ground, even before I started flying, and it's helped me a lot in flying, too. When you're flying in bad weather or in rough terrain, it's pretty important to know if you're going upstream or downstream.

"If you're going upstream, it means you're flying uphill and you could very soon be in the soup," he explains. "The cloud level is sitting there and the terrain is going up. A time or two, that knowledge really saved my bacon. I had to figure real quick where I was in relation to whatever map I was reading."

In the winter, when you can't see river-flow, Tompkins says you can still use this system. "There's got to be a lot of snow for you not to be able to tell which is upstream and which is downstream. You know just by looking at the terrain, at the banks of the river to see where the wash is, where the driftwood happens to be on the corners, that sort of thing. You have to know your land."

Although Short needed only a private pilot's licence for his work, he's had his night endorsement "you might say 'forever'," his float endorsement "forever," and has been licensed for multi-engine for many years.

Close calls have come often to Short Tompkins. One cold October day in the 1960s, Short landed at the mouth of the North Nahanni River where it empties into the Mackenzie, and parked the Cessna 180 upstream by heeling the back ends of the floats into the riverbank. Immediately, some people arrived in a helicopter and asked if he could fly out and meet them at a lake back in the mountains to look at a road site. He agreed, but said he wanted to warm up first and would meet them in a half-hour.

Returning to the airplane, he walked past seven or eight barges that were tied in a row, nosed into the bank. He got into his Cessna and wound it up. When the airplane came off the bank, the iced rudders on the heels of the floats were frozen at an angle, which instantly turned his aircraft downstream toward the barges. He could do nothing to turn away in the short distance.

"I was upstream quite a ways, so this didn't bother me too much. I just cut the power and jumped out onto the float," Short says. "I was going to drift down to the barges, and I thought I could somehow salvage the situation there."

He was standing on the front of the float when he reached the first barge. He leaned over and put out his hand to catch the barge, rather than let the float hit it. But the end of one wing touched the barge, jerking him off the float and plunging him into the water.

He was wearing heavy clothing, including high boots that were laced part-way up and tied. Being a good swimmer he didn't panic when he hit the water, just swam for shore. He had almost reached the shoreline when he looked back and saw that his airplane was heading around the end of the barge, from where it would surely drift out into the river. He couldn't let the airplane go! He'd swim back out and crawl up onto a float.

He started swimming toward the airplane when he was suddenly slapped up against the edge of a barge by an undercurrent. He wasn't going to make it to the airplane. He changed his direction to go back to shore, but he couldn't move!

The current wasn't strong, but it was relentless as it beat against the side of the seven-foot high loaded barge, pinning him against its steel side. Slap! Slap! Slap! It's rhythmic force sucked him down. He went underwater, scrambled back up and swam a bit closer to shore along the edge of the barge. The current slapped him down again, and again. The third time he went down, he knew the current was going to win.

This particular barge was a closed-in structure with a house on it. When the airplane had floated around the open end of the barge, somebody working on the deck saw it and looked around for a pilot. The man spotted Short seven feet below, pinned against the side of the barge and "going down every couple of minutes."

"Get a rope!" the man hollered to one of the other workers. Somebody else yelled "Get a plank!" But the man who'd spotted him "used his head."

"I'll never forget this," Short says. "The man threw himself over the side of the barge, holding onto a handrail, and let his feet hang down so I could grab them. He had on rubber boots with the tops turned down. I grabbed those boots and held on until they got a rope down to me and hoisted me up. I was played right out. If I'd have gone underneath that barge they'd never have found me. The suction from the river current was so strong it rolled the upper parts of my leather boots right back."

Nothing happened to the drifting airplane. "Didn't hurt it at all. Somebody got a canoe and brought it back to shore. I could have lost my life trying to rescue it."

Even recalling the situation makes him shudder, knowing how close he came to drowning in the icy waters of the Mackenzie River.

When asked of the number of airplanes he has owned how many have been wrecked, Short's answer is candid. "I'm not happy to have to tell you," he says, "but I believe I demolished four."

Although that equals 25 percent, it must be remembered that Tompkins has spent his life flying in wild remote country, often carrying horrendous loads, and has encountered the worst weather conditions in Canada. But Short doesn't use these factors as excuses.

"I think it's fair to say that weather was never a contributing factor to any of the wrecks I had. I think they were basically due to having too many other things on my mind. Too big a hurry.

"But," he adds, "I was the only one who got any serious injuries out of them – and I got a broken back, out of the Super Cub [CF-PNN]."

Short had taken the aircraft to Dawson Creek for an inspection and now wanted to pick it up. "I caught a ride to Dawson with Pen Powell. A fellow named Phil Miller came along with us. I was going to fly my airplane back from Dawson Creek, and Miller wanted to ride with me so I let him get in the back seat."

A personal conflict ensued while in the air. The Fort St. John *Alaska Highway News*, dated August 27, 1969, reports what happened:

> Fort St. John businessmen, Short Tompkins and Phil Miller, escaped a brush with death last Wednesday, August 20, when the light plane piloted by Tompkins plunged to earth from 1 000 feet above the Dawson Creek Airport.
>
> The damage to the plane was extensive enough for it to be considered a total write-off and an investigation of the crash is underway by the Department of Transport . . .
>
> As a result of the crash Tompkins sustained back injuries in which one vertebra is badly damaged. . . . Miller . . . suffered a cut jugular vein and a broken nose. . . . A registered nurse who was on the scene of the accident almost immediately stemmed the bleeding from Miller's main artery until he arrived at hospital.

"Well, the last thing I remember was jerking on the flaps. But the aircraft, instead of hitting the ground nose-first, hit flat and just collapsed everything," Short says. "Right on the weeds, flat. We got pulled out of that and I spent about two months in the hospital."

The accident resulted in a nasty court case, with Miller and Tompkins suing and counter-suing one other. At the same time, the Tompkins family was going through trying times, dealing with their business ownership and operation.

"When I look back – which I often do as I get older and I have less to do – and reflect on what happened to what we had and see the mistakes I made in terms of dealing with the others, and I see what others did wrong, it looks so much different now than it did when it happened," Short says philosophically.

"Our family thing blew up. It started coming apart when I was in the hospital with my back broken. By the time I got in the saddle again, it was coming to pieces. I was hurt in the autumn of 1969, we were in court in late '71, and I think the family got squared away with each other sometime in 1972."

The Tompkins Contracting operation was, in its heyday, one of the largest corporations in the Peace River country.

"At one time we had offices in Grande Prairie, at Mile 54 of the Alaska Highway, Fort Nelson and Whitehorse. We had a service station at Mile 54 and one in Fort Nelson, too. We had airstrips both here and Fort Nelson, at our places. At one time we had the largest payroll in the North Peace."

The service stations complemented the contracting, because the company had trucks as well as heavy equipment. At one point they were running over 60 trucks, half company-owned and half driver-owned. Their equipment included Caterpillars from D-6s to D-9s. "When we sold the company we had between 40 and 50 pieces of Caterpillar equipment, D-6s, D-7s, D-8s, D-9s, graders and motor scrapers. It was a tremendous operation."

When the company was sold in 1981, Tompkins Contracting Limited had also owned a total of 13 airplanes. Super Cub CF-LKR was replaced by Super Cub CF-PNN. Then came a Cessna 180 CF-TRC and four different Cessna 185s, two Piper Navajo twins, another couple of Super Cubs, a twin-engine Britten Norman Islander, and a Cessna 207 ("a long-bodied 206"). For a time, the company also rented a Cessna 210 and a Cessna 182.

"The most we had at one time were two 185s and the Islander. And a Super Cub, with wide tundra tires. I don't think we were ever without a Super Cub as long as we had the company."

Tompkins' advice now, contained in a theory that covers everything from flying to finance, is "Never get in too big a hurry." He maintains that flying is safe if you take your time. "The only time I ever got in trouble was when I was in too big a hurry. Once you learn to fly – and I think it's the same with most people who fly – a lot of what you do is instinctive. Give your instincts lots of time to work."

He believes that flying has enhanced his life and his work, although hindsight provides a lot of wisdom.

"I look back and see all the mistakes. Some were connected with the aircraft operation, because there was jealousy over who had the aircraft and who didn't. I managed our operations, and you might say I was the aggressive one. I was always in charge of the aircraft because I was the pilot.

"For years we didn't have a commercial pilot, and it wasn't until I had my back broken that we hired one. By the time I was well enough to fly again, Elmer Olson was on the job and doing it well. He stayed with us right up until we sold the company."

One of the most traumatic events in Short Tompkins' life, outside of the family matters, occurred when Elmer Olson went missing.

"Elmer was a good friend of mine. He'd flown for our company for 11 years and I spent a lot of time in the front with him, in the Twins. About four o'clock one afternoon I got word that he'd gone missing on a flight to Fort Ware. It was in March when the days got dark about seven o'clock."

Short took his Cessna 185 and, along with his youngest son, Michael, went to see if they could pick up an ELT signal. Other aircraft were also on the search. When two pilots reported picking up a signal, he set one of his aircraft radios on that frequency.

"The clouds were just below the mountain tops, so we couldn't fly above the mountains on the flight path to Fort Ware," Tompkins recalls. "We were in the valley of the Prophet River when we came around the side of a mountain and this ELT signal came in on the receiver. It's a spooky sounding signal, like a siren only short blasts. I said, 'He's here, somewhere close!'"

Tompkins circled around and around the mountain. The signal came and went, as if the downed pilot was making a desperate attempt to get through. But the signal led them nowhere. When darkness fell, they had to go back to Beattie's place at the Sikanni Chief River to spend the night. During the early morning hours, search and rescue aircraft flying above the cloud were able to get a fix on the signal.

"It was at least 30 miles from where we were, but it just happened that the signal bounced off that particular mountain.

"I'll never forget that experience because we were so sure we'd found him. It turned out he'd hit the side of Lloyd George Mountain head-on with a Britten Norman Islander [not a Tompkins Contracting aircraft], so it was over real quick for him."

It is not pleasant to count the friends who've crashed in flights, and pilots' photo albums and log books bring back many dramatic scenes.

"This 180 that I wrecked belonged to John Okranic," Short says, pointing to a photograph. "He was killed down here in the lake [Charlie Lake]. He and I shared the same dock all the time."

Short's third airplane crash occurred in the 180 that he'd borrowed from Okranic. It happened "because I forgot to set the flap."

"Too much hurry." Cessna 180 ran off No-Name Lake, north of Worsely, 1976.
Short Tompkins Collection

"Too big a hurry!" son Russell adds.

"Yes," Short agrees. "When you're coming off a small lake or a small strip on skis, you depend on 'the right feel in your tailbone.' At a certain point in your takeoff run you decide whether you're going to fly or not. I made up my mind that we were away, and when I reached the edge of the lake – it didn't fly.

"If I'd had the flaps set when I went to raise the nose at the edge of the lake it would have gone. But in doing the spin around the lake I dumped the flaps and forgot to reset them, so it went right off the edge of the lake, into the bush. Wrecked."

While Short states that weather has never been a factor in his crashes, he has encountered – and overcome – some tough situations that could easily have resulted in calamity. One such time occurred en route from Fort St. John to Fort Nelson in the Cessna 207 on wheels.

"I'd talked to the weather office in Fort St. John and was told there was a front between here and Fort Nelson," Short says. "I knew that at Fort Nelson there was enough visibility to land at our strip, but I'd have to go through that front between here and there. There were four of us in the 207, all pilots.

"We took off, and I made up my mind I would simply climb to 7 000 or 7 500 feet to get above any icing conditions, fly to Fort Nelson, let down and land.

"I climbed into the cloud and was heading toward the Blueberry beacon, the first radio beacon north of here. By the time we got there, we'd picked up so much ice that the 207 wouldn't climb any more. I think we were about 5 000 feet above sea level when it quit climbing, which put us about 2 000 feet above the ground. I knew I was in trouble. I wouldn't be able to get up to 7 500 feet where I wanted to be, so I thought I'd better get back.

"I was north of the beacon so I made a turn, heading back. In making that turn I lost better than 1 000 feet. Ted Pickell was sitting in the front with me, and I said to him, 'I'm going to fly this thing on the clocks. I want you to be VFR [Visual Flight Rules]. As soon as we see the ground, you let me know.'"

Concentrating on the instruments while Ted watched for the ground, Short continued to fly back the direction they'd come. When they had gone about 20 miles, Ted said, "I'm starting to pick up the ground." Short knew from his instruments that he must be very close to the ground.

"I was at full power. By this time I'd even set a notch of flap, but I was still losing a bit of altitude," Short recalls. "As soon as Ted told me he could see the ground, I switched from IFR [Instrument Flight Rules] to VFR, in other words to visual flying. I very quickly picked a familiar spot and found my way back to Mile 54. I was able to hold an altitude by this time, but just. I'd set a notch of flap, was on full power, the ice was still on the airplane, and I knew that I couldn't land on the short strip at Mile 54. I had to get slowed down.

"I didn't want to go to the airport with all that ice on the airplane because I'd get a violation filed against me for even flying that day – I wasn't an IFR pilot. I still had lots of fuel, so I decided to go over the hump into the Peace River valley and get down close to the water where it would be warmer, so the ice would come off.

"I went over, dropped and flew a ways up the valley. The ice all came off, I came back and landed at Mile 54!"

The Cessna 207 "bit the dust" in 1979. Short had been to Fort Nelson doing a tour of Tompkins' truck stops and their facilities with some Imperial Oil personnel.

"I was bringing three Imperial Oil credit people back from Fort Nelson to Mile 54. Rather than take off from our airstrip in Fort Nelson, which was quite short, I elected to go over to the airport and meet them there. Because we'd had breakfast at our place at Mile 293, one person rode with me over to the airport and I was to meet the other two there," Short recalls.

"When I was radioing for takeoff at Mile 293, I noticed that the passengers' seat was further ahead than I liked to see it for travel with the 207. At the airport, when I loaded up the other two passengers, I would move that seat back.

"We got over to the airport, loaded the other two passengers, we got talking and I forgot to move the seat back. That meant my passenger was sitting with his knees up a bit. I did my run-up and everything, and we taxied for takeoff on a beautiful long tarmac runway.

"With the 207 we used to set 30 degrees of flap, two notches, using an electric switch on the dash. The 207 was a bit of a dog in many ways. It didn't get off the ground like the others because it was a lot of airplane for the amount of power it had, so with that amount of flap you always took off and flew quite a distance before you let the flap off."

He did his run-up, taxied out and took off. He was starting to gain speed about 50 feet up when the aircraft began to sink. "My head wasn't working right or I would have realized what was happening. My passenger had hit that flap button with his knee!" Tompkins says.

"When it started to sink I had full power on, and I instinctively tried to hold the machine level. As the flap came off I lost lift very quickly, to the point where one wing stalled and tipped down. It wasn't long until we hit the ground and were over on our back.

"That was a great old airplane, the 207. It broke my heart to see that happen. We had it insured and the insurance company wrote it off. Nobody was hurt. Just my pride."

Pen Powell, who has crashed two of his own airplanes, is quite familiar with Short's accident record. "Short Tompkins has wrecked lots of them," Powell says, as if passing over the torch. "He's an expert at it."

Being the head of a large business brought about a fair amount of pressure. One the things Short loved about flying was the release it gave him from commercial concerns. "When I left the office and crawled into that airplane it was a different world. I did a lot of little 'gippo' flying jobs that had nothing to do with our business. I'd help

Short Tompkins – operator change on Murray River in Grizzly Valley.
Short Tompkins Collection

out the guide-outfitters, prospectors and trappers, stuff like that. I'd take trappers in and out, haul their dogs. I always enjoyed doing that. A lot of it I never got paid for, but that didn't seem important.

"I flew prospectors like Art Pollon in to the strip on the Gataga River several times. One thing about Art, he always made sure I got something for it, my gas or something. Art didn't have much in the way of supplies – I could load Art, his dog and his supplies in the Super Cub and still have room. He'd stay out there six weeks. Go back to get him, there'd be no dog. He always ate the dog" (Footnote 1).

In the early 1960s Short staked some gold claims on the Turnagain River southeast of Dease Lake, and at one time thought seriously of spending more time prospecting. The contracting business, however, took precedence. "I envied the freedom these prospectors and trappers had, but I got a little share of what they were doing with some of the work I did for them. And I could fly back!"

Short has strong views on the conditions he has seen others fly under, as well as about his own experiences. One subject is "drinking and flying."

"I probably flew the odd time when I was hung over, but I've seen very few people who mixed alcohol with flying," he says. "I drank on the ground, but never, ever in the airplane. And no drinking and then climbing into the cockpit. I'd sometimes spend the night uptown in the bar and go flying the next day and maybe shouldn't have, but I don't think very often.

"Like they say, 'there should be eight hours from bottle to throttle.'"

Short believes he has accumulated around 9 000 flying hours. He has flown throughout northeastern British Columbia, northern Alberta, and the Northwest Territories to Inuvik, and the Yukon. "We worked in the northern part of the Yukon, what they call the Eagle Plains, and the Peel area. We did all our flying work out of Whitehorse. In 1971 and 1972 we worked on three different oil jobs out of Inuvik that were big rig drilling projects."

The Alaska Highway, built in 1942, changed the social, economic and environmental fabric of northern B.C. and the Yukon. Tompkins saw those changes and participated in them, from driving trucks up the highway as soon as it was navigable, to flying over every mile of the country.

"In the years I've been flying, agriculture has pushed north nearly 100 miles in a line across the western provinces," Short says. "But I think the biggest thing I've seen over the last 10 or 15 years is the clear-cutting in British Columbia. Boy, that really shocks me when I fly and see that."

Aviation, says Tompkins, has left its own particular mark on the North. "One thing it's done, it's scattered a lot of fuel drums all over the north country. You go into the Arctic, every lake you're on, every place where aircraft have been, you'll see fuel drums. They may be picking them up now – I haven't been up around the north country since about 1988 – but there were fuel drums everywhere. People left garbage around. But now a lot of the commercial charter outfits, when they fly hunters into an area and go back to pick them up, ask their pilots to look the campsite over and make sure they bring the garbage out. It's being done more now."

Tompkins maintains that camp clean-up was one of the things his company was always careful about. "Sure we knocked down a lot of trees when we were building roads, and in the early days you didn't need to clean them up. Now you're supposed to clean that up. But as far as leaving fuel drums and our refuse along the way, no. We either buried it or took it with us."

In 1988, Short Tompkins did some flying of a different sort, taking Reform Party of Canada members on a tour of the North.

"I was on the executive council of the Reform Party, and was named 'Chairman of the Big Eight' constituencies in northwestern Canada," Short says proudly. "It was my mission to spread the word across that area that we'd formed the Reform party. I spent a month doing that in my Cessna 185, myself and Bob Van Wegen, a public relations man for the party."

Short Tompkins at Charlie Lake, 1991. *Photo: Jack Baker*

He flew the 185 as far east as Churchill, Manitoba, and to Yellowknife and Whitehorse, with party leader Preston Manning and Senator Stan Waters. "Preston and I flew in the 185 various times, and he and his two boys have been fishing with me at Kitchener Lake."

For all his escapades, Short Tompkins has had a lot of luck – both good and bad – perhaps because of his ambivalent Number 13. By his own admission, some of his accomplishments were won by tough and unbending determination, which follows a Tompkins family tradition. In a local history of the North Peace (Footnote 2), Short's father, Phil, is described as a forceful and high-strung man, active in mind and body, who thrived on adventure and excitement. "He was happier when he had to strive or fight for something than when he got it easily." The article concludes by stating, however, that "if anyone was in need in any way, the Tompkins family were there. Their home welcomed travellers along the road. If ever there is a prize given to a family for unselfish service to a country, it should go to the Tompkins."

Short feels there was good camaraderie among the Peace River people, especially among the pilots. "There was something there, all right. If there was something I could help them with, I'd help them. There would be very few people in that fraternity that I'd turn down."

There were old trails for Short Tompkins to follow, and many new trails to break. If he sometimes did it in "too much hurry," so be it. Time is a benevolent judge.

Footnote 1:

For a longer account of Art Pollon, see "The Jackpine Savage" story in *Flying the Frontiers, Volume I.*

Footnote 2:

Kyllo, Edith: *The Peacemakers, Hudson's Hope Section*, self-published, 1973.

The Tail-Gunner

There is, perhaps, one more story that represents our history in the skies as well as some of the others, although the teller, Jack Horne of Victoria, B.C., was not a pilot, but a tail-gunner in World War II.

The story unfolded in Powell River, B.C., in 1966, at a lonely construction site out in the bush. Seven guys were sitting around in camp, talking, whiling away a rainy evening. One man had a noticeably scarred face, and finally one of the fellows got up the nerve to ask him how he'd got that way.

"Some beggar ruffled my goose feathers," was the curt response.

Jack Horne, a carpenter on the construction project, looked up, his interest piqued. "Were you in the air force?"

"Yeah," the man replied cautiously.

"Not Canadian," Jack said, noting the man's accent.

"No. Luftwaffe. I'm Finnish. We were forced into the German army, 187 Squadron."

"Flying yellow spinners?" Jack asked. "Focke-Wulf 190s?"

"How d'you know?"

The two men eyed one another across the now silent room.

"They were the best."

"And you?"

"Tail-gunner, R289013, attached to RAF Squadron 115, number three group."

"How many raids?"

"Twenty-seven."

"Pretty lucky." The Finn sucked hard on his hand-rolled cigarette.

"Yeah."

Both men knew the risks. The life-expectancy of a tail-gunner was said to have been three-and-a-half minutes.

"When were you shot down?" Jack asked quietly.

"March 25, 1945."

Jack Horne's memories leapt back over 20 years.

"Four or five of them came out of the sky that afternoon," he said, looking over at the men who sat quietly in the darkened, smoke-filled room. "They shot the hell out of my two wing men. Then one came over the top, trying to get rid of me – but I was waiting with four guns, each repeating 1 150 rounds per minute."

The two men stared at each other, their eyes shaded by the cigarette smoke curling up from tightly clenched fingers.

"Never had a chance," grunted the Finn.

The veterans took turns completing each other's thoughts, while their audience was held to silence.

"I must have hit his canopy and he couldn't get out. He went down into a mist, ground haze. Never saw him crash. It was unconfirmed," Jack said.

The Finn butted his cigarette. "You bastard," he said quietly. "*You're* the one who ruffled my goose feathers!"

"Unconfirmed," Jack repeated.

"If you want, I'll go to Ottawa and confirm the record of a hit."

Tail-gunner Jack Horne, 115 Squadron, R.A.F. Witchford, Elycambs. Taken V.E. Day, May 8, 1945. Lancaster bomber "I.L. Easy". *Jack Horne Collection*

The men looked at each other.

"There's no need," Jack said. "It's all over now."

The other men in camp sat back, reflecting on what they'd heard, what Canada meant to so many and what peace is all about.

Tail-gunner Jack Horne, 115 Squadron R.A.F., Witchford, Elycambs. *Jack Horne Collection*

The End